Dedicated to Melvyn,
the ideal overlander.

AFRICA OVERLAND

A Route and Planning Guide

David Brydon

Roger Lascelles, Cartographic and Travel Publisher
47 York Road, Brentford, Middlesex TW8 0QP Telephone: 01-847 0935

Publication Data

Title Africa Overland — A Route and Planning Guide
Typeface Phototypeset in Compugraphic Palacio
Printing Kelso Graphics, Kelso, Scotland.
ISBN 0 903909 58 8
Edition This First September 1987.
Publisher Roger Lascelles
47 York Road, Brentford, Middlesex, TW8 0QP.
Copyright David Brydon

Distribution

Africa:	South Africa —	Faradawn, Box 17161, Hillbrow 2038
Americas:	Canada —	International Travel Maps & Books, P.O. Box 2290, Vancouver BC V6B 3W5.
	U.S.A. —	Hunter Publishing Inc, 155 Riverside Dr, New York NY 10024 (212) 595 8933
Asia:	Hong Kong —	The Book Society, G.P.O. Box 7804, Hong Kong 5-241901
	India —	English Book Store, 17-L Connaught Circus/P.O. Box 328, New Delhi 110 001
	Singapore —	Graham Brash Pte Ltd., 36-C Prinsep St.
Australasia	Australia —	Rex Publications, 413 Pacific Highway, Artarmon NSW 2064. 428 3566
	New Zealand —	Enquiries invited.
Europe:	Belgium —	Brussels - Peuples et Continents
	Germany —	Available through major booksellers with good foreign travel sections
	GB/Irleand —	Available through all booksellers with good foreign travel sections.
	Italy —	Libreria dell'Automobile, Milano
	Netherlands —	Nilsson & Lamm BV, Weesp
	Denmark —	Copenhagen - Arnold Busck, G.E.C. Gad, Boghallen, G.E.C. Gad
	Finland —	Helsinki — Akateeminen Kirjakauppa
	Norway —	Oslo - Arne Gimnes/J.G. Tanum
	Sweden —	Stockholm/Esselte, Akademi Bokhandel, Fritzes, Hedengrens. Gothenburg/Gumperts, Esselte Lund/Gleerupska
	Switzerland —	Basel/Bider: Berne/Atlas; Geneve/Artou; Lausanne/Artou: Zurich/Travel Bookshop

Contents

Part 2 Route guides

Part 3 Background notes on African countries

Part 4 Route Commentary

Tunisia

Algeria

Niger

Mali

Burkina Fasso

Ivory Coast

Foreword

Africa, the world's second largest continent, comprises 56 states or countries of which 17 are completely landlocked or, as with Transkei and Ciskei, have no port of their own.

Large areas of this continent remain unexplored and its riches have been barely tapped. Enormous mineral wealth lies unmined beneath its soil, and the full agricultural potential of Africa has yet to be seen.

Much of the continent is desert and there are vast areas of water and jungle. It is a continent of extremes: from the snow capped peaks of mountains like Kilimanjaro and Kenya, to the scorching heat of the desert; from the impenetrable jungles of Zaire and Congo, to the silver-sanded beaches bordering the Indian Ocean. It is a continent full of culture and design, of music and dancing, with a wealth of wildlife, flora and fauna, new species of which are still being recorded.

There is something for everyone in Africa, for Africa has it all. A journey across this great continent, the dark continent, is not to be undertaken lightly. It will not be a holiday but it will be an unforgettable experience and one that most people will never repeat. It is a journey that should not be rushed, for only by taking one's time can all of the knowledge and beauty that the African continent has to offer be fully appreciated and absorbed.

Introduction

The overland trip across the African continent, no matter which route is taken — and there are many — is still one of the greatest motoring challenges in the world today. One does not need a great deal of money, just the ambition to undertake such an expedition, and the perseverance to push through with the planning and the actual trip until the end. Anybody can do it provided they are reasonably fit and able, medical fitness being the one main precondition for any likely traveller and visitor to Africa. Marriage is no obstacle, neither are children unless they are very young, say under 7 years of age when the heat could prove too much for them. It will be an experience that no-one will ever forget, and you need to do it only once to gain a lifelong memory. Experience! That's exactly what it is — an experience and an adventure rolled into one.

This book provides all the information you need to undertake the Trans-African Journey, and it details the various steps to be taken en route to ensure a trouble-free and successful trip. I am no stranger to Africa, having undertaken the overland trip on no fewer than four occasions (the latest in 1982) and I would recommend it to anybody.

Nowadays one can read of travellers getting lost, and into trouble, or even dying in the attempt to cross Africa but the reasons for these tragedies are simple and there for anyone to see. The first and most important reason is insufficient planning. Such a trip must not be undertaken lightly, and should be planned on an expedition basis with the whole of the planning for the trip spread over a period of at least one year. It is not the sort of journey that can be conceived today and executed tomorrow, next week, or next month. The second reason is an inadequately prepared or equipped vehicle, or even an overloaded vehicle. The third reason is lack of respect and appreciation of the elements that are to be faced.

Prospective travellers should not listen to rumours and hear-say of crime, muggings, abductions and other bad reports of happenings in African countries. If any doubts about safety arise on a trip such as this the wisest thing to do is to consult the consul of your nationality in the neighbouring country to the next one you wish to visit. This will give you a true picture of events. I have travelled hundreds of thousands of miles across Africa without incident and I can assure anyone who intends worrying about rumours that they will be much better off staying at home.

Africa as a whole is shrouded in mystery and intrigue. Africa is huge and exciting. It is also a country of extremes. It features the hottest spot in the world, and some of the wettest. It has snow, desert, jungle, valleys, mountains and warm silver sanded beaches. Amongst the natives are the tallest people in the world, the Masai and Watutsi of Kenya, and the shortest, the pygmies of Zaire.

Nowadays there are organised tour operators who drive groups of travellers across the continent for a sum that is modest by normal holiday standards. The advantage is that you will be travelling under an experienced leader who knows what he is doing and where he is going. Amongst the disadvantages is the fact that you will not know your fellow travellers in advance and that you may not grow to like them, which would most likely ruin your trip. Remember you will be living, eating and sleeping in close harmony with your fellow travellers for several weeks and at times the strain can be immense. Also remember that travelling with an organised tour you will not have the freedom of your dictates and will have to abide by the regulations and planning of the expedition leader. By planning your own trip you can go where you wish, when you wish.

People from all walks of life are now undertaking this trip and in all sorts of vehicles, each with their own advantage. Many people are also hitch-hiking across the continent (something that I did in 1972) and this again has advantages particularly when one's finances are limited. Popular travelling groups appear to be the boy and girl or two boys and two girls group, and on my trips I have also met many husband and wife teams, occasionally with children. I have also met a group of three girls from Australia. Sex is no obstacle given lust for adventure and ambition to travel. The age of travellers ranges widely too: I met a couple in their late sixties with their adult son on my last trip. The number of people travelling together is not important but the optimum is two. If avoidable one should never travel alone; yet I have met many successful "loners", and nowadays they are becoming more frequent as they travel the continent on their motorbikes. Even pushbikes are becoming more common, a most economical means of transport but hard work at times. Ordinary saloon cars are also now crossing the Sahara, relying mainly on speed and lightness to take them over areas of soft sand that will trap slower and heavier vehicles. On my last trip I met a single African driving a Peugeot 504 who had completed the journey from France to Benin in five days! The best vehicle that anyone can travel in, however, is one with a high ground clearance — one inch can make a lot of difference — and four-wheel drive. It must be a rugged vehicle, and comfort should not be taken into consideration as this is something you will have to forego on such a trip. There are many rugged four-wheel drive vehicles with a high ground clearance on the market, but by far the best, the most tried, and most popular is the Land Rover.

It must be emphasised that the Trans African trip will not be a holiday, enjoyable as it will be, and that there will inevitably be difficulties. If you are able to accept this, you will see an Africa that the normal tourist finds difficult to discover; you will appreciate the vast size of the continent and enjoy a personal freedom, independence, and sense of peace you have not experienced before; you will lose completely the worries and inhibitions associated with the dull confines of civilisation. Whatever your reasons for embarking on such an expedition, you will return with memories to savour for the rest of your life. You will achieve what many people would like to achieve but get no further than discussing: everybody's dream but few people's reality. The chance of a lifetime.

The beautiful and serene Arak Gorge, from the top of the road that descends to the river bed running through it. Scenery in stark contrast to the normal sand of the desert.

Part 1
Preparations and essential information

Planning the trip

First stage

The very first thing to do is to decide roughly which route you intend to take, and list the countries you intend to pass through. At the time of writing for various reasons it may not be advisable to include Libya or Angola on your itinerary, but the situation is changing all the time. The next stage is to write to the consul/legation of the countries that you wish to visit which are represented in your capital, and ask for:

(a) Visa application forms for the number of people travelling (always add one more person in case you should make a mistake and ruin a form). Most embassies require the completion of forms in triplicate.

(b) Tourist information on that particular country.

If the representative you write to cannot provide all the information you require he will invariably send you the address of their National Tourist Office who will be able to help you. A list of representatives of African Governments in London is given in Appendix A.

It will probably be some time before you will need to apply for visas if they are required, and if they are not the representative will tell you. In the meantime you can study the visa application forms to see what information is required and how many photographs you need.

As the tourist information arrives, study it carefully and learn as much about that particular country as you can. All of this will occupy a great deal of your time and at this stage no further action is necessary.

It is advisable to start a file and keep all of your paperwork in order. This will help you at a later stage when paperwork increases dramatically; the whole planning will be a lot easier if you know where everything is.

It will also help if you purchase some useful publications to study thoroughly. Recommended are: *Africa* (magazine; African Journal Ltd; this is a must!); *East Africa travellers guide* (Thornton Cox); *South Africa travellers guide* (Thornton Cox); *National Geographic* (magazine); *The Great Sahara* by J. Wellard (Hutchinson); *Sahara Handbook* by Simon and Jan Glen (Roger Lascelles, 1987); *The Secret of the Sahara* by Rosita Forbes; *Africa South of the*

14

Sahara by G. Kingsworth (Cambridge University Press). There are many more but these are the important publications and will give you some idea what to expect on your travels.

Step by step preparation

- Obtain and read as much information as you can on the countries you wish to visit.
- Plan your route.
- Select your travelling companions and your vehicle.
- Obtain your passport(s).
- Visit your medical practitioner for a medical examination to satisfy yourself that you are fit to travel. Sometimes people who think they are fit enough are not.
- Obtain all the passport size photographs you will need. Some visa applications require 3 photographs, and it is best to have 12 to 15 extra to take with you for any additional visa you may need, or for any other use that may occur.
- Arrange with your local automobile club for the issue of
  (a) Carnet de Passage (this can be post dated)
  (b) International Certificate for motor vehicles
  (c) International driving licences
  (d) Camping Carnet.
- Arrange the necessary vaccinations through your doctor. Application of all vaccinations could take 2 or 3 months.
- If you have ferry crossings on route, such as across the Mediterranean, it is advisable to book them.
- Arrange personal medical and baggage insurance, and vehicle insurance.
- Visit your dentist for a check up and any treatment that may be required.
- Arrange with your bank for the required amount of cash and travellers' cheques you wish to take with you.
- Begin to apply for visas.
- Double check that you have forgotten nothing, and mark off everything that you must take with you against a check list.
- Your vehicle must be given a thorough check, and this can be done, together with fitting out with spares and extras, while you are going through the rest of the planning as detailed above.

The route

There are many routes that can be followed, depending on where you wish to go and what you wish to see. Political restrictions can, however, dictate the route that you take. Drought, flooding, confrontation, border closure, and coups can all force deviations and also make it impossible to stick rigidly to any one particular route.

While on the actual trip you may find a reason to take a different route from the one originally planned. Maybe you are running short of time, or even wish to visit another country not originally on your itinerary. This is no problem until you reach central Africa. At that point there are only two countries straddled across the whole width of the continent. One is Sudan and the other is Zaire so you must pass through one of these if you are to travel farther south on your journey. Each can be unco-operative in its own way, closing and opening borders unpredictably — but nowadays with so many people making the overland trip these two countries are becoming more sympathetic to the overlander. Sudan is the more difficult of the two to gain entry to, as visa applications are referred to Khartoum and take 3-4 weeks to process; but it is possible to obtain a visa for Zaire at the border while you wait, or at the Zaire embassy in a neighbouring country such as Central African Republic. This takes 24 hours.

When it comes to starting the actual trip there are only three main starting points in Africa. **Tangiers** with two routes south: either following through the kingdom of Morocco, then Mauritania and Senegal before heading eastwards; or travelling eastwards to Oujda or Algiers and then southwards across the Sahara. **Algiers,** the most popular, heading directly south across the Sahara. **Tunisia,** again heading south across the Sahara.

The route through Morocco, Mauritania, and Senegal is not to be recommended to 'first-timers' as there are some difficult sections in southern Morocco and Mauritania where four-wheel drive is essential. Also this route does not take you across the centre of the Sahara but hugs the edge of it and little of the actual desert is seen.

There are three main routes across the Sahara desert and by far the most popular and the one recommended to 'first timers' is via In Salah, Tamanrasset, and Agadez. This route is now open to all: there are no restrictions, no vehicle checks and no permission needed to cross the desert. The other two desert routes are via Hassi Messaoud, and Djanet into Tchad; and via Reggane, Bordj Moktar, and Gao. For both these routes the crossing is extremely difficult, and permission is required which can often be refused or withdrawn when you are halfway across. Vehicles are rigidly checked for robustness and to ensure they are sufficiently equipped for such a voyage. (This was once the case on the Tamanrasset crossing but is not so now.) Also, the crossing via Djanet into Tchad, just about the hardest of all, is not recommended owing to the civil unrest in Tchad at the moment.

Another route that is becoming more and more popular is the one straight down from Cairo in Egypt to Nairobi in Kenya through the Sudan. On this route there are two approaches. Firstly by ship into Alexandria; and secondly by driving across Europe, through Turkey, Syria, Jordan and into Israel, crossing the Sinai desert into Egypt. At the moment Land Rovers are not permitted across the Sinai as they are classed as "caravans", and all such vehicles are prohibited. Only saloon cars are currently allowed. Range Rovers come into this category.

I have listed here the main routes, but it is possible to deviate from these routes and make up one of your own. Wherever you go in Africa the only problems you are likely to encounter in any country will be of a political nature; therefore it is wise to keep abreast of current developments in all the countries you intend to visit.

More details of the routes mentioned here are given on pages 90-168. Special attention should be paid to the type of road you will be driving on for remember that your vehicle will be your refuge and your home for the duration of the journey and should be nursed along with the utmost care. Soft sand and dirt can exert tremendous pressure on the vehicle as well as yourself, so drive within its limitations and do not work it too hard.

On route shipping

There are occasions when you may resort to shipping your vehicle in Africa — for instance through Lake Nasser, and along the Zaire River.

Nile River Service (Lake Nasser)
This is operated by Nile Valley River Transport Corporation, P.O. Box 122, Aswan, Egypt (Tel. 3348). There are two departures every week, each way, as follows:
- Depart Aswan Monday at 1600, arrive Wadi Halfa Tuesday at 0800.
- Depart Aswan Thursday at 1600, arrive Waddi Halfa Sunday at 0800.
- Depart Wadi Halfa Wednesday at 1600, arrive Aswan Thursday at 0800.
- Depart Wadi Halfa Saturday at 1600, arrive Aswan Sunday at 0800.

No food is provided and travellers should take sufficient supplies for their needs. Approximate fares are: First class £E36.00 or £S80.00; Tourist class £E15.50 or £S38.50. Rates for vehicles are not known but are normally around three times the first class passenger fare. Refer to the currency conversion chart (page 24) for equivalent rate in dollars or sterling of Egyptian and Sudanese pounds.

Nile River Service (Sudan)
This is operated by Sudan River Transport Corporation, P.O. Box 29, Khartoum North, Sudan. Owing to insufficient navigable water in the upper sections of the River Nile, the boat trip which normally travels to Juba now turns round at Malakal. There is a weekly service each way as follows:
- Depart Kosti Thursday at 1000 hours, arrive Malakal Saturday at 0700
- Depart Malakal Sunday at 1000 hours, arrive Kosti Tuesday at 0700

Food is available on board, but passengers may take and cook their own food if they wish. Vehicle fares are not known but passenger fares are: First class £S33.00 to £S120.00; Second class £S26.00 to £S70.00. These fares do not include meals.

Zaire River Service
This is operated by Onatra, Office National des Transports, B.P. 78 Kinshasa, Zaire (Tel. 24769 or 22424; Telex 21017ZR); also B.P. 162, Kisangani, Zaire (Tel. 254).

Boats capable of carrying passengers and vehicles run regularly between Kinshasa and Kisangani. It is recommended that overlanders take advantage of this service, which makes an interesting addition to the trip as well as providing a break from driving. You can ferry your vehicle from Lisala or Bumba to Kisangani, and see the beauty of the dense jungle, teeming with wildlife, from one of Africa's greatest rivers, also teeming with wildlife.

There is a weekly service, departing Kinshasa every Monday, and arriving in Kisangani 9 days later. The downstream trip from Kisangani to Kinshasa (1,080 miles/1740 km) takes 5 days. Each trip calls at Bolobo; Mbandaka; Lisala; Bumba; Basoko; and Kisangani. There are also several unscheduled minor stops. It is not possible to give an accurate account of costs, but the trip from Lisala to Kisangani for vehicle and driver is about £45 sterling, or from Kinshasa to Kisangani, £145 sterling.

Travelling companions

The choice of persons or person to accompany you is of paramount importance and the success or failure of the whole trip can depend upon your choice. The reasons are obvious; you will be spending practically every minute of the day and night together, in the cramped confinement of your vehicle or tent for most of the time, and any clash of personalities could be disastrous.

Age is not really important but character is and you must ensure as far as possible that those in the group are of similar habits and character, that they are known to one other, and are capable of amicable association. Make it clear who will be in charge, and that instructions must be adhered to: it is advisable to draw up a list of regulations before setting out. Remember, on a trip such as this there can be only one leader, one person who will make the final decisions, albeit in consultation with the others.

Physical fitness is an important factor in selecting your travelling companions, as there will be some extremes in temperature to contend with, and times when everybody will be required to push and heave when the vehicle becomes stuck, or to lift when it comes to changing a wheel. Bear this in mind when deciding whether or not to take young children.

Any persons suffering from a chronic illness or ailment should really be excluded, for you could spend the entire trip nursing that person; if the condition deteriorates and urgent medical attention is required, you could find yourself in a position where that particular treatment is not available, as is often the case in certain areas of Africa.

Most important, at least one member of your group should be a professional motor mechanic or have sound mechanical knowledge.

Travel restrictions

From time to time politics, civil wars and natural disasters may force a country to close its borders or roads. In such cases it is nearly always possible to make a detour by road, and where this is not possible there is nearly always a cargo ship in the nearest port willing to take you and your vehicle around the troubled country so that you may continue your journey. If any trouble does develop the first people to hear of it are the representatives of that country in Embassies and Consuls throughout the world, who will immediately advise any prospective visitor to that country on application. If the problem is severe then that country will instruct its representatives not to issue any further visas or entry permits. If you are in any doubt about entering any particular country then don't. Always keep abreast of developing political situations by keeping in regular contact with representatives of your own country; such representatives are stationed in most of the countries you will visit. If you happen to get caught up in any particular situation, whether political or otherwise, contact your nearest Embassy or Consul immediately. A full list of addresses and telephone numbers is given in Appendix 2. It should be noted that they can only give immediate advice. Should you require practical assistance, this could take time.

Rain chart

It must be emphasised that this chart is intended solely as a guide, that African weather can be totally unpredictable and the rainy season can pass without a drop of rain falling. On the other hand it can rain in the dry seasons.

0 No rain expected L Light rains expected M Medium rains expected H Heavy rains expected	January	February	March	April	May	June	July	August	September	October	November	December
North African Coast	L	L	0	0	0	0	0	0	0	0	L	M
Northern Sahara	0	0	0	0	0	0	0	0	0	0	0	0
Morocco	0	0	0	0	0	0	0	0	0	0	0	0
Mid Sahara	0	0	0	0	0	0	0	0	0	0	0	0
Senegal	0	0	0	0	0	0	L	M	L	0	0	0
Ivory Coast	0	0	L	M	H	H	M	0	L	M	M	M
Southern Sahara	0	0	0	0	L	M	M	M	0	0	0	0
Northern Nigeria	0	0	0	0	L	M	H	H	M	0	0	0
Southern Nigeria	0	0	L	L	M	H	H	H	H	M	L	0
Central African Republic	0	0	M	M	M	M	M	H	H	H	L	0
Northern Zaire	L	M	M	H	M	M	M	H	H	H	M	L
Southern Zaire	H	H	H	L	0	0	0	0	0	0	M	H
Kenya	0	L	M	H	M	0	0	0	0	L	L	L
Western Tanzania	M	M	H	M	0	0	0	0	0	M	M	M
Tanzanian Coast	L	L	M	H	M	0	0	0	0	0	L	L
Zambia	H	M	M	0	0	0	0	0	0	0	M	M
Botswana	L	0	0	0	0	0	0	0	0	0	0	0
South Africa (Johannesburg)	M	M	L	0	0	0	0	0	M	M	M	H
Egypt	0	0	0	0	0	0	0	0	0	0	0	0
Northern Sudan	0	0	0	0	0	0	0	L	0	0	0	0
Southern Sudan	0	0	0	0	0	M	M	M	L	0	0	0
Zimbabwe	H	M	M	0	0	0	0	0	0	0	L	M

Temperature chart

The number given in each square represents the average maximum temperature in celsius (centigrade)

	January	February	March	April	May	June	July	August	September	October	November	December
North African Coast	15	16	18	21	24	28	31	32	29	25	20	16
Northern Sahara	18	21	25	30	34	40	43	42	38	31	24	18
Morocco	19	21	23	26	29	33	38	38	32	29	23	19
Mid Sahara	22	25	29	34	38	43	46	46	43	37	29	22
Senegal	32	33	35	37	38	38	35	33	35	36	34	32
Ivory Coast	30	31	31	32	31	29	28	28	28	29	31	31
Southern Sahara	34	36	39	41	41	38	34	32	34	36	37	34
Northern Nigeria	36	38	41	42	41	38	34	33	34	35	37	36
Southern Nigeria	33	34	35	34	33	32	32	31	32	32	33	33
Central African Republic	33	34	34	33	32	31	30	30	31	31	32	32
Northern Zaire	31	31	31	31	31	30	29	28	29	30	29	30
Southern Zaire	29	29	30	30	31	31	29	30	29	29	29	29
Kenya	27	28	28	27	25	24	24	23	25	25	24	24
Western Tanzania	28	28	28	28	28	28	28	29	31	32	31	28
Tanzanian Coast	31	31	31	30	29	29	28	28	28	29	30	31
Zambia	26	26	26	26	25	23	23	25	29	31	29	27
Botswana	31	30	29	28	26	23	24	26	30	32	32	32
South Africa (Johannesburg)	26	25	24	22	19	17	17	20	23	25	25	26
Egypt	24	26	30	35	39	42	41	41	39	37	31	25
Northern Sudan	28	29	34	39	43	43	42	42	41	40	33	29
Southern Sudan	31	33	36	39	39	37	33	32	37	36	34	31
Zimbabwe	26	26	26	26	23	21	21	23	26	28	27	26

Crossing the Sahara

It is possible to cross the Sahara desert only by one of the three main routes mentioned earlier, and it is wise to keep to these routes and not deviate from them as it is so easy to get lost. Many of the minor roads/tracks, and some of the major roads/tracks, across the desert are closed to tourists and are so marked on any good map. This is mainly due to lack of facilities, extreme heat, or the isolation of such roads. On the other hand the restriction might be owing to the presence of military installations or top secret work of some type so *always* stick to the given routes.

When to travel

Your trip should be planned so that you travel at a time when weather conditions are favourable: when the desert heat is at its lowest, and when the heavy rains have ceased or not yet started.

When it comes to crossing the Sahara, this should be undertaken between October, when temperatures start subsiding, through to March or April, when they begin rising again.

The rainy season throughout Africa must be avoided at all costs. In general, the rainy months fall between the beginning of May and the end of September, but they can start early and finish late; and in Central Africa and Zaire rain can be expected at any time, although the main seasons are September/October, end of January into February, and May/June. In the southern region of Africa the rain starts in October through to February. For more detailed information refer to the Rain Chart and Heat Chart on pages 19 and 20.

The ideal month to cross the Sahara is December, when the desert is at its coolest and there is less likelihood of violent sand storms, another element to beware of.

Length of journey

How long it takes you to travel across Africa, from your chosen starting point, depends entirely on the amount of time you have available, whether you are out of work or on extended leave, and also how much money you have.

No-one can lay down any specific time limit for the trip, although tour operators normally take around 8 weeks to travel from London to Nairobi, and 12 weeks to Johannesburg. One important thing to bear in mind is this: the longer the trip takes you, the more you will see and learn, the more friends you will make, and the more you will enjoy. The person that rushes from A to B misses the important items, learns nothing apart from how to wreck his vehicle quickly, and meets only the border officials.

You must, however, work out a timed routine to allow for missing adverse weather conditions such as the Sahara heat and the Central African rains, and also to keep within the time limit of your visas (although it is possible to renew visas on route). This routine need not be rigid: allow enough flexibility for such mishaps as illness or vehicle breakdowns. Take your time and make the journey last. It is most likely a 'once in a lifetime' trip, and I have met many people who have done the trip, and reminisced 'I wish I had made it last longer'.

If you allow for an average of 100 miles per day, this will allow plenty of time for sightseeing, and prolonged stays in some areas. There are times when you could quite comfortably cover 300 miles in a day on some tarmac roads such as in Nigeria, Cameroun, or from Kenya south; but there are also times when you will be hard pushed to travel 50 miles in a day such as in the Sahara region, and on the dirt roads of Zaire.

The total mileage you are likely to cover is entirely dependent on the route you choose and the deviations you may make.

Finance

A lot of your expenditure will be incurred before you leave your home country, on such things as visas, vaccinations, photographs, passports, first aid kit, vehicle spares and extras.

Budgeting for your trip
You should make allowance for expenditure on the following items when budgeting for your trip.

● Before departure

Passports
Photos
Visas
Insurances
Carnet de Passage
International driving permits
International Certificate for motor
  vehicles
Cost of travellers cheques
Sleeping bags
Tents
Other camping equipment

Special clothing
Post
Stationery
Maps and reference books
Photographic equipment
Vaccinations
Medical and dental examinations
First aid kit
Vehicle spares
Vehicle equipment
Shipping

● During the trip

Additional spares for vehicle
Additional visas
Emergency funds (fines, detours
  breakdowns etc.)
Entry to game parks
Ferry crossings

Food and drink
Fuel (petrol or diesel) and
  lubricants
Hotel/camping accommodation
Medical expenses

No actual costs have been stated as these will vary considerably with nationality (visas required), individual needs and requirements, chosen route, vehicle and inflation.

Expenditure along the way
It is not possible to detail the expenditure likely during the journey as this, like time limits, will depend upon your chosen route and many other factors. But the main expenditure once you have left home will be for food, petrol and spending money.

Ample allowance should be made for unexpected emergencies such as

22

vehicle breakdown or diversion. Whatever you do, don't penny pinch. Having spent so much time and money on planning the trip of a lifetime, you would be foolish indeed to jeopardise the whole expedition by running short of money on the way.

As far as money for petrol or diesel fuel is concerned, you should get to know your vehicle before you depart and therefore be aware how many miles it will do to the gallon in different circumstances. A good guide is to deduct 33% from the normal fuel consumption to calculate your average in Africa, for although at times you will be able to cruise long distances on quiet tarmac roads (there is little traffic outside main towns across the continent), in Zaire and across the desert your fuel consumption will be increased considerably as you will either be struggling through soft sand, or crawling along on rutted dirt tracks. This 33% will also allow for unexpected mileage.

I did my latest trip in a 4 cylinder petrol Land Rover which averaged 17 miles to the gallon at home. During the trip I was lucky to get 10 miles to the gallon in the desert, yet on the good tarmac roads I was averaging 24 miles to the gallon and my average for the whole trip was 16½ mpg.

Whether your chosen vehicle is a Land Rover V8 petrol, 4 cylinder petrol, or 4 cylinder diesel, Toyota Land Cruiser or Volkswagen Combi, it is impossible to provide accurate expenditure costs as far as fuel consumption is concerned. These three makes of vehicle are by far the most popular encountered during a Trans African Safari, but each one reacts differently. The driver can affect the fuel consumption considerably, some being heavy footed on the accelerator and others more gentle. Speed, traffic, stopping and starting, roads, altitude, and even weather, all contribute to the variation in fuel consumption of any vehicle, so work out before you leave home approximately what your consumption will be, and be generous in your allowance.

Carrying your money
Travellers cheques are the safest means of carrying money, provided you keep a note of the numbers of each cheque — this enables lost or stolen cheques to be replaced in almost any country within hours. Cash should also be carried, particularly in international currencies such as sterling, dollars, French francs, or Deutschmarks, as certain banks will not accept travellers' cheques, and hard cash is acceptable to any finance house anywhere. It is also handy for exchanging on the black market when no other source is available, such as weekends or public holidays.

It is not advisable to rely on 'transferred' money, i.e. money sent from your bank to a bank in the country where you happen to be when you need it, as this procedure is not at all reliable in Africa, with the exception of one or two capitals such as Lagos, or Nairobi. Even by the quickest method this could take a week or more.

Personal expenditure
As with general finance, it would not be wise or possible to detail exactly how much you will require for your personal expenditure as this will vary considerably from person to person. Apart from food and drink, you will go for several days in uninhabited areas without spending anything. Only when you come to a town will you find the need to purchase some item for yourself, such as an ice cream or a pint of beer. The time will arise when you may need to stock up on medicines or film for your camera or decide to purchase a souvenir of your trip. This should be taken into consideration

+ Price varies depending on currency exchange rate which is nearly all black market.
+ + Drastic shortage of fuel from normal sources.

FUEL COST AND CURRENCY EXCHANGE	Fuel price quoted is at December 1985 and is given only as a guide to help calculate the difference in price from one country to the next and to enable you to fill your tanks when you know the next country charges more. The end column gives the currency for that country and the exchange rate for £1 sterling (approximate)

	Petrol Cost (in sterling per gallon)	Currency & Exchange	
Algeria	£1.32	Dinar	6.90
Benin	£1.80	CFA France	550
Botswana	£1.47 S.A. Rand accepted	Pula	3.10
Burkina Fasso	£2.24	CFA	550
Cameroun	£1.65	CFA	550
C.A.R.	£2.40	CFA	550
Congo	£2.82	CFA	550
Egypt	£1.20	Pound	1.20
Gabon	£1.84	CFA	550
Ghana	£0.80 to £4.20 + (black market, shortage)	Cedi	86.00
Ivory Coast	£2.60	CFA	550
Kenya	£1.80	Shilling	23.45
Liberia	£1.20	Dollar	1.43
Libya	£1.04	Dinar	0.42
Malawi	£2.55	Kwacha	2.38
Mali	£3.50 (shortage)	CFA	550
Mauritania	£1.48	Ouguiya	110.8
Morocco	£1.34	Dirham	13.8
Mozambique	£2.05 + +	Metical	59.84
Niger	£1.45	CFA	550
Nigeria	£0.62	Naira	1.432
Rwanda	£2.40	Franc	134.26
Senegal	£2.04	CFA	550
Sierra Leone	N/A	Leone	7.60
South Africa	£1.68	Rand	3.72
Sudan	N/A	Pound	3.6
Swaziland	£1.35 S.A. Rand accepted	Lilangeni	3.72
Tanzania	£2.22 (about £3.00 black market)	Shilling	23.45
Tchad	£1.82	CFA	550
Togo	£1.96	CFA	550
Tunisia	£1.39	Dinar	1.08
Uganda	£4.20 + +	Shilling	1.99
U.K.	£1.79		
Zaire	£3.50 + + (£4.40 to £7.20 black market)	Zaire	78.71
Zambia	£2.85	Kwacha	7.95
Zimbabwe	£2.40 (slight shortage)	Dollar	2.38

This is a fairly good road but one that can cause a lot of vehicle damage if not negotiated with care.

when calculating your personal allowance. For normal expenditure without any unforeseen purchases, you could work on an amount of £2.50 per day as a rough guide. Obviously, if you decide to drink a lot of African beer, at £2 or more a pint, you will require a lot of money. Remember also that there will be occasions when you will want to stay in a hotel, or you may have to pay for camping. There will also be entrance fees into game parks, gratuities, and ferry crossings.

In an absolute emergency, your High Commission or Consul in the country you are currently travelling in may assist you with a loan, but they are unsympathetic towards travellers who through their own bad planning and carelessness have run out of money. Ensure from the start that your finances are sufficient.

CFA franc

Several African countries have unified currency known as the CFA franc (Communauté Financière Africaine franc), and you are strongly advised to carry large amounts of this currency with you. As the CFA franc is not always easily obtained outside Africa, you should make a point of obtaining some at the first country you reach that uses this currency (refer to map on page 27). By carrying large amounts of CFA francs you will avoid the interest rates payable when exchanging other currency for the CFA, also when you cross the border into the next CFA country you will have currency available for your purchases — invaluable on a Sunday or public holiday or when the banks are closed, or when the nearest bank is a long way from the border.

There is no restriction on the amount that you may take out of or into any particular country if the adjoining country uses the same CFA franc. But beware, there are two types of CFA franc, one for use in Central African countries (Centrale), and one for use in West African countries (Ouest), and they are *not* interchangeable although the exchange rate is exactly the same, around 550 to the pound sterling (see chart page 24).

Although currency exchange rates fluctuate the exchange rate for the French franc/CFA franc remains constant at 50 CFA: 1FF.

CFA franc regulations

In the event of your leaving a country that uses CFA francs and entering a country that uses a different currency the amount of CFA francs that you can take out with you is around 100,000 francs although some countries do not stipulate any limit.

The CFA franc is issued in notes of 500, 1,000 and 5,000, and coins of 5, 10, 25, and 100. Each note and coin is marked 'Ouest' or 'Centrale', and some notes or coins are also marked with the name of the country of issue such as Tchad, but this does mean it is not acceptable in, for example, Gabon, provided the countries are all in the same West or Central group.

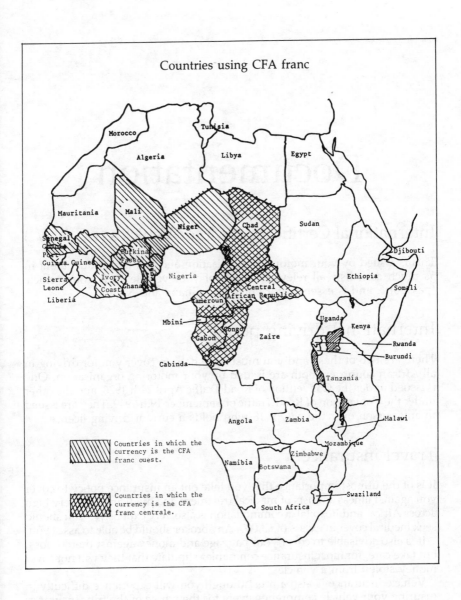

Countries using CFA franc

Countries in which the currency is the CFA franc ouest.

Countries in which the currency is the CFA franc centrale.

Documentation

International Certificate of Motor Vehicles (I.C.M.V.)

This is issued by your motoring organisation and is a useful document in as much as it lists all relevant details of your vehicle. It is your vehicle 'passport', and is essential for entry into Ghana and Nigeria.

International driving permit

There are two of these and you must have both to cover you for driving in all African countries. Both are issued by your motoring organisation. One is issued under the Convention of Road Traffic April 24th 1926, and the other under the Convention of Road Traffic of September 19th 1949. They are issued to any person over the age of 18 who holds a current driving licence.

Travel insurance

It is of the utmost importance that you take out an insurance policy to cover you against illness as costs of medical treatment and medicines are very high across Africa, and hospital accommodation is also very expensive. You should seek medical cover in excess of £3,000. Any broker should be able to assist you.

It is also advisable to cover your baggage and money against theft or loss, but take care, for most insurance companies stipulate that they will not cover money stolen from a vehicle.

Vehicle insurance is also a must though you will experience difficulty in insuring your vehicle comprehensively for the whole of the trip. Insurance can be purchased for your vehicle at most border points; in fact it is required at some borders that you purchase vehicle insurance as they will not recognise insurance policies issued by other countries even if it is worldwide cover.

Carnet de Passages en Douanes

This can be one of the most expensive items of your trip and is essential to enable you temporarily to import your vehicle into most countries outside Europe. It takes the place of import duty for which every vehicle is liable, and tax deposits, for the automobile organisation that issues it guarantees these charges on your behalf. It is issued by the automobile organisation in return for an indemnity which can be in the form of a cash deposit lodged with them and returned to you on surrender of the Carnet upon the return of you and your vehicle, or a bankers guarantee stating that they are holding the required cash deposits, or by insurance. The cash deposit methods are the cheapest as you lose nothing on surrender of your Carnet. The insurance method has its advantages, though, as you will not have to lodge a deposit, the insurers doing it for you; but you will have to pay a non-returnable premium which can be very high depending upon the value of your vehicle.

Almost every African country has regulations concerning the temporary importation of a vehicle and the amount of import duty payable, and this varies from one country to another. The only alternative to the Carnet is to carry large amounts of money with you and lodge the required deposit at the entry point into a country, and collect it back when you leave the country, but this method is neither wise nor practical. Two of the countries in Africa with the highest duty rate are Nigeria and Egypt at 250% times the value of your vehicle. This means that should your vehicle be worth £10,000, the duty on it would amount to £25,000. This would be the amount you would be required to lodge with the bank or the automobile organisation, and the amount the insurers would lodge on your behalf. And if for some reason you left your vehicle in any country as a permanent import, you would most likely lose your deposit when the customs of that country lodge a claim for duty to your automobile organisation.

The insurance works in a similar way. Although you pay the premium, this in no way clears you of any possible claim that may arise through your leaving the vehicle in a country as a permanent import. You would still have to pay it, although originally you do not have to lodge the large amount of money as a deposit. Generally the premium required by insurance companies in this case is around 7% of the highest claim likely on your journey and the Carnet deposit is calculated by the same method, i.e. the deposit you would have to lodge would be equal to the highest duty claim likely. In the case of Nigeria or Egypt your required premium would be 7% of 250% times the value of your vehicle; thus if your vehicle is worth £10,000, the required duty would be £25,000, and 7% of this amounts to £1,750, which would be the premium payable. This method is by far the best for people who do not have large amounts of money to lodge as deposit. Most African countries have import duties at a rate in excess of 100% times your vehicle value.

When applying for a visa for entry into Nigeria, and Zaire, the Carnet must be produced in lieu of a return air ticket before a visa will be issued. This is also the case with some other countries in Africa.

Tunisia and Algeria do not require the Carnet for entry, and it will not be issued to include Zimbabwe. Here they will view the Carnet and then charge you a small deposit, non-returnable, which only amounts to two or three pounds sterling. Zambia and Botswana are likely to refuse to accept the Carnet and will also charge a small deposit which will be nominal.

Using the Carnet
This is one of the most valuable documents you will have with you and must be carefully guarded for its loss or theft could prove very expensive. Whenever you enter a country, it is important that your entry is recorded by the customs officials on the counterfoil of each Carnet page. They will then remove a section of the page, retain it and return the Carnet to you. It is the duty of the customs official to carry out this procedure but it is your responsibility to ensure that it is carried out correctly. You must make sure that the Carnet is stamped in the correct place and that the correct page is removed. The same procedure is carried out upon departure from the country. Whenever the carnet is stamped upon entry to a country, it *must* also be stamped at the point of departure, and it is up to you to see that this happens. If you fail to do so you could be liable for the payment of customs duty and taxes. Should you be unable to get the Carnet stamped for any reason at the exit point of any country, your liability will remain until you can prove conclusively that the vehicle has been exported from that country. In such a case, at the end of your journey you should take your vehicle to a Police or Customs Office and ask them to inspect the vehicle and sign and stamp the Carnet on the 'certificate of location' which is on the back page.

The Carnet is valid for only a year from date of issue, but this can be postdated to the date of commencement of your journey in which case the Carnet will be valid for one year from the latter date. In many countries you may temporarily import your vehicle for up to a maximum of only six months and in some cases less than this, or to the expiry date of the Carnet whichever comes first. If through serious illness or an accident your vehicle is likely to remain beyond the limit, or after your departure, you should immediately contact your issuing motoring organisation, or the local agent in the country where the vehicle is, or the customs of that country, for advice.

Road fund licence

Commonly known as car tax, the disc in your window is accepted in most African countries, even if it is out of date, except perhaps Nigeria. Officials do not seem to bother about it much but if it has run out it is best to remove it from sight. You will only be required to purchase a road fund licence of the country you are in if you are going to stay for any length of time, normally over 3 months. The one exception to this is Botswana where every tourist has to purchase a 'visitors' road fund licence disc at a cost of 1 pula (which is about 1 dollar or £0.65 sterling) irrespective of the amount of time you plan to spend in that country.

Nationality plates

All vehicles must have a nationality plate affixed to the rear of the vehicle. These are normally available from your motoring organisation, who will also advise whether any of the countries you are visiting require a translation into Arabic of your number plate.

Documentation requirements for driver and vehicle

	Carnet de Passage	V.R.B. or I.C.M.V.	I.D.P. or N.D.L.	3rd party insurance	Road tax	Drive on left or right
Algeria	N/C	VRB	NDL	C	N/C	right
Benin	C	ICMV	IDP	N/C	N/C	right
Botswana	N/C	VRB	IDP	C	C	left
Burkina Fasso	C	ICMV	IDP	N/C	N/R	right
Cameroun	C	ICMV	IDP	N/C	N/C	right
C.A.R.	C	ICMV	IDP	N/C	N/C	right
Congo	C	ICMV	IDP	N/C	N/C	right
Egypt	C	ICMV	IDP	C	N/C	right
Gabon	C	N/C	IDP	N/C	N/C	right
Ghana	C	VRB	NDL	N/C	N/C	right
Ivory Coast	C	ICMV	IDP	N/C	N/C	right
Kenya	C	VRB	NDL	C	N/C+	left
Liberia	C	ICMV	NDL	N/C	N/R	right
Libya	C	ICMV	NDL	N/C	N/C	right
Malawi	C	N/C	NDL	C	N/R	left
Mali	C	ICMV	IDP	N/C	N/R	right
Mauritania	C	ICMV	IDP	N/C	N/R	right
Morocco	N/R	VRB	NDL	C	N/C	right
Mozambique	C	ICMV	IDP	N/C	N/C	right
Niger	C	ICMV	IDP	C	N/R	right
Nigeria	C	ICMV	IDP	C	C	right
Rwanda	C	ICMV	IDP	N/C	N/R	right
Senegal	C	ICMV	IDP	C	N/C+	right
Sierra Leone	C	ICMV	IDP	N/C	N/C	right
South Africa	C	VRB	NDL/IDP	C	C	left
Sudan	C	ICMV	IDP	N/C	N/C+	left
Swaziland	C	VRB	NDL	C	N/C	left
Tanzania	C	ICMV	IDP	N/C	N/R	left
Tchad	C	VRB	IDP	N/C	N/R	right
Togo	C	ICMV	IDP	N/C	N/R	right
Tunisia	N/R	VRB	NDL	C	N/C	right
Uganda	C	ICMV	NDL	N/C	N/R	left
Zaire	C	ICMV	IDP	N/C	N/R	right
Zambia	C	ICMV	NDL	C	N/C	left
Zimbabwe	N/C	VRB	IDP	C	N/C	left

C = Compulsory. N/C = Not Compulsory. IDP = International Driving Permit. N/R = Not Required. NDL = National Driving Licence (from your home country). ICMV = International Certificate for Motor Vehicles. VRB = Vehicle Registration Book. + = Circulation permit req.

Proof of ownership of vehicle

All travellers should take with them some sort of proof of ownership of the vehicle, such as an authenticated receipt for moneys paid. The vehicle registration book does not constitute proof of ownership. If you do not own the vehicle, then you should carry written authorisation from the owner showing he/she has no objection to your using it.

Special permits/restrictions

Egypt Permission is required to drive a right-hand drive vehicle in Egypt. This can be obtained from the Traffic Department on arrival.

Kenya A circulation permit must be obtained for all foreign vehicles touring in Kenya. A temporary permit is issued at the border, giving the driver 7 days to obtain the necessary permit from the Registrar of Motor Vehicles, 1st floor, Gill House, Moi Avenue, Nairobi (opposite the 'Kenya' cinema). A small fee is payable for the permit which is valid for 3 months and is equivalent to road tax. After 3 months, if the vehicle remains in Kenya, the full rates are payable which for a Land Rover would be around 350 Kenya Shillings.

Kenya/Tanzania border closure In November, 1983, the Kenya Tanzania border re-opened and overlanders no longer required permission to cross between these two countries. However, the current situation is somewhat unclear and, should permits be required, those needed are:
(a) Permit to leave Kenya via the closed border.
(b) Permit to enter Tanzania via the closed border.

The procedure for obtaining these permits is this; first of all you must write to the Commissioner of Police, Police Headquarters, Dar-es-Salaam, Tanzania, if you are in Kenya travelling south, or visit personally if you are in Tanzania travelling north. State that you wish to apply for permission to cross the border into Kenya and enclose the following information:
1. Your vehicle type
2. Registration, engine, and chassis numbers
3. Number of passengers, their names and passport numbers
4. Citizenship of passengers
5. Date you wish to cross
Allow two or three weeks for a reply. When the permit arrives, take it personally to the Commissioner of Police Headquarters, Nairobi, Kenya, and he will issue you the permit to cross the border from the Kenyan side. He will not issue the Kenyan permit until he has seen the Tanzanian permit.

If you are in Tanzania travelling north, write to the Commissioner of Police first, then apply to the Tanzanian Police.

Overlanders will be issued with a permit to cross the border only at Namanga, and in doing so must report to Customs, Immigration, and Police.

Nigeria It should be noted that green coloured Land Rovers are liable to be refused admittance to Nigeria, mainly because government vehicles in Nigeria are green, and could be confused with overlanders' vehicles of that colour.

Senegal The visitor arriving by road receives a temporary pass at the border valid for ten days. In that time he must take the temporary pass to either Touring Club de Senegal, 28, Avenue Roume, Dakar; or Ministry of Finance, Avenue Charles Haisne, Dakar, if he/she intends to stay in Senegal longer than that time. A deposit of around £100 sterling (50,000CFA) is required for a car permit.

Sudan All vehicles travelling in the Sudan must have a transit permit for the vehicle. It is issued by applying direct to the Ministry of the Interior, (Passports and Immigration), P.O. Box 770, Khartoum, Sudan, allowing plenty of time for the permit to be issued. It is also available from Sudanese Embassies when applying for entry visas if the Carnet de Passage is produced at the time of application. Visas and permits can be obtained in the Sudanese Embassies of border countries such as Kenya (Nairobi), Central African Republic (Bangui), or Egypt (Cairo). The cost is around £40 sterling. Issue could take up to two weeks as the applications have to be referred to Khartoum.

Passports

These are required by every traveller before he or she is permitted to enter a foreign country. It should be applied for well in advance of your departure as it could take some time to issue. British passport holders, once they have received their passport, may, on personal application to their passport office, be issued with a second passport, valid for one year only. This can be beneficial in obtaining visas when a large number have to be obtained in a short period of time, but the main reason for the issue is to enable the holder to visit certain countries in conflict with others. For example any person with an Israeli stamp in his passport, or known to have visited or intending to visit Israel, will not be allowed entry into an Arab country; and anyone with a South African stamp in his passport, or who is known to have visited or be intending to visit South Africa, will be refused entry into Nigeria, Kenya, and many other black African states. Thus the second passport comes in handy. It is not wise to advertise the fact that you possess a second passport to anybody, and it should be kept concealed at all times.

Personal bank guarantee/credit letter

This is a very useful piece of paper, worth nothing as far as cash is concerned, but it could prove invaluable. It should be drafted on the headed paper of your bank and worded as follows:

"I declare that this Bank holds the sum of £.......... in the name of .... which can be used for the purpose of purchasing air or sea travel tickets only, from any country in the world to a destination in the United Kingdom. This Bank will be responsible for the cost of such travel tickets.

This Letter of Credit shall be cancelled and endorsed thereon on exchange for the tickets and duly returned to this Bank for payment."
It is important that this letter be dated on the day of issue but clearly marked 'valid indefinitely'.

The reason for the above letter is this. Some countries will want to know exactly what money you have with you, and also what arrangements you have made to return home in the event of vehicle breakdown. The above letter is as good as a one-way air ticket out of the country, which is all that the authorities require, but it *must* be marked for indefinite validity otherwise you are likely to be told 'it is too old,' or 'it is out of date'. I have experienced this on more than one occasion. One country that is very particular about visitors having a return ticket or bank guarantee is South Africa, where they often insist on a deposit equal to the cost of an air ticket home if the traveller has neither.

Another useful letter of credit that it would be advisable to take with you should be drafted as follows:

"I declare that this Bank holds the sum of £......... in the name of .... which can be transferred to any country in the world at the request of the above named person on immediate notice in writing, identification, or telephone call. I confirm that these funds will be available in case of need to meet such a transfer."

This also should be marked for indefinite validity, and will cover you in the event of certain countries, such as Zaire and Nigeria, stipulating that you have a certain amount of money for each day you intend to spend in their country. If you are getting towards the end of your trip and your finances are low then this letter could prove invaluable to you.

It is advisable to have these credit letters drafted for each and every member of your party, and to take them with you when you apply for visas, as most Embassies insist on a return air ticket before issuing a visa, even if you have a Carnet de Passage with you.

I have never had any problems since I began carrying the above two letters of credit with me.

Sudan A deposit is sometimes required for each person travelling in Sudan and costs around £100 sterling. This deposit is required to ensure that the visitor has sufficient funds for maintenance during the stay in Sudan and is refunded on leaving the country. More often than not the 'Bank Guarantee/Credit letter' will be accepted in lieu of a deposit provided it is drawn up correctly (see above).

International certificates of vaccination.

There are certain vaccinations that a visitor to Africa must have before being allowed into most of the countries, and there are others that are strongly advisable. The necessary vaccinations are given by your local G.P. or, in the case of yellow fever, by a hospital in your area, and an international certificate issued that will have to be produced at border crossings to enable the officials to see that you have been vaccinated. As more and more diseases are being eliminated, so fewer vaccinations are required. Cholera is on the way out, and smallpox has been eliminated.

It is recommended that travellers also be vaccinated against typhoid and paratyphoid. Tetanus is another vaccination that no traveller to Africa should go without. Vaccination against these three gives protection for up to 5 years. It is also highly recommended that travellers be inoculated against polio and hepatitus. There are two main types of malaria and both are prevalent in Africa so each traveller should carry a supply of the necessary prophylactic. Your doctor will advise.

The Embassies where you obtain your visas will advise which vaccinations you should have, and some will wish to see your vaccination certificates when

Health and vaccination requirement chart

	Yellow Fever	Cholera	Tetanus	Typhoid, Para-typhoid, Tab.	Polio	Hepatitis
Algeria	no	no	advised	advised	no	no
Benin	yes	advised	advised	advised	advised	advised
Botswana	yes	advised	advised	no	no	no
Burkina Fasso	yes	advised	advised	advised	advised	advised
Cameroun	yes	yes	advised	no	no	advised
C.A.R.	yes	yes	advised	no	advised	advised
Congo	yes	yes	advised	no	no	advised
Egypt	no	advised	advised	advised	no	no
Gabon	yes	yes	advised	advised	no	advised
Ghana	yes	yes	advised	no	no	advised
Ivory Coast	yes	yes	advised	advised	no	advised
Kenya	yes	no	advised	advised	no	no
Liberia	yes	yes	advised	no	advised	advised
Libya	no	advised	advised	advised	no	no
Malawi	yes	yes	advised	no	no	no
Mali	yes	yes	advised	advised	no	advised
Mauritania	yes	yes	advised	advised	no	advised
Morocco	no	advised	advised	advised	no	no
Mozambique	yes	yes	advised	advised	advised	advised
Niger	yes	advised	advised	no	no	advised
Nigeria	yes	yes	advised	no	no	no
Rwanda	yes	no	advised	advised	no	no
Senegal	yes	yes	advised	no	advised	advised
Sierra Leone	yes	yes	advised	no	advised	advised
South Africa	yes	no	advised	advised	yes	advised
Sudan	no	yes	advised	advised	advised	advised
Swaziland	yes	yes	advised	advised	advised	advised
Tanzania	yes	no	advised	advised	no	no
Tchad	yes	yes	advised	advised	no	advised
Togo	yes	yes	advised	advised	no	advised
Tunisia	no	advised	advised	advised	no	no
Uganda	yes	yes	advised	advised	no	no
Zaire	yes	yes	advised	no	advised	advised
Zambia	yes	yes	advised	advised	no	advised
Zimbabwe	yes	yes	advised	advised	advised	no

Malaria prophylactics should be taken for all countries you intend visiting, commencing 6 weeks before your departure and finishing 4 weeks after your return.

Visa/entry permit requirements

"Yes" indicates either visa or entry permit required, "No" indicates neither needed. If a visa or entry permit is required, it should be obtained before departure wherever possible.

	British	Irish	French	German (West)	American	New Zealand	Canadian	Australian	Approx. cost of Visa.
Algeria	no	yes	no	yes	yes	yes	yes	yes	-
Benin	yes	yes	no	no	yes	yes	yes	yes	£5.00
Botswana	no	no	no	no	no	no	no	no	-
Burkina Fasso	yes	yes	no	yes	yes	yes	yes	yes	£7.20
Cameroun	yes	yes	yes	yes	yes	yes	yes	yes	£3.00
C.A.R.	yes	yes	no	yes	yes	yes	yes	yes	£4.00
Congo	yes	yes	no	no	yes	yes	yes	yes	£6.50
Egypt	yes	yes	yes	yes	yes	yes	yes	yes	£7.00
Gabon	yes	yes	no	no	yes	yes	yes	yes	£5.00
Ghana	yes	yes	yes	yes	yes	yes	yes	no	£2.50
Ivory Coast	no	yes	no	no	yes	yes	yes	yes	-
Kenya	no	no	yes	no	yes	no	no	yes	-
Liberia	yes	yes	yes	yes	yes	yes	yes	yes	£4.00
Libya	yes	yes	yes	yes	yes	yes	yes	yes	£7.00
Malawi	no	no	yes	no	no	no	no	no	-
Mali	yes	yes	no	yes	yes	yes	yes	yes	£5.00
Mauritania	yes	yes	no	yes	yes	yes	yes	yes	-
Morocco	no	no	no	no	no	no	no	no	-
Mozambique	yes	yes	yes	yes	yes	yes	yes	yes	-
Niger	no	no	no	no	yes	yes	yes	yes	£2.00
Nigeria	yes	yes	yes	yes	yes	yes	yes	yes	£2.50
Rwanda	yes	yes	no	yes	yes	yes	yes	yes	£4.00
Senegal	yes	yes	no	yes	yes	yes	yes	yes	£1.25
Sierra Leone	no	yes	yes	yes	yes	yes	yes	yes	£5.50
South Africa	no	no	yes	yes	yes	yes	no	yes	-
Sudan	yes	yes	yes	yes	yes	yes	yes	yes	£6.00
Swaziland	no	no	yes	yes	no	no	no	no	-
Tanzania	no	no	yes	yes	yes	no	no	no	-
Tchad	yes	yes	no	yes	yes	yes	yes	yes	£5.50
Togo	yes	yes	no	no	yes	yes	no	yes	£3.50
Tunisia	no	no	no	no	no	yes	no	yes	-
Uganda	yes	yes	yes	no	yes	yes	no	yes	no charge
Zaire	yes	yes	yes	yes	yes	yes	yes	yes	£8.00
Zambia	no	no	yes	yes	yes	no	no	no	-
Zimbabwe	no	yes	no	yes	no	no	no	no	-

VISA APPLICATION FORM

(Fill this form in triplicate and attach)
3 passports size photographs

Full name of the applicant (capital letters) .... *FRED SMITH*

Marital status (give full name of Wife/Husband or ex-wife/husband if applicable) .... *SINGLE*

Present address .... *2, ANY PLACE, FALLINGDOWN, HERTS.*

Occupation .... *CARPENTER*   Nationality .... *BRITISH*

Place of birth .... *LONDON*   Date of birth *25-DEC-1950*

Passport No. .... *A 10000*   Date of issue .... *1ST APRIL 1980*

Issuing Authority .... *PASSPORT OFFICE*   Place of issue .... *LONDON*

Date of Expiry .... *31ST MARCH 1990*

Full names of father .... *JOHN SMITH.*   Nationality .... *BRITISH*

Full names of mother .... *ELIZABETH SMITH*   Nationality .... *BRITISH*

Type of visa required (please delete) Voyage Transit/Return, Special, Diplomatic *TRANSIT (OR TOURIST)*

Date of entry in Republic of Zaire and via frontier of .... *10TH JULY 1983*

.... *BANGUI - ZONGO*

Has the applicant previously stayed in Zaire (Please delete) ~~YES~~ — NO

Where .... — .... When .... —

In which capacity : ....

Capacity he now wishes to stay in Zaire .... *TOURIST*

Reason of the actual journey .... *TOURISM/TRANSIT*

Place where the applicant intends to work .... *NONE*

Full name of the Manager of the Company or Mission (please attach appropriate documents)

.... *NONE - TRAVELLING ON OWN INITIATIVE*

and address ....

Full names and addresses of persons able to give charter references in respect of the Applicant

BANK MANAGER ANY BANK, FALLINGDOWN, HERTS.

MANAGER, ANY CARPENTERS FALLINGDOWN, HERTS

My Signature binds me and makes me liable to prosecution in case of false declaration and to refusal of any visa in the future.

London, date .... *10TH JUNE 1983*   Signature .... *F. Smith*

Official use only

Genre de visa accordé ....   No. 05846/

Date de délivrance ....   Durée du séjour ....

Date d'expiration ....

Pour .... entrée(s)

A Londres, le .... 19........

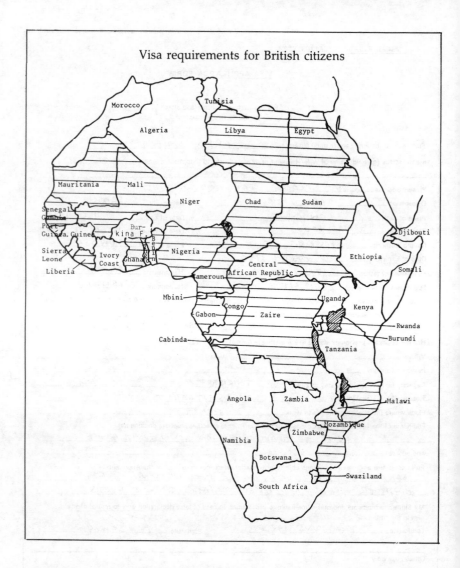

Visa requirements for British citizens

you apply for your visas. Make sure you have all your certificates up to date for you could be refused entry without them. Cholera and hepatitis vaccinations are valid for only 6 months, so if you plan to make your trip a long one you will have to have these two renewed.

Vaccination requirements may not be 100% accurate and travellers should double check with the authorities concerned as to what vaccinations may be required, and to bear in mind that requirements can change at very short notice, even during the journey.

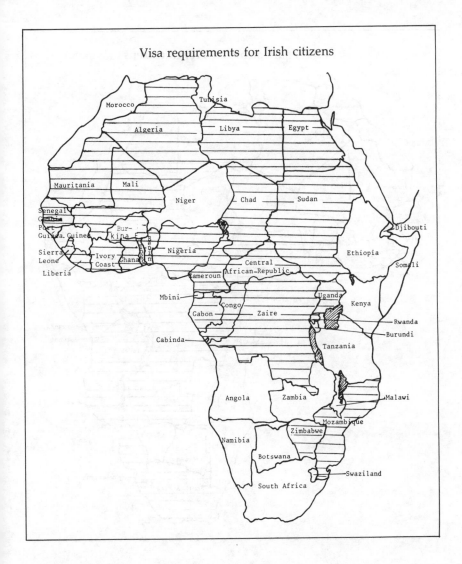

Visa requirements for Irish citizens

Visas, visitors passes and entry permits

These are things you cannot undertake your journey without. They are
required for most of the countries you visit and if possible should all be
obtained before you commence your trip. Visas are required for foreign
countries, while entry permits and visitors passes are required by British
passport holders who wish to gain entry into Commonwealth countries.

It is important that wherever possible you should visit the Embassies and

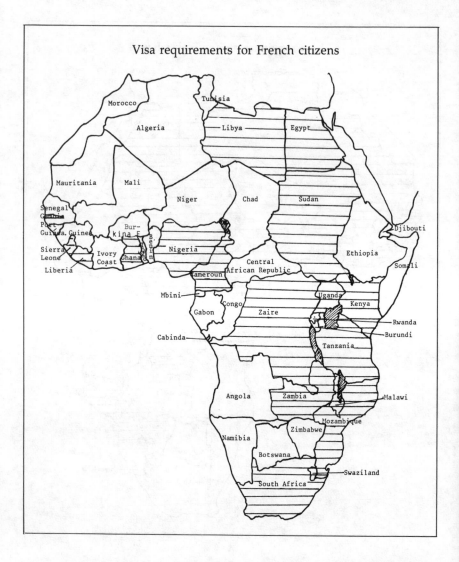

Visa requirements for French citizens

Consulates personally to collect the visas and entry permits you require as a passport lost in the post can cause you considerable delays — particularly one that already has visas in it. (See Appendix A for addresses.) It should also be remembered that visas collected by post can take a long time, a week or more per visa, while collecting personally eliminates postal delays.

When you receive your visa application forms, you will find that each embassy will tell you how long it takes to issue each visa/entry permit, and you can work out from there just when to start collecting them. Always leave

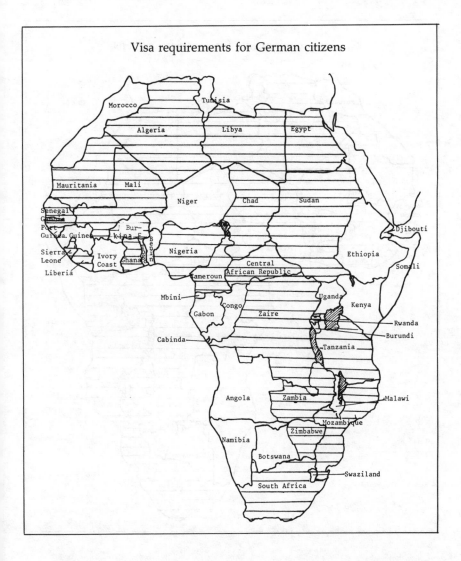

Visa requirements for German citizens

it until as late as practical for visas are not valid for long. Some allow you 6 months to use them, most are 3 months, but some are only one month. By spending a week in your capital collecting visas, you will save 3 or 4 weeks over postal collection. Most visas will be ready for you the next day but some will be issued on the spot while you wait. Note that the Government of Libya stipulates that all visa applications must be on a form printed in the Arabic language, and must be completed in Arabic. No other application will be accepted.

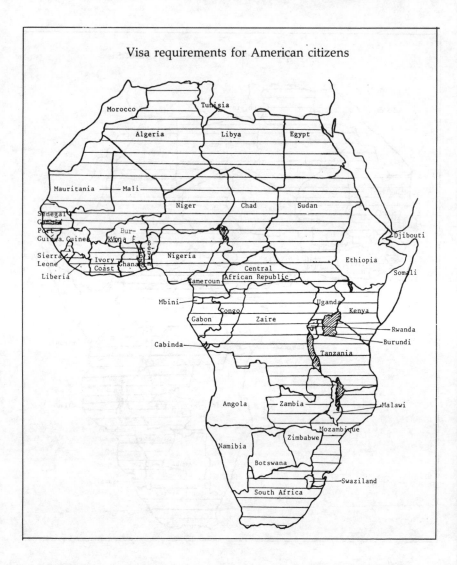

Visa requirements for American citizens

Remember that possession of a visa does not guarantee your entry to a country. For instance, travellers to Nigeria can expect much fluctuation in the opening and closing of borders. This is discussed further on page 64.

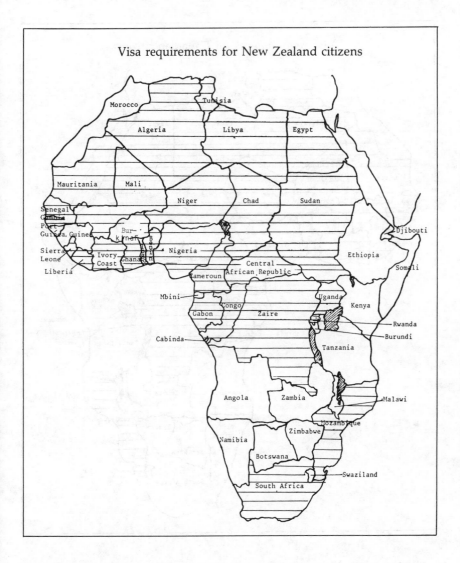

Visa requirements for New Zealand citizens

International Camping Carnet

This is a useful means of identification as far as camping is concerned. It is issued by the International Automobile Federation, a parent body to many national automobile organisations. It shows that the holder is a decent and respectable person and allows entry into many private camping sites. Some sites will allow a reduction on production of this Carnet. You may apply for one through your local motoring association, remembering to submit a photograph of yourself for attaching to the Carnet.

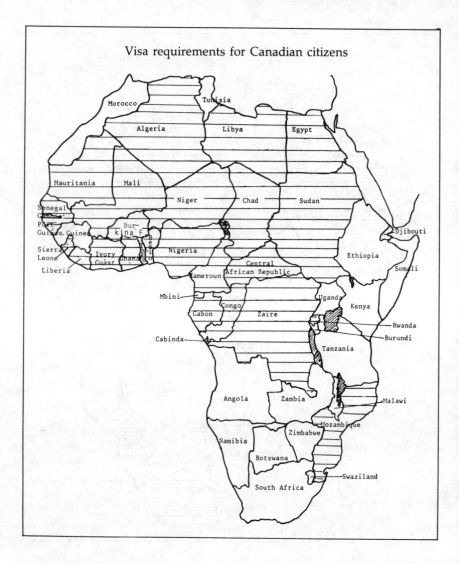

Visa requirements for Canadian citizens

The Internationl Camping Carnet will often be accepted in place of your passport for security when booking into a camp site but ensure that you collect it again when leaving.

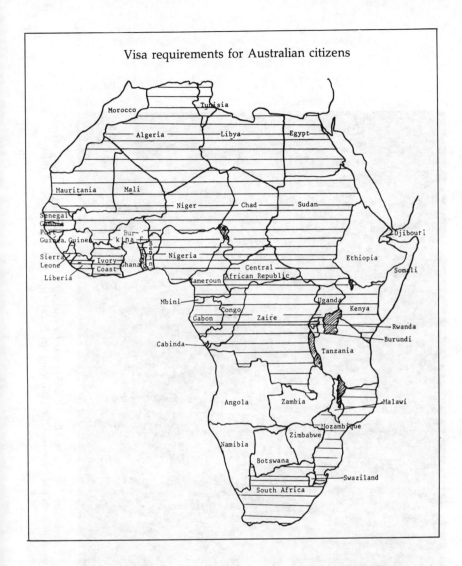

Visa requirements for Australian citizens

Proof of ownership of photographic equipment

It is advisable to carry receipts for all of your photographic equipment to show that it was purchased in your home country. Some countries are very particular about the import/export of cameras etc., and you could be charged duty if you cannot prove ownership and place of purchase.

The author and a fellow "overlander" in the middle of the Sahara. He was a Frenchman cycling his way across Africa and we came across him early one morning after following his tracks for 2 to 3 days. Note the thick sweaters both are wearing.

Vehicle and Equipment

Your most important piece of equipment is, of course, your means of transport and nowadays that can be so varied I will deal with a few in turn.

Bicycle

To cross Africa on a bike you must be really fit and ambitious, although many people are doing it now, some even pulling a trailer behind. With this means of transport you do not have to worry about fuel or engine breakdown or becoming stuck in soft sand, and if you should have any serious breakdown you can just leave your bicycle in the hedge and fly home, as a Carnet is not required. Disadvantages are the small amount of provisions and water that you are able to take with you, and the lack of protection you will have from the scorching sun and other elements. Not a method that I would recommend.

Motor cycle

At one time a motor cycle would not be allowed across the desert but now they are widely accepted on all routes. In fact, this method is becoming more and more popular; there are travellers alone or in groups, particularly with 'tracking' or 'scrambling' motor cycles, sometimes accompanied by motor vehicles. Carrying parts is no great problem as the engine is so small that a spare could almost be taken and the low fuel consumption means no jerry cans need be carried. There is no risk of getting stuck in soft sand and a motor cycle has many advantages over a four-wheel vehicle particularly when it comes to driving on rough roads. Care must be taken as far as security is concerned as valuable items such as cameras are not so safe as they would be in a vehicle. Many overlanders are now using a motorcyclist as pathfinder, to ride ahead to seek the best route across the desert so that soft sand patches and other hazards can be avoided.

47

Saloon car

Not an advisable method unless you are travelling alone with the minimum of luggage, spares and other equipment, since weight will make the vehicle prone to sink in soft sand and without four-wheel drive extricating yourself could be a problem and could lead to vehicle damage, miles from anywhere. A very lightly laden saloon may be able to maintain a high speed to take you over any soft sandy spots, but the ground clearance would not be sufficient for rough roads. Those saloon cars that I have encountered have merely crossed the Sahara desert and then gone no further.

It should also be remembered that saloon cars are not permitted to travel on certain routes.

4 x 4 vehicle

General requirements are for a strong robust vehicle, with high ground clearance and four-wheel drive, such as a Land Rover, which is strongly recommended.

Many overlanders are doing the trip in large ex-army 4 x 4 vehicles and there is nothing wrong with this but it must be remembered that these affect the route you can follow, as some bridges and all ferries have weight restrictions, which may force you to make lengthy detours.

You have to take into consideration the number of passengers you intend to take when selecting your vehicle. For example, no more than four with their equipment should be carried in a Land Rover. If you intend taking two Land Rovers this could be increased to seven or eight persons, with all the equipment being carried in the second vehicle. Calculate carefully the weight of each person, and the weight of all the spares and luggage you will be taking and keep well within (up to about 80% of) the recommended limit of the vehicle manufacturer. Remember that the Land Rover's recommended roof rack limit is 112lb or 50kg, and the roof rack itself can weigh this. Many people exceed this limit and get away with it, but when you are travelling on very rough roads or sand where the vehicle is going to be swaying from side to side like a ship in a storm, exceeding this weight limit could result in the vehicle cracking up, so take care. A great danger is in having the centre of gravity so high — for example, with eight full jerry cans — that the vehicle will tip over on slopes and split tracks. Many trips have been abandoned as a result of overloading (see 'Vehicle strengthening', page 54).

An extra fuel tank should be fitted to your vehicle if this is possible. This will be more convenient than carrying jerry cans, and if this gives you a range of 500 miles or more you need not take so many jerry cans, thus reducing your weight commitment. However, the further your motoring range the better. You will want to take full advantage of your fuel capacity when you come to a country where fuel is very cheap (see fuel cost chart on page 24) particularly when it is followed by a country where fuel is expensive. Care should be taken when opening jerry cans in the heat — this can result in expansion inside the can and the fuel may rush out into your face, particularly if the can is extra full.

Petrol or diesel

This is a difficult choice, each type of engine having its advantages and disadvantages. Both types of fuel are readily available across Africa. Diesel fuel in general is cheaper than petrol so if economy is your prime factor in deciding, diesel must be your choice. On top of this a diesel-engined vehicle will travel more miles to the gallon than a petrol-engined one of roughly the same size. In a 4-cylinder petrol-engined Land Rover you can average around 17 miles to the gallon while with a 4 cylinder diesel-engined Land Rover your average would be around 22 miles to the gallon. This difference, combined with the cheaper cost of diesel fuel, can mean quite a saving over 10,000 miles, which is the distance that most people travel in a trip across Africa. Diesel fuel carries less risk of fire than petrol and as the diesel engine has no electrical system it is advantageous when it comes to fording streams or driving through deep puddles of water. Electrical power is used on a diesel engine only to start it; from there on the ignition can be switched off and the engine will continue running.

A petrol-powered engine is however easier to maintain, parts will be more readily available, petrol itself is a cleaner fuel, and the petrol engine is quieter than the diesel engine. It also has a higher power output, is a higher revving engine and is more easily understood. Although a petrol engine is more expensive to run, spare parts and repairs will be cheaper.

Tyres

This could be a difficult choice as there are so many to choose from but it is important that an all round tyre for use both on and off roads be fitted. Personally, I favour the Michelin XZY for its vehicle performance and comfortable ride, and it's an ideal tyre for the Land Rover. Although expensive they are among the hardest wearing tyres — my sets have lasted around 50,000 miles, and that is hard driving across Africa. These tyres are also readily available right across the continent, should they need replacing. It must be emphasised that one should fit a 'general tyre' and not a strictly 'off road' or road tyre. Whatever your choice you should avoid tubeless tyres, and if possible stick to radials, and not crossply.

Registration plates

Whatever registration plates are on your vehicle will be acceptable throughout Africa, but each vehicle must have a nationality plate affixed as close as possible to the registration plate. These are obtainable from your automobile organisation or shipping agent.

Caravans and trailers

Caravans may be towed on most roads in North Africa, and as far south as the Aswan Dam in Egypt, but under no circumstances should they be towed across Africa owing to the difficult terrain that will be encountered. Some trailers are often towed behind Land Rovers and ex-army vehicles, but this is a practice that should be avoided.

Spare parts

Motor mechanics on your route can be few and far between so it is important that someone in the party has a sound mechanical knowledge. Once you have started crossing Africa you will find spares difficult to obtain outside main cities, and even then they will be very expensive so take as many with you as your weight limit will allow.

Obtain a workshop manual for your vehicle from your nearest agent, if possible the type issued by the manufacturers. It will also assist to carry a spares manual. You should also carry the following spares:

Set of rear half shafts
Set of gaskets
Fan belt
Water pump
Spark plugs (petrol only)
Points (petrol only)
Condenser (petrol only)
Complete set spare bulbs
Two spare wheels with tyres and
 tubes fitted
Two spare tubes
Puncture outfit with tube and tyre
 patches
Fuel pump repair kit
Fuel pipe
Fuel filter

Two oil filters
Radiator hoses
Distributor cap
Rotor arm
H.T. lead
Fuses
Ignition coil
Carburettor repair kit
Set of ball joints
Injectors (diesel only)
Clutch assembly
Brake shoes
Lengths electrical wire with
 insulating tape
Spare speedometer cable
Wandering lead light

A comprehensive tool kit should be carried ensuring that you have a spanner to fit every nut and bolt on your vehicle. Your tool kit should include the following:

Warning triangle
Strong tow rope with shackles
Assortment of self tapping screws,
 nuts, bolts, split pins and
 washers
Tyre levers
Tyre pump

Tyre pressure gauge
Wheel brace
Club hammer
Wrecking bar
Hydraulic jack
Pair high lift jacks
Engine oil and grease

Navigation

The most important navigational aids you will have with you are map and compass but these are no use if you do not know how to use them so if this is the case take lessons in mapreading before you leave home.

Make sure you select a good comprehensive map to cover the route you will be travelling on. The best available for the whole of Africa is the Michelin range at around 63 miles to the inch, and numbers 153 (Africa North & West), 154 (Africa North East), and 155 (Africa Centre and South), cover the whole of the African continent and even show you where petrol and water are available.

You should also take a good map reading compass besides having one affixed to the dashboard of your vehicle, and ensure that both are

50

compensated, a job that you can do yourself although you will normally find someone to do it for you through a yacht chandler.

A ruler and dividers will come in useful for plotting your course, and you should not be without a good pair of binoculars for spotting the desert route markers.

You should keep a log and, at regular intervals and at the end of each day, calculate your position on the map and how far you have travelled that day by checking the vehicle's speedometer and making a note of the distance travelled. It is important that the vehicle speedometer is kept in good working order. The above is important in case a sandstorm should develop during the night and cover your tracks. Without a good compass and record of distances travelled, you could get lost. You should never wander far from the road either, for the same reason, for sandstorms can appear from nowhere and within a short while the road is gone and there is nothing but sand all around you.

When using the compass never check your position on top of the vehicle bonnet or anywhere near the vehicle where the metal parts can give a false reading. Move well away from the vehicle and check the direction on flat ground.

Emergency equipment

This is the equipment you should carry in case of breakdown, getting stuck in sand or mud, encountering fallen trees, collapsed bridges or roads blocked by other broken down vehicles forcing you to divert through the jungle.

These are all hazards that you are quite likely to encounter at some time during your journey, and it is important that you have the tools to get you out of the situation that you find yourself in.

Quite often you may have to 're-build' a collapsed or weak bridge before you are able to cross it, and at some river crossings you may have to 'build' your own ferry out of planks and dugout canoes to take you to the other side.

One of the most useful items of emergency equipment is the sand ladder used mainly to extricate you from the sand or mud when you become stuck. It is placed under the driving wheels to give them the necessary traction to drive out and on to firmer ground. Two of these must be carried, the normal dimensions being 12 inches by 6 ft, but they can be any size within reason. Remember that the width must comfortably take the width of the wheels of your vehicle with some 3 inches of sand ladder protruding either side, and the length should be no longer than the distance between the front and rear wheels of your vehicle.

A useful alternative to the sand ladder is the PSP, or pierced steel plank, used for emergency tracks during the war, and still obtainable from breaker's yards, and ex-government stores, or army and navy stores. The PSP comprises a sheet of steel, 10 ft by 15 inches, which is grooved and has holes punched in it along the length at regular intervals. The edges of the holes protrude to give a rough surface affording maximum grip for the wheels of the vehicle under which it is placed. These planks, although excellent for their purpose, are also fairly heavy.

Both the PSP and the sand ladder are ideal for bridging a narrow ravine, filling gaps on dilapidated bridges, or as a ramp to board a 'canoe' ferry.

Besides the above, you should also carry the following for emergencies:

Bow saw and spare blades
Folding shovel (two, for removing
  sand from wheels etc.)
Axe, or panga
Carborundum stone for
  sharpening

Lengths of securing rope (about
  ½" diameter)
Wrecking or crow bar
Two sheets of steel, 12 inches
  square, ¼ inch thick (as base for
  jacks in soft sand or dirt)
Club hammer.

The axe or panga is for use when you find it necessary to cut your own path through the bush, or when you encounter a fallen tree and in this respect it would be useful to carry a small chain saw if you can make room for one as this would ease your labours considerably.

The wrecking bar and club hammer will come in handy should you have an accident and have to effect emergency bodywork repairs on your vehicle.

Warning triangles

These are obligatory in most countries and you are required to place them on the road a reasonable distance from the rear of your vehicle if you breakdown or are halted on the road, particularly at night or in poor visibility. Keep the triangle in your sight all the time for it is not unknown for locals, particularly kids, to pick it up and run off with it.

Vehicle extras

There is a never ending list of extras that can be fitted to a vehicle about to undertake a journey across Africa, each item adding to the total weight of the vehicle, but here I will list the items that I consider necessary for a Land Rover but applicable to all vehicles.

All of the items can be obtained with comparative ease and four recommended suppliers are:
— Big J Safari Equipment, Leighton Buzzard, Bucks.
— Brooklyn Engineering, Chandlers Ford, Hants.
— Brownchurch Brothers, London.
— Overland Vehicles and Supplies Ltd., Fareham, Hants.

● **General**
Roof rack with ladder
Winch (Big J supply one usable on
  front and rear of vehicle)
Light guards
Sump shield (very important)
Engine shield (very important)
Extra fuel tank
Fire extinguisher
Hand throttle (useful in obtaining
  good mileage to gallon)
Security box

● **Electrical**
High power coil
Extra battery
Rear wiper/washer
Rear spot light
Front fog lights
Electric fan
Engine compartment light
Map reading light
● **Gauges**
Ammeter
Oil temperature
Oil pressure
Water temperature
Altimeter

● Mechanical
Free wheeling hubs
Oil cooler
Steering damper
H.D. suspension
Overdrive

● Security
Fuel cut out
Vibratory alarm
Ultra sonic alarm

The sump and engine guards are important for protecting your gearbox, sump and engine particularly on the roads of the Sahara deep south and Zaire.

The hand throttle is a money saving device when you are on good straight roads for you can set it at the speed you desire and remove your foot from the accelerator. The vehicle will then maintain the speed you set it for unless you come to a hilly stretch when you should resort to the accelerator again. Do not forget to disengage the hand throttle when slowing down. By using this you will achieve your best mileage per gallon for the vehicle will be running at a steady setting, and the fuel economy will also be steady and not fluctuate as it does when someone's foot is on the accelerator. No matter how steady your foot, there is always the bump or dip in the road ahead that will jolt the vehicle and cause your foot momentarily to put a little more pressure on the accelerator and so pump that extra amount of fuel through to the engine thereby affecting your consumption slightly.

The security box must be concealed in your vehicle where no one can find it and have access to it. The best place is in the floor somewhere. In this you can keep your papers, money, passports and other valuables.

Free wheeling hubs are affixed to the front wheels and are used to allow the wheels to move freely when not in four-wheel drive. When the hubs are engaged four-wheel drive may be engaged also but you should never engage four-wheel drive while the hubs are disengaged. These also are a fuel saving device when disengaged.

An oil cooler is a must in hot countries as the engine cannot normally cope in keeping the engine oil cool enough. On running the engine oil through the oil cooler, which is placed in front of the radiator normally, there is less chance of the engine overheating as it is likely to when you combine the heat, weight of vehicle, and the soft sand that the vehicle will have to plough through at times.

The steering damper acts to take the shock out of the steering which would normally be there on rough tracks.

Heavy duty suspension refers to stronger suspension, as the normal suspension is not sufficient on some roads in Zaire.

Overdrive adds an extra gear and a half gear between the normal gears, another fuel saving device as it can be used in any gear.

The extra battery is strongly advisable as there are no service stations to assist should you have a flat battery in the middle of the desert. Each battery could be used in turn to ensure that they are both kept fully charged. On Land Rovers, the extra battery can be located beneath one of the front seats.

Rear wiper washers will come in very handy as you will be forever towing a cloud of dust behind you, much of which will settle on the rear window.

An electric fan is another device used to keep the engine cool and is operated manually from inside the cab when the engine temperature begins to rise. It is used in conjunction with the normal fan.

An engine light is useful if you should have a breakdown at night.

The altimeter is useful in calculating your height above sea level. Why is this important? Because the vehicle will perform less satisfactorily the higher the altitude. If you know the height you are at you can adjust the carburettor or replace the existing jets in the carburettor with high altitude jets to counteract the performance. Refer to Effect of Altitude section in Appendix C.

Security alarms — refer to General Security on page 66.

One item that should never be fitted to a vehicle on such a trip as this is a Citizens Band Radio (C.B.) In some countries it is illegal while others allow it, but border guards are naturally suspicious of tourists crossing in a vehicle and you are likely to find yourself in severe trouble on crossing the borders, if you are equipped with this form of communicating with other vehicles or persons.

An air filter of the 'oil bath' type is strongly advisable and this should be cleaned regularly. You will be amazed at the amount of dust and sand you find in the oil.

Vehicle strengthening

The construction of the Land Rover is ideal for many off road purposes, however the soft metal (aluminium) construction of the body work renders it susceptible to strain and stress under certain conditions and loads. An example of such conditions is an overland trip across Africa and in particular when a roof rack is fitted and well laden. An empty Land Rover can be likened to a tall flag pole, whereas a loaded Land Rover can be likened to a flag pole with a weight (such as a man or ape) perched on top (i.e. it is more prone to swaying to and fro). On an overland trip a lot of equipment needs to be carried, and the weight of this equipment, particularly on a roof rack when fitted adds greatly to sideways motion of the vehicle body, especially when driving along potholed or rutted or bumpy roads; soft sandy stretches; and even turning corners. All of the momentum moves to one side and then back to the other like a pendulum, causing distortion to the body of the vehicle and cracking in the weakest points. To counteract this and prevent what could amount to permanent damage of the vheicle, reinforcements as illustrated should be applied before the journey commences.

There are three main points of weakness but only two are dealt with here as the third, although important, is in the bulkhead of the engine compartment and difficult to locate and illustrate. In any case the strengthening in each of the lower corners of the front window will help considerably. The weak area around the rear side windows applies only to the Land Rover Station Wagon, as in theory a section of bodywork has been removed to fit the windows.

The way to avoid much of the abovementioned stress is to keep the carried weight to a minimum, and if at all possible do not use a roof rack. When it was necessary to carry a great deal of fuel and water, a roof rack was essential, but nowadays with refuelling and watering points more readily available, a roof rack can often be left behind, especially if extra fuel tanks are fitted beneath the vehicle. British Leyland advocate a maximum weight of around 165 lb on top of a LWB Land Rover, and when you consider the weight of the larger roof racks are around 230 lb unladen, there is not much room for anything else up there. If you must have a roof rack, load it only with light articles.

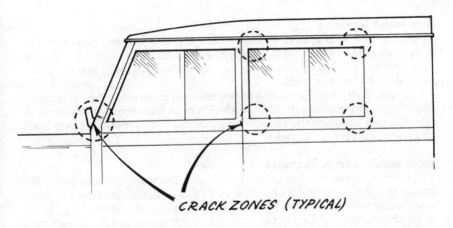

CRACK ZONES (TYPICAL)

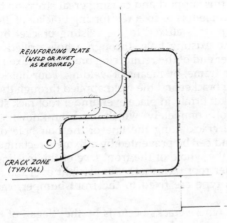

REINFORCING PLATE
(WELD OR RIVET
AS REQUIRED)

CRACK ZONE
(TYPICAL)

SIDESCREEN REINFORCEMENT

WINDSCREEN REINFORCING BRACKET

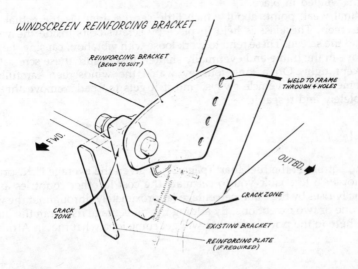

REINFORCING BRACKET
(BEND TO SUIT)

WELD TO FRAME
THROUGH 4 HOLES

FWD.

OUTBD.

CRACK ZONE

CRACK
ZONE

EXISTING BRACKET

REINFORCING PLATE
(IF REQUIRED)

Rear (side) windows

Cracks are likely to appear in each of the top and bottom corners of the bodywork around these windows as depicted in the illustration. To prevent this, affix an "L" shaped bracket using a robust piece of steel, to each corner as shown, by rivet or weld.

It is also likely that the windows will become more and more difficult to slide open and eventually may break. There is little that can be done to alleviate this although the strengthening of the body around the windows as mentioned above will help.

Front windscreen/bracket area

The bracket serves two purposes; (a) holding the windscreen in place; (b) acting as main support for the type of roof rack that overhangs the front windscreen, the struts of this roof rack being bolted to this bracket. This is the main cause of cracking in this area with the main weight on the roof rack pushing against this support and causing great stress on bumpy roads. The answer to this problem is to fix a reinforcing bracket of 3/4mm thickness as in the illustration. It is affixed to the existing bracket by means of a bolt threaded into the existing hole, through a hole drilled in the reinforcing bracket. The other end of the reinforcing bracket is affixed to the edge of the front windscreen frame, by means of welding. Four holes should be drilled in the reinforcing bracket and the weld applied through these. This will hold the existing bracket firmly in place even under roof rack strain, and prevent it being broken off completely, which has been known.

The horizontal crack along the line of the bolt hole only occurs under extreme stress and can be prevented by affixing a rectangular piece of steel, by weld, across the whole of the front face of the existing vehicle bracket.

There is another roof rack that extends right over the front bonnet. The supports of this type are fixed to the front bumper, causing little or no problem.

Another point where cracks occur is by the "legs" of the roof racks, no matter which type is used. An appropriate method of strengthening here would be strips of steel on the outside of each leg, extending the complete length, welded in place.

A final weak point, about which little can be done, is the actual front windscreen. The glass is held in place by screws/bolts inside the vehicle around the screen. These tend to work loose with vibration, causing the glass to move in the frame and eventually shatter. Just ensure these screws/bolts are kept tight. On a long journey watch the windscreen carefully for movement as the vehicle sways, and if it gets too bad, remove the glass completely and reseal it.

Fuel

At the bottom of the fuel chart (page 24) is given the average U.K. price of fuel for 1986 to enable you to calculate the cost in other countries as fuel normally rises by the same percentage (approximately) throughout the world with one or two exceptions. By adding the percentage rise from the quoted price here to the price today you will get some idea what fuel in Africa will cost.

Camping equipment

Basically this consists of tents and sleeping bags and you can obtain both from any camping store of which there are many. One of the best equipped that caters for travellers is the Youth Hostels Association shop in Southampton Street, London. As there will be no accommodation in most of the areas you will be travelling through, you will be sleeping in tents or under the stars for most of the time, so ensure your equipment is adequate.

Occasionally you may sleep in a hotel in order to have a good clean up. It is recommended that you become a member of the Youth Hostels Association, for they have hostels throughout the world and those in Kenya, in particular Nairobi, are very good and all are reasonably priced. They offer simple but clean accommodation for the traveller, irrespective of age, and many also provide meals. If they do not there are always facilities for cooking your own food. You join by paying an annual membership fee or you may become a life member on payment of one fee, neither of which is excessive, and that entitles you to use any hostel with all its facilities throughout the world. A handbook listing regulations and giving details of Youth Hostels is issued on joining. You may join at the Southampton Street shop (as above), or write for full information to the head office: Youth Hostels Association, Trevelyan House, St. Albans, Herts, England.

Sleeping bag
This should be of the zip-up type, and quilted. It should also be 100% Terylene inside and out, and around 35 to 40 ounces in weight or 1000 to 1140 grams. You will find that this sort of bag will keep you cool in the hot regions, and warm during the cold nights in the desert. Ensure that the length of the bag is suitable for you as they come in different lengths. The zip-up type of sleeping bag can also be opened out into a double quilt, for airing and using as a cover.

Tent
Your tent must have a built-in heavy duty ground sheet, a zip down the centre between the doors to close them, and zips along the base of the doors to seal you in completely. For security you can always affix a small padlock to the zipper handles and so lock the tents up. If possible obtain a tent that has an inner mosquito net door or mosquito ventilation. Nylon is the best tent material as it is lighter, more waterproof, and dries quicker after a night of heavy dew. Fly sheets are also a great advantage, not only in keeping the main tent dry, but if they have a sealed back and zip-up front you can close the fly sheet and leave the tent open for the night in the hotter climates, without fear of too many mosquitoes invading your privacy.

Mosquito nets are useful if you intend sleeping 'under the stars'. One useful method is to have a mosquito net made into a tent!

Water containers and purifiers
Water containers for each person are a must and a one- to two-litre metal (aluminium or alloy) container will be ideal. It can be filled at the start of each day and replenished as necessary, to give each person water to hand for his consumption. Avoid plastic water bottles, and even plastic jerry cans, for not only do they puncture easily but plastic tends to taint the water and give it an unpleasant taste.

Some method of water purification is essential on your trip. Chlorine tablets such as Puritabs are ideal when washing fruit and vegetables, but can leave an unpleasant taste in drinking water. By far the most efficient way of purifying water is by means of a water purifier working on the charcoal filter system; take plenty of spare filters with you as in Africa the amount of water that one filter will purify is less than 20% of what the manufacturers recommend. This method of purification not only removes bacteria and dirt from the water, but it leaves the natural mineral element of the water intact.

Water purifiers are small compact items and can be electrically operated from your vehicle supply, or by means of a hand pump. They can be coupled to an existing water supply system, or used as a portable system by dipping the inlet pipe into one of your water cans.

Water need only be purified for actual consumption, and only when you need it. Do not drink purified water that has stood for more than 24 hours without re-purifying.

Most water purifiers will claim to purify 100 gallons or more per cartridge, but to ensure you do not run out of cartridges, and therefore clean water for drinking, calculate 30 gallons per cartridge across Africa.

One of the best purifiers on the market, although a little expensive, is distributed by Safari (Water Treatments) Ltd of Basingstoke, Hants., and their purifiers are also obtainable from Brownchurch (Safari Equipment) Bros, of East London. On application, Safari (Water Treatments) Ltd. will supply you with full details of their purifiers together with laboratory test results.

Cooking stoves
These should be of the methylated spirit, petrol, or paraffin type as gas cartridges for gas stoves are unavailable across most of Africa.

Camping security

When it comes to camping out in the bush you should ensure that no-one sees you leave the road to erect camp, and also ensure that your camp is far enough away from the road as not to be seen by passing vehicles or persons. Try and conceal yourself by bushes or trees. This way you will not run the risk of attracting persons with criminal intent during the night when you are asleep, intent on relieving you of some of your equipment, such as a towel hung up to dry or a spotlight from your vehicle.

It is always best to seek permission to camp in the grounds of a mission, or at a native village. Here you will invariably find someone offering to guard your vehicle and possessions for you and it is a good idea to accept. Do not forget to give him something for his troubles before you leave — not necessarily money, for most people will be more than pleased with an old shirt or pair of shoes, or even a handful of salt or rice.

If in doubt, or you have even the slightest suspicion that you are being watched, ensure that someone sleeps the night in the vehicle and do not leave any loose item hanging about your campsite.

Refer to the section on General security on page 66.

Clothing

Each person's clothing and baggage must be kept to a minimum for weight reasons, and as far as the container is concerned I would recommend a soft holdall approximately 24 inches by 18 inches by 10 inches, as this will twist and bend itself into a confined space, which a rigid suitcase cannot do.

Owing to the variations in climate you will be experiencing you should take both light and warm clothing, although for much of the trip you will live in shorts, with a T-shirt or sweat shirt, and pair of sandals.

The following list is the maximum recommended for any one person. It is tempting to take more than is required, but you will find that this list includes everything that is necessary for a man (women can adapt it accordingly), and includes clothing worn at departure:

2 pair shorts	1 pair sandals/sneakers
2 pairs trousers	1 towel
3 shirts/T-shirts	handkerchiefs
(one with long sleeves)	1 strong pair shoes
3 sets underwear	1 swimming costume
4 pairs socks	1 anorak
1 warm jumper	1 sunhat

Clothing should be cotton or linen as man-made fibres such as nylon can be very uncomfortable in the heat and do not permit the body to 'breathe' properly. Cotton and linen articles are also more easily washed.

Other personal items that should not be forgotten are:

1 water bottle (drinking)	sewing repair kit
toilet bag and toiletries	sunglasses (polaroid)
torch	camera and films
penknife	

It is advisable to take a pair of polaroid sunglasses as these are the most suitable to counteract the extreme brightness you will be encountering.

In the desert the temperature at night will be very low and you will feel cold. The temperature at night often drops to around 4°-5°C while during the day it rises to 30°C or more — the great difference causing you to feel the cold more than you normally would.

When you arrive in Algiers or wherever you start your journey, try to purchase a *cheche* from an Arab market. This is the headgear that Arabs wear to protect their head and neck against the sun, wind, and sandstorms.

At night, to protect yourself from biting insects, wear long-sleeved shirts and jeans if the temperature permits. Try to obtain some Mijex before you leave home and spray it on your skin when insects are about. It affords good protection against mosquitoes and other insects and has a rather pleasant lemon scent.

Correct dress for men and women
You should be most careful to ensure that you and the members of your party always dress adequately and correctly and do not give offence. There are certain customs and laws that could result in imprisonment if not observed. For example, in Malawi women may not wear mini skirts, and in some countries such as Nigeria and Niger, shorts or slacks are forbidden on women. All female travellers should ensure that they take dresses that are at least knee length for wear in public, and that these cover the body fully.

In Malawi men are forbidden to wear bell-bottom or flared trousers — another arrestable offence — and men should ensure that they do not go anywhere in public in *any* African country shirtless and bare-chested. This shows disrespect and it is also an offence. Particular care should be taken not to cross a border shirtless — even if you are sitting in your vehicle — for the border officials often approach the vehicle for inspection. The same applies when entering immigration or customs buildings or a police station. Always put your shirt on before you leave the vehicle. Walking around an African market bare-chested can cause pandemonium.

You will often see local men and women naked, washing in the river. Do not think that this means it is all right for you to do so, for it is not. When you wish to strip off for a bath do it well away from other people. In the same context, a bare-breasted African woman walking the streets is commonplace, but a white woman doing the same is likely to be arrested. Play safe. Cover up. (Refer also to section on General Appearance.)

Survival

The most important item here is water. You should ensure that you carry sufficient both for yourselves and your vehicle, and you should keep your water containers topped up for the emergency that is always possible: that of being stranded through vehicle breakdown or some other calamity.

Food for yourselves is not so important as long as you have sufficient water, for man *can* go two to three weeks without solid food provided the liquid intake is there. Nevertheless you should always keep your food supply stocked up. It is just as important to have adequate supplies of fuel for your vehicle. Apart from first aid, which will be dealt with next, your survival kit should include the following:

- Mirror (for signalling)
- Matches (for firelighting)
- Orange or red smokebombs or flares (obtainable from yacht chandlers)
- Plastic sheet

The latter when slung between four posts or the branches of a tree serves to collect the dew during the night which can then be used for drinking purposes.

It is also wise to carry a bottle of distilled water for topping up your vehicle battery, although rain water will do in an emergency.

First aid

The first aid kit you carry must be comprehensive as it is one of the most important items in the vehicle. You must take all your medical requirements with you as they are extremely expensive to buy in Africa. Here is a list of your minimum requirements:

Bandages
Lint
Adhesive waterproof plasters
    (assorted sizes)
Roll adhesive plaster
Scissors
Lancet
Eye bath
Acriflex or Betadine ointment

Tetracycline (antibiotic tablet,
    useful against infection)
Thalazole (for use against
    bacillary dysentery)
Salt tablets
Vitamin tablets
Antihistamine (for allergy)
Furamide (for amoebic dysentery)
Steri-strip skin closures

Anadin (pain killer)
Codis (pain suppressor, and useful in eliminating diarrhoea)
Nivaquine/Chloroquine/Maloprim (anti-malaria)
Lomotil (excellent for stomach pain and diarrhoea)

Cotton wool
TCP or similar antiseptic
Vaccines against scorpion and snake bite, 5ml syringes and needles (disposable)

The latter can be obtained from the Pasteur Institute in Algiers, or free of charge from the clinic in Touggourt, or any clinic or hospital en route. These vaccines must be kept as cool as possible otherwise they will be of little use when required. It is advisable to renew them occasionally to ensure you have a fresh and good supply. Your local hospital will advise you on the use of syringes and applications of vaccine if you do not already know.

All medicines and drugs must be kept in their original packing as far as possible and clearly marked. The international campaign against drug smuggling is very evident in Africa and an unmarked tin of chalk powder that you would use when mending a puncture could be mistaken for narcotics, involving you in lengthy delays while it is being analysed.

Always consult your doctor for practical advice on the medicines to take with you, as some of those listed above will not be obtainable without prescription, even some anti-malaria tablets. Your doctor will also advise on the method of application of medicines, and the frequency and dosage.

Do not forget to take moisturising cream for your face, hands and arms, and 'lipseal' or plain vaseline for your lips and knuckles to prevent them cracking. Also, any other cosmetic you think you may need.

General advice for the trip

Customs and immigration

The method by which you approach and deal with the authorities of other countries, your general manner and attitude, can have a direct bearing on your enjoyment and the success of your trip.

The customs and immigration officials at each border crossing are there to do a job. They have many regulations to enforce, and they have to ensure that visitors abide by them. They have to be constantly on the alert for terrorists, drug smugglers, currency smugglers, espionage agents, assassins or the journalist that intends sneaking into a country unauthorised to scoop a story. It is a complex and difficult profession. By making life easier for them, you make it easier for yourselves.

This is the best way to approach border officials:

1. Make sure you have all your papers in order and ready. Appoint one member of your party — the most amiable — to approach the customs or immigration with all of the papers. Normally one person can handle all the necessary paperwork. If the officials wish to see all members of the party they will say so.

2. Approach the office with a smile on your face, pass the time of day with all officials you encounter, and go out of your way to be friendly to everyone, even if their attitude seems negative.

3. Keep smiling and try to engage them in friendly chat. Discuss your travels, family and weather, even while they are going through your documents.

4. Appoint one or more members of your party (always trying to leave one in the vehicle), to walk around and start friendly conversations with other officials, particularly customs officials who may be waiting to inspect a vehicle. (Do not approach them if they are busy with someone else or going through a vehicle.)

5. Never disagree with any official. If he finds something wrong with any of your documents, or cannot find a visa, or page to stamp, then humour him and assist him in every way you can.

6. Joke with the officials if you can but do not persist if they appear uninterested.

7. If the customs wish to search your vehicle, then assist them by removing all of your baggage etc., opening your bags for their inspection, helping them on to the roof rack or to open any box they may want to look in. Remember all the time to smile and be friendly and courteous. Exchange names and addresses, and say you will write, even if you do not intend to.

8. You may feel frustrated at times, but don't show it; you may feel like losing your temper, but suppress it!

9. Do not give officials any gifts, apart from a newspaper or magazine which those in remote border controls are often very pleased to receive particularly if it is in English. Many officials will ask for certain items, like toothpaste, soap, biscuits, fruit etc. Do not succumb, for it could get you into trouble for bribery which is an offence in every country. Keep within the law at all times. No matter how much they persist, refuse politely, but maintain your friendly manner. You will not be denied entry into a country for failing to bribe the officials, or refusing their demands.

10. If a customs official or policeman wants a lift it can be to your advantage to give him one, but the decision is yours and you must consider the distance, the room you have in your vehicle, and your weight capacity.

11. If the officials pick you up on some mistake you have made, or find something in your vehicle that you should not have, be apologetic; never argue with them.

In short, when dealing with officials at borders or elsewhere, smile, be friendly, courteous and helpful. Never disagree or argue. Be patient and, if it comes to it, apologetic — even beg forgiveness, on bended knee if necessary! All of this may be hard for you, but you will be helping yourself. You must remember that the decision rests with the customs and immigration officials whether or not to let you into their country. If they refuse you entry there is absolutely nothing you can do about it, and you will have real problems if there is no alternative route available.

If you upset them they could keep you waiting at the border for a couple of hours or even days! It is of no consequence to them if you are short of food or water, or have a sick passenger. If for some reason you are made to wait, accept it and be patient, for provided you have not broken any laws or deeply offended the officials they will let you in eventually. Sometimes, particularly at remote border controls, you are made to wait for the sheer devilment of it, or because someone before you has upset them. Just sit tight and wait without losing your patience, and every couple of hours go and ask if you can go yet. Always deal with the same person and do not try to go over his head for this could make things worse. If he has ended his shift for the day, then wait for his next shift to start.

Although there will be times when you are kept waiting, in general tourists are given preference, particularly if they can speak some local language. Once at a border control in Ghana, the native bus passengers in front of us were having a hard time, having to tip all of their luggage out on to the ground for inspection. I thought "Here we go, we'll be here for some time!" The same official then approached us with a big smile on his face, stamped our passports, and said to us "You are my friends, you can go". We were away in five minutes.

In another incident at the Niger border in the desert, we encountered a group of Swiss overlanders who had been there five days! They were early; their visa did not start for another 3 days, but the immigration officer had been prepared to let them enter, until one of the party started laying down the law. When we got there they were out of food and water and were relying on the kindness of other travellers to assist them. We were away in a couple of hours leaving them still waiting at the border.

Once at the Zambian border, a traveller had to produce his money before entry so they could see if he had enough to maintain himself. The officials counted his travellers cheques, but miscalculated the amount and told him he had insufficient money for entry. Instead of politely pointing out their mistake, he became annoyed, banged his fist on the desk, and demanded that they stamp his passport. They stamped his passport all right.... 'Refused entry — offence against the state'. This traveller had to return from whence he came with no chance of ever entering that country with the same passport.

So take my advice, and at all times respect the authority of the officials you encounter everywhere. You will be helping yourself and your fellow travellers.

Nigeria

There is often fluctuation in the opening and closing of the borders of Nigeria. Although travel in the country is as safe as it ever was for tourists, the borders are frequently closed and sometimes for long periods, mainly to restrict the influx of indigenous people from neighbouring states such as Benin and Cameroon. The one exception is the border at Birni-Nkonni in the north of the country which for much of the time appears to operate normally. All travellers in order to eliminate any great inconvenience should follow this advice:

1. Apply for a visa in the normal way before leaving on your trip.
2. Confirm the validity of your visa, and enquire as to the border situation at the Nigerian Mission in the country prior to entering Nigeria, i.e. Benin, Niger, Cameroon etc. Also visit the mission of your own country in the bordering state and state your intentions, seeking advice.

If you are unable to enter Nigeria you must go round it, thus. From Birni-Nkonni the road eastwards through Zinder (Niger) to Gouré (Niger) is good tarmac for most of the way. From there to Mainé-Soroa is a mixture of sand/dirt, undulating and potholed. From Mainé-Soroa to Garoumele (visit the old legionaires fort here, very interesting) there are two roads:

(a) Via Diffa and Gagam is dirt/sand, firm but potholed in places with the latter section liable to flooding at times (127 mls)

(b) Turn left in Mainé-Soroa and head north east on what can only be described as a track. Soft sand through dune country. Very soft in places of drifting sands. A picturesque route (but advised for 4x4 vehicles only) 106 miles long, with no water or fuel. This second route is largely uninhabited and desolate.

From Garoumele to Nguigmi, dirt road then tarmac to town. Clear customs and immigration here for entry into Tchad. Fill up with fuel and water as no certainty of either till Mao in Tchad 230 miles away. Nguigmi to Niger/Tchad border is 70 miles. Mainly firm but corrugated sand. Interesting route around the northern end of Lake Tchad. From the border to Mao the track winds through sand dunes and is sand for most of the way. Clear customs and immigration in Mao. From Mao take the route via Bir Grat to

Wherever overlanders stop in Africa, they are soon approached by curious, friendly natives.

Massakori. Dirt and sand. Danger of flooding when it rains. From Massakori to the capital of Tchad, Fort Lamy (now N'Djamena). Broken tarmac. All facilities in Djamena.

Language

Throughout Africa, the majority of countries use one of two European languages as well as their native tongue (see the Language Map on page 67). These are French, in the countries that were once French colonies, or English in the countries that were once British colonies. However, you will find that in every country you visit English is used, particularly amongst the school children who now learn it in school, and educated adults. But if you can speak French and English you will get by in every country. Only in remote country areas are you likely to find nobody who speaks French or English.

General security

This is something to be very aware of: personal security, security of possessions, and security of vehicle.

Wherever you go in Africa people will look up to you, and will gather around you in hordes. Partly this is because white people and overlanders in general are not often seen; but also it is because, with your large expensive vehicle full of expensive possessions, you appear to live like a king compared to the poverty in which they live. Children in particular will gather around and although you may gain satisfaction from it, you must remember to remain watchful or they may lift something from your vehicle and be away with it. Even an old spotlight cover would make a good hat for some African child.

It is this wealth that you display — obvious even from the untorn clothing you wear — that will attract thieves to you, your camp site, and your vehicle.

On my latest trip, I managed to cover the whole of Africa without a single incident of theft, while the overlanders I met had nearly all been robbed at some time during the trip. I attribute this to these simple precautions:

1. Never display your wealth, be it watch, bracelet or money. Keep any valuables in the vehicle security box.
2. Keep away from the dark and lonely places, particularly at night, even if you are in a group.
3. Keep away from unlit streets at night.
4. Never retaliate against a thief or robber.
5. Keep away from large crowds, particularly if there are signs of rowdiness.
6. Do not encourage children to stay around you by giving them gifts such as food. They will beg but ignore them for they can be as light fingered as anyone.
7. Do not give lifts to strangers.
8. Watch your possessions all the time, particularly when camping and there are Africans around you. Most of them are just curious but there is usually one who will try to help himself to something.
9. Never carry large amounts of money with you. Leave it in the security box.
10. Never carry your camera in your hand; wear it on a strap around your neck.
11. Never leave your vehicle alone in lonely places, or so far away that you

Language map

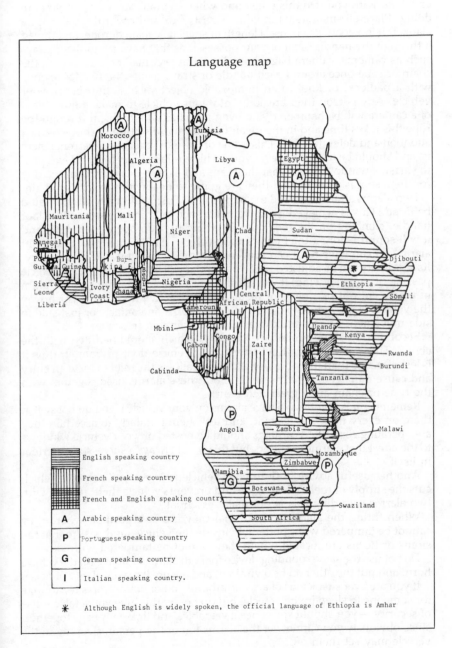

English speaking country

French speaking country

French and English speaking country

A Arabic speaking country

P Portuguese speaking country

G German speaking country

I Italian speaking country.

* Although English is widely spoken, the official language of Ethiopia is Amhar

will be unable to hear the alarm.

12. When you leave your vehicle, conceal any valuables that you will not be taking with you. Do this when and where no-one can see what you are doing. Place all small items in your security box and cover the rest with a blanket. It is a good idea to use a length of small link chain or rope, and thread it through the handle of all of your possessions that have a handle or strap, such as cameras, camera bags, holdalls, kettle etc. making a turn with the chain or rope once around each handle or strap; secure the two loose ends with a padlock, or knot to an immovable object such as the seat of your vehicle. Any person then breaking into your vehicle to make a quick grab of a camera will be hampered and even if he has a knife to cut through the rope this takes time and in the meantime the alarm sounding should attract attention and deter the thief. This is one of the most effective deterrents there is, and should be used whenever your vehicle is left alone. Most thieves plan to smash a window, grab what they can, and escape in a car that is waiting for them so it is unlikely that they are going to deal with the rope or chain.

Two alarms should be fitted to your vehicle. First a **vibratory alarm** should be fitted. This is achieved by movement, such as someone trying the door handle, climbing on the roof rack, or trying to slide open a window, and it will sound before a thief enters your vehicle. This is the most important alarm you can have for it can prevent vehicle damage by thieves on entry. Its sensitivity can be adjusted — too fine and it will be set off by a large vehicle passing or a gust of wind. It works on the principle of a swinging pendulum in a hole cut out of a piece of metal and is effective no matter which way the vehicle is moved. Avoid the type that works on contacts or just side to side movement of a pendulum as these are limited in scope.

Second is the **door/bonnet switch alarm** which should be fitted with the above. This operates as a thief opens your vehicle door or bonnet; thus it is less effective than the vibratory alarm as it allows the thief to force an entry and cause damage before it sounds. Both these alarms used together with the rope or chain are a great deterrent.

Remember it is pointless to have alarms on your vehicle if you do not switch them on every time you leave it, and test them regularly to ascertain they are operating correctly. Warnings should be posted on your vehicle windows to the effect that alarms are fitted, but this is not always a successful deterrent in itself.

Another useful advice to fit to your vehicle is a 'cut-out' solenoid which cuts the supply of fuel to the engine and prevents vehicle theft; though with two alarms sounding this is not really essential.

When fitting the alarms, ensure that they are in a position where they cannot be tampered with, preferably inside the vehicle, and ensure that the sirens or horns are located where they cannot be tampered with either.

Do not use the same sounding device for both alarms. Put one on the vehicle horn, and put the other on its own siren, and ensure it makes plenty of noise.

If you are ever suspicious of anyone around you or your camp site, arrange for someone to sleep in the vehicle, but do not let this give you a false sense of security — you should still conceal valuables and link your bags together, since obviously you cannot set the alarms too or the person sleeping in the vehicle may set them off.

When you camp, place one tent either side of the vehicle, facing opposite directions so that you can view both sides of the vehicle in case of intruders at night. It is also a good idea to extend one of your tent guy lines and fix it to the vehicle, so that a prowler is likely to fall over it, shake the tent in the process, and waken you.

Any valuables you take into your tent with you at night should be concealed and placed in the centre of the tent, if possible, between two persons, and not under your pillow, or in a corner; thieves have been known to slit the tent open quietly, look around, and swiftly lift anything of value such as a wallet in your trousers. This method of stealing occurs even in organised camp sites, so beware. I always place my wallet and money in the bottom of my sleeping bag.

Finally, whenever you leave your vehicle to go shopping or whatever, try to leave someone with your vehicle, even in daylight, or try and keep it in sight. If you all wish to visit somewhere special, take turns.

All equipment loaded outside your vehicle such as spare wheels, and loose equipment on the roof rack, should be secured with chain and padlock. You should also have a locking fuel filler cap, and fix a hasp and staple and padlock to your vehicle's bonnet. This latter is essential. Other security devices include hasp and staple and padlock to all doors and window grills, although this gives the vehicle the appearance of a security van! For convenience purchase your required padlocks in one go and ask for a common key for all padlocks. This relieves you of having to carry a large bunch of keys around and also gives you ample spare keys. As an added security measure you could have tinted glass fitted to your vehicle. This enables you to see out but likely thieves are unable to see in. It also reduces the glare of the sun and keeps the inside of the vehicle cooler.

The security advice given here is sound and comprehensive and by adhering to it you will not fall victim to the thief that constantly has you and your vehicle under surveillance, waiting for the moment when your alertness slips.

Finding your way

In the desert there are no roads or signposts so care must be taken in navigation. Some navigation experience — even marine navigation — is necessary as you should be able to read the sun and stars, and use landmarks such as hills, rivers, or power lines to guide you. A compass and dead reckoning are features in desert navigation. Consult your map regularly and identify your landmarks. Rivers and railway lines can be followed and in places you will find the route marked with beacons or 45 gallon drums, placed 1-2km apart; or the marker may be a pile of stones, whitewashed.

More recently, T.V. and radio receiver masts have been erected and these invariably lead you to a town. They are normally 15 to 20 miles apart but one can be clearly seen from the other, particularly with a pair of binoculars.

As mentioned on page 51, a log should be kept and your mileage recorded each hour. You should also make a note of hills, track junctions, towns, railways, radio masts, and the type of terrain you are travelling over. If you happen to get lost or take the wrong track, back track to your last known position and then record and allow for the extra mileage you have travelled. You can then calculate roughly how much fuel you have lost from what you allowed to get you from A to B.

If you become completely lost, and do not know which route to take, whatever you do, don't panic. Consider alternatives very, very carefully before taking any action. Under no circumstances should you move far away from your vehicle for without its shelter you will not survive long in the heat of the desert (see Breakdown, page 70).

Driving

Try not to drive for long periods during the heat of the day without stopping for at least half an hour to rest your vehicle, particularly in the desert where the soft sand exerts tremendous strain and loose sand will increase above normal the wear and tear on moving parts. Never attempt to drive in the desert at night, which in any case is forbidden in most areas.

Breakdown

The first thing you should do if you happen to break down is to ascertain your exact location and the distance to the nearest village or town. Never walk for help alone, and never walk if it is dark. Wait till daylight (but do not walk in the full heat of the day). If you are too far from any civilisation to walk then stay with your vehicle and wait for a fellow traveller or local to pass, then beg a lift or ask him to deliver a message.

If you break down in a remote area, do not waste wood or rags lighting a fire until you are sure it will be seen by passers-by or aircraft. Remember that one of the best means of attracting someone's attention is by using a shiny piece of metal or a mirror as a reflector, provided the sun is shining. In dull and cloudy weather a white sheet waved from the top of your vehicle should be visible.

There is no step-by-step procedure for emergency survival as circumstances differ. The most important thing is to keep a clear head and think logically. It is wise to read a little more about the subject than can be written here. A short and informative book on the subject is K.E.M. Melville's **Stay Alive in the Desert** (published by Roger Lascelles, London).

Sand storms

If you encounter a severe sandstorm stop immediately, no matter where you are, and manoeuvre your vehicle so that the engine faces in the direction that the sand is blowing, and not into it. This will prevent sand blowing into the engine compartment and clogging up the works.

Driving in soft sand

When you encounter soft sandy sections you should approach them in a low gear with the engine revs fairly high — but not too high or the wheels will spin and sink you into the sand, and not too low, or the slowing action of the soft sand will cause the engine to stall, and on moving out of the soft area from a standstill you are likely to become stuck. Approach the area reasonably fast and you will stand more chance of riding over the soft area; but beware if the surrounding area is rocky, for hitting rocks hidden beneath soft sand at speed may damage the vehicle or cause you to lose control and even overturn. If in doubt have someone reconnoitre on foot with a stick to ascertain the extent of the soft area. It may be possible to drive around it.

When driving for long distances in soft sand, it is recommended to deflate the tyres a little and so afford you better flotation, but keep your eyes on the vehicle temperature gauges as this will create more labour on the engine and cause it to overheat quicker. Always re-inflate your tyres immediately you are clear of the soft sandy area.

If you become stuck, dig the sand out from around your drive wheels, place your sand ladders or PSP down, and drive slowly forward. If you have enough people in your party, put one person in charge of each sand ladder or PSP to remove it immediately you have driven off it, and place it under the wheels again, repeating the process until you reach solid ground.

Driving in mud

This is entirely different from driving in soft sand but the techniques are the same as far as the sand ladders or PSP are concerned. With mud you slide, which you do not do in sand, and care must be taken that you do not slide sideways or you could end up in a ditch or in the jungle. If you can see soft mud ahead, try and rush through it without stopping. If you are compelled to stop, lay stones, branches or anything firm under your wheels to give you a grip, but do not use leaves. You may have to jack the wheels clear of the ground to get your sand ladders or PSP underneath.

Take care when driving in Zaire or elsewhere along wet, rutted roads, for if you happen to slide into the ruts, not only will they damage the vehicle if they are deep, but they will control your direction and it will be difficult to get out of them again. Whatever you do, try not to oversteer the vehicle or you are likely to lose your rear wheels, i.e. have them slide out from under you. A quick jerk of the steering wheel will often extricate the front wheels from the ruts, but the rear wheels will not always follow and you may have to resort to making a ramp in the ruts by digging the soil away from the sides and pushing it down in front of the rear wheels so that they can climb out on it.

Hitch-hikers

Overlanders nowadays are likely to encounter many hitch-hikers. Whether or not you give them lifts is entirely your choice. Remember that among many bona fide hitch-hikers are some who are drug traffickers, and others who are out to make a quick buck from anyone they meet, particularly a lone driver. Take great care, for you will not know until it is too late if the hitch-hiker you pick up is a threat to your security or not. That hitch-hiker could be carrying drugs, and if you are stopped and searched at one of the many roadblocks in Africa, and those drugs are found, you too could be held as a trafficker or accomplice. Ignorance is no defence when it comes to drug offences. On the other hand your hitch-hiker could be a genuine, innocent traveller. You must make the decision but take care.

Road checks

During your journey you will encounter road checks in most countries. They are intended largely for the local inhabitants, in order to reduce the smuggling of food from one state to another, and to winkle out drivers breaking the law by driving without a licence or overloading their vehicle. However, tourists do get caught up in these road blocks, and the vehicle may be

Throughout Africa, whenever overlanders stop to take pictures they are surrounded by hordes of locals wishing to be included, and it is difficult to accommodate them all as they clamour to get in the picture, sometimes only a few inches from the lens. These impoverished but extremely sociable people can make you feel like royalty. Note the Land Rover, centre photo.

searched although usually only papers are checked. You must report to all checks, for failure to do so could result in arrest and lengthy delays. If the police check or customs check is unmanned, but there is a barrier across the road, always stop and find the officials before you proceed. If the barrier is open, and there are no officials present, it is safe to proceed.

Radio and recording equipment

Radios If a radio is to be taken on the journey, it should be a permanent fixture in the vehicle if at all possible. Portable radios are a much sought-after luxury in many parts of Africa. A portable radio left lying in a visible position inside a vehicle is an invitation to someone to break into the vehicle to steal it. It is not unknown for murder to be committed merely to obtain another person's radio.

Tape recorders If a tape recorder is taken along, keep it as small and simple as possible, but avoid pocket-sized models which some officials could interpret as 'spying equipment'. As with radios, tape recorders are also a much sought-after luxury, which some people will go to any lengths to obtain.

Citizens Band Radio These should be avoided. Whereas CB radios may be operated legally in many countries with the necessary licences, in other countries the mere possession of one is illegal. A CB radio is clearly 'communicating equipment' and as such can easily be interpreted as 'spying equipment' in many countries. Suspected espionage can result in lengthy delays, embarrassment, and/or imprisonment, with confiscation ranging from the actual CB radio set to the whole vehicle. So leave your CB at home.

Photography

Caution must be exercised in taking photographs as this can be a touchy subject. Never photograph individuals without their permission. Never photograph any government or official building without first seeking permission — and this includes railway stations, radio stations, dams, bridges, airports, police stations and, most important, frontiers and borders. You should never raise your camera at crowd disturbances either, or public gatherings of any kind. If in doubt always ask permission. Some countries require you to have special permission, or a photographic visa.

Photographic equipment
Everybody will want to take a camera to record the journey, and particularly for use in the game parks and reserves of Africa, but care must be taken not to overload yourself. One camera should be sufficient; never take more than two, and steer clear of extra powerful telephoto lenses. A telephoto lens of 200 or 300m should be the maximum and to exceed this could be asking for trouble when it comes to crossing international borders or even at road blocks for the police and customs associate large amounts of photographic equipment and lenses with journalists, and journalists require special permission to enter a country. If you are mistaken for a journalist or reporter, your equipment could be confiscated. Remember, insurance does not cover confiscation.

Your stated profession or trade will not help matters. In most countries

73

where important game parks are situated, like Ivory Coast and Kenya, there are shops where large telephoto lenses can be hired. In Kenya these can also be purchased and the prices are not much higher than London. Film in Kenya is cheap and this is worth remembering. If possible, take all you need with you, but remember that film must be kept cool at all times. Any large amount of film discovered at borders could also spell trouble. Many countries (mainly in Europe) stipulate that no more than 10 films per person may be imported. Tunisia stipulates 20 films, still or cine. If you intend taking large amounts of film, secure them in your vehicle strong box, and insulate against extreme heat.

A recent innovation is the 'instant' or Polaroid camera and so successful has it been that I would now class it as essential for an overlander, though it should not replace the more conventional type of camera. Where once we used to persuade people to be photographed by giving rice or salt, now they can be presented with a copy of the photograph on the spot. It is the closest thing to white man's Ju Ju! Indeed today's travellers will often be confronted by local people actually begging to have their photographs taken, for they are beginning to understand that a camera is not an evil device in which to trap their spirit. Some people can become quite aggressive if they are not given a photograph and the instant camera can alleviate this problem. However, remember to carry plenty of instant film; for every person you want to photograph, there may be another 30 or 40 asking you to take their picture. In the past 18 months, particularly in Central and West Africa, this type of camera has also proved itself an instant pass towards speedy border clearance, especially when the officials are invited to stand with your group against your vehicle!

Politics

This is a delicate subject, and for obvious reasons you should never discuss or become involved in any form of political activity or even discussion while you are in a foreign country.

Alcohol

In many of the countries you will be visiting strict regulations are in force regarding drink and driving which can result in immediate imprisonment, so take care. In some countries, mainly where the Moslem religion prevails, it is illegal even to possess alcohol of any kind. Again, you could be imprisoned if any is found in your possession.

Firearms

You should never carry firearms, even if they are fully licenced. Many border officials frown on them, and in the (unlikely) event of your being held up by someone with a firearm, he will not hesitate to shoot if he finds you are armed and his own life could be at stake.

74

Water

In Europe we are all accustomed to having water on tap and often take it for granted. In Africa the situation is entirely different. Droughts and famine persist all the time, caused by insufficient water. It is commonplace to pass through areas of Africa that have not seen rain for several years. In such places you may have to pay for the water you require. You should always ask permission to use local sources of water where it is obviously scarce, and take care that you do not pollute any water supply. Treat it as the rare commodity it is in Africa and do not waste any.

With the exception of bottled (spa) water sold in some areas, all drinking water should be purified, preferably by running through a water purifier (see page 58). Water sterilisation tablets can be used but this will leave an unpleasant taste in the water. The other method is to boil the water, though it then has to cool before you can drink it, and in cooling re-contamination is likely. Also boiling removes oxygen from the water and leaves it very distasteful. By far the best method is to pump it through a purification system as this also removes dirt and discoloration.

It is preferable to keep your water for emergencies, and to drink minerals to quench your thirst. These, being in sealed bottles, are safe. Drinks such as Coca Cola, Pepsi, Fanta, Mirabelle, 7-Up, and Sprite are commonly available in every country in Africa, and are cheap too. Most of the time you can buy minerals ice-cold from the roadside stalls. However, bottles are scarce throughout the continent, and wherever you buy your mineral you will have to consume it on the spot unless you pay a deposit (normally three times what the drink costs) or can supply an already empty bottle. So carry a few empties of the drink you like best, and then you can buy a supply of full ones to take away, repeating the process when these have been drunk.

Under no circumstances buy bottles of minerals that are not sealed. In many markets you will find 'locally bottled' minerals, where someone has made their own mixture and put it into any old bottle they can lay their hands on. It may be a Coke bottle and can look like the real thing, so take care.

Health

The need to look after your health can never be over-emphasised. In Africa the diseases and illnesses you can contract outnumber those contractable in Europe by ten to one. Many of them can be so easily picked up by the unwary. There are precautions that must be taken to avoid these health hazards.

Heat and diet
Heat in itself can endanger your health if you are not careful and sensible. Fluid loss is a very real risk in hot climates, where perspiration is increased. To counteract it **you must increase your fluid intake.** Although the human body can go for several days without solids even a few hours without intake of fluid can be fatal. When it is extremely hot you may not feel inclined to eat; this is normal and nothing to worry about. It is probably best not to force yourself to eat. But you must supply your body with fluids regularly. Man can comfortably go for three weeks on fluids alone without ill effects. To allow for the lack of solid intake, you must take your vitamin tablets regularly, and to prevent heat exhaustion, which can lead to heat stroke, you must regularly take salt tablets.

The only source of water in the desert is subterranean. This well is over 350 feet deep.

For most of the time your diet will be supplemented with fresh fruit purchased from market stalls and roadside vendors, and this will be beneficial as fresh fruit is a good source of vitamins. Make sure you wash fruit thoroughly in clean water before eating it. The best fruit to relieve hunger pangs you may develop is the banana. You may wish to take the opportunity of eating at native stalls, and here I would recommend fried yams and cassavas, and fried plantain, a type of cooking banana. In most markets you will find these being cooked in curved metal dishes over a fire, but make sure that whatever you purchase is freshly cooked and hot when you buy it. This applies particularly to meat which you will find being grilled over a form of barbecue. Most of the meat available will be monkey, and it is delicious; but as with all meat it must be well cooked. Sausages should be avoided.

Never drink milk unless it has been boiled first (except, possibly, in Kenya or South Africa). It is also unwise to purchase bazaar ice, or iced lollies, as these may be made from unpurified water and freezing alone will not kill any bacteria present.

Disease and infection

Intestinal disorders such as dysenteries and diarrhoea can result from eating contaminated food and drinking impure water. These disorders can be very unpleasant. Make sure your medical kit is equipped to treat them.

Bilharzia is a disease prevalent throughout Africa and very common in Central Africa. It can be fatal. It is contracted via a minute water snail which transmits the infection to you through the soles of your feet.

To ensure you do not contract this disease you must make sure that you do not walk barefoot anywhere; and, more important, if you enter any water to swim or wash make sure it is fresh running water and keep your feet off the bottom as much as possible; the bilharzia snail is commonly found in stagnant water amongst the mud. Another precaution is to place a rock or piece of board in the water to stand on if you are due for a wash.

Hookworm This also enters the body through the soles of the feet, and is commonly found in damp ground around villages. The general rule once more is, keep your shoes on.

Sleeping sickness This is brought on by the bite of the tsetse fly. Although this is gradually being eliminated, you should beware.

Malaria This is transmitted by the Anopheles mosquito. Not all mosquitoes carry malaria, and only females bite, but you cannot know the difference, so try to avoid being bitten and take your prophylactics regularly. They may not guarantee that you will not contract malaria if bitten, but they give your body some resistance to the disease. As there are several types of malaria transmitted by several types of mosquito, consult your doctor as to the best preventative medicine. At the moment work is in progress on the development of an anti-malaria vaccine.

Camping

It is difficult to find official camp sites in Africa, except in South Africa, some large capitals, and game reserves, so you must make the best of what is available and camp where you can. Always ask permission if you wish to camp on somebody's land; and try to camp well away from water otherwise you will be plagued by flying insects.

Border officials will often allow you to camp at the border, and most hotels will let you camp in their grounds although they may make a small charge. In Togo and Benin you can camp on the sandy beach.

Try to camp either *in* a village or well away from it, and if you camp in a village try to do so within the confines of a police post or similar official concern.

Many a church mission will be only too pleased to let you erect your tent in their grounds and some may even offer you a bed inside and the use of their cooking facilities. They will not charge you for camping but gratefully accept a donation to their cause.

Camping in the open is likely to attract many curious and inquisitive villagers who make a good photographic subject but can prove a nuisance by their sheer numbers.

Always try to erect tents before darkness falls — which throughout Africa is around 1900 hours. At night it is so easy to lose some item, and flies and mosquitoes will be attracted by your lights.

Hotels throughout Africa are modestly priced, and rest houses offer cheap but clean accommodation.

Personal appearance

See also the section on correct dress on page 59. More and more people in Africa are now wearing western type clothing, and are beginning to accept the European mode of dress of which they were critical a few years ago, but male travellers with long hair are often treated with contempt. In fact in some countries, such as Kenya, there are limits to the length of a person's hair and regulations are laid down as to what length constitutes grounds for refusal of entry. Some tourist hotels, even in Malawi, tend to relax the regulations regarding clothing.

Ferries

At some time or another you are going to have to cross a river, sea, or lake by ferry. It could be by the conventional motorised means, or it could be by a couple of dug-out canoes roped together and paddled across or pulled by a rope from the other shore. You must therefore be prepared for the unexpected, like removing your car battery to start the engine (many ferries in isolated positions stand idle for long periods and their batteries are often removed or stolen); or having your crew grab a piece of wood to paddle your vehicle across the river. You may have to wait a day or two before you can cross; or perhaps the ferry skipper, so pleased with having a vehicle on board (some ferry a vehicle only once in 8 or 9 months) might decide to give you a guided tour of the river and so make a ten-minute crossing into a four-hour one. Be patient and join in the fun. You will get there in the end.

Once in Africa the ferries are treated as part of the road, and as such there is no charge for them; but some crews will ask you for payment, and the amount you give is your personal choice.

Minefields

Never attempt to cross into another country by any means other than the offical border crossing. Various political struggles have resulted in the laying of minefields, civilian as well as military, and no charts as to their location are available, making it difficult to clear them all (although much of this has been undertaken). Morocco, Libya, and Tchad are no exception. Play safe and cross only at the recognised border posts.

The African peoples

There are hundreds of different tribes in Africa, and the customs of the people vary considerably, but you will find that although many people are of a shy reserved nature, particularly the pygmies, they will almost invariably express friendship towards you. Africans are by nature very friendly people, none more so than the peoples of Zaire, Niger and Burkina Fasso. They will share their home and their food with you and want nothing in return. They will go out of their way to assist you for the sheer pleasure of it. You will have no problem with the language barrier for despite the many languages you will hear you will always know what they are talking about.

Once in Africa you will soon realise that many things you take for granted back home, even seemingly trivial things, now appear exceedingly important. You will stand next to people who have nothing at all in this world apart from the clothing they stand in and you will realise just how fortunate you are. Despite poverty, disease, starvation and other misfortunes, people manage to live from day to day as if they haven't a care in the world, and you would find it difficult to locate more cheerful, happy-go-lucky acquaintances. Wherever and whenever you stop, you will soon be surrounded by the local people, mainly children who want nothing more than to talk to you and shake the hand of a 'white man', who after all is a rare visitor to their part of the world.

You will notice that conditions and lifestyles in many of the places you visit will be decidedly primitive compared with European standards, so you must be prepared to respect, understand, and accept, without prejudice, cultures alien to your own.

As already mentioned, you may often feel utter frustration when confronted by the petty officialdom of some functionaries, but they are in private life just another friendly helpful villager of Africa. In their official capacity, however, they have a job to do, and that job can be difficult particularly as they have to bridge a language and culture barrier alien to their own in their dealings with you. So remember, be cheerful and helpful and, whatever you do, never force anyone into a position from which retreat would cause embarrassment.

Smuggling

Never resort to smuggling — that is carrying 'forbidden' goods either from one country to another or from one state to another in the same country — whether for yourself or as a favour for someone else. Beware of strangers asking you to carry or deliver a parcel for them. Remember that your vehicle is liable to be searched at any border or check point, or at any time in a foreign

It is always a pleasure to meet various tribes and discuss their way of life. Here we meet the elders of a desert nomad tribe.

country, and the driver is responsible at all times for everything inside that vehicle.

Any large amounts of salt or rice can, in some areas, be classified as smuggled goods, with heavy penalties for offenders, and things like flour in unmarked containers could easily be suspected as narcotics, submitting you to long delays and embarrassment while it is chemically analysed.

Fuel availability

It is a well known fact that wherever there are propelled vehicles, petrol is available, somewhere; and this is the case throughout Africa. No matter where you travel you will find other vehicles and, accordingly, fuel will always be available on your route, but you must use your ingenuity and find it. You then have to negotiate the cost. It may be very high but if you are desperate for fuel it is a price that must be paid. The best way to find fuel is to ask other drivers where their supply is. It could be a café, hotel, grocery store, or the local police station. It could be a factory, plantation, or even a boat on the river. Use your imagination at all times.

Black market

It must be stressed that dealing on the black market is illegal in most countries and heavy penalties are imposed on offenders who are caught. This applies particularly to currency exchange offences. You should therefore exchange currency only at the authorised places of exchange such as banks, hotels, and, occasionally, border controls where the customs officials operate exchange facilities.

Raw gold

It is an offence to purchase or even possess raw gold in the form of nuggets or dust in many countries, unless a certificate is issued with purchase.

Diamonds

It is a serious offence to purchase or be in possession of uncut diamonds in most countries without a licence. It is also a risky procedure to purchase them from unauthorised dealers.

The Sahara: a reminder for overlanders

Your vehicle
Check your fuel, water, battery, and oil levels *daily*, and keep them all topped up.

Fellow travellers
Always get to know any fellow travellers you may meet, and discuss your route and destination amongst other things. You never know when you may

AO6

Sunset at a camp site alongside the River Niger.

need their assistance.

Consider travelling in convoy with other travellers if they do not object.

Camping
Erect your camp well away from an oasis whether large or small if you wish to avoid being plagued by flies.

Travelling permission
Where permission is needed to travel certain routes, ensure that you have your permit *before* entering the desert region. Permits are usually obtainable from the local town hall or police station, and are issued by the administrative authorities of that town after careful inspection of your vehicle and its equipment. You will have to provide the following information:

—Make of vehicle
—Registration number
—Type of vehicle
—Names of all passengers and their passport numbers
—Departure point
—Destination
—Approximate time of arrival at destination
—Each stopping place

Even if permission is not required for the route that you choose to travel on, it is advisable to leave this information with the authorities at your point of departure in case some calamity should befall you. The search party will then have information to assist them. Remember that if you are in need of search and rescue, the costs for these are entirely your responsibility. The permit merely authorises you to travel on the stated route, and acknowledges that your equipment is in order. It does not in any way signify an acknowledgement of responsibility for your safety and wellbeing by the authorities concerned.

Keep to your route
Whatever route you decide to take, do not diverge from it, or change your mind and take another route. Your permit authorises you to travel the stated route only and separate permission is required to take another course.

There are several 'linking' roads between the main routes across the desert, such as In Amguel to Djanet, or Bordj Omar Driss to In Ecker. Under no circumstances should you take any of these routes. Tourist travel is strictly forbidden on some of these, while those that are open to travellers require special permission to travel on them. In any case, many of these 'linking' routes are highly dangerous. You may find a signpost at the junction of the main route you are travelling on, but this is often the only route indication you will find. The road will suddenly end and you will find yourself alone in a vast expanse of sand, with nobody around to ask the way, or you may find the road splits up and there are several vehicle tracks heading in all directions. These tracks are made by locals who know exactly where they are going, but there is no guarantee on following a chosen set of tracks that you will find the vehicle. The tracks could disappear, or go on for many miles.

If there is a particular linking road that you wish to take, enquire about the possibility of using it from the authorities before you begin your desert crossing, and if it is all right to use it, ensure that you have a permit if it is required.

Be sensible, do not take chances, and you will have an enjoyable experience.

Part 2
Route Guides

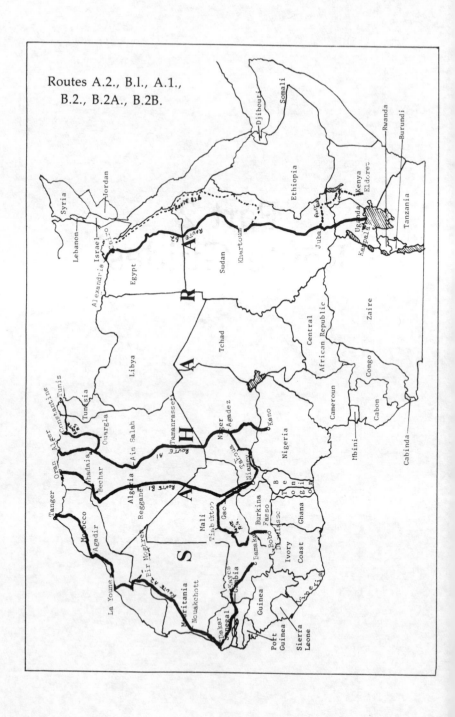

Routes A.2., B.1., A.1.,
B.2., B.2A., B.2B.

Routes A.5., A.6., A.7.

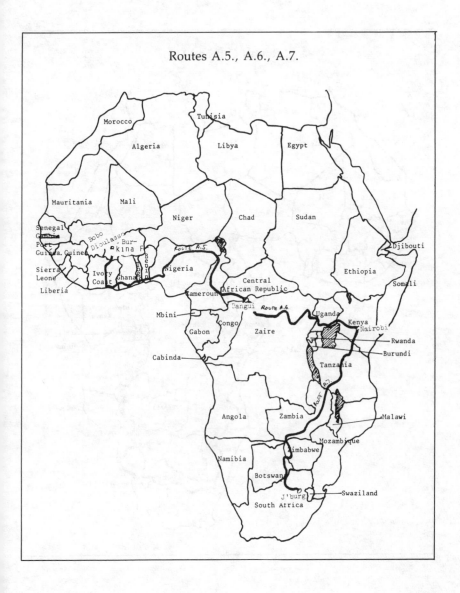

Routes C.1. and C.2.

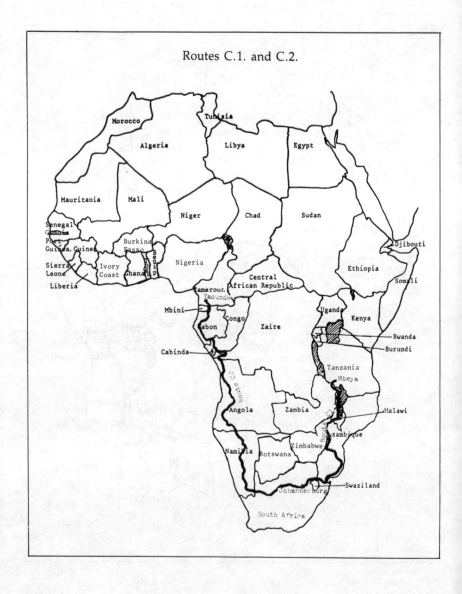

Route guide index

The following two routes are fairly new and as yet travelled over by few people; very little concrete information is available and therefore caution should be exercised — i.e. enquire from your consul in the preceding country regarding the route ahead.

Route C.1.   153
Mbeya to Nkhotakota
Nkhotakota to Catandica
Catandica to Inhambane
Inhambane to Belfast
Belfast to Johannesburg
Route mileage 2,203 (3,532k)

(Note: No shortage of fuel, water or provisions on this route)

Route C.2.   159
Yaoundé to Lambarene
Lambarene to Mindouli
Mindouli to Camabatela
Camabatela to Caconda
Caconda to Oshikango
Oshikango to Windhoek
Windhoek to Karasburg
Karasburg to Vryburg
Vryburg to Johannesburg
Route mileage 4,180 (6,688k)

(Note: This is a very interesting route but recommended only for 4-wheel drives. Fuel and water are always available but "at a price" in Gabon and Zaire.)

How to read the route guides

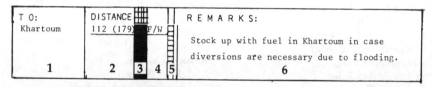

T O: Khartoum	DISTANCE 112 (179)		F/W		R E M A R K S: Stock up with fuel in Khartoum in case diversions are necessary due to flooding.
1	2	3	4	5	6

Column 1 Lists the names of towns through which you will be travelling.
Column 2 Gives the distance from the last named town directly above it. The first figure gives the miles and the figure in brackets gives the kilometres.
Column 3 Gives an indication of the road condition — see chart below.
Column 4 States what facilities are available in that town. F = Fuel, W = Water, F/W = Both.
Column 5 Is a mileage scale in 50 mile sections made up with 10x5 mile sub-sections. Its main use is to calculate distances between sand/dirt/tarmac road sections, and length of each section.
Column 6 Gives general remarks on road conditions, and facilities in and between towns on route.

Basically there are three types of road and they are indicated as follows:

Indicates a sealed tarmac surface which can be sub divided into broken or pothol-ed surface under "remarks".

 Indicates a dirt road or track which can be sub divided into potholed or cor-rugated surface under "remarks".

 Indicates a sand surfaced road or desert sand track. "Remarks" will indicate sand con-dition, such as "soft" or "drifting".

Before setting out on any journey through the desert, you are advised to read again the section The Sahara: a reminder for overlanders **on page 81.**

Route A.1.
Algiers to Kano

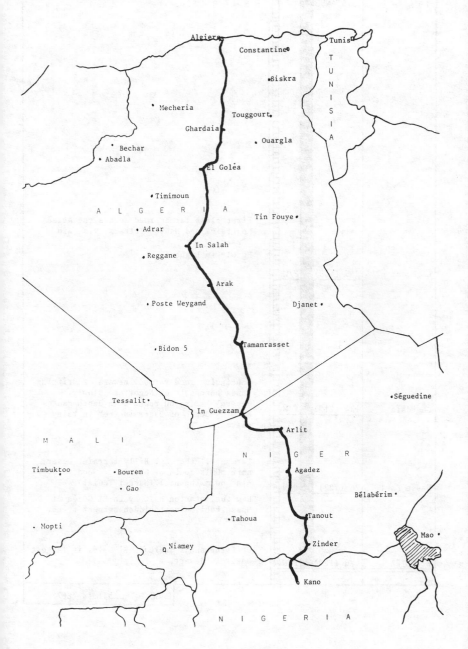

TO:	DISTANCE		REMARKS:
			First class tarmac road across the Atlas Mountains and Hauts Plateaux, via Ain Oussera. Hotels in Laghouat.
Laghouat	255 (408)	F/W	
			Continuing good tarmac. Beware of drifting sands across road. Negotiate slowly. Several Wadis on route with depth gauges showing depth of water in them in rainy season.
Ghardaïa	134 (215)	F/W	
			Tarmac all the way. Hilly terrain. Desert café 50mls south of Ghardaia. Good food. Also swimming pool.(Hassai Touiel)
Hasse Fahl	76 (122)	F/W	New fuel station halfway to El Goléa at Hasse Fahl, almost hidden amongst trees.
El Goléa	76 (122)	F/W	Drifting sands on road. El Goléa is largest oasis in desert.

PAGE TOTAL. 541mls (867)

TO:	DISTANCE			REMARKS:

REMARKS:

Road narrows after El-Goléa but still of tarmac. Desert flat and stoney with hills and sand dunes. Beware of trucks on narrow road occupying whole width.

Water at Fort Miribel, abandoned fort 400 yards to your left about 53 miles south of El-Goléa.
Tademait Plateau between El-Goléa and In Salah.

145 miles from El-Goléa, road is tarmac with large potholes appearing. Surrounding desert flat.

Ain-el-Hadjadj	57 (91)	W	Large sand dunes now appearing. From here road descends Plateau Tademait with 20% gradient. Ahead, 4 distinctive plateaux.

Scattered potholes to In Salah, otherwise tarmac surface.

In Salah	250 (400)	F/W	Good tarmac after In Salah for about 20 miles, then road through to Arak in bad state of repair, washed away in places necessitating a detour through soft sinking sand. Very bad through Arak Gorge.

More comfortable to drive on sand.

Arak	185 (296)	F/W	Petrol available in Arak Gorge. Picturesque area. Tarmac road washed away by flooding. Heavy trucks frequent this area.

Dangerous section as road begins to climb Mouydir Mountains. Still tarmac but broken up and potholed. Several wadis pass under road between Arak and Marabout leading to possibility of flash floods when it rains. Be cautious.

Marabout	85(136)	W	Long sections of tarmac broken up by heavy trucks that frequently travel this route.

PAGE TOTAL. 577 (923)

TO:	DISTANCE		REMARKS:
			Tarmac road badly broken up, but still some good long tarmac sections. Military fort at In Ecker still in use. Drifting sands across road in places.
In Ecker	52 (83)	F/W	Liable to flooding in rainy season.
In Amguel	20 (32)	W	Abandoned fort at In Amguel Begin ascent of Hoggar mountains. First 30 miles from In Amguel, road is tarmac with good surface as potholes have been filled in. Liable to flooding in rainy
Tit	26 (42)	W	season. 35 miles from In Amguel bad potholes again, for 15 miles then excellent tarmac to Tamanrasset.
Tamanrasset	75 (120)	F/W	All facilities including Safari Hotels here but water scarce. Large supermarket with fresh French cheese flown in from Algiers.
			Clear Immigration & Frontier Police at fort on north side of main street in Tamanrasset.
			Good tarmac from Tamanrasset for 70 miles, then under construction to the border.
			Driving now on sand. Keep out of other vehicle tracks. Navigate with care. No signposts or markers. Good flat sand. Firm but soft patches occasionally. 60 miles from Tamanrasset markers every 2 kilometres consisting of 45 gallon drums and/or metal or wooden poles.
In Guezzam	260 (417)	F/W	Petrol not always available at In Guezzam but small provisions shop. Report to Customs and Immigration. Check
Algeria ++++++++++ Niger			out of Niger. 16 miles over flat firm sand to Assamaka, border control in Niger, though first 4 miles soft. Follow marker posts, every 5 kilometres.
			Good firm sand to Arlit. Occasional soft stretch, and rocky areas that require careful negotiation. 3 miles from Arlit, track passes uranium mine and dual carriageway begins. Dirt surface.
			Clear Police and Customs in Arlit.
Arlit	130 (208)	F/W	

PAGE TOTAL. 563 (902)

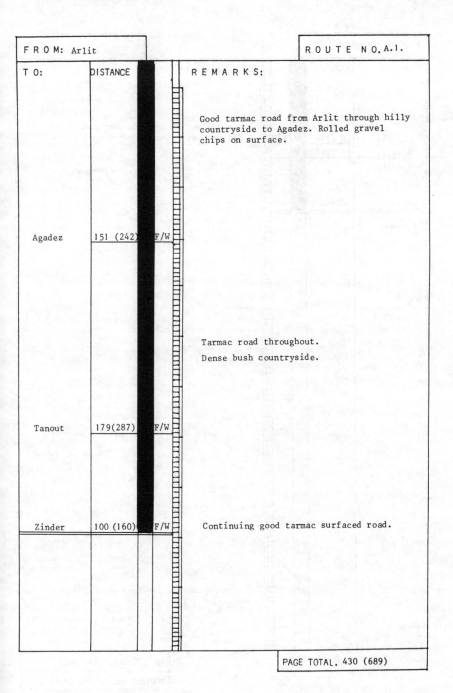

FROM: Arlit				ROUTE NO. A.1.
TO:	DISTANCE			REMARKS:

Good tarmac road from Arlit through hilly countryside to Agadez. Rolled gravel chips on surface.

Agadez   151 (242)   F/W

Tarmac road throughout.
Dense bush countryside.

Tanout   179(287)   F/W

Zinder   100 (160)   F/W   Continuing good tarmac surfaced road.

PAGE TOTAL. 430 (689)

| FROM: Zinder | | | | ROUTE NO. A.1. |

T O:	DISTANCE			REMARKS:
Magaria	59 (95)	F/W		Clear Niger Customs and Immigration at Magaria and at border.
Niger ++++++++++++ Nigeria	14 (22)			
Kano	77 (123)	F/W		

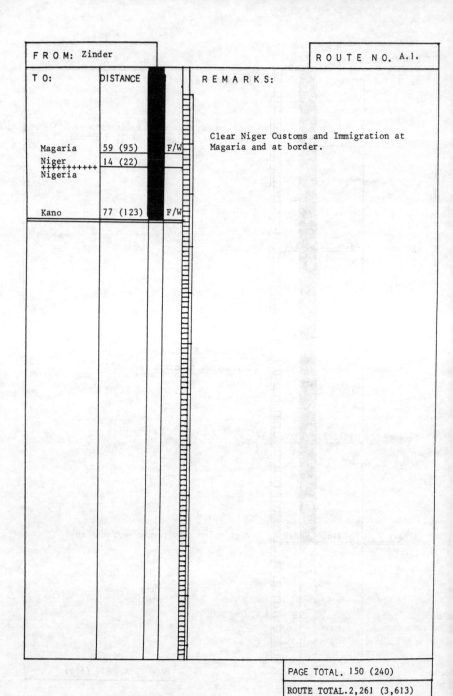

PAGE TOTAL. 150 (240)

ROUTE TOTAL. 2,261 (3,613)

Route B.1.
Oran to Niamey

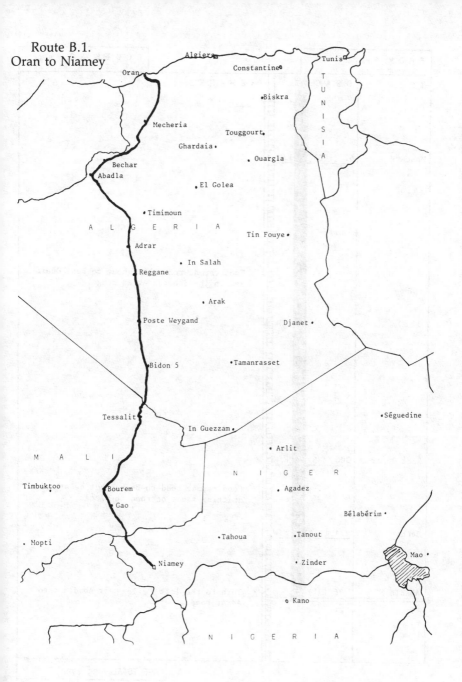

97

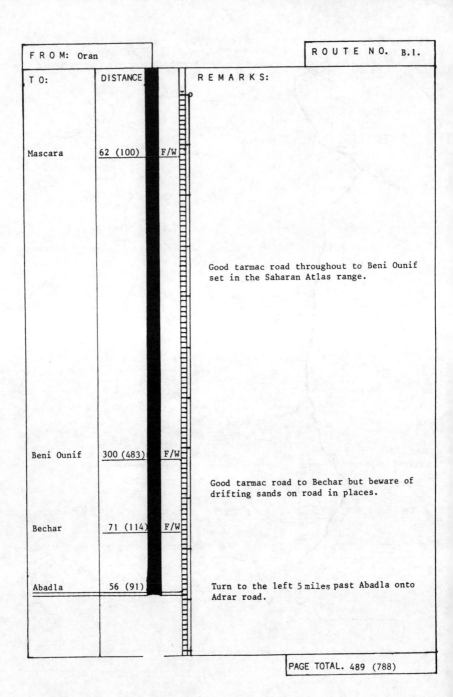

FROM: Oran			ROUTE NO. B.1.
TO:	DISTANCE		REMARKS:
Mascara	62 (100)	F/W	
			Good tarmac road throughout to Beni Ounif set in the Saharan Atlas range.
Beni Ounif	300 (483)	F/W	
			Good tarmac road to Bechar but beware of drifting sands on road in places.
Bechar	71 (114)	F/W	
Abadla	56 (91)		Turn to the left 5 miles past Abadla onto Adrar road.

PAGE TOTAL. 489 (788)

FROM: Abadla				ROUTE NO. B.1.

TO:	DISTANCE			REMARKS:
				A picturesque route through avenues of oasis and sand dunes.
Guerzim	129 (206)			
Kerzaz	26 (42)	F		Road liable to flooding at these three positions.
Foum-el-Kheneg	49 (78)			
Adrar	106 (169)	F/W		Good tarmac road to Adrar where all facilities available. Report to Police to ascertain if permission is required to cross desert. Fill up with fuel and water.
Reggane	83 (133)	F/W		Ensure you are on the right road to Reggane. No signposts. Road lined with palm trees. Fill up with fuel and water. No more fuel for 800 miles unless Tessalit has stocks but do not bank on it.

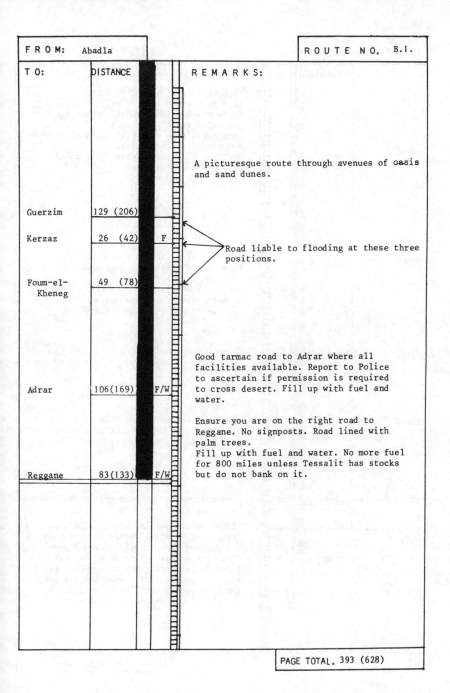

PAGE TOTAL. 393 (628)

99

FROM: Reggane				ROUTE NO. B.1.

TO:	DISTANCE			REMARKS:
				(Link road from Reggane to In Salah.) Take road south towards Mali border. Sandy track with corrugations and concealed rocks. Take care. Good navigation essential as no signposts and many markers missing. Small sand dunes on route. Good speed possible over flat sand.
Poste Weygand	170 (272)			Deserted area. Just a few ruins. Sandy track continues, occasionally dirt and stones. Many soft sandy sections. Corrugations taken at speed less bumpy. 80 miles south of Poste Weygand route crosses Tropic of Cancer(signposted).
Bidon 5	160 (256)			Another deserted area with a couple of old water tanks. Road continues sand, bumpy in places but mainly flat
Bordj Mohktar	75 (120)	W		Customs/Immigration at Bordj Mohktar, and an old military fort.
Algeria +++++++++++++ Mali	20 (32)			Travel South East for border with Mali, travelling 17 miles where you will pass a lone dead tree. 3 miles further you will come across a line of trees. Follow these to the border which is marked by a plain lump of concrete on the edge of the road. Sandy track heads west for a short distance before swinging south.

PAGE TOTAL. 425 (680)

FROM:	Algeria/Mali Border.			

TO:	DISTANCE			REMARKS:
				Road to Tessalit is of undulating sand with many bumps. About 8 miles from Tessalit, road diverts around the airport and military base. Report to Customs and Immigration. Fuel may occasionally be available at Tessalit.
Tessalit	80 (128)	W		
				Route from Tessalit winds its way through the Tilemsi Valley, with rough crumbling hills on either side of the corrugated sand and dirt track. Difficult and slow route liable to flooding and becoming impassable at times when it rains.
				Military checkpoint on entry to Anefis.
Anefis	176 (283)	W		
				Drinking water available from a well at Tassit, 48 miles south of Anefis.
				Route from Anefis to Gao is very badly marked with vehicle tracks leading off in all directions. Compass navigation necessary. Route can be impassable during rains and diversion via Almoustarat and Bourem may be necessary.
Gao	146(234)	F/W		At Gao, report to Police Post(in town next to market). Travelling permit will be issued here for Mali, and photographic permit if you intend taking photographs in the area. Could take 2 or 3 days for issue of permits. (Hard cash often expedites the process).
Ansongo	60 (95)	W		Leave Gao on road following course of Niger River. Police check on outskirts and again at Ansongo. Road surface improved; of sand and dirt but soft in places. Becomes rough dirt with sandy patches.
				Clear Customs and Immigration at Ansongo.
Labézanga	62 (99)	W		Mali/Niger border town. Customs/Police check

PAGE TOTAL. 524 (839)

FROM: Labézanga				ROUTE NO. B.1.

TO:	DISTANCE			REMARKS:
Mali ++++++++++ Niger				
Ayorou	26 (42)		F/W	Very rough dirt road to Ayorou over several weak bridges. Some washed away. Diversion over rocks and large stones in bed of wadi often necessary.
Tillabery	55 (88)		F/W	Well graded gravel surface to Tillabery, Road about 20 ft wide.
Niamey	75 (120)		F/W	Good tarmac surface from Tillabery to Niamey through open countryside. Police check on entering Niamey.

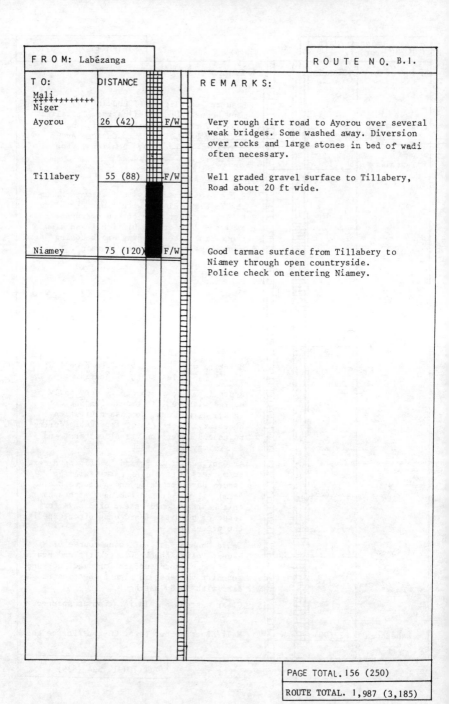

PAGE TOTAL. 156 (250)

ROUTE TOTAL. 1,987 (3,185)

Route A.2. Tangiers to Bamako

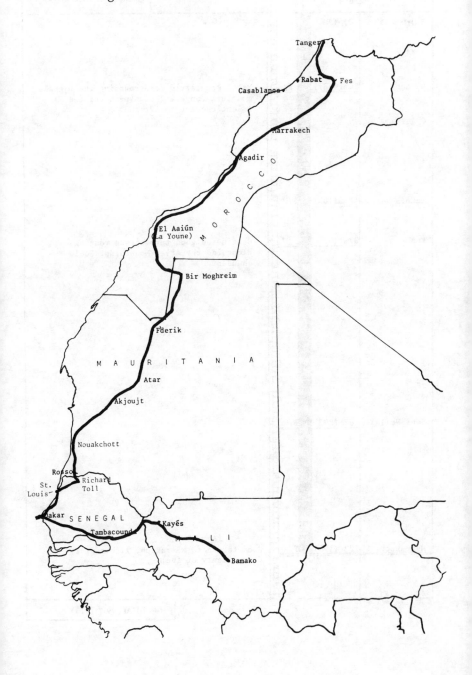

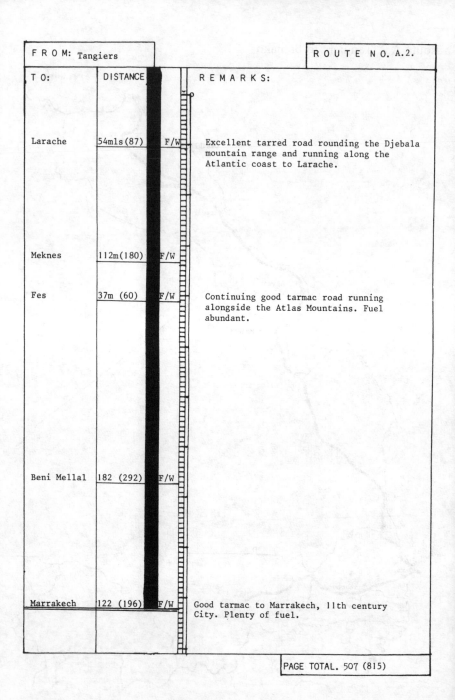

FROM: Tangiers			ROUTE NO. A.2.
TO:	DISTANCE		REMARKS:
Larache	54mls(87)	F/W	Excellent tarred road rounding the Djebala mountain range and running along the Atlantic coast to Larache.
Meknes	112m(180)	F/W	
Fes	37m (60)	F/W	Continuing good tarmac road running alongside the Atlas Mountains. Fuel abundant.
Beni Mellal	182 (292)	F/W	
Marrakech	122 (196)	F/W	Good tarmac to Marrakech, 11th century City. Plenty of fuel.

PAGE TOTAL. 507 (815)

T O:	DISTANCE		REMARKS:
Tizi-n-Test	85(135)		Mountain pass at 2,092 metres. Difficult Section. Exercise caution.
Agadir	106 (171)	F/W	Twisting, winding tarmac across the Atlas Mountains to Agadir on the coast. Very picturesque route.
Goulimime	123(198)	F/W	Road descends from the Atlas Mountains to desert town of Goulimime. Petrol and water available.
Tan Tan	78 (125)	F/W	Narrow tarmac road to Tan Tan in the Western Sahara. Still plenty of fuel. Route to Tan Tan passes through area of sand dunes. Watch for sand on road in places.

PAGE TOTAL. 392 (627)

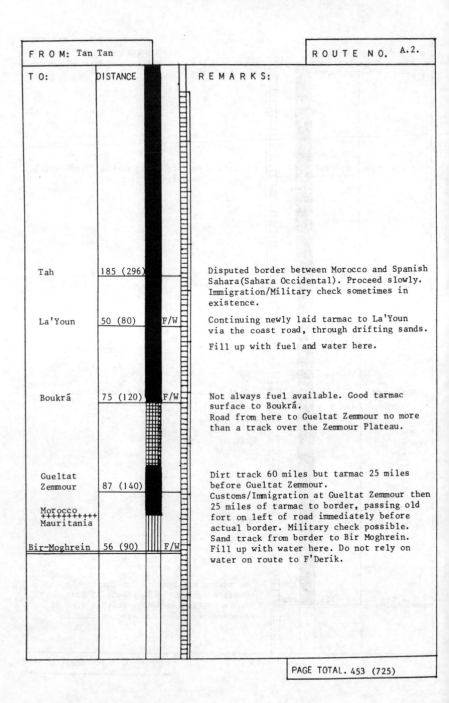

F R O M: Tan Tan				ROUTE NO. A.2.

T O:	DISTANCE			R E M A R K S:
Tah	185 (296)			Disputed border between Morocco and Spanish Sahara(Sahara Occidental). Proceed slowly. Immigration/Military check sometimes in existence.
La'Youn	50 (80)	F/W		Continuing newly laid tarmac to La'Youn via the coast road, through drifting sands. Fill up with fuel and water here.
Boukrá	75 (120)	F/W		Not always fuel available. Good tarmac surface to Boukrá. Road from here to Gueltat Zemmour no more than a track over the Zemmour Plateau.
Gueltat Zemmour	87 (140)			Dirt track 60 miles but tarmac 25 miles before Gueltat Zemmour. Customs/Immigration at Gueltat Zemmour then 25 miles of tarmac to border, passing old fort on left of road immediately before actual border. Military check possible. Sand track from border to Bir Moghrein.
Morocco +++++++++++ Mauritania				
Bir-Moghrein	56 (90)	F/W		Fill up with water here. Do not rely on water on route to F'Derik.

PAGE TOTAL. 453 (725)

FROM: Bir-Moghrein				ROUTE NO. A.2.
TO:	DISTANCE			REMARKS:
F'Derik	249(400)	F/W		Sand track throughout. Detours required at times to avoid drifting sands.
Atar	180(287)	F/W		Sand track through hilly terrain. Water and fuel at Choum. Tunnel(rail) at Choum. Railway follows road to this point. Gravel before Atar as road climbs through two passes. All facilities at Atar.

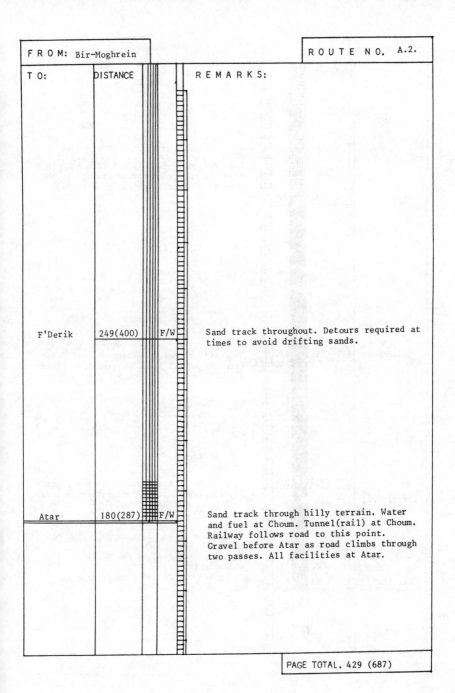

PAGE TOTAL. 429 (687)

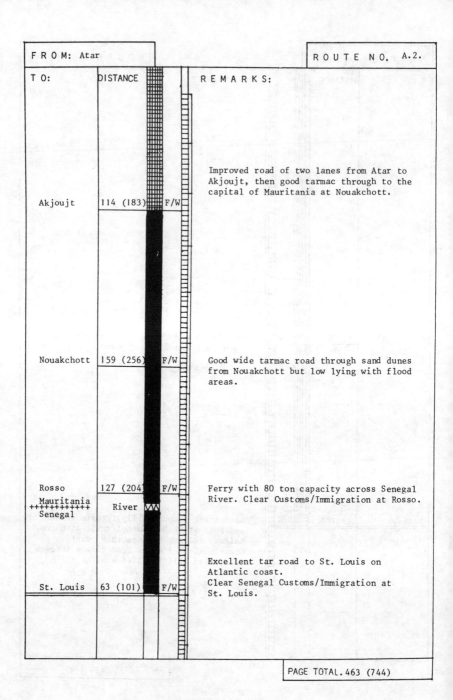

FROM: Atar			ROUTE NO. A.2.

T O:	DISTANCE		REMARKS:
Akjoujt	114 (183)	F/W	Improved road of two lanes from Atar to Akjoujt, then good tarmac through to the capital of Mauritania at Nouakchott.
Nouakchott	159 (256)	F/W	Good wide tarmac road through sand dunes from Nouakchott but low lying with flood areas.
Rosso	127 (204)	F/W	Ferry with 80 ton capacity across Senegal River. Clear Customs/Immigration at Rosso.
Mauritania ++++++++++++ Senegal	River		
St. Louis	63 (101)	F/W	Excellent tar road to St. Louis on Atlantic coast. Clear Senegal Customs/Immigration at St. Louis.

PAGE TOTAL. 463 (744)

T O:	DISTANCE		REMARKS:
			Tarmac road throughout to Dakar Petrol and water plentiful on route.
Dakar	166 (268)	F/W	
Kaolack	115 (184)	F/W	Good tarmac road. No fuel shortage.
Maleme Hodar	85 (135)	F/W	Good tarmac through to Maleme Hodar then well graded gravel on dirt to Tambacounda.
Tambacounda	81 (131)	F/W	Busy market town at Tambacounda and end of decent roads. Roads to Kayes often washed away by floods, together with bridges. Vehicles may be railed from Tambacounda to Kayes if roads too bad. Cost cheap but travel slow. Enquire at Tambacounda if ferry at Kidira is running. Fair dirt road to Goudiry.
Goudiry	70 (113)	W	Very badly rutted dirt road to Mali border. Customs/Immigration at Kidira.
Kidira Senegal ========== Mali	42 (67)	W	

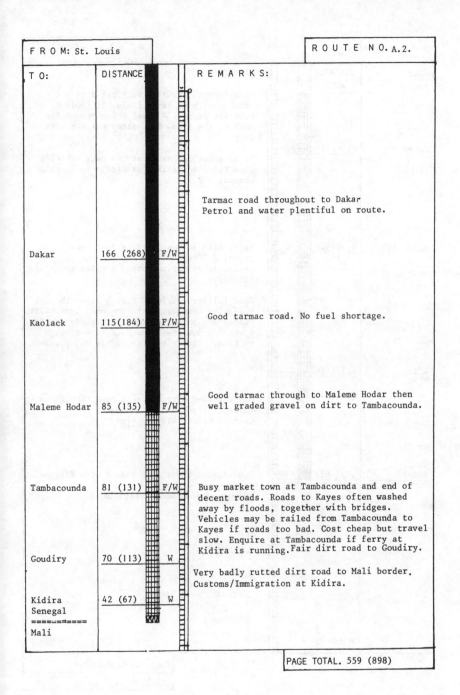

PAGE TOTAL. 559 (898)

TO: ++++++++++++	DISTANCE		REMARKS:
Diboli			Road through to Kayes very bad dirt and sand. Low lying land liable to flooding in rainy season. 4 wheel drive needed for much of the time. Some sandy patches very deep.
Kayes	65 (105)	F/W	It is sometimes necessary to rail vehicles from Kayes to Bamako, particularly in rainy season.
Bafoulabe	96 (154)	W	Ferry with 20 ton limit at Bafoulabe crossing River Bafing. Petrol sometimes available at Mahina, about 6 miles south of Bafoulabe.
			Road follows course of Bakoye River through beautiful countryside to Toucoto. Very badly rutted and potholed. Many soft sandy patches. 4 wheel drive needed much of time through to Kita. Liable to flooding in rainy season.
Kita	121 (194)	F/W	Badly rutted dirt and sand road through to Bamako. Caution needed all the time.
Bamako	102(163)	F/W	Good tarmac roads link Bamako with Sikasso, Segou, and beyond. Plenty of fuel when available.

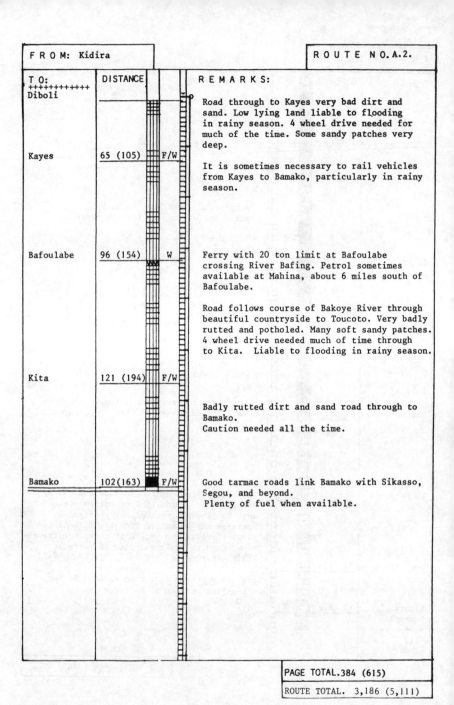

PAGE TOTAL. 384 (615)

ROUTE TOTAL. 3,186 (5,111)

Route A.3.
Tunis to Ghardaia

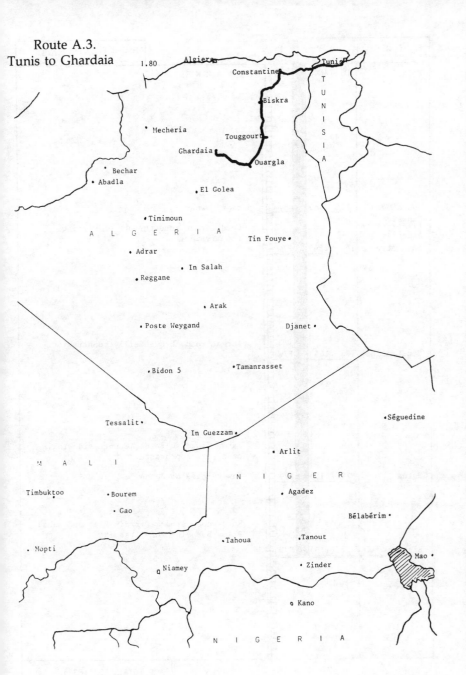

T O:	DISTANCE		REMARKS:
Ghardimaon Tunisia ++++++++++++ Algeria	115 (185)	F/W	Border town. Good tarmac road through undulating countryside.
Souk Ahras	159 (254)	F/W	
Constantine	102 (164)	F/W	Tarmac road through hilly countryside.
Batna	74 (119)	F/W	Tarmac road to Batna. Countryside taking on desert appearance. New by-pass at Batna.
Biskra	72 (115)	F/W	Road good tarmac. Terrain flat and sandy. Palms becoming more frequent.

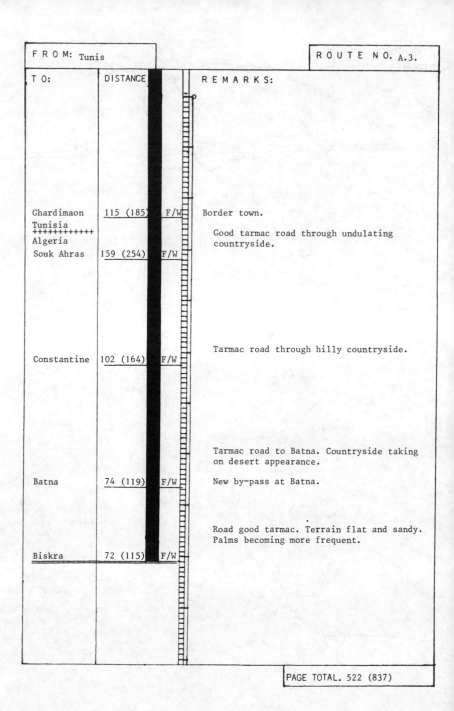

PAGE TOTAL. 522 (837)

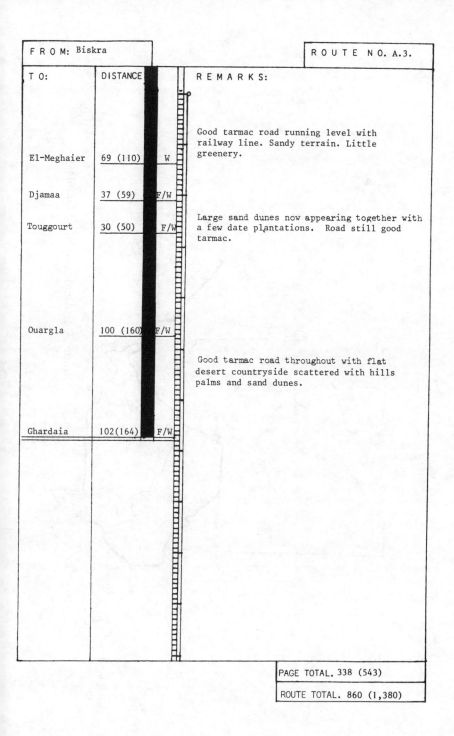

T O:	DISTANCE		REMARKS:
			Good tarmac road running level with railway line. Sandy terrain. Little greenery.
El-Meghaier	69 (110)	W	
Djamaa	37 (59)	F/W	
Touggourt	30 (50)	F/W	Large sand dunes now appearing together with a few date plantations. Road still good tarmac.
Ouargla	100 (160)	F/W	
			Good tarmac road throughout with flat desert countryside scattered with hills palms and sand dunes.
Ghardaia	102(164)	F/W	

PAGE TOTAL. 338 (543)

ROUTE TOTAL. 860 (1,380)

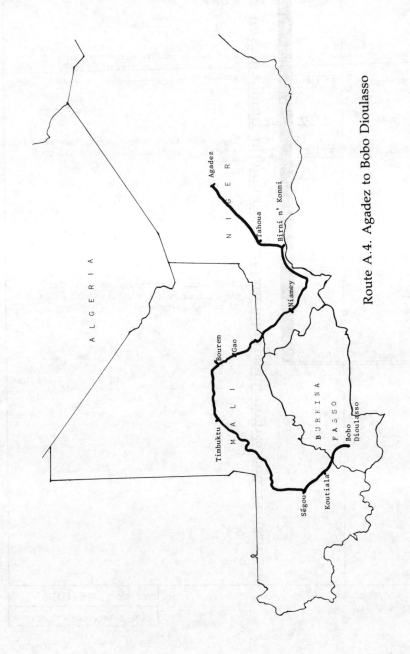

Route A.4. Agadez to Bobo Dioulasso

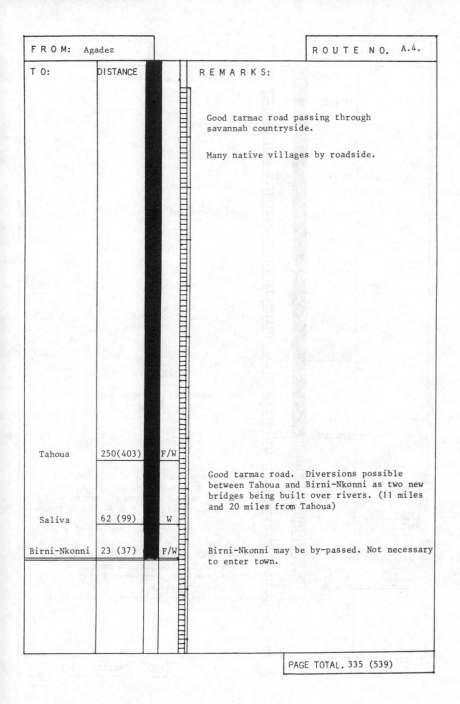

TO:	DISTANCE			REMARKS:
				Good tarmac road passing through savannah countryside.
				Many native villages by roadside.
Tahoua	250(403)	F/W		
				Good tarmac road. Diversions possible between Tahoua and Birni-Nkonni as two new bridges being built over rivers. (11 miles and 20 miles from Tahoua)
Saliva	62 (99)	W		
Birni-Nkonni	23 (37)	F/W		Birni-Nkonni may be by-passed. Not necessary to enter town.

PAGE TOTAL. 335 (539)

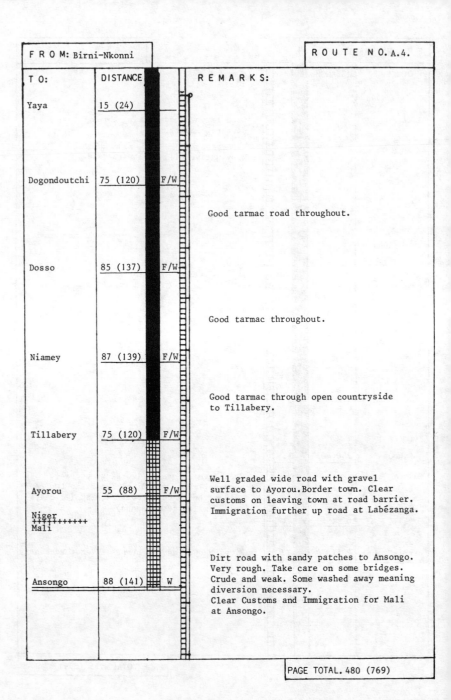

FROM: Birni-Nkonni			ROUTE NO. A.4.
TO:	**DISTANCE**		**REMARKS:**
Yaya	15 (24)		
Dogondoutchi	75 (120)	F/W	Good tarmac road throughout.
Dosso	85 (137)	F/W	Good tarmac throughout.
Niamey	87 (139)	F/W	Good tarmac through open countryside to Tillabery.
Tillabery	75 (120)	F/W	Well graded wide road with gravel surface to Ayorou. Border town. Clear customs on leaving town at road barrier. Immigration further up road at Labézanga.
Ayorou	55 (88)	F/W	
Niger +++++++++++ Mali			Dirt road with sandy patches to Ansongo. Very rough. Take care on some bridges. Crude and weak. Some washed away meaning diversion necessary. Clear Customs and Immigration for Mali at Ansongo.
Ansongo	88 (141)	W	

PAGE TOTAL. 480 (769)

116

T O:	DISTANCE		REMARKS:
			Rough dirt road to Gao with sandy sections, some soft, in places.
Gao	60 (96)	F/W	Report to Police post in Gao for permit to travel to Timbuktoo, and photographic permit if you intend taking photographs. Permits can take a day or two to issue.
Bourem	59 (95)	W	Road to Bourem leaves Gao through avenue of palms. Sandy road but fairly firm. Drive carefully as giraffes and other wildlife wander the area. Towards Bourem road becomes corrugated and rutted dirt. Care needed as many ruts filled with sand. Road floods in rainy season.
Bamba	85 (137)		Ask directions for Timbuktoo in Bourem as there are no roads. To be safe keep the River Niger on left. 4 wheel drive essential for this route.
			Precise navigation needed as no signposts or markers. Only tracks of other vehicles heading in all directions. Very soft sand throughout and 4 wheel drive needed much of time. Route through dense shrubbery restricting range of vision.
Timbuktoo	120 (192)	F/W	Advisable to deflate tyres somewhat, temporarily.
			Report to police in Timbuktoo for visa for photography if you intend taking photographs in the town. All streets of sand except for short stretch of tar by post office. Only one petrol pump at market.
Goundam	60 (97)	W	Road to Goundam sand. Soft in places.
			Fuel at Diré. 2·1 miles south east of Goundam.
Niafounké	55 (88)	W	Road to Niafounké sand, some soft. Many dunes. Beware drifting sand on road. Soft and deep. 4 wheel drive essential.
			Road from Niafounké still sandy but diversion around lake necessary which requires a long section driving over rock.
Léré	85 (136)		Road becomes hard dirt towards Léré, but with a covering of sand in places.
			Section from Timbuktoo to Léré either badly marked or not marked at all.

PAGE TOTAL. 524 (841)

TO:	DISTANCE		REMARKS:
Nampala	57 (91)	W	Road of hard packed dirt, rutted in places. Careful navigation from Timbuktoo to Nampala essential as route unmarked and diversions through dense bush making your own route necessary at times particularly in rainy season when road floods. Compass navigation section.
Kogoni	83 (133)		Dirt road, bumpy in places. 10 miles from Kogoni, road joins and runs parallel with canal. An active waterway and one of the main means of transportation in the area. Kogoni is as far as large vessels are able to travel, from where barges take over. Road now fairly smooth but large humps at intersections and lock gates.
Niono	30 (50)	F/W	Road floods in rainy season.
Markala	43 (69)		Road condition improves as it leaves canals on approach to Markala, and crosses River Niger. Road tarmac with good surface from Niono.
Ségou	24 (38)	F/W	
Bla	55 (88)	F/W	Fuel now available in most towns, but not plentiful and some filling stations may be closed. Good tarmac now.
Koutiala	46 (74)	F/W	
Mali ++++++++++ Burkina Fasso			Clear Mali Customs and Immigration at Kouri. Police check at Falamana. Good tarmac road throughout Clear Burkina Fasso Customs/Immigration at at Falamana and Fo.
Bobo-Dioulasso	133(213)	F/W	

PAGE TOTAL. 471 (756)

ROUTE TOTAL. 1,801 (2,891)

Route A.5. Bobo Dioulasso to Bangui

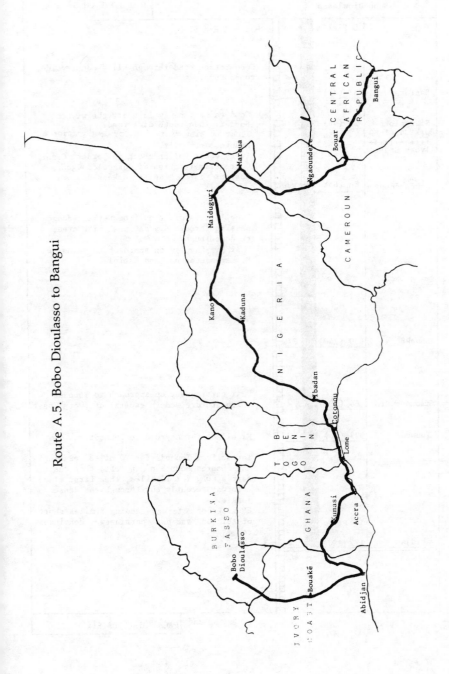

119

| FROM: Bobo-Dioulasso | | | ROUTE NO. A.5. |

TO:	DISTANCE		REMARKS:
			Good tarmac road through hilly countryside to Banfora.
Banfora	53 (85)	F/W	
Niangoloko	29 (46)	F/W	Good tarmac, newly laid all the way to Border, then rough dirt road.
Burkina Fasso			Clear Burkina Fasso Customs/Immigration at Niangoloko.
++++++++++++			
Ivory Coast			Ivory Coast Police check on border. Clear Customs/Immigration at Ouangolodougou.
Ferkéssédougou	60 (97)	F/W	Customs check also at Ferkéssédougou.
			Excellent tarmac road from Ferkéssédougou passing through dry savannah with areas of dense bush. Dual carriageway on approach to towns of Niakaramandougou, and Katiola.
Bouake	150 (240)	F/W	
Yamoussoukro	66 (105)	F/W	Dual carriageway on approach to Yamoussoukro, future modern capital of Ivory Coast.
Toumodi	29 (46)	F/W	Excellent tarmac road to Toumodi.
			Tarmac from Toumodi for 20 miles, passing the 'Sacred Mountain' on left, then dual carriageway for 12 miles, then first class motorway recently cut through the dense jungle. 80 miles of motorway ending 8 miles short of Abidjan, and dual carriageway continues to capital.
Abidjan	122 (197)	F/W	

PAGE TOTAL. 509(814)

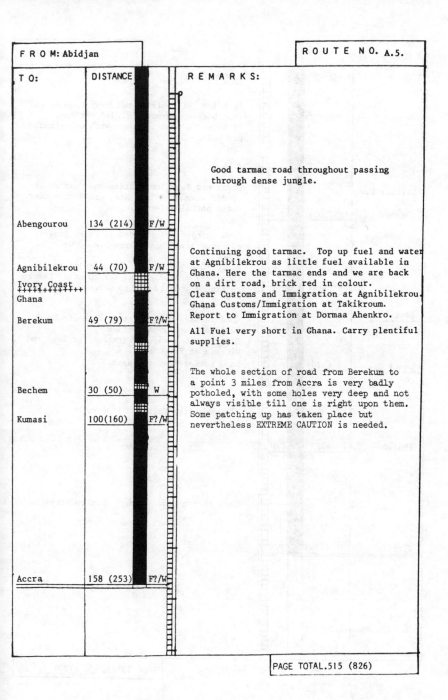

FROM: Abidjan			ROUTE NO. A.5.
TO:	DISTANCE		REMARKS:
			Good tarmac road throughout passing through dense jungle.
Abengourou	134 (214)	F/W	
Agnibilekrou	44 (70)	F/W	Continuing good tarmac. Top up fuel and water at Agnibilekrou as little fuel available in Ghana. Here the tarmac ends and we are back on a dirt road, brick red in colour.
Ivory Coast ++++++++++++++ Ghana			Clear Customs and Immigration at Agnibilekrou. Ghana Customs/Immigration at Takikroum. Report to Immigration at Dormaa Ahenkro.
Berekum	49 (79)	F?/W	All Fuel very short in Ghana. Carry plentiful supplies.
Bechem	30 (50)	W	The whole section of road from Berekum to a point 3 miles from Accra is very badly potholed, with some holes very deep and not always visible till one is right upon them.
Kumasi	100 (160)	F?/W	Some patching up has taken place but nevertheless EXTREME CAUTION is needed.
Accra	158 (253)	F?/W	

PAGE TOTAL. 515 (826)

TO:	DISTANCE			REMARKS:
				18 miles of concrete motorway from Accra, then back to tarmac potholed surface. At Sogakofe road improves with occasional pot hole.
Ghana ++++++++++++ Togo Lome	125(200)		F/W	Ghana and Togo Immigration and Customs at border town of Aflao. Road crossing border badly potholed tarmac.
Cotonou	79 (126)		F/W	Good tarmac surface through Lome. Road running along coast through coconut plantations. First 10 miles into Benin potholed tarmac, then well graded gravel for 10 miles before rejoining good tarmac to Cotonou.
Benin +++++++++++ Nigeria Lagos	75 (120)			Good tarmac to border town of Porto Novo. Dual carriageway at border. Clear Customs and Immigration for Togo and Nigeria at Porto Novo. Good tarmac road to Lagos.
Ibadan	78 (125)		F/W	Motorway from Lagos to Ibadan, and by-passing city.
Ilorin	99 (159)		F/W	Good tarmac road through open countryside.

PAGE TOTAL. 456 (730)

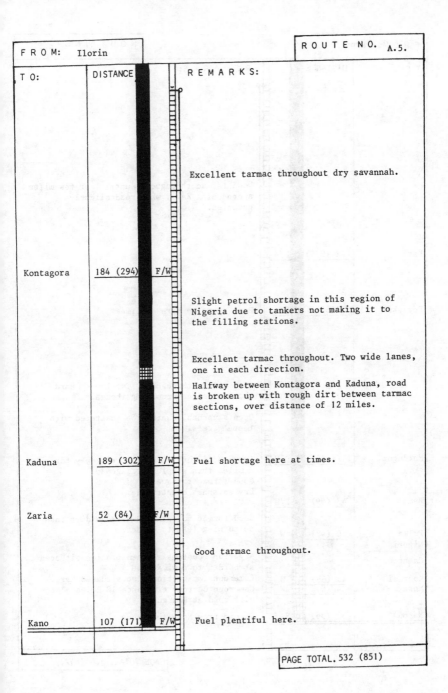

FROM:	Ilorin		ROUTE NO. A.5.
TO:	DISTANCE		REMARKS:

Excellent tarmac throughout dry savannah.

| Kontagora | 184 (294) | F/W | |

Slight petrol shortage in this region of Nigeria due to tankers not making it to the filling stations.

Excellent tarmac throughout. Two wide lanes, one in each direction.

Halfway between Kontagora and Kaduna, road is broken up with rough dirt between tarmac sections, over distance of 12 miles.

| Kaduna | 189 (302) | F/W | Fuel shortage here at times. |

| Zaria | 52 (84) | F/W | |

Good tarmac throughout.

| Kano | 107 (171) | F/W | Fuel plentiful here. |

PAGE TOTAL. 532 (851)

FROM: Kano			ROUTE NO. A.5.

T O:	DISTANCE		REMARKS:
			Good tarmac throughout, until last few miles approaching Kari, when road slightly potholed.
Kari	172 (275)	F/W	
Potiskum	52(84)	F/W	Fuel shortage here at times.
			Good tarmac throughout. Two lanes. Hard shoulder edges crumbling though. Open savannah countryside scattered with baobab trees.
Maiduguri	147(235)	F/W	Leave Maiduguri on dual carriageway for 8 miles then single carriageway. Good tarmac surface. Dry savannah countryside.
Bama	43 (69)	F/W	
Pulka	30 (48)	W	Good tarmac to Pulka, then rough dirt road on turning left to border.
Nigeria ++++++++++++ Cameroun			Nigerian Customs and Immigration situated at border town of Kirawa.
Kourgui	43 (69)	W	Cameroun Immigration also situated here.
Mora	4 (6)	W	Cameroun Customs clearance 18 miles along dirt road at Kourgui.
Maroua	35 (56)	F/W	Tarmac from Mora to Maroua.

PAGE TOTAL. 526 (842)

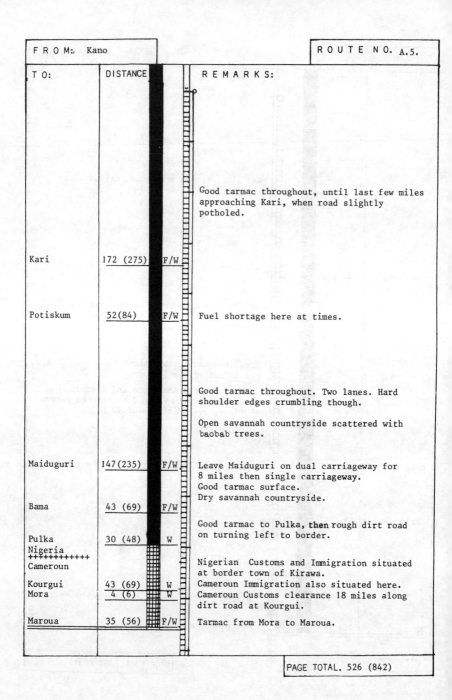

FROM: Maroua			
TO:	DISTANCE		REMARKS:

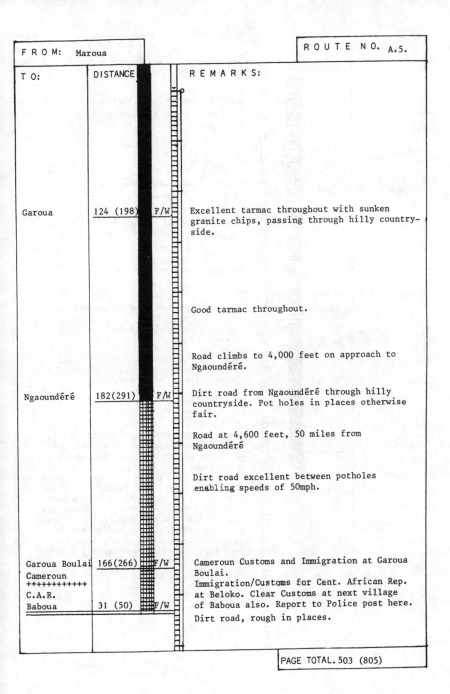

TO:	DISTANCE		REMARKS:
Garoua	124 (198)	F/W	Excellent tarmac throughout with sunken granite chips, passing through hilly countryside.
			Good tarmac throughout.
			Road climbs to 4,000 feet on approach to Ngaoundéré.
Ngaoundéré	182(291)	F/W	Dirt road from Ngaoundéré through hilly countryside. Pot holes in places otherwise fair.
			Road at 4,600 feet, 50 miles from Ngaoundéré
			Dirt road excellent between potholes enabling speeds of 50mph.
Garoua Boulai	166(266)	F/W	Cameroun Customs and Immigration at Garoua Boulai.
Cameroun ++++++++++++ C.A.R.			Immigration/Customs for Cent. African Rep. at Beloko. Clear Customs at next village
Baboua	31 (50)	F/W	of Baboua also. Report to Police post here.
			Dirt road, rough in places.

PAGE TOTAL. 503 (805)

FROM: Baboua			ROUTE NO. A.5.

TO:	DISTANCE		REMARKS:
			Take care on wooden bridges. Dirt road, potholed and corrugated in places. Hilly countryside.
Bouar	67 (107)	F/W	
Baoro	38 (61)	W	Dirt road improves. Some bends to negotiate.
			After Baoro road becomes very good. Dirt and gravel surface. Well graded.
			Negotiate bridges with care.
Yaloké	105 (168)	F/W	Now excellent dirt road to Bossembélé.
Bossembélé	42 (67)	F/W	
			Excellent tarmac road from Bossembélé to Bangui, through thick forest.
Bangui C.A.R. +++++++++++++++++++++++ Zaire	98 (157)	F/W	Clear Customs and Immigration at Yimibi, 8 miles from Bangui on the way in. Road from here tarmac but potholed. Beware pedestrians. Book ferry across river to Zongo. Best route. Alternative via Sibut, Bambari and Bangassou, then across to Ndu, but not recommended as roads very poor and ferry often missing. Clear C.A.R. Customs/Immigration in Bangui before boarding ferry. Immigration in docks, Customs next to ferry embarkation point. Toll ferry. Fill up with petrol. Supply scarce in Zaire.

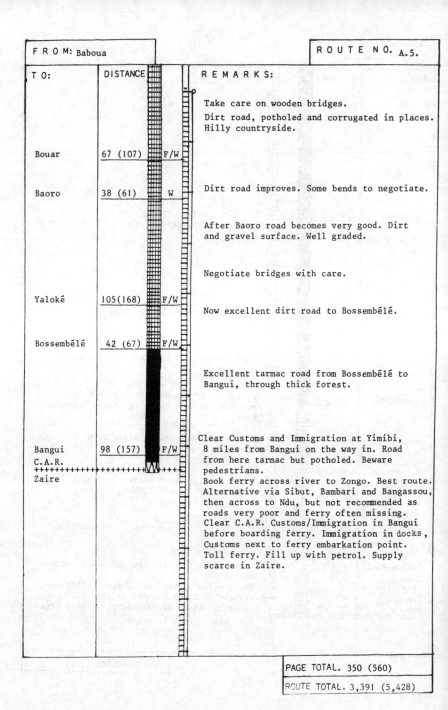

PAGE TOTAL. 350 (560)

ROUTE TOTAL. 3,391 (5,428)

Route A.6. Bangui to Nairobi

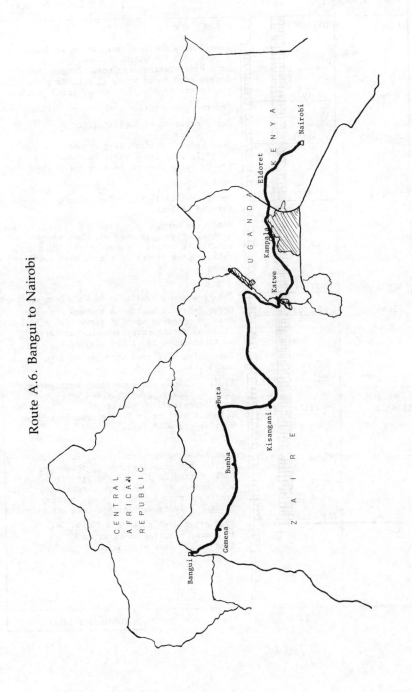

FROM: Bangui		ROUTE NO. A.6.

TO:	DISTANCE	REMARKS:
		Clear Zaire Customs/Immigration at Zongo, ½ mile from ferry. Minimal delay. Very badly rutted dirt road. Single track Recommended speed 10 to 12 mph. Many
Boyabo	58 (93)	pot holes. Road winds through thick jungle.
		Proceed with caution over wooden bridges.
		Ferry crossing at Bogilima(free).
Bogilima	43 (69)	Road remains rutted. Keep out of ruts and holes left by trucks that have become stuck in the rainy season. Average speed 15mph.
Gemena	97 (155) F?/W	Petrol available at 'Coton Zaire'; European farming combine.
		Road from Gemena soft sand for first 6 miles. 4-wheel drive often needed. Then sandy patches to Akula. Average speed 12mph with walking pace speeds at times. Dirt sections bumpy.
Akula	89 (142)	Fuel sometimes available in Binga from planters
Diobo	23 (37)	Cross ferry at Akula (no charge) Road on opposite side of ferry liable to flooding during rainy season, and large sections could be washed away by floods.
		Continuing dirt road with bad rain gullies and holes.
Lisala	98 (157) F?/W	Sandy sections and some rocky sections on road to Lisala. Average speed 18mph. Road corrugated in places. Catholic Mission in Lisala sometimes helps overlanders with fuel.
		Road to Bumba much the same. Dirt with rain gullies and potholes through thick jungle. Badly rutted in places. Average speed 20mph with speeds of up to 35mph possible at times. Bamboo overhangs road at times cutting sun off and leaving wet patches that are slippery.
Bumba	105 (168) F?/W	Fuel often available from 'Scibe Zaire' at Bumba, situated on river bank. Road passes many plantations.

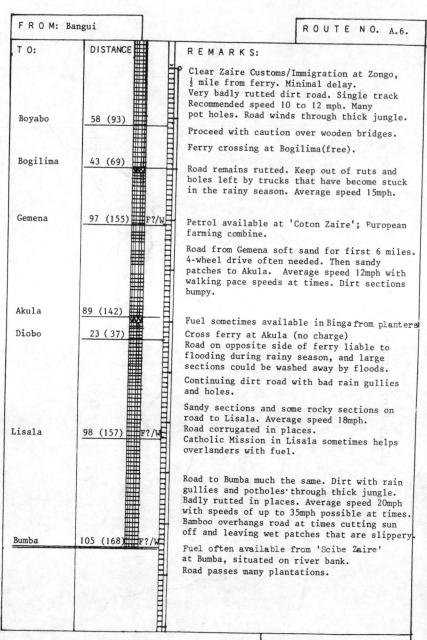

	PAGE TOTAL. 513 (821)

| FROM: Bumba | | | ROUTE NO. A.6. |

TO:	DISTANCE		REMARKS:
			Road to Aketi flanked by dense jungle and overhanging bamboo. The dirt road is good in places, but in general well rutted and bumpy. Beware of trees across road when it rains. Single track about 8 to 10 ft wide. No fuel on route.
Aketi	119(190)	W	Cross river at Aketi on railway bridge.
			Many large dips in road, often giant puddles. Almost one long bamboo archway across the 10 foot road. Beware fallen trees when it rains. Take care on wooden bridges. Dirt road improves on approach to Buta.
Buta	77 (123)	W	Average speed 25mph. Beware animals on road around villages. No fuel on route.
			Road from Buta to Banalia very good dirt and gravel. Corrugated in places. Very wide. Running through dense jungle and bamboo archways. Average speed 30mph.
Banalia	120 (192)	W	Cross River Aruwimi by ferry at Banalia. No charge for crossing. Runs all night.
			Very good dirt road to Kisangani. Average speed 35mph. Few corrugations. Jungle now thinning.
Kisangani	81 (130)	F/W	Fuel available at the pumps in Kisangani. Fill up for rest of journey through Zaire. They will not fill jerry cans. Good hotels and eating places in town.
			Good tarmac road to Madula where we turn left for Bafwasende onto red dirt road with close corrugations. Road potholed in places. Average 30mph. Sections of this road liable to flooding. Road deteriorates at Batama. Badly rutted especially through bamboo archways. Many deep holes, often filled to 2 or 3 feet with water. Negotiate with care. Bottom often rocky.
Bafwasende	163(261)	W	

PAGE TOTAL. 560 (896)

AO9

FROM: Bafwasende			ROUTE NO. A.6.

T O:	DISTANCE		REMARKS:
			Undulating bumpy dirt track crossing several wooden bridges. Care needed. Average speed 18mph.
Nia Nia	49 (78)	W	
			Road remains dirt though a little wider. still corrugated in places and with the odd pothole. Passing dense jungle. Some sections liable to flooding.
			Some deep dips that fill with water to 2ft deep when it rains.
Mambasa	122(195)	W	Road improves towards Mambasa but still rutted. Passes through dense jungle. Pygmies often seen on route. Average 20mph. Road from Mambasa liable to flooding.
Komanda	59 (94)	W	Road very bad from Mambasa. Many water filled dips and several rain gullies across the whole width for long distances. Dense jungle on either side. Very soft road surface. Keep away from edges.
Beni	78 (125)	F?/W	Hard dirt road, gravel covered in places. After Atunukwe road becomes very bad. Long sections of rock, sunk into surface with top protruding making going very rough. Average speed 8mph. Sometimes quicker to walk. 8 mile section of laid rock at Oysha. Improves towards Beni.
Katwe	50 (80)		Fuel sometimes at Beni. Several private sources for fuel at Butembo. Price high. Fill up if possible. Little fuel in Uganda.
Zaire +++++++++++ Uganda			Very rough road through Virunga National Park improving towards border (on equator). Clear Zaire Customs/Immigration at Katwe. Uganda Customs/Immigration 3 miles up road.
Mbarara	80 (128)	F?/W	Excellent 4 lane dirt road from border, recently scraped in preparation for sealing. To form part of Trans African Highway. 14 miles from border we are back on tarmac. Tarmac right through Ruwenzori Nat. Park to Mbarara. Occasional pothole.
Masaka	86 (138)	F?/W	Continuing tarmac through hilly countryside passing tea plantation area. Odd pothole.

PAGE TOTAL. 524 (838)

130

TO:	DISTANCE		REMARKS:
			Good tarmac road throughout with just the odd pothole.
			Fuel often available in Kampala.
Kampala	81 (130)	F/W	
			Good tarmac road passing Owen Falls dam at Jinja. No stopping allowed here.
Iganga	74 (118)		Excellent tarmac after Iganga for 10 miles then broken up until the border at Malaba.
Tororo	57 (91)	F/W	
Malaba	10 (16)	F/W	Clear Ugandan Customs/Immigration at Malaba.
Uganda +++++++++ Kenya			Kenya Customs/Immigration at same place a few yards further up road. Have currency ready for checking.
			No fuel shortage in Kenya.
			Good tarmac road with occasional pothole.
Eldoret	80 (128)	F/W	
			Fair tarmac but potholed in places. Travelling through pine forest area at up to 9,000 feet above sea level (Mau Escarpment.)
Timboroa	40 (64)		
Eldama Ravine	79 (126)		Leave main road past Timboroa as remainder to Nakuru very badly broken up and potholed. New laid excellent tarmac through Eldama Ravine(C55) to Nakuru.(Turn to left just past
Nakuru	29(46)	F/W	equator sign, for Majimazuri)
			Tarmac road, very badly potholed in places for long distances. Last 10 miles to Naivasha excellent new laid tarmac.
Naivasha	42 (67)	F/W	
			Excellent new tarmac road from Naivasha to Nairobi. Part of Trans-African Highway. Travels past Mount Longonot, extinct volcano, and along the ridge of the Rift Valley, giving breathtaking views of the valley below.
Nairobi	55 (88)	F/W	
			All facilities in Nairobi. Cooper Motors(CMC) is Land Rover Agent.

PAGE TOTAL. 547 (874)

ROUTE TOTAL. 2,144 (3,429)

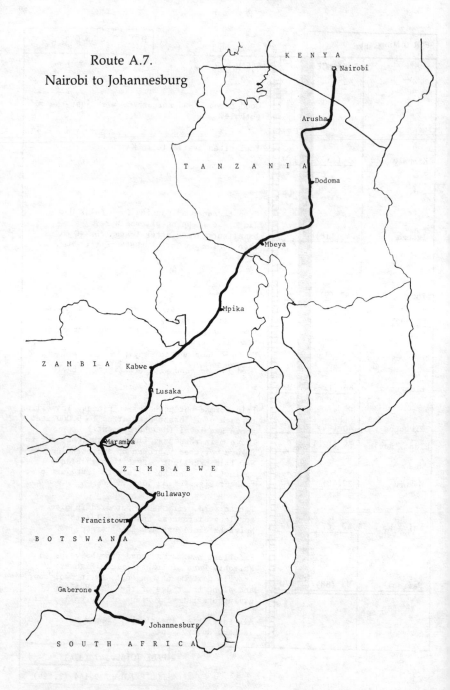

Route A.7.
Nairobi to Johannesburg

FROM: Nairobi			ROUTE NO. A.7.
TO:	DISTANCE		REMARKS:

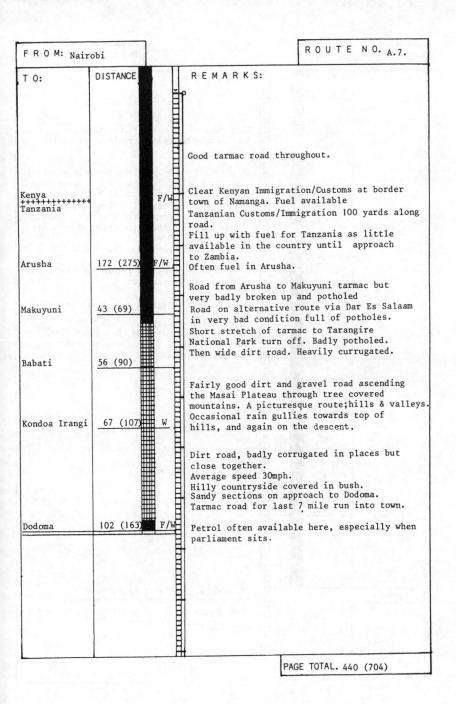

TO:	DISTANCE		REMARKS:
			Good tarmac road throughout.
Kenya ++++++++++++ Tanzania		F/W	Clear Kenyan Immigration/Customs at border town of Namanga. Fuel available Tanzanian Customs/Immigration 100 yards along road. Fill up with fuel for Tanzania as little available in the country until approach to Zambia.
Arusha	172 (275)	F/W	Often fuel in Arusha.
Makuyuni	43 (69)		Road from Arusha to Makuyuni tarmac but very badly broken up and potholed Road on alternative route via Dar Es Salaam in very bad condition full of potholes.
Babati	56 (90)		Short stretch of tarmac to Tarangire National Park turn off. Badly potholed. Then wide dirt road. Heavily currugated.
Kondoa Irangi	67 (107)	W	Fairly good dirt and gravel road ascending the Masai Plateau through tree covered mountains. A picturesque route; hills & valleys. Occasional rain gullies towards top of hills, and again on the descent.
Dodoma	102 (163)	F/W	Dirt road, badly corrugated in places but close together. Average speed 30mph. Hilly countryside covered in bush. Sandy sections on approach to Dodoma. Tarmac road for last 7 mile run into town. Petrol often available here, especially when parliament sits.

PAGE TOTAL. 440 (704)

TO:	DISTANCE		REMARKS:

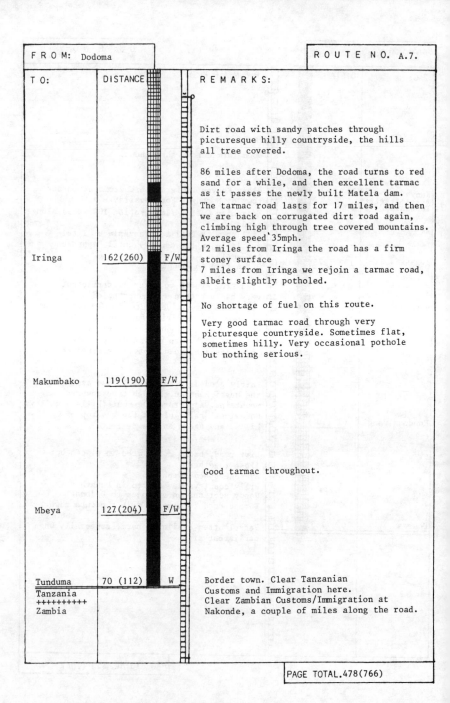

Dirt road with sandy patches through
picturesque hilly countryside, the hills
all tree covered.

86 miles after Dodoma, the road turns to red
sand for a while, and then excellent tarmac
as it passes the newly built Matela dam.
The tarmac road lasts for 17 miles, and then
we are back on corrugated dirt road again,
climbing high through tree covered mountains.
Average speed 35mph.
12 miles from Iringa the road has a firm
stoney surface
7 miles from Iringa we rejoin a tarmac road,
albeit slightly potholed.

Iringa — 162(260) — F/W

No shortage of fuel on this route.

Very good tarmac road through very
picturesque countryside. Sometimes flat,
sometimes hilly. Very occasional pothole
but nothing serious.

Makumbako — 119(190) — F/W

Good tarmac throughout.

Mbeya — 127(204) — F/W

Tunduma — 70 (112) — W

Border town. Clear Tanzanian
Customs and Immigration here.
Clear Zambian Customs/Immigration at
Nakonde, a couple of miles along the road.

Tanzania
++++++++++
Zambia

PAGE TOTAL. 478(766)

FROM: Tunduma

TO:	DISTANCE		REMARKS:
Tanzania ++++++++++ Zambia			
Isoka	73 (117)	F/W	Excellent tarmac road through dense bush country. Little to be seen due to bush bordering roadside.
			Petrol generally available but long distances between pumps.
Mpika	151 (241)	F/W	Bushes thinning slightly and hills now coming into view. Still good tarmac road.
			Good tarmac road throughout.
Chifwefwe	213(341)	F/W	
			Average speed 50mph. Roads have little traffic using them.
Kabwe	98 (157)	F/W	All facilities.

PAGE TOTAL. 535 (856)

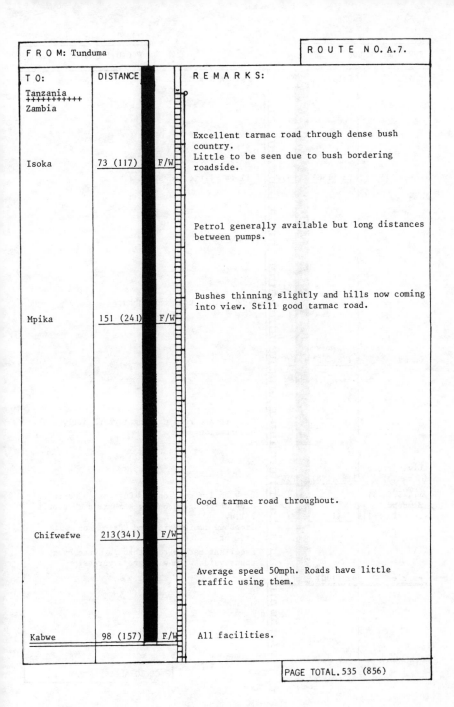

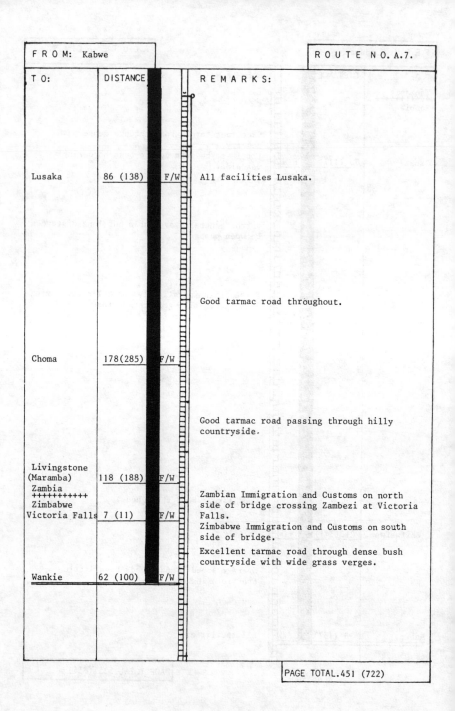

FROM: Kabwe			ROUTE NO. A.7.

T O:	DISTANCE		REMARKS:
Lusaka	86 (138)	F/W	All facilities Lusaka.
			Good tarmac road throughout.
Choma	178 (285)	F/W	
			Good tarmac road passing through hilly countryside.
Livingstone (Maramba)	118 (188)	F/W	
Zambia +++++++++++ Zimbabwe Victoria Falls	7 (11)	F/W	Zambian Immigration and Customs on north side of bridge crossing Zambezi at Victoria Falls. Zimbabwe Immigration and Customs on south side of bridge.
			Excellent tarmac road through dense bush countryside with wide grass verges.
Wankie	62 (100)	F/W	

PAGE TOTAL. 451 (722)

FROM: Wankie			ROUTE NO. A.7.
TO:	DISTANCE		REMARKS:
			Excellent tarmac road throughout, passing through dense bush country.
Bulawayo	210(336)	F/W	All facilities Bulawayo.
			Good tarmac road through bushy savannah.
Plumtree	62 (100)	W	
Zimbabwe ++++++++++++ Botswana			Clear Zimbabwe Immigration and Customs 6 miles past Plumtree Clear Botswana Immigration and Customs a short distance farther on the other side of
Francistown	58 (93)	F/W	the Shashi River, which forms the border. Good tarmac road throughout.
			Good tarmac road passing through semi-desert.
Palapye	99 (158)	F/W	
Mahalapye	40 (64)	F/W	Good tarmac road throughout. Beware cattle on road.

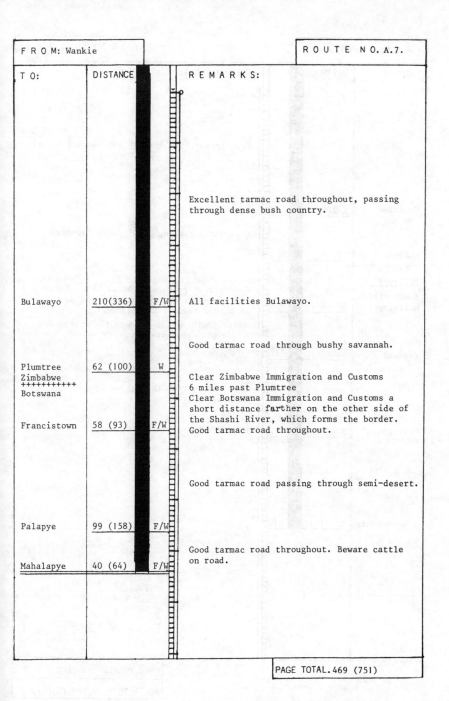

PAGE TOTAL. 469 (751)

FROM: Mahalapye			ROUTE NO. A.7.
TO:	**DISTANCE**		**REMARKS:**
			Good tarmac road through semi-desert country.
Gaberone	122(195)	F/W	
			Good tarmac through hilly bush country.
Lobatse	45 (72)	F/W	
Botswana +++++++++++ South Africa Mafeking	50 (80)	F/W	Good tarmac road throughout. Clear Botswana and South African Immigration and Customs at border town of Ramatlabama. Enter South Africa through the independent state of Bophuthatswana.
Zeerust	44 (70)	F/W	
			Good tarmac road throughout to Johannesburg.
Rustenburg	76 (122)	F/W	
Johannesburg	88 (141)	F/W	

PAGE TOTAL. 425 (680)

ROUTE TOTAL. 2,798 (4,479)

Route B.2. Alexandria to Kampala
Route B.2A. Juba to Eldoret
Route B.2B. Cairo to Wad Medani

139

FROM: Alexandria			ROUTE NO. B.2.
TO:	DISTANCE		REMARKS:
			You have a choice of two routes here, both good tarmac roads. (a) The main route via Tanta. (b) The desert route via Moudirièt El Tahrir and the Pyramids.
Cairo	140(224)	F/W	
			Good tarmac road throughout, road following course of Nile on west bank.
El Minya	152(243)	F/W	
			Good tarmac road crossing to east bank of Nile at Nag Hammâdi and continuing through the Nile Valley.
Qena	238(381)	F/W	

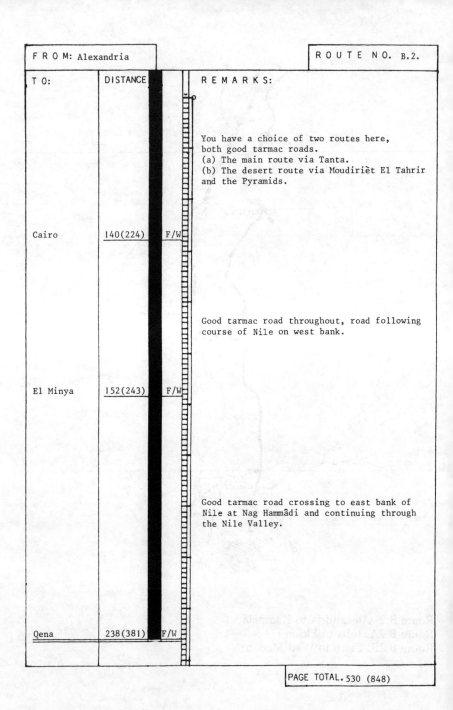

PAGE TOTAL. 530 (848)

FROM: Qena			ROUTE NO. B.2.
T O:	DISTANCE		R E M A R K S:
			Good tarmac road through the eastern desert, passing through the Nile Valley and the tombs of the great kings and queens of Egypt, including Tutankhamun and Rameses.
Aswan	188(301)	F/W	Although it is possible to drive to Wadi Halfa around the western side of Lake Nasser, it is not advisable as the route is very dangerous. A boat trip is therefore necessary to Wadi Halfa along the length of Lake Nasser. See section on 'shipping'.
		L A K E N A S S E R	Permission required to drive to Wadi Halfa. Enquire at authorities(police) in Aswan if you are determined to take this route.
Egypt +++++++++++ Sudan			Clear Egyptian Customs/Immigration at Aswan. Clear Sudanese Customs/Immigration at Wadi Halfa.
Wadi Halfa	225(360)	F/W	
			ALL DIRT (UNSEALED) ROADS IN SUDAN, EAST OF THE WHITE NILE TO THE ETHIOPIAN BORDER, BETWEEN KHARTOUM AND JUBA, ARE DRY SEASON ROADS ONLY.

PAGE TOTAL. 413(661)

TO:	DISTANCE		REMARKS:
			Rough dirt track through the Nubian desert. Many soft sandy patches. Becomes sand track past station 6.
			First section of road stoney. Care should be taken. Route follows railway line
			PERMISSION IS OFTEN REQUIRED TO TRAVEL THIS ROUTE THROUGH NUBIAN DESERT; ENQUIRE AT WADI HALFA BEFORE SETTING OUT. CONVOY TRAVEL NECESSARY.
			Vehicles may be railed to Khartoum.
Abu Hamed	230 (368)	W	Fuel not always available
			Continuing sand/dirt track to Atbara.
Atbara	153(245)	F/W	
			Improved dirt road, heavily corrugated in places, following east bank of Nile River.
Shendi	82 (131)	F/W	

PAGE TOTAL. 465(744)

FROM: Shendi			ROUTE NO. B.2.
T O:	DISTANCE		REMARKS:

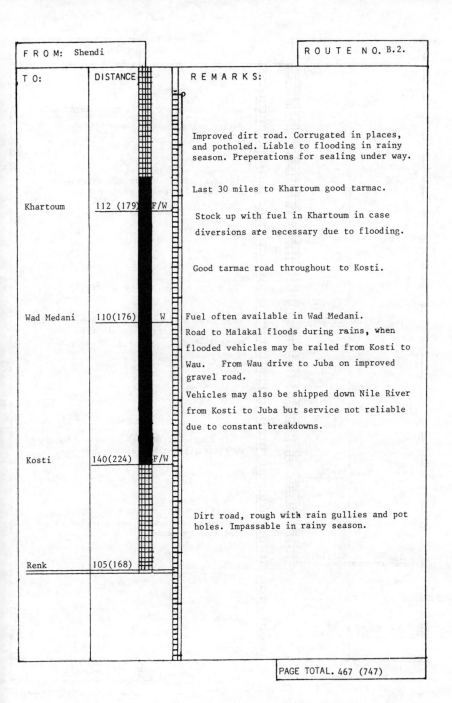

TO:	DISTANCE		REMARKS:
			Improved dirt road. Corrugated in places, and potholed. Liable to flooding in rainy season. Preperations for sealing under way.
			Last 30 miles to Khartoum good tarmac.
Khartoum	112 (179)	F/W	Stock up with fuel in Khartoum in case diversions are necessary due to flooding.
			Good tarmac road throughout to Kosti.
Wad Medani	110(176)	W	Fuel often available in Wad Medani. Road to Malakal floods during rains, when flooded vehicles may be railed from Kosti to Wau. From Wau drive to Juba on improved gravel road. Vehicles may also be shipped down Nile River from Kosti to Juba but service not reliable due to constant breakdowns.
Kosti	140(224)	F/W	
			Dirt road, rough with rain gullies and pot holes. Impassable in rainy season.
Renk	105(168)		

PAGE TOTAL. 467 (747)

FROM: Renk				ROUTE NO. B.2.
TO:	DISTANCE			REMARKS:

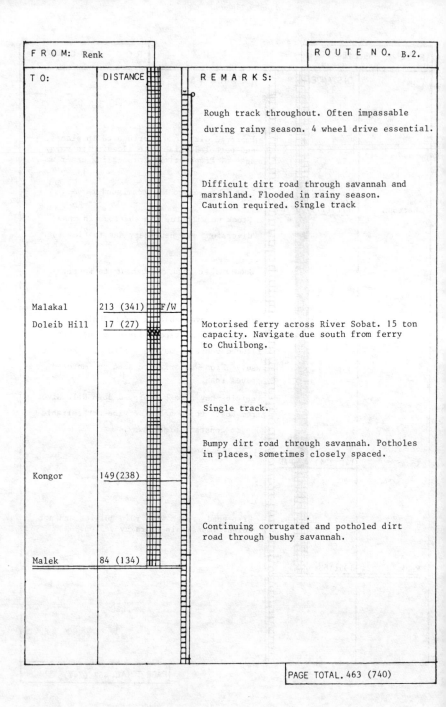

Rough track throughout. Often impassable during rainy season. 4 wheel drive essential.

Difficult dirt road through savannah and marshland. Flooded in rainy season. Caution required. Single track

Malakal	213 (341)	F/W
Doleib Hill	17 (27)	

Motorised ferry across River Sobat. 15 ton capacity. Navigate due south from ferry to Chuilbong.

Single track.

Bumpy dirt road through savannah. Potholes in places, sometimes closely spaced.

Kongor	149(238)

Continuing corrugated and potholed dirt road through bushy savannah.

Malek	84 (134)

PAGE TOTAL. 463 (740)

144

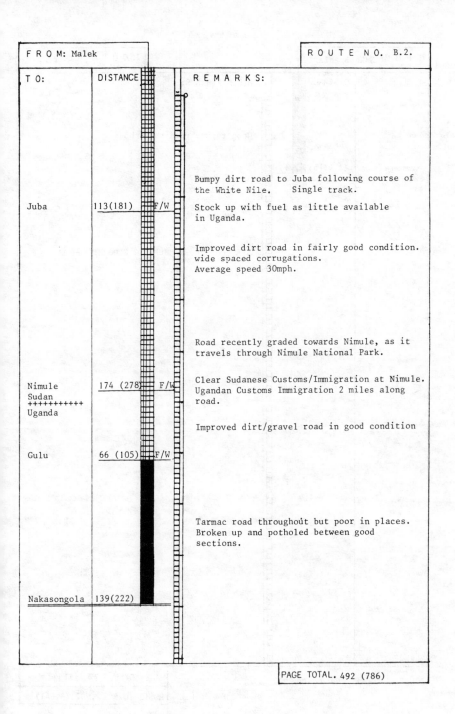

FROM: Malek		ROUTE NO. B.2.

TO:	DISTANCE	REMARKS:
		Bumpy dirt road to Juba following course of the White Nile. Single track.
Juba	113(181) F/W	Stock up with fuel as little available in Uganda.
		Improved dirt road in fairly good condition. wide spaced corrugations. Average speed 30mph.
		Road recently graded towards Nimule, as it travels through Nimule National Park.
Nimule Sudan ++++++++++ Uganda	174 (278) F/W	Clear Sudanese Customs/Immigration at Nimule. Ugandan Customs Immigration 2 miles along road.
		Improved dirt/gravel road in good condition
Gulu	66 (105) F/W	
		Tarmac road throughout but poor in places. Broken up and potholed between good sections.
Nakasongola	139(222)	

PAGE TOTAL. 492 (786)

AO10

F R O M: Nakasongola			R O U T E N O. B.2.
T O:	DISTANCE	REMARKS:	

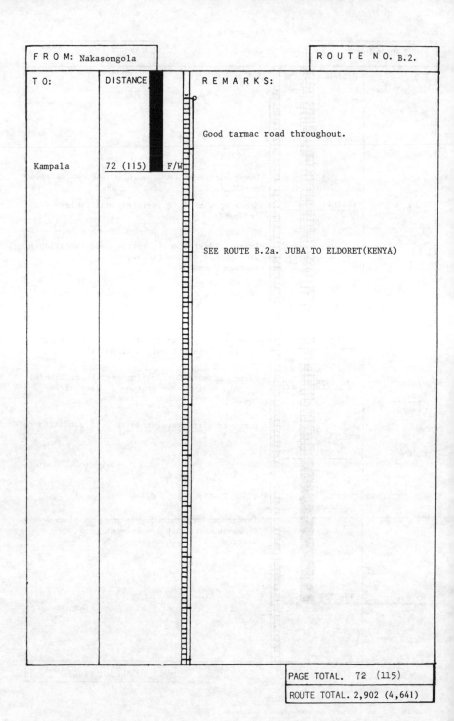

Good tarmac road throughout.

Kampala   72 (115)   F/W

SEE ROUTE B.2a. JUBA TO ELDORET(KENYA)

PAGE TOTAL. 72 (115)

ROUTE TOTAL. 2,902 (4,641)

FROM: Juba		

T O:	DISTANCE		REMARKS:

Plans in progress for new road from Juba
through to Lodwar.

Graded dirt road through dry savannah.
Very bumpy road.

| Torit | 84(134) | W |

Very rough dirt track through Imatong
mountains. Many potholes. Caution needed.
Heavy corrugations to Kenya border.

Report Sudan Immigration/Customs at Kappeta.

| Kappeta | 106(170) | |

Badly marked track with several branch-offs.
Mainly dirt/gravel but sandy patches towards
Lodwar.

Report Kenyan Immigration/Customs at
Lokichokio and Lodwar. Road bad during rains.

Sudan
+++++++++++
Kenya

Road from border to Lodwar is currently
being upgraded.

| Lodwar | 221(354) | F/W |

PAGE TOTAL. 411 (658)

F R O M: Lodwar			ROUTE NO. B.2A.

T O:	DISTANCE		REMARKS:
			Excellent dirt/gravel road through to Kitale. Average speed 35mph. Route through Cherengani hills, on approach to Kitale is tricky. Road is paved in places and there are many sharp bends.
Kitale	190(304)	F/W	
			Good tarmac road through to Eldoret.
Eldoret	45 (72)	F/W	

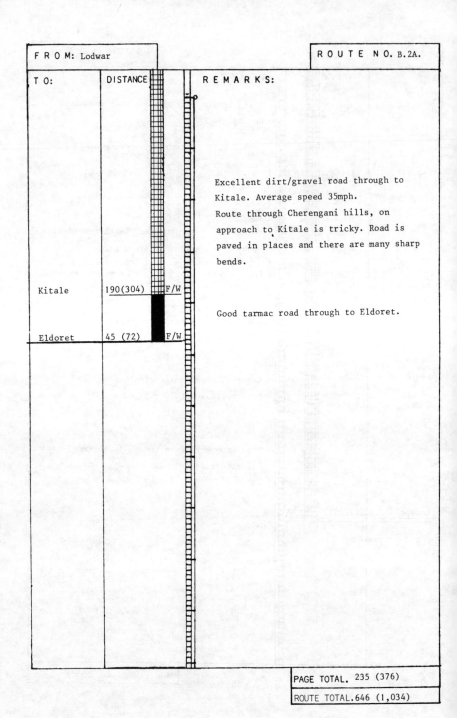

PAGE TOTAL. 235 (376)

ROUTE TOTAL.646 (1,034)

| FROM: Cairo | | ROUTE NO. B.2B. |

T O:	DISTANCE		REMARKS:
			A good alternative route skirting the Gulf of Suez and the red sea, and so avoiding the road from Wadi Halfa to Atbara which is closed at certain times of year.
Suez	83 (133)	F/W	Good tarmac road to Suez. Fill up with fuel here as future supplies are uncertain before Port Sudan.
			Good tarmac road through mountainous countryside. Very hilly.
Ghardaka	272(436)	W	Fuel sometimes available at Ghardaka.
Port Safaga	33 (53)	W	Turn to right just before Port Safaga for Qena and the Nile Valley. 100 miles of good tarmac. Fuel sometimes at Port Safaga.
			Good tarmac road throughout.
Marsa Alam	144(230)	W	

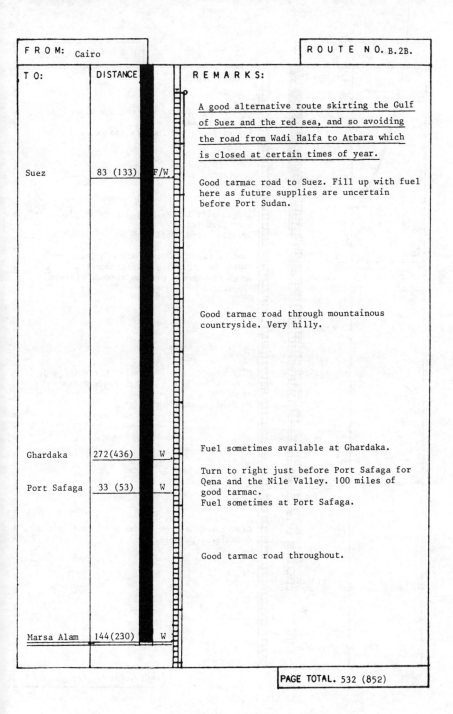

PAGE TOTAL. 532 (852)

FROM: Marsa Alam				ROUTE NO. B.2B.

T O:	DISTANCE			REMARKS:
				Continuing good tarmac through hilly terrain to Ras Banas. Report to Police/Immigration here.
Ras Banas	90 (144)	W		
				Single dirt track. Very stoney in places and many potholes. Average speed 25mph.
Egypt ++++++++++++ Sudan	72 (115)	W		Road to right at Bir Shalatein leads to Aswan. No more than mountainous track. Very rough in places. Caution needed. Distance 230 miles.
				Dirt road in poor condition but with good view of Red Sea. Beware loose rocks on road. No fuel on this route
Muhammad Qol	222(355)			
				Gravel road to Port Sudan with sandy patches. Occasional pothole.
Port Sudan	96 (154)	F/W		

PAGE TOTAL. 480 (768)

FROM: Port Sudan			ROUTE NO. B.2B.
TO:	DISTANCE		REMARKS:
			Good tarmac road, ascending and winding to a height of 2,000 feet.
			Picturesque route through the Akaba Pass.
Sinkat	86 (138)	F/W	
			Good tarmac road through desert country. Sand on road in places.
Kassala	274(438)	F/W	
			Excellent tarmac road.
Gedaref	87 (140)	F/W	

PAGE TOTAL. 447 (716)

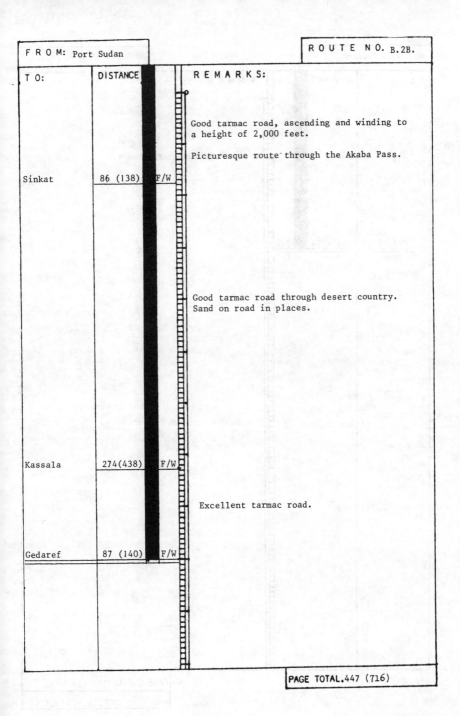

FROM: Gedaref			ROUTE NO. B.2B.

T O:	DISTANCE		REMARKS:
			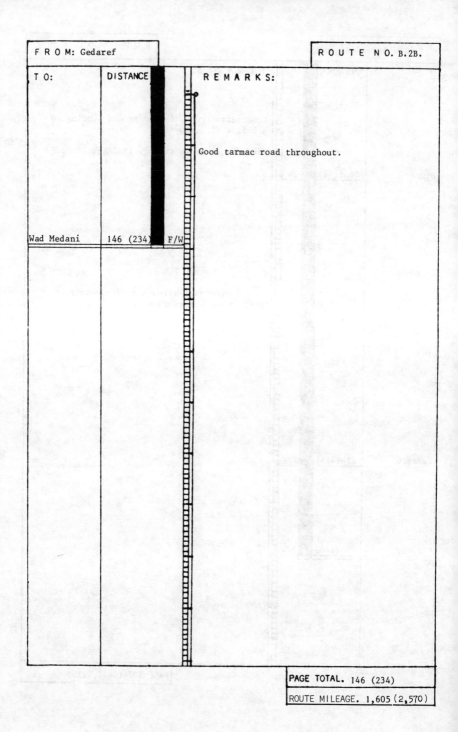 Good tarmac road throughout.
Wad Medani	146 (234)	F/W	

PAGE TOTAL. 146 (234)

ROUTE MILEAGE. 1,605 (2,570)

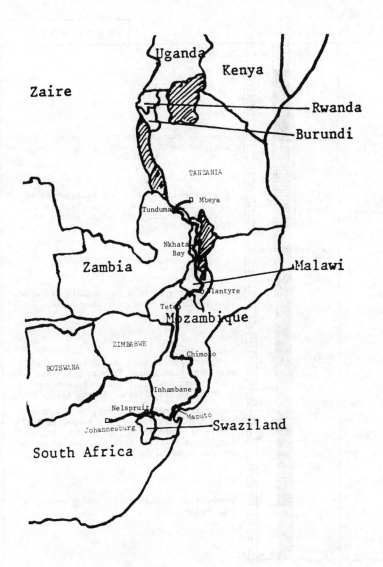

Route C.1. Mbeya to Johannesburg

FROM: Mbeya				ROUTE NO.C.1.

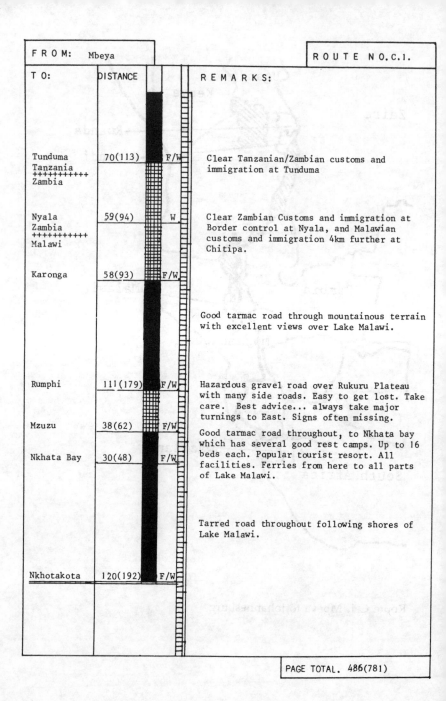

TO:	DISTANCE			REMARKS:
Tunduma Tanzania ++++++++++++ Zambia	70(113)		F/W	Clear Tanzanian/Zambian customs and immigration at Tunduma
Nyala Zambia ++++++++++++ Malawi	59(94)		W	Clear Zambian Customs and immigration at Border control at Nyala, and Malawian customs and immigration 4km further at Chitipa.
Karonga	58(93)		F/W	Good tarmac road through mountainous terrain with excellent views over Lake Malawi.
Rumphi	111(179)		F/W	Hazardous gravel road over Rukuru Plateau with many side roads. Easy to get lost. Take care. Best advice... always take major turnings to East. Signs often missing.
Mzuzu	38(62)		F/W	Good tarmac road throughout, to Nkhata bay which has several good rest camps. Up to 16 beds each. Popular tourist resort. All facilities. Ferries from here to all parts of Lake Malawi.
Nkhata Bay	30(48)		F/W	
Nkhotakota	120(192)		F/W	Tarred road throughout following shores of Lake Malawi.

PAGE TOTAL. 486(781)

F R O M: Nkhotakota			ROUTE NO. C.1.

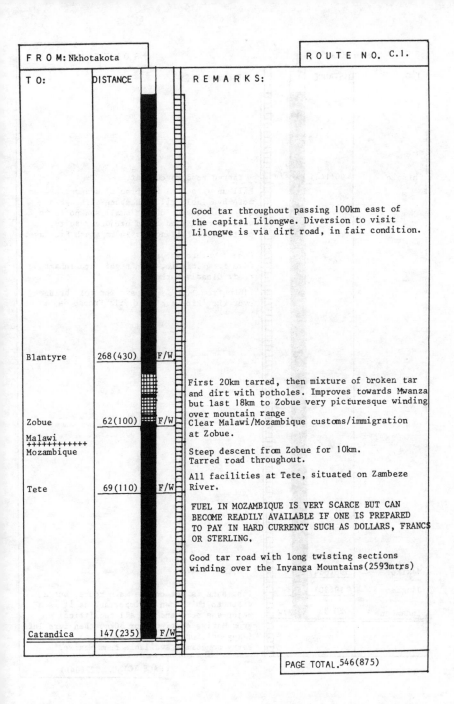

T O:	DISTANCE		REMARKS:
			Good tar throughout passing 100km east of the capital Lilongwe. Diversion to visit Lilongwe is via dirt road, in fair condition.
Blantyre	268(430)	F/W	
			First 20km tarred, then mixture of broken tar and dirt with potholes. Improves towards Mwanza but last 18km to Zobue very picturesque winding over mountain range
Zobue	62(100)	F/W	Clear Malawi/Mozambique customs/immigration at Zobue.
Malawi ++++++++++++ Mozambique			Steep descent from Zobue for 10km. Tarred road throughout.
			All facilities at Tete, situated on Zambeze River.
Tete	69(110)	F/W	
			FUEL IN MOZAMBIQUE IS VERY SCARCE BUT CAN BECOME READILY AVAILABLE IF ONE IS PREPARED TO PAY IN HARD CURRENCY SUCH AS DOLLARS, FRANCS OR STERLING.
			Good tar road with long twisting sections winding over the Inyanga Mountains(2593mtrs)
Catandica	147(235)	F/W	

PAGE TOTAL.546(875)

| FROM: Catandica | | | | ROUTE NO. C.1. |

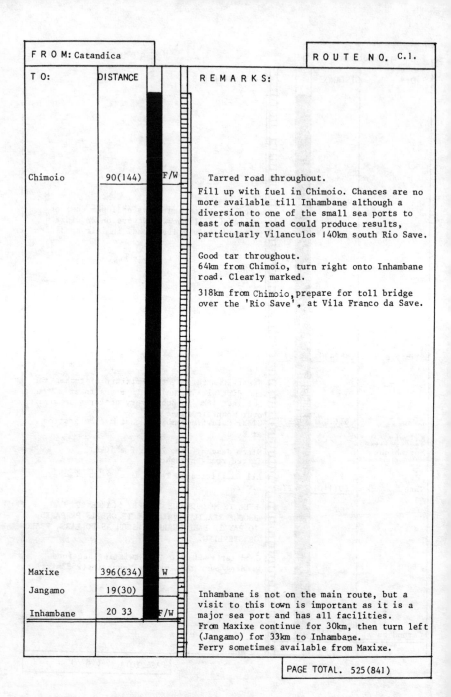

TO:	DISTANCE			REMARKS:
Chimoio	90(144)	F/W		Tarred road throughout.

Fill up with fuel in Chimoio. Chances are no more available till Inhambane although a diversion to one of the small sea ports to east of main road could produce results, particularly Vilanculos 140km south Rio Save.

Good tar throughout.
64km from Chimoio, turn right onto Inhambane road. Clearly marked.

318km from Chimoio, prepare for toll bridge over the 'Rio Save', at Vila Franco da Save.

Maxixe	396(634)	W	
Jangamo	19(30)		
Inhambane	20 33	F/W	

Inhambane is not on the main route, but a visit to this town is important as it is a major sea port and has all facilities.
From Maxixe continue for 30km, then turn left (Jangamo) for 33km to Inhambane.
Ferry sometimes available from Maxixe.

PAGE TOTAL. 525(841)

FROM: Inhambane				ROUTE NO. C.1.
TO:	DISTANCE			REMARKS:

Good tar road throughout

| Xai-Xai | 167(267) | F/W |

Toll bridge on leaving Xai-Xai, over the
Limpopo River.

Good tar road through to the capital of
Maputo.

| Maputo | 127(204) | F/W |

Good tar road throughout. All facilities at
Maputo.

| Ressano Garcia | 57(92) |

Tar road throughout but broken in places.

Mozambique
++++++++++++
South Africa

Clear Mozambique customs/immigration at
Ressano Garcia, and South African customs/
immigration at Komatiport.

Good tar road throughout.

| Belfast | 164(262) | F/W |

PAGE TOTAL. 515(825)

157

FROM: Belfast				ROUTE NO. C.1.

T O:	DISTANCE			REMARKS:
Witbank	45(72)		F/W	Good tarred road to Witbank.
				Witbank to Johannesburg is via motorway.
Johannesburg	86(138)		F/W	All facilities.

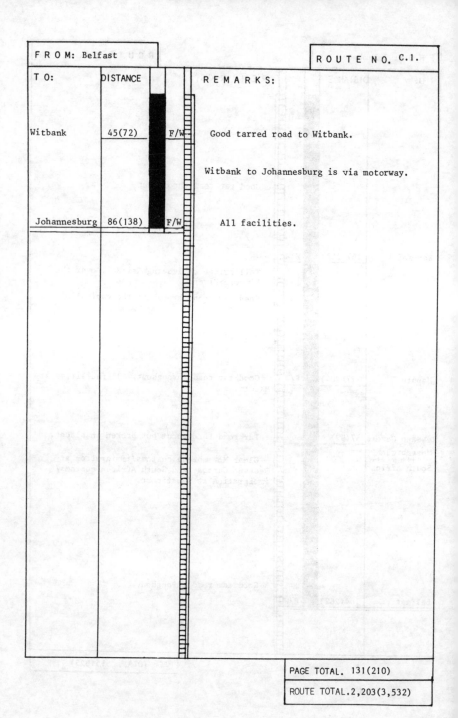

PAGE TOTAL.	131(210)
ROUTE TOTAL.	2,203(3,532)

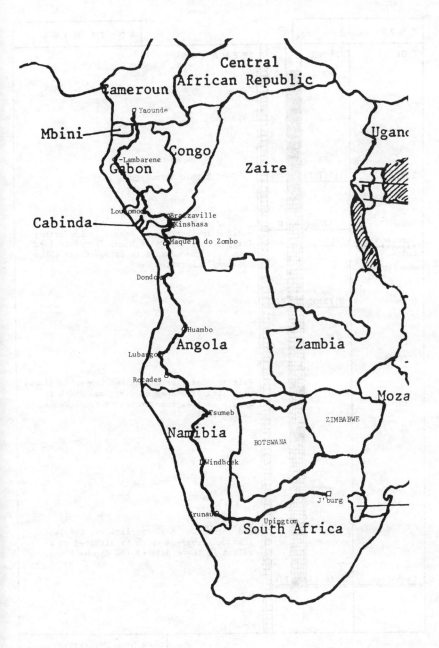

Route C.2. Yaoundé to Johannesburg

TO:	DISTANCE			REMARKS:

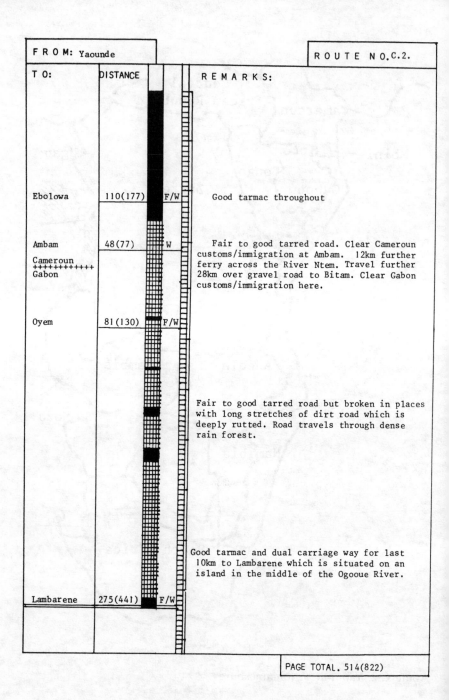

Ebolowa	110(177)	F/W		Good tarmac throughout
Ambam	48(77)	W		Fair to good tarred road. Clear Cameroun customs/immigration at Ambam. 12km further ferry across the River Ntem. Travel further 28km over gravel road to Bitam. Clear Gabon customs/immigration here.

Cameroun
++++++++++++
Gabon

Oyem	81(130)	F/W		

Fair to good tarred road but broken in places with long stretches of dirt road which is deeply rutted. Road travels through dense rain forest.

Good tarmac and dual carriage way for last 10km to Lambarene which is situated on an island in the middle of the Ogooue River.

Lambarene	275(441)	F/W		

PAGE TOTAL. 514(822)

T O:	DISTANCE		REMARKS:
			Good tarred road for 10km from Lambarene, then only fair condition to Fougamou.
			Road currugated and potholed dirt and gravel to N'Dende, through rain forest.
			Road approaching N'Dende through hilly terrain.
N'Dende	185(297)	F/W	All facilities. Clear Gabon and Congo customs/immigration at Rve du Mt. Fouari, 48km south of N'Dende.
Gabon ++++++++++++ Congo			Very few facilities available at border control at Fouari apart from tinned pilchards and soap, so stock up in N'Dende. Several safari bungalows available to travellers along this stretch, and at Moungoudi, 24km into Congo.
			Descending road from Kibangou to Loubomo is improved tar.
Loubomo	177(284)	F/W	All facilities.
			A dirt/sand road throughout badly rutted and very soft in places. The last 30km before Mindouli is over the Bateke mountain range and affords magnificent views over the surrounding countryside.
Mindouli	151(243)	W	

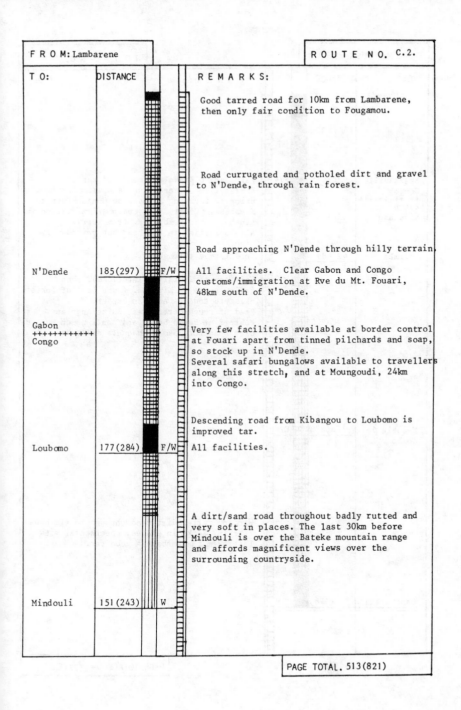

PAGE TOTAL. 513(821)

AO11

FROM: Mindouli			ROUTE NO. C.2.

T O:	DISTANCE		REMARKS:
Brazzaville Congo	92(147)	F/W	Fair tar to Kinkala, then good tar to Brazzaville. Clear Congo customs/immigration prior to ferrying across the Congo River to Kinshasa. Clear Zaire customs/immigration in Kinshasa on disembarking from ferry. All facilities in Kinshasa but prices very high.
+++++++++++++ Zaire Kinshasa	2(3)	F/W	
Madimba	42(68)	W	Good tarmac throughout.
			Fair tar to Inkisi-Kisantu(18km), then follow signs to Kipemba. (Turn left at Inkisi-Kisantu towards Angolan border. Road of rough dirt. Clear Zaire/Angolan customs at Banza Sosso and continue on rutted dirt road for 35km to Maquela do Zombo.
Maquela do Zombo	173(278)	F/W	
			Winding rutted dirt road through mountainous terrain. Rocky in places. Spectacular view. Last 52km to Camabatela good tar.
Camabatela	173(278)	F/W	

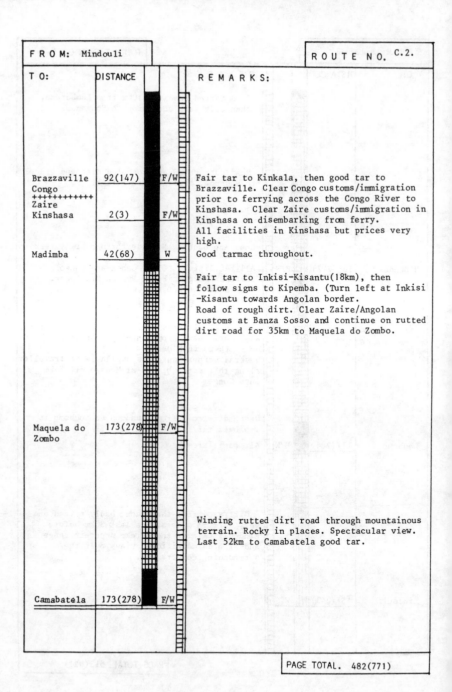

PAGE TOTAL. 482(771)

| FROM: Camabatela | | | ROUTE NO. C.2. |

T O:	DISTANCE		REMARKS:
Lucala	93(149)	F/W	Good tarred road.
			Good tarred road throughout. Turn left onto Quibala road, 5km before Dondo. A picturesque route through hilly countryside, the road crossing many streams and cataracts.
			Occasional security checks.
Huambo	323(517)	F/W	
			Good tarmac through hilly terrain.
Caconda	105(169)	F/W	

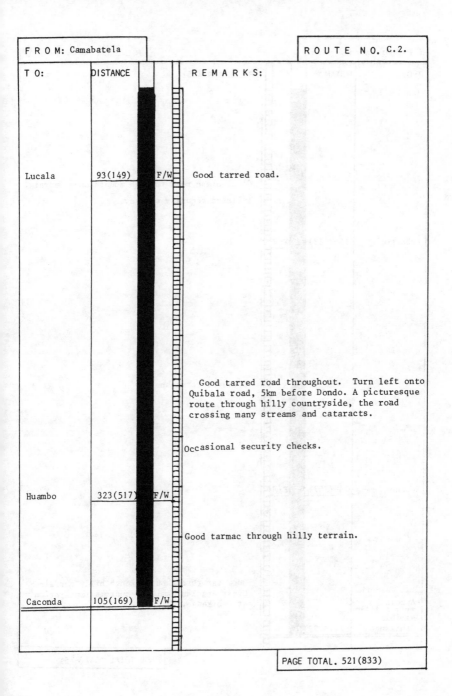

PAGE TOTAL. 521(833)

F R O M: Caconda					ROUTE NO. C.2.

T O:	DISTANCE			REMARKS:

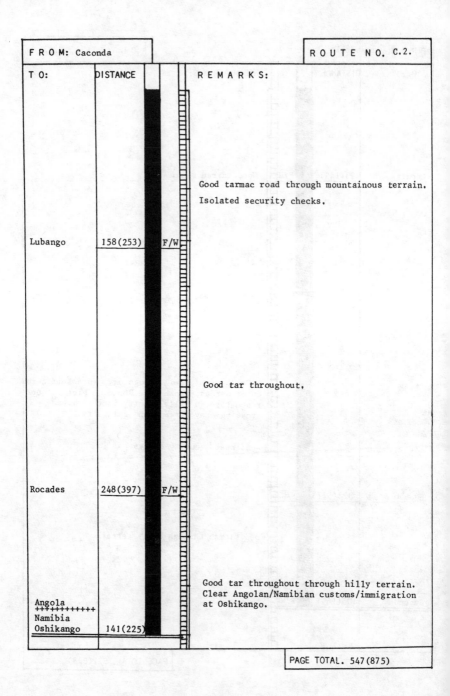

Good tarmac road through mountainous terrain.
Isolated security checks.

Lubango — 158(253) — F/W

Good tar throughout.

Rocades — 248(397) — F/W

Good tar throughout through hilly terrain.
Clear Angolan/Namibian customs/immigration
at Oshikango.

Angola
++++++++++++
Namibia
Oshikango — 141(225)

PAGE TOTAL. 547(875)

164

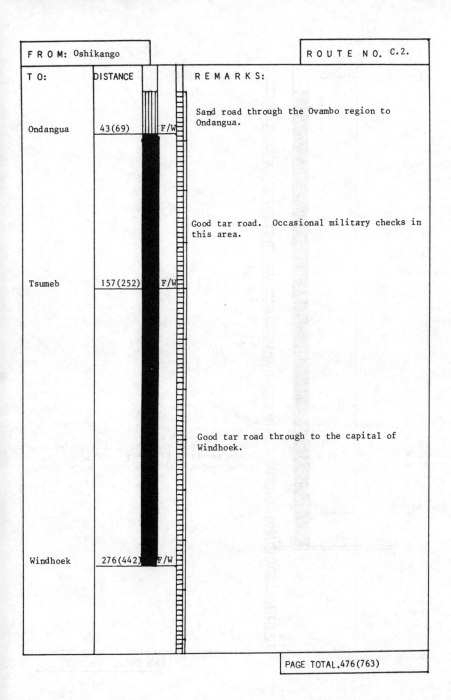

FROM: Oshikango				ROUTE NO. C.2.
TO:	DISTANCE			REMARKS:
Ondangua	43(69)	F/W		Sand road through the Ovambo region to Ondangua.
Tsumeb	157(252)	F/W		Good tar road. Occasional military checks in this area.
Windhoek	276(442)	F/W		Good tar road through to the capital of Windhoek.

PAGE TOTAL.476(763)

TO:	DISTANCE		REMARKS:
			Good tarmac road throughout. A diversion from Grunau to visit the Fish River Canyon, Africa's "Grand Canyon", would be really worth while.
Grunau	424(679)	F/W	
Karasburg	35(56)	F/W	

PAGE TOTAL. 459(735)

T O:	DISTANCE			R E M A R K S:
Namibia ++++++++++++ South Africa Nakop	87(140)			Common border, Occasional check but no customs/immigration formalities.
Upington	88(141)	F/W		
				Picturesque route through Namaqualand, at its best in September.
				Good tarmac throughout
Vryburg	258(413)	F/W		

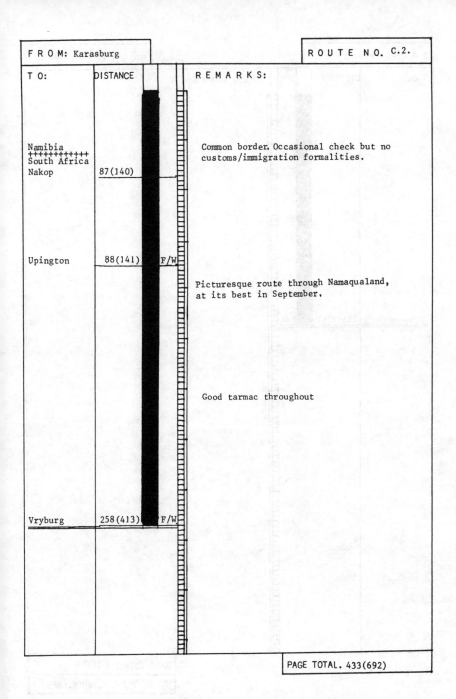

PAGE TOTAL. 433(692)

F R O M: Vryburg

T O:	DISTANCE		R E M A R K S:
Johannesburg	235(376)	F/W	

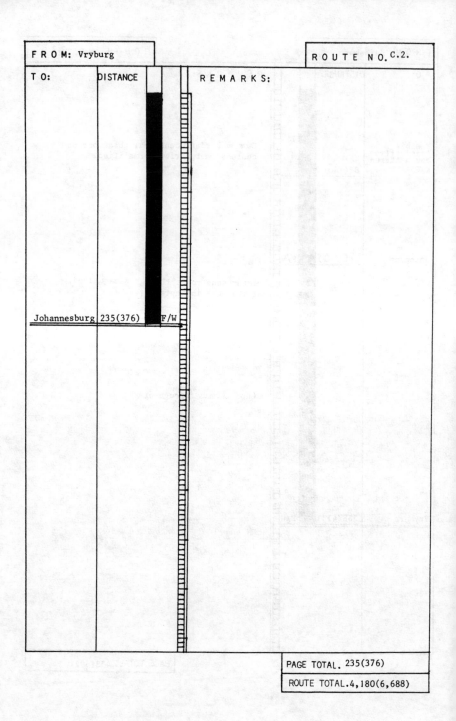

PAGE TOTAL. 235(376)

ROUTE TOTAL. 4,180(6,688)

Part 3
Background notes on African countries

Background notes on African countries

Algeria

This is Africa's second largest country with an area of 920,000 square miles. The terrain is mainly of desert, but there are beautiful mountain ranges, plains and gorges in the north and in the coastal region. The Atlas range extends into Algeria, and deep in the desert lies Mount Tamanrasset at 7,000 feet. Orange groves, olive groves and cork oak plantations thrive in the northern region, while the deep south is barren. There are 750 miles of coastline filled with delightful beaches and on the northern-most point of the coast lies the capital of Algiers (population 2 million).

The population of Algeria is 19.1 million. Originally under French rule, Algeria gained independence in July 1962. The President is Colonel Chadly Benjedid.

There is a very good road system in the tourist area of the north, whilst the roads in the south are no more than desert tracks. Algeria is the country from where most people begin their overland expeditions: three of the main routes run from north to south down the length of the country.

The average daytime temperature in Algeria is 80°F but can rise well above this when the hot Sirocco wind blows off the desert.

In the far south, during the summer months from May to September, the temperature can rise to 120°F or more when many of the roads are closed to visitors. Rainfall in this region is less than minimal, while in the coastal region there is a rainy season from November to February.

There is no limit to the amount of foreign currency that may be taken into or out of Algeria, but the import of Algerian money is limited to 50 dinars. The unit of currency is the dinar, divided into 100 centimes. Most hotels and banks in the north of Algeria will exchange travellers cheques or European currency.

Angola

Angola covers an area of 481,351 square miles and Luanda, the capital, is also the main sea port. The population is 6,759,000.

Formerly a Portuguese colony, Angola became independent on 11 November 1975, and is led by President José Dos Santos.

The road system throughout the country is very good despite the many mountainous regions in the coastal area. Further inland the country consists of one huge plateau with an average height of 3,600 ft. Driving is on the right and a carnet de passage, ICMV and IDL are required.

Along the coastal half of the country the wet season temperatures range from 12°-28°C and the season extends from October to April. In the dry season from May to September the temperatures average the same maximum of 28°C but drop to 6°C or 7°C. Inland the weather is very similar but can be much hotter with average temperatures reaching 32°C throughout the year.

Visas are required by all foreign visitors, as are cholera and yellow fever vaccination certificates. Vaccination against hepatitus is also advised.

The unit of currency is the kwanza which presently (1986) stands at 42.74 to the £1 sterling. Travellers may import and export as much foreign currency as they wish provided it is declared at the border control. Foreign currency is readily accepted at most hotels.

The British Embassy is to be found at Rua Diogo Cao, Luanda; P.O. Box 1244; telephone Luanda 34582/3. The Director of Immigration is at Fronteiras de Angola, Defa, Luanda; telephone 30314/30019, telex 3127 MIREX AN.

Benin

The country covers an area of 44,699 square miles and although the coast line is only 75 miles long, a distance of over 400 miles lies between the coast and the northern border. The main port on the coast is Cotonou while the capital, slightly inland, is Porto Novo.

Once a French colony, it gained independence in August 1960 after 67 years of French rule. As Dahomey, it was under the leadership of President Hubert Maga, and in November 1975 became Benin under the leadership of Lieutenant Colonel Mathieu Kerekou.

The population of Benin is 3.4 million and geographically the country varies considerably from the equatorial south to the arid savanna in the north where the northern capital of Kandi stands at over 4,200 feet above sea level. Its stilted villages, in particular Ganvi, are a characteristic feature.

Many crops are grown and Benin is self sufficient in food. The main cash crop is palm and its produce like palm oil and palm kernel. Maize, cassava, sorghum, yams and millet are among the most popular crops that are grown.

Road conditions are fairly good even on the dirt roads, and in the coastal region the roads are tarmac.

There is no limit to the amount of foreign currency that may be imported into Benin and, provided it is declared, you may take out as much as you take in. The currency is the CFA franc which is divided into 100 centimes.

Botswana

Botswana covers an area of 222,000 square miles, and has an average temperature of 83°F. It is almost one huge desert. The Kalahari desert occupies all of the southern region while the north of the country contains the famous Okavango Delta and the Makgadikgadi pan.

The Okavango is the greatest inland delta system in the world, forming over 7,000 square miles of swampland. Originally a river flowing into the Indian Ocean, the Okavango now dwindles away its vitality far from the sea as a result of shifts of the earth's surface in a remote geological era, during which many of the continental features such as the Great Rift Valley, were formed.

The country's population is 960,000 and their leader is President Quett Masire. Botswana gained independence from Britain in September 1966 and is now a member of the British Commonwealth.

Most of the towns are situated along the eastern border where the shortage of water is not so great. The main road network runs from Francistown in the north, close to the border with Zimbabwe, to the capital, Gaberone, in the south, near to the border with South Africa.

The unit of currency is the pula and there is no limit to the amount that may be imported or taken out. The South African rand is also accepted as legal tender, and most hotels and banks readily exchange travellers cheques and cash.

Burkina Fasso

Burkina Fasso (formerly Upper Volta) covers an area of 106,000 square miles and today is famous for its wood and bronze carvings. Ouagadougou is the capital and Bobo Dioulasso the second city.

This country was established in 1919 when it was carved out of the colonies of Upper Senegal and Niger. In 1932 it was suppressed and the territory divided between the Ivory Coast, Sudan and Niger, only to be re-established in 1947. It became an independent state on 5 August 1960. The population is 7 million, and the head of state is Captain Thomas Sankara. A return to civilian rule is planned.

This landlocked country is famous for its red, white and black Volta rivers, which flow into Lake Volta in Ghana. It has some interesting waterfalls and rapids, particularly in the "Bobo" region, where one of Africa's oldest villages is also to be found at Koumi. In Bobo itself is one of the largest and most active markets in Africa. The ground on which the market stands was once a trading centre for slaves. The rest of the country is mainly savanna with desert in the extreme north. The rainy season is from June to September, and the average temperature around Ouagadougou in the centre is 90°F with the hottest period period from March to May.

The unit of currency is the CFA franc and currency regulations are as for other CFA franc countries.

Despite the coup in this country at the end of 1983, overland travel is still possible and travellers are still made very welcome. However certain areas of the country now register a change in attitude: instead of the usual "Hello Tooreest (Tourist)" travellers can occasionally expect "Hail Comrade".

Cameroon

It covers an area of 201,348 square miles and varies geographically from savanna in the north, scattered with craggy hills, to the equatorial rain forest in the south coastal region. Along the border with Nigeria are the Cameroon Highlands and the Adamaoua range which runs from Mount Cameroon (13,300 feet) in the south to Garoua.

The country gained independence in 1961 and was originally jointly administered as two separate territories by the French and British. The population of Cameroon is 8.5 million. Following the sudden resignation of Ahmadou Ahidjo who had ruled since independence in 1961, President Paul Biya, a Christian from the south, took over in November 1982 as head of Cameroon.

There are some very good game reserves in Cameroon, one of the best being the Waza National Park in the extreme north, and the present government is fully conscious of the need to preserve the country's wild life.

There is a very good road network which is being improved all the time and even the dirt roads are of excellent quality, ranking amongst the best dirt roads in Africa.

The climate varies considerably from one end of the country to the other. In the north the climate is dry with an average of 80°F, while the south is humid with an average of 75°F. In the winter months of December/January the temperature in the north can drop to 35°F or lower at night. It can also drop to this temperature in the Highlands.

The currency is the CFA franc and the usual regulations regarding the CFA franc apply. Visitors are not restricted in the amount of foreign currency that they may take in or out of the country.

Central African Republic

The country covers an area of 241,408 square miles, and the temperatures range from 58°F to 110°F. It lies in the heart of Africa and is famed for its luscious tropical fruits, exotic butterflies, and thick equatorial jungles.

Originally under French administration as Oubangui-Chari, it gained independence in 1960 becoming the Central African Republic. General André Kolingba is the head of the ruling military committee.

The road network is small and most of the country's 2.3 million people live in the capital of Bangui. The extreme north east, and areas in the north, are uninhabited arid lands while the south west is thick equatorial jungle. This is where the pygmies can be found.

The currency is the Communauté Financière Africaine franc (CFA franc). One franc is equal to 100 centimes (cents). Unless you are going straight into another country that has the CFA franc as its currency, you are limited to taking 15,000 CFA out of C.A.R. There is no limit to the amount of foreign currency that may be taken into C.A.R., and you may take out as much as you take in. Travellers cheques are readily cashed at banks and most hotels, and French francs are accepted as payment of bills in most hotels and restaurants.

Congo

The area of the Congo is 132,103 square miles. It was first allocated to France in 1882 and became part of French West Africa in 1908 through to 1958 when it became a member state of the French community. It became independent in August 1960. Congo has a population of 1.6 million, and head of state is Colonel Denis Sassou Nguesso.

The north is dense rain forest and almost impenetrable swamp. Dense jungle also occupies the south west while the south east is hilly terrain rising to 3,300 feet. Apart from a short section at the capital of Brazzaville, tarmac roads are non-existent and many of the dirt roads are liable to flooding in the rainy season, which is all the year round in the north with the heaviest falls in September/October. The average temperature in the north is 86°F, while in the south the average temperature is 82°F and the rainy season is from October to May.

The unit of currency is the CFA franc and regulations are as generally apply to countries using this currency. There is no limit to the amount of foreign currency that may be imported or exported provided it is declared on entry.

Egypt

Egypt covers an area of 386,198 square miles including the Sinai Desert. It has one of the largest cities in Africa as its capital: Cairo. It is one of the host countries of Africa's largest river, the Nile, yet over 80% of Egypt is desert. Most of the country's agriculture is on the banks of the river Nile, which are very heavily populated by most of the country's 43 million people.

Rainfall in Egypt is negligible. Temperatures range from a winter average of 70°F to a summer high of around 120°F. Aswan, in the south of the country is one of the hottest towns in Africa with an average throughout the year of 94°F (34° Celsius). Temperature during the daytime rarely drops below 70°F.

Egypt has been independent since 1922. The current president is Hosni Mubarak.

Most of the main roads have a good tarmac surface while the desert roads are no more than sand tracks.

The currency of Egypt is the Egyptian pound and visitors may not import or export any local currency. Any amount of foreign currency may be exported provided it is declared on entry. Travellers cheques are cashable at all banks.

Gabon

Gabon, with an area of 103,391 square miles, is almost one mass of dense jungle with the Chaillu mountain range in the south running northwards and linking up with the Cristal mountains in the north west corner.

The country gained independence from France in August 1960. Its population is 1.4 million and President Omar Bongo is the leader. The capital Libreville is also the main port.

The rainy season lasts from September to June, and from November to March some very heavy rains fall. Temperatures in the dry season reach around 80°F which is the coolest time of year. During the rains temperatures rise to 90°F or more.

The only tarred section of road is on the bridge that spans the river Ogooué at Lambaréné, a town which is perched on an island in the middle of the river. The main dirt road runs from the northern border with Cameroon to the southern border with Congo and is fairly good apart from a rough section through the Chaillu Mountains.

The unit of currency is the CFA franc and the usual CFA regulations apply. There is no limit to the amount of foreign currency that may be imported but it must be declared, and the amount exported must not exceed the declared amount. Deposits or guarantees are needed in Gabon with the amount ranging from 40,000 CFA to 300,000 CFA (£80 to £600 sterling). These are refundable on leaving.

Ghana

Covering 92,010 square miles, Ghana became independent in March 1957 when the state was created from British Togoland and the Gold Coast. The south of the country is bushland, ranging through dense forest in the west and central regions to savanna in the north. In the centre of Ghana is Lake Volta.

The population of Ghana is 11.4 million and the capital is Accra, situated on the coast overlooking the Gulf of Guinea; once one of the world's great cocoa exporters, and Africa's largest grower, Ghana has declined somewhat in recent years due mainly to several attempted or successful coups, the latest being in 1981 when Flight Lieutenant Jerry Rawlings, the current military leader of the country, was returned to power. The situation in Ghana is now stable, but security is still fairly tight and tourists should expect the odd thorough search on entry. Despite this inconvenience, the officials still maintain their friendly disposition.

The road network consists of tarmac roads between all the main towns but these roads are poorly maintained and it is safer and more comfortable to drive on the dirt roads.

The currency is the cedi, divided into 100 pesewas. There are strict regulations in force governing the import and export of Ghanaian currency, but there is no limit to the amount of foreign currency that may be taken into or out of the country. It must, however, be declared on entry. Only exchange the amount of money you are likely to need as it is extremely difficult to change cedis back to foreign currency.

Guinea

Guinea has an area of 94,964 square miles and is very mountainous apart from the Malinke region which is fairly flat at around 1,300 feet above sea level. Most of the coastal region north west of the capital of Conakry is flat and marshy, the dirt roads here are liable to flooding in the rainy season. The highest mountains are to be found in the south eastern corner where they rise to 5,500 feet above sea level, while the Djalon range north of Conakry are picturesque, with several high waterfalls and cascades. The rainfall in this region lasts from May to October with the heaviest falls, sometimes as much as 20 inches in a month, being during July, August and September. The average temperature in this region is 85°F. In the east of the country the temperature averages 90°F and the rainy season is also from May to October but the falls are not so heavy.

Originally part of French West Africa, Guinea became independent in October 1958. Its population is 5 million. Until his death in March 1984, the country's leader was President Ahmed Sakou Toure, a founder of

175

independence on the African continent. He was Africa's longest serving president. He was succeeded by Mr Lansana Beavogui.

There is a fairly good road system by African standards. Tarred roads lead from Conakry to Kambia on the Sierra Leone border and to Kissidougou in the east. There is also a short section at Labe. The dirt roads are good during the dry season but during the torrential rains can become rivers.

The unit of currency is the syli, and the normal exchange rate gives approximately 40 to the £ sterling. Visitors must declare their foreign currency on arrival.

Ivory Coast

Ivory Coast covers an area of 127,000 square miles; and consists of dry savanna plains in the north while the southern region, below central, is dense humid jungle with humidity as much as one hundred per cent at times after rains. The country has one of the heaviest rainfalls in West Africa, with an annual figure of up to 90 inches. The rainy season lasts from March through to December, often with a dry break for a few weeks around August.

Originally part of French West Africa, the Ivory Coast gained independence in August 1960 and is led by President Felix Houphouet Boigny. The population of the Ivory Coast is 8.3 million and comprises over 60 different tribes.

Ivory Coast is one of the African countries that has its plans for the Trans African Highway well in progress, and in fact there is an excellent section of motorway now in use from south of Toumodi to the capital, Yamoussoukro. In general though, tarred roads are few, and the only sections are from Yamoussoukro to Daloa in the east, and north westwards to Ouélle, and Agnibilekrou at the border with Ghana. The rest of the towns are connected by dirt or gravel roads, some of which are very good.

The unit of currency is the CFA franc and regulations are as for other CFA franc countries. Any amount of foreign currency may be taken in to or out of the Ivory Coast and all banks and hotels exchange travellers cheques, although hotels will often do this only for their own residents.

Kenya

The country covers an area of 225,000 square miles and is one of extremes, being savanna in the south and desert in the north, while the west is forest and the eastern border is silver-sanded beaches flanked by the Indian Ocean.

Kenya gained its independence from Britain in December 1963 under the leadership of President Jomo Kenyatta. Upon his death Daniel Arap Moi became president.

Nairobi, the capital, is one of Africa's most modern cities and stands at a height of 5,450 feet above sea level. It has a pleasant climate, being hot at times but without the humidity of the coastal region, where Mombasa is the main sea port.

Kenya lies astride the equator, which runs through the perpetually snow-capped Mount Kenya, Africa's second highest mountain at 17,058 feet (after Mount Kilimanjaro on the Tanzanian border). In the south western region, the highlands are bisected by the Great Rift Valley, one of Africa's most spectacular sights with its vast plateaux and escarpments descending to the valley floor, as wide as 40 miles in places. It is in the highlands that Kenya's main crop, coffee, is grown along with the many tea plantations. In the far south western corner is Lake Victoria (24,300 square miles), which is shared by Kenya, Tanzania, and Uganda, the three countries that make up the East African Community. The main language of these three countries is English while the native language is Swahili.

The rainfall can be heavy, and the wet season is usually around Easter time when some of the dirt roads become impassable due to flooding or washing away; on the whole though the majority of dirt roads are excellent. All of the main roads in Kenya, however, are tarmac, from the coast to the border with Uganda, and from Isiolo in the north to the border with Tanzania. Note that northern frontier districts of Kenya (and the southern frontier districts of Sudan) may be closed to private motor traffic (depending on rains) during the periods 15 March to 15 June and 15 October to 15 December owing to seasonal rains. Advance enquiries should be made, directed to Kenya/Sudan Automobile clubs or respective consular departments.

Kenya has some of the world's greatest game parks and reserves, the largest being Tsavo which boasts elephant herds totalling 25,000. There was a decline in the elephant population owing to poaching, but since the government imposed a ban on the sale of animal trophies and ivory, the numbers are increasing once more.

Kenya's largest lake is Lake Turkana (originally Lake Rudolf) in the extreme north, re-named after the tribe that inhabits the area. It covers an area of 2,473 square miles. The longest river is the Tana, 440 miles long.

There is a large detachment of white people in the total population of 15.5 million, spread throughout the country. The most populous area is the highlands where most of the agriculture is carried out.

The currency is the shilling made up of 100 cents. There are notes of 5, 10, 20, and 100 shillings, while the coins are 5, 10, 25, and 50 cents. There are also coins of 1 and 2 shillings. No Kenya currency may be taken into or out of the country, but there is no limit of foreign currency, which must be declared on entry.

Liberia

Liberia has 350 miles of coastline, and at the widest point between the coast and the inland border is over 250 miles. The country covers an area of 43,000 square miles. Geographically the country is fairly flat with a belt of rain forest in the south, and hills rising to 3,000 feet in the north.

The country is presided over by Master Sergeant Samuel Doe who is the head of the military council. It was constituted as the Free Independent Republic of Liberia on 27 July 1847 and was first recognised by Britain and France. Most of the country's 1.9 million people live in the area between the capital, Monrovia, and the port of Buchanan where the main section of tarmac road is. The only other section of tarmac runs north from Monrovia to Gbarnga. The rest of the roads are of dirt or gravel and there are two large barren areas practically free of habitation; one is east of Buchanan and the other is the Gola region in the north west of the country where a lot of the country's diamond wealth comes from.

Liberia's annual rainfall is very heavy, often in excess of 130 inches. January is the only dry month, with the heaviest rains falling between May and October. The temperature is fairly constant throughout the year and ranges from a minimum of 65°F to a maximum of 90°F.

The currency is the Liberian dollar, and strict regulations are in force regarding the export of local currency, which is forbidden to non-residents. Any amount of foreign currency may be imported or exported but the exported amount must not exceed what a visitor declares on entry.

Libya

The whole of the country is one large plateau broken only by rifts and basins. It is ninety per cent desert, being straddled across the Sahara. It covers an area of 680,000 square miles.

Libya became independent in December 1951 and is ruled by Colonel Muammar Gaddafi who is head of the military council. The population of Libya is 3 million. The road network is poor with the only tarmac roads being along the coastal region and from Misurata on the coast to Ubari in the desert. Routes in the desert are no more than sand tracks, many of which are closed to tourists.

As tourists are not always welcomed in this country, it is wise to ascertain the situation regarding visitors well in advance.

The coastal climate is typical of the Mediterranean, with an average temperature during the year of 80°F. This can be much higher at times particularly when the hot sirocco blows from the desert. In the south of the country, deep into the desert region, temperatures of 120°F or more are not unexpected, especially during the summer months of June to August.

The unit of currency is the Libyan dinar and visitors may import or export up to 20 of these in bank notes. There is no limit to the amount of foreign currency that may be imported or exported. It is required that every visitor completes a currency declaration form on entry, and possesses at least £300 sterling.

Malawi

It covers an area of 36,325 square miles including Lake Malawi and has Lilongwe as its capital. Often referred to as "little Switzerland", Malawi is one of the most beautiful countries on the African continent, and is comprised wholly of mountains, hills, and valleys with the 355-mile long Lake Malawi occupying most of the eastern boundary. The country lies in the Great Rift Valley, which runs northwards through Kenya.

Malawi was formerly called Nyasaland and became independent in July 1964. The population of 6.1 million, ruled over by President Hastings Banda, live mainly in the central and southern regions.

The rainy season is from December to March, when the temperature averages 80°F, with October and November the hottest months. June and July are the coolest months with an average temperature of 70°F.

A tarmac road runs from the northern town of Karonga, alongside Lake Malawi, to Milange on the Mozambique border, with a small break at Mzuzu. There is also tarmac from Chipata on the Zambian border, through Lilongwe to Blantyre. The rest of the roads are dirt and are not too good, being through mountainous country.

The unit of currency is the kwacha which is divided into 100 tambala. Up to 20 kwacha may be taken in or out of the country in notes. There is no restriction on the amount of foreign currency that may be taken in or out. Travellers cheques are cashed by banks and hotels.

Mali

Mali covers an area of 478,832 square miles and has a population of 6.7 million people. The present leader is President General Moussa Traore.

This is an enchanting country, hosting the great River Niger and containing such historic places as Mopti, the "Venice of Mali", which was founded in the 13th century, and the legendary Timbuktoo. More than half the country is desert and the rest savanna. Despite the River Niger running through it, Mali is one of the most drought-ridden countries in West Africa. The rainy season is from June to September, when the temperature is around 88°F. March to May are the hottest months with temperatures well over 100°F, and often 120°F. Kayes in the far west of the country is reputedly the hottest town on earth with temperatures of up to 140°F in the shade being recorded.

Of the 7,000 miles of roads in the country, less than two thirds are usable throughout the year, and some of the dirt roads are in very bad condition. Much of the transport is by rail. The only tarmac roads are in the east linking the capital, Bamako, with Segou, Mopti, Sikasso, and 'Bobo' in Burkina Fasso. These tarmac roads are in good condition.

The currency is the CFA franc (Ouest) and the usual rules apply. There is no limit to the amount of foreign currency that may be taken in or out of Mali. International travellers cheques can be exchanged at any Malian bank and some hotels.

Mauritania

Originally part of French West Africa, Mauritania occupies most of the western end of the Sahara desert, and has its coastline on the Atlantic Ocean. It covers an area of 398,000 square miles, mainly desert.

Mauritania became independent in November 1960. The country's leader is President Lieutenant Colonel Mohamed Khouna Oulid Haidalla.

Most of the country's irrigation comes from the Senegal River which forms the southern border and provides much of the water requirements for the 1.6 million population, as there is little rainfall. Only in the capital of Nouakchott and towards the southern border does occasional rain fall during the 'wet' month of August. The coolest time of year is December/January with temperatures from 60°F to 78°F. During the summer months the temperature ranges from 70°F to 90°F. The hottest months are September/October, after the rainy season.

Apart from a tarred system north and south from the capital, the roads are mainly sand or dirt, and in places no more than tracks.

There is no limit to the amount of foreign currency that may be taken into Mauritania, and the amount taken out may be equal to this provided it has been declared on entry. The Mauritania currency unit is the ouguiya; no local currency may be taken into or out of the country. All banks cash travellers cheques, as do some hotels.

Morocco

Situated in the top north western corner of Africa, Morocco covers an area of 266,524 square miles. The north is mountainous with the Atlas range running the width of the country, while in the south the country terminates in the Sahara Desert.

Morocco gained independence from Spain in March 1956. It is a monarchy, and King Hassan II rules over the population of 20 million people, of which 2 million live in the main town of Casablanca. Rabat, the capital, has a population of 700,000 people.

The climate is pleasant with an average temperature of 65°F in winter, November to April. The summer temperature (May to October) can reach over 100°F but averages around 85°F.

The road system is one of the best in Africa, and petrol stations are within short distances of each other along the roads. In the south, though, many of the minor roads are simply dirt or gravel tracks.

The currency is the dirham, divided into 100 cents. No Moroccan money may be imported or exported. There is no limit to the amount of foreign currency that may be imported or exported but in the event of foreign currency with an exchange value of 5,000 dirham being imported, a *declaration de devises* must be completed. Surplus dirhams may be re-converted to foreign currency on departure only on production of exchange receipts.

Mozambique

Mozambique has a population of 12.4 million, and covers an area of 303,070 square miles. The president is Joaqueim Chissano. Originally a Portuguese colony, Mozambique gained independence in June 1975.

Situated on the east coast it enjoys more of the Indian Ocean on its beaches than any other African country. The climate is tropical. The rainy season ranges from November through April when the temperature is at its highest, averaging 85°F. During the dry season the temperature averages 75°F.

The road network is poor, with the only tarmac roads running from the capital of Maputo to Beira, and then north to Blantyre in Malawi, and from Beira to Umtali on the Zimbabwean border. Apart from a small mountain range to the north of the Rio Zambezi, the country is fairly flat, with the southern section mainly swamp.

The unit of currency is the escudo, divided into 100 centavos. Visitors may take as much foreign currency into Mozambique as they wish and may export up to the same amount. Up to 3,000 escudos may be taken into or out of the country. International travellers cheques are readily cashed at banks.

There is a drastic shortage of fuel in Mozambique. However, supplies are always found, and priority given, at garages if the purchaser pays with hard currency.

Namibia

Namibia covers an area of 318,261 square miles, excluding Walvis Bay (434 square miles) which forms part of the South African Cape Province although it is administered as part of Namibia. It is essentially a desert land with the eastern section forming part of the Kalahari Desert. The main port is Walvis Bay and the capital, Windhoek, lies 205 miles inland from Walvis Bay at an altitude of 5,870 ft. There is a central plateau with an average altitude of 3,300 ft.

The coastal region on the western seaboard has very little rainfall and temperatures throughout the year range from an average minimum 10°C to an average maximum of 23°C. Further inland rain can be expected from January to March and, although the average minimum temperatures are the same, the average maximum is 28°C.

There is an excellent road system throughout the country.

Currency, currency regulations, visa, passport entry and health requirements are all the same as those for South Africa.

Niger

This landlocked country covering an area of 489,398 square miles was originally part of French West Africa until it gained independence in August 1960. It has a population of 5.3 million. President of the military council is Lieutenant Colonel Seyni Kountche.

More than half of Niger is desert and uninhabited, though the southern region is mountainous with many small hills from 1,300 to 1,650 feet in height. This area is more populous. The river Niger, 2,610 miles long, is the third longest in Africa. Rising in Guinea, it flows away from the sea towards the north west, before turning and heading east and then south, finally entering the sea in Nigeria. It flows for a distance of 342 miles in Niger.

Niamey is the capital with 140,000 people. The temperature here and throughout the rest of the country can be very hot during the summer months from March to May. The best time to visit is between October and February when the temperature is at its lowest. As the country is mainly desert, only the roads in the south and south west are tarred, but these are very good.

Currency is the CFA franc, and there is no limit to the amount that may be taken into the country, or out, if the next country is also one that uses the CFA franc. Nor is there a limit to the amount of foreign currency that may be taken in or out. Travellers cheques and international currencies can be exchanged freely.

Nigeria

Nigeria covers an area of 356,670 square miles. It is a country with a unique atmosphere, and brash yet friendly people. In the south is the capital, Lagos, a large modern city. Nigeria gained independence from Britain in October 1960, and is led by Major General Ibrahim Babangida. It is the most densely populated country in Africa with a population of over 100 million people. It has some of the most interesting market places on the African continent.

In the south of the country, the thick rain forests make the climate hot and humid with an average temperature of 92°F, which is fairly constant throughout the year. The rainy season in the south lasts from March to November, and the rains in this region are very extensive particularly between June and September when 15 to 20 inches can fall in a month. The north of the country is savanna and the average temperature 98 to 100°F. The hottest period is March to May when the temperature can be 110°F or higher, and the rainy season is June to September. During winter in the northern region, which is from November to February, the harmattan wind blows across

Nigeria from the Sahara desert creating a haze with the fine particles of sand that it carries, and visibility is considerably reduced. Sometimes the countryside and the sun are completely obscured.

The roads in this country are excellent, with tarmac linking all major and many minor towns. Although the majority are all weather roads, it is best to avoid Nigeria in the rainy season, as rainfalls are torrential.

The unit of currency is the naira, divided into 100 kobo. Strict currency regulations are in force and no Nigerian money may be taken out of or into the country. All visitors must complete a declaration of the foreign currency they have in their possession and a minimum amount is required to be shown for each visitor which varies from £30 sterling to £100 sterling per day. Letters of credit and travellers cheques etc. are accepted.

Rwanda

Rwanda is a small country covering 10,166 square miles. The capital is Kigali. It was originally administered by Belgium, and became independent in 1962. Major General Juvenal Habyalimana is head of the military council.

Rwanda is a green mountainous country with fertile, terraced hillsides bisected by rivers and lakes. It is the home of some of the tallest people in the world, the Watutsi tribe, who also inhabit Uganda and Kenya. These people grow to a height of 7 feet or more.

The population of Rwanda is 5.1 million. Owing to the general high altitude the climate is comparatively cool, averaging 65 to 70°F throughout the year. The rainy season is from October to May. Therefore June to September are the best months to visit as driving can be extremely hazardous during the wet season.

It is a picturesque region. The only tarmac road is one from Kigali to Kabale in Uganda, a total distance of 62 miles. The rest of the roads are dirt or gravel and are very dusty. Outside of Kigali, camping sites are scarce, and camping is not advisable unless you can obtain permission to camp in the grounds of a police station.

The currency used is the Rwandan franc. Although up to 5,000 francs may be taken out of or into the country by residents or visitors, it should be noted that this currency is not exchangeable through normal sources outside Rwanda. Visitors may import and export as much foreign currency as they wish and currency declaration forms are not necessary.

Senegal

Covering an area of 76,000 square miles, Senegal was formerly part of French West Africa. The country gained independence in August 1960. The head of state is President Abdou Diouf. The population is 5.7 million, most of whom live in the west of the country.

The country is almost one mass of dry flat arid countryside, with its highest point Mount Kossanto at 1,367 feet above sea level. Temperatures range from 60°F to 90°F. The road system is mainly dirt or gravel road, the only tarred surfaces being in the west of the country around the coastal region. The roads to the east are no more than rough dirt tracks and are often impassable.

Currency is the CFA franc and the same regulations apply as for other CFA countries. There is no limit to the amount of foreign currency that may be imported, and the same amount may be exported provided it is declared on entry. Travellers cheques are readily cashed.

Sierra Leone

Situated in the south western corner of West Africa, Sierra Leone covers an area of 27,925 square miles and has a population of 3.5 million, of which 2,000 are Europeans. The colony of Sierra Leone originated in the sale and cession to English settlers in the year 1787, and became a British Protectorate in August 1896. On 27 April 1961 the country became independent. Freetown is the capital and President Dr Siaka Stevens leads the country.

There is a large area of rain forest in the north west and south east regions, while to the north east the area is mountainous, with the Loma mountains being the highest point in the country at 6,390 feet. These mountains form part of the border with Guinea, and it is in the Loma Mountains on the Guinea side that the River Niger rises.

There are several tarmac roads, mainly in the central and coastal regions, reaching as far inland as Makeni and Sefadu. The rest of the roads are dirt or gravel and usable throughout the year.

The annual rainfall is high with the wet season between May and November. Travel in the mountainous region during this period can be dangerous as torrential rain turns the roads into rivers. The temperature is cooled by the rains and rises again in November towards the end of the rainy season. The average temperature throughout the year is 86°F.

The unit of currency is the leone, and none may be exported from the country. There is no limit to the amount of foreign currency that may be imported but often there is a minimum spending limit applied.

South Africa

South Africa covers an area of 472,000 square miles, and has a population of 24 million. The country is led by President P.W. Botha. South Africa has been independent since 1910, and an independent republic since 1961, when it withdrew from the Commonwealth. Its coastline is embraced by both the Indian and Atlantic Oceans, but it has few rivers to rely on for its water supplies. It has large areas of semi-desert in the north, central and north western regions and many dry veld or savanna type regions. The majority of the country inland is at around 6,000 feet above sea level. The climate inland is sub tropical, while places on the coast, such as Durban, have a more tropical climate.

During the winter months the temperature averages 65°F during the daytime in the north region where frost occurs at night. The winter ranges from May to August. On the east coast the daytime temperature averages 70°F in the winter dropping to around 52°F at night. The rainy season here is from September to April. No rain falls from May to August which are the winter months. The summer average in both regions is 90°F. In the south of the country the pattern is different: the rains fall during the winter months and the winter temperature ranges from a minimum of around 46°F to 65°F during the summer months although it can rise much higher.

The road system in the country is excellent with tarmac roads linking all major towns and many minor ones, and there are some very good motorways.

The unit of currency is the rand divided into 100 cents. Notes in circulation are 2, 5, 10, and 20 rands while the coins are 1, 2, 5, 10, 20, and 50 cents. There is also a 1 rand coin. The 1 and 2 cent coins are nickel. There is no limit to the amount of foreign currency that a visitor may take into South Africa, but a lower limit is stipulated to ensure that the visitor has sufficient means to maintain him/herself. This figure varies, but visitors with insufficient means are often required to lodge a deposit in cash ranging from R400 to R1000 before they are allowed entry. Visitors may meet this requirement by means of travellers cheques, credit letters, bank drafts, or other instruments of international exchange, negotiable in South Africa.

The South African rand is also legal tender in South West Africa (Namibia), Botswana, Lesotho, Transkei, and Swaziland.

Sudan

Africa's largest country, covering an area of 967,500 square miles, Sudan is bisected by the River Nile, which supplies most of the country's irrigation. Accordingly the majority of the population of 18.4 million are to be found living along the banks of the Nile or in the large cities such as Khartoum, the capital (population 1 million). The country became independent in 1956. The president of Sudan is General Swareddahab.

Rain is negligible in the northern regions, while in the swampy south heavy rains can fall during the period June to September. A visit to Sudan should be avoided during this period if at all possible as many of the southern region roads will be under water. In the north, too, the roads can be closed during the rainy season. Around towns the roads are good tarmac while the rural roads are poor and often no more than tracks, particularly in the south.

Currency is the Sudanese pound divided into 100 pastres and 1000 milliemes. Sudanese currency may not be taken out of the country and all foreign currency must be declared on arrival, and a record kept of all transactions, whether travellers cheques or cash.

Swaziland

Swaziland, only 6,705 square miles, with a population of 530,000, became independent of British rule on 5 September 1968 and is now an independent state within the Commonwealth. King Sobhuza died in 1982 after a reign of 61 years. Queen Mother Ntombi acted as regent for the youthful crown Prince Makhosetive until his enthronement as King Mswati III in April, 1986.

Swaziland is one of the most delightful countries you could wish to visit. This tiny kingdom offers its visitors an unbelievably wide variety of scenery for such a small area and has one of the finest climates in the world. From the magnificent mountain ranges guarding the western boundaries numerous streams and rivers carve their way eastwards, creating a series of picturesque waterfalls, rapids and gorges and then continue through thick forests and fertile rolling grasslands to the flat, distinctive bush country of the eastern region.

Swaziland is fast becoming a modern country with new hotels, casinos, and nightclubs being erected in and around the capital of Mbabane; but at the same time it still retains its culture. Swazi warriors still carry shields, knobkerries and battleaxes, while the women wear colourful attire and all follow a lifestyle where age-old doctrines, rituals and ceremonies play an important role.

The currency of Swaziland is the lilangeni with the same value and exchange rate as the South African rand, which is also legal tender.

Tanzania

Tanzania has an area of 362,820 square miles. Originally known as Tanganyika, the country became Tanzania and gained independence in December 1961. The leader is President Ali Hassam Mwinyi. It has a population of 18 million, 757,000 of whom live in the former capital of Dar-es-Salaam. The new capital, Dodoma, has a present population of 46,000.

A country richly endowed by nature, Tanzania has a coastline which stretches for 500 miles with tropical palm clad beaches and undersea coral gardens. In the north, on the border with Kenya, looms the constantly snow-capped Mount Kilimanjaro, a mystical mountain and the highest in Africa at 19,340 feet above sea level. Also in Tanzania is Lake Tanganyika, the world's second deepest lake, situated in a deep trough-like depression within the Great Rift Valley. The country rolls down from dense forested mountains in the north and south to great plains of rich brown savanna grass and bush inland from the sea.

Tanzania, like Kenya, has some excellent game parks and reserves and more than 70,000 square miles of land are permanently dedicated to the preservation of wildlife.

Although Tanzania lies in the tropics, its temperatures depend more on altitude than season. Dar-es-Salaam and the coastal plains are hot but pleasant with average temperatures of 70 to 80°F during the day and cool evenings. The best time to visit is May to October when the climate is superb. Heavy rains fall from March to May. The central plateau is hot, dry and always cool at nights.

All the main roads to and from the capital are tarred, as are some of the inland roads, and the majority of them are all weather roads. Tanzania requires foreign private and commercial vehicles to be in possession of a circulation permit, obtainable free of charge from one of the licence (revenue) offices. (Refer to address list.)

The first "tourist" reputedly visited Tanzania 1.75 million years ago and his remains have recently been found in the Olduvai Gorge in the Serengeti Plains. His name was Zinjanthropus and many other remains of early man are now being uncovered in this area.

The currency of Tanzania is the shilling divided into 100 cents. It is illegal to import or export, even to Uganda or Kenya, any Tanzanian currency. Tanzanian currency may be taken out of the country, however, in the form of travellers cheques, and may be imported in the same way.

Tchad

The country covers an area of 501,000 square miles and the capital is N'Djamena, originally called Fort Lamy. Formerly part of French Equatorial Africa, Tchad gained independence in August 1960. The leadership of the 4.5 million population is currently disputed, after the invasion by President

Goukhouni Oueddi supported by Libyan troops in late 1982, following a coup by Hissene Habre.

Tchad is the largest landlocked country in Africa and is mostly desert or grassland. Roads are fairly good by African standards, and even the dirt roads take some beating.

Currency is the CFA franc and the regulations regarding exchange control are the same as for other CFA countries.

Togo

Togo is the smallest of the African states that were once under French administration. It has a coastline of 35 miles and extends inland for more than 400 miles, covering an area of 22,000 square miles. At its widest point the country has a width no greater than 100 miles.

Togo achieved independence in April 1960. It has a population of 2.7 million. The president is General Etienne Eyadema. The capital is Lome, on the coast of the Gulf of Guinea, where beaches fringed with coconut palms highlight the area.

The average temperature is 80°F on the coast and 90°F inland, and the main rains fall between May and August.

The centre of Togo is covered by thick deciduous forest and is the least populated in contrast to the north and south where savanna lands stretch out.

Togo is fast becoming a popular holiday resort, and first class hotels are springing up all over the place but mainly in the coastal region. There is a very good road network through the country, but particularly in the coastal region.

The currency is the CFA franc. For regulations on currency control refer to Benin.

Tunisia

Although the country is small, with an area of 64,000 square miles, Tunisia has a population of over 6.4 million, and has a coastline of 750 miles occupying nearly half of the borders. A former French protectorate, Tunisia became independent in March 1956.

The northern region encompasses the eastern extremity of the Atlas Mountains, while the south extends into the Sahara Desert. Summertime temperatures (May to September) average 85 to 90°F, while winter temperatures (December to March) average 60°F.

The road network is good and all the main towns are connected by tarred roads.

The Tunisian unit of currency is the dinar, divided into 1,000 millimes. It is forbidden to import or export any Tunisian dinars. There are no restrictions on foreign currency. On leaving the country visitors can re-convert Tunisian currency only on production of an exchange control form showing where and when the money was obtained; and the amount re-converted may not exceed 500 dinars. If you are likely to have more than 500 dinars to re-convert, you *must* make a declaration at the Customs office at your point of entry.

Uganda

Uganda covers an area of 91,343 square miles, over a quarter of which is accounted for by the waters of Lake Victoria, Lake Kyoga, and Lake Albert.

A British protectorate since 1894, Uganda gained independence on 9 October 1962. In 1971 Dr Milton Obote was overthrown by Idi Amin and a year later in 1972 Idi Amin evicted the country's 27,200 Asians, most of whom went to Britain. In April 1979, a combined force of Tanzanian Army and Ugandan exiles advanced into Uganda and a few days later took Kampala. Idi Amin fled the country. Dr Binaisa was installed as president only to be overthrown by the army of Uganda in May 1980. Elections followed and Dr Milton Obote was returned to power. He was overthrown for the second time in the coup of July 1985. Mr Yoweri Museveni now leads the country's 12.6 million people.

The country is mainly open bushland with several hilly regions, particularly in the south east. There are also vast areas of tea and coffee plantations. Uganda has some excellent game parks and reserves, two of the best being the Kabalega (formerly Murchison) and Ruwenzori (formerly Queen Elizabeth) national parks.

There are two rainy seasons, from February to May and from August to December. The average temperature throughout the country is 78°F. Altitude throughout the country varies from 3,000 to 4,500 feet, hence the moderate climate.

There are some good tarmac roads all over Uganda but at present these are not in the best of conditions, with scattered potholes on most of them.

The unit of currency is the Ugandan shilling.

Zaire

The country covers an area of over 895,348 square miles, and lies astride the equator. Formerly a Belgian colony known as the Belgian Congo, Zaire was granted independence in June 1960. The population is 26 million and the president General Mobuto Sese-Seko. The capital is Kinshasa.

In the north the terrain is dry savannah while the central and southern regions are thick humid jungle, much of which is unexplored. Zaire has a 25-mile long coast on the Atlantic, where the Zaire river (formerly called the Congo) enters the sea. The south east of the country is mountainous with heights up to 8,000 feet. Rains in this country can be expected at any time and are invariably heavy. The average temperature throughout the country is around 80°F.

The road network is very small, owing to the dense jungle, and the majority of transport uses the vast river network. Only around the main towns will decent roads be found. In rural areas the roads are poor and rarely maintained since they are little used.

The hydrographical network of Zaire is exceptionally extensive. The Zaire river — sixth longest in the world and second in Africa at around 2,718 miles — has many tributaries, the most important being the Oubangi, which flows along the northern border with C.A.R., and the Kasai in the south. Zaire has a riverine network of 15,000 miles of which 9,000 miles are navigable. This makes it possible to link Kinshasa by water with any other main part of the country. From the tourist point of view, travelling by river in Zaire is a unique and unforgettable experience.

The unit of currency is the Zaire, made up of 100 makuta or 1,000 sengi. It is forbidden to import or export Zairean currency, but there is no limit to the amount of foreign currency that may be taken into or out of the country. On entry, visitors must complete a currency declaration form which also doubles as a record of currency exchange and must be produced whenever money is exchanged. At one time, visitors had to show evidence of spending at least Z25 a day during their stay but this rule has recently been relaxed. In any case, it would not be difficult for overlanders to spend this amount daily, particularly when it comes to fuel purchase.

Zambia

Zambia has a population of 6 million people and covers an area of 290,586 square miles. Originally called Northern Rhodesia, Zambia became independent in October 1964. The capital is Lusaka and the President is Kenneth Kaunda. Zambia is one of Africa's greatest exporters of copper, with the main belt in the Ndola region against the Zaire border.

The southern half of the country acts a catchment area for the Zambezi river which forms the southern border; the country in general is one vast plateau with an average height of 4,000 feet above sea level. The terrain is mainly bush and woodland, very dense in some areas. The average temperature is 80°F. The wet season is from November to March depending on altitude.

There is a very good road system throughout the country with all of the main roads being tarred. It is an offence to camp or even stop or park under or near any road or rail bridge.

The unit of currency is the kwacha divided into 100 ngwee. Small amounts of Zambian currency may be taken out of or into the country and there is no limit to the amount of foreign currency that may be imported or exported. A currency declaration must be completed to enable visitors to take out up to the amount that they imported. Travellers cheques can be cashed at all banks.

Zimbabwe

Zimbabwe covers an area of 150,699 square miles and has a population of 7.4 million.

In 1963, the states of Rhodesia and Nyasaland were dissolved and the self governing state of Southern Rhodesia was formed. On 14 April 1964 Ian Smith became Prime Minister. On 5 November 1965 he declared a state of emergency and issued a unilateral declaration of independence. On 2 March 1970 Ian Smith and his government declared Rhodesia a republic. Talks were held with the British government towards legal independence and as a result elections were held and a new government was formed. On 18 April 1980 Rhodesia became the republic of Zimbabwe. The President is Canaan Banana and the Prime Minister Robert Mugabe. The capital, once Salisbury, is now called Harare.

Zimbabwe is composed of several plateaux with heights ranging from 3,000 to over 8,000 feet above sea level, and this contributes towards the temperate climate. The rainy season is from November to March and this is the hottest time of year with temperatures reaching 85° or more. During the dry season temperatures average 70°F.

The road system is excellent and first class tarred roads link all of the main towns.

The unit of currency is the Zimbabwean dollar and strict regulations are in force to ensure no dollars leave the country. There are no limits on foreign exchange.

Part 4
Route Commentary

The author's latest journey

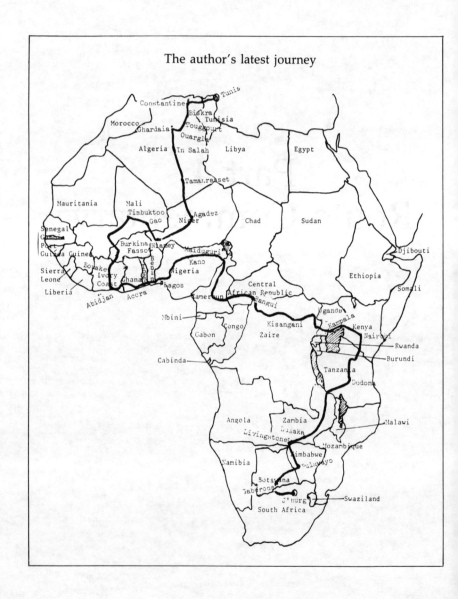

Tunisia

There were four of us on this trip: myself, Mick, Mel and Tony. Mick was a motor mechanic from the Isle of Wight whom I knew personally for a while before departure and who immediately jumped at the opportunity to 'travel the Dark Continent and visit foreign lands', when I approached him with the offer. Mel worked with him as a motor mechanic and had experience of this sort of trip as he had accompanied me on other occasions. Tony was an outsider, an unknown quantity whose place on this trip was arranged by his parents in response to an advertisement placed in a national magazine. He was something of a 'problem' child who at the age of 16 had no academic qualifications and was finding it difficult to secure employment. He was toying with the idea of joining the army until his parents read my advertisement and decided to obtain further details. Liking what they received in the way of information, they decided to book him a place. Up to the day of departure the only contact I had had with him was by telephone, and the only sight a rather grainy machine taken photograph, so none of us knew what to expect of him. The rest of us had a good personal knowledge of each other's way of life — very important on a trip such as this where you are living, eating and sleeping in close proximity for the next few months.

Despite postponements over a period of seven months, owing to shipping problems, visa difficulties and vehicle preparations, the departure day finally arrived with about three weeks to spare. Timing is vitally important on a trip like this as the desert can be crossed only at certain times of the year and the journey has to be planned to coincide with the dry seasons in the various countries concerned. Otherwise you can end up in serious difficulties as tropical rain storms can create flash floods capable of washing away a vehicle.

On departure day Mick, Mel and I had our first sight of Tony, and realised immediately that we were going to have our hands full keeping him in check. All 6ft 3 inches of him. I lumbered Mick with this responsibility as, at 25, he was the nearest in age to Tony.

Palermo to Tunis

Our departure from Palermo, Sicily, was on a warm mid-November day. There was a clear blue sky, with the occasional wisp of white fluffy cloud. Our thoughts were on the adventure and excitement of Africa, now only 24 hours away, and the hot sunny days which would fill our lives for several weeks to come. From now on we would be concerned only with essentials; certain things at home previously so important would become trivial, while certain luxuries that at home we take so much for granted, we would sorely miss.

The vessel due to take us across the Mediterranean to Tunis was the Expresso Venezia, which had not berthed when we arrived at the quayside so we had some time to kill.

My time was filled in compensating our compass, a lengthy job which involved manoeuvring the Land Rover into different positions, and adjusting the compass each time so that when the vehicle faced north the compass read north, and so on. Readings have to be very precise; there is little room for error when the compass is the main means of knowing your way across the Sahara desert. Mick and Mel checked the mechanical aspects of the vehicle and then sat on the sea wall and read their camera instruction books.

While we were doing our respective jobs, Tony was making a general nuisance of himself, so I decided that some shock treatment might do him good. With Mick and Mel we coaxed him to the edge of the water but he realised what we were up to and exploded with temper as soon as Mick and Mel grabbed him. We hoped the shock of the ducking would cool him down; meanwhile, we did discover one thing to remember on our trip — Tony was short fused.

At 1700 hours our boat docked, and daylight began to fade, the warmth of the day merging into a cool evening. We drove the Land Rover to the quayside to join the other vehicles waiting to board and duly proceeded to passport control, and then returned to the vehicle to wait.

On boarding an hour later we had to park in the hold, lock the vehicle, leave the ship, and re-embark up a gangway to the side. This meant we would be unable to leave someone with the vehicle overnight as originally planned but as everyone was in the same situation we decided it ought to be safe. We therefore removed our sleeping bags and toiletries, locked the Land Rover and made our way to the gangway at the side of the ship. By then, the ship was very full, with all seats taken, so we resigned ourselves to spending the night on the deck in our sleeping bags. But first of all we had a meal and a hot shower, then completed our immigration forms for entry into Tunisia. The majority of people on board the Expresso Venezia were Arabs, on their way home from enormous shopping expeditions in Palermo where things are much cheaper than in Tunis or Algeria. Many were laden with blankets, clothing and electrical goods, blocking the gangways and reception areas of the ship.

At 2120 hours the ship's mooring ropes were cast off, and we slowly edged our way out of the harbour into the open waters of the Mediterranean which looked a murky grey except for the white water churned up by the ship's propellors. It had been a warm day, but now there was a cold night wind so we headed for a secluded part of the upper deck and snuggled into our sleeping bags for the night.

Around 0730 hours when it was becoming a little warmer and the sun was beginning to break through, we all went inside into the warmth of the ship and had a good wash and clean up before proceeding to breakfast. We returned to the deck to find Tunis now in sight: for Mick and Tony their first view of Africa. The sun was by now blazing down on us as if to say "You will have to put up with me for the next few months".

Tunis to the Algerian border

The ship docked and we were all allowed to proceed to our vehicles on the car deck, to drive off the boat onto African soil and join the queue for customs clearance. I was given a form to complete by an official. It asked details of vehicle and passengers, and our length of stay in Tunis. This took about 10 minutes to fill in and just as I finished the same official returned, took the form from me, took one look at it and, to my amazement, tore it up in front of me, did a sharp about turn and promptly disappeared without a word. Shortly afterwards, while we were all still sitting in the Land Rover looking rather bemused, a smartly dressed Arab appeared at the window, speaking good English, and after confirming that we were getting nowhere with our customs clearance, promptly led me to the far side of the building where he helped me complete the correct forms. But on our return to the Land Rover he insisted on payment for his 'service'. It appeared he was merely an Arab who understood customs procedure and was out to make a quick buck. When I refused to pay him, he disappeared as quickly as the first official , taking my papers with him. Mel immediately gave chase and returned with a uniformed customs officer, who was most helpful and within a few minutes we were on our way.

Our first priority was to obtain some local currency, so we drove to a bank in the centre of Tunis and changed a little money into Tunisian dinars before leaving the busy capital, with its snake-charmers, dancers and market activity.

Our route towards Medjez-el-Bab and westwards towards the Algerian border took us along winding roads, and gave us our first sight of the African countryside. As we drove along at 40 to 50 mph we passed through a large plain sprouting with next season's corn supply. To our right was the start of the huge Atlas Mountain range which winds its way across to Morocco on Africa's west coast. The plain then rose slightly before a steep drop into a valley bed with mountains on one side, and green rolling hills on the other. Not the sort of sight one generally associates with Africa, but nevertheless quite picturesque. The whole area was one of ploughed fields ready for seeding, interspersed with olive groves. We also passed some small wooded areas which reminded us very much of English forests.

Our first stop was the town of Beja where we stocked up with provisions — milk, biscuits, bread etc. — and then we went through Jendouba, the last town in Tunisia and on to the Algerian border. As I was driver and navigator, I had allocated Mel the job of liaising with the border officials, his duty being to clear all paper work, as he had previous experience of this. At the border Mel took the Carnet and other documents into the office while the rest of us waited in the vehicle expecting to be called in at any minute, but Mel soon returned with the paperwork completed. The barrier was lifted and we were on our way out of Tunisia after a very brief visit of about 8 hours and heading towards the Algerian border post. This was about 4 miles ahead along a winding narrow road that took us over a small but steep mountain and here, in complete contrast, it was a case of 'everyone out' and into the building, where we each had to complete an entry card and a form stating what money we were each carrying. This time we had to wait at least 1½ hours while the Carnet was completed and our forms checked. All done, the customs officials accompanied us to our vehicle for a brief inspection and then we were on our way.

Although the sun had been shining since we left the ferry, we could feel the cold when not in the sun.

Algeria

From the Algerian border, the road continues to climb the mountain, twisting all the way, and passing clusters of trees of the species *Quercus Suber*. This is the cork oak whose bark is harvested, and we could see trees where the bark had been stripped some time ago which were already growing a new layer of bark.

Souk-Ahras and our first night in Africa

At 4,000 ft the road began to level off once more but still followed a twisting course, hugging the mountainside with a layer of fresh green grass on both sides of the road. After a gentle descent we came into the town of Souk-Ahras where we planned to obtain some Algerian money. However on entering town we were stopped at a police check-point and so missed the banks, which closed at 1600 hours. Fortunately we were lucky enough to find a money-changer in one of the local shops who accepted French francs for Algerian dinars.

We then had to find our way out of town — not so easy as you might think. We wanted to head for Constantine, a fairly large town near the north coast of Algeria, yet out of four people asked no two indicated the same direction. By now we were on the outskirts of the town where there were few signposts and those we saw did not help much, so we stopped a car, and the driver kindly showed us on the map which way to go. But first we pulled off the road and had tea; it was 1700 hours and this was our first meal, apart from fruit at lunchtime, since leaving the ferry. Back on the road again I became unhappy about the directions the driver had given us so I decided to take a road which headed in the approximate direction we had to go. By now it was 1800 hours and darkness was falling, a time when we would normally stop to erect our tents for the night, but on this occasion it was decided to drive on through the darkness to make up some of the mileage lost in the last town.

After about 20 miles we came across the first signpost pointing towards

Guelma, which is situated halfway between the border and Constantine; confident we were on the right road at last, we decided to stop for the night. It was already 1930 hours, and we soon found a suitable area to pitch camp for the night. It was quite chilly so we soon had the tents up and the vehicle alarms switched on, and retired for our first night in Africa.

Constantine to Biskra

We awoke the next morning feeling rather cold, and emerged from the tents to discover there had been a frost. However, the sun was up and soon warming the air. After breakfast, and packing the tents away, we were soon on the road again, passing through green countryside although still in the mountains.

We passed through Guelma and followed the twisty road to Constantine, arriving around midday. But once again we were out of luck for the banks were closed and we were now getting low on fuel so it was important we find a money-changer. It did not take too long to find someone at the local station although he would not change all we wanted. Our next quest was for fuel so we joined a queue at the first filling station we found and waited our turn. Came our turn and the attendant began to fill our tank, but luck was against us once more. After 5 gallons the pump ran dry and that was all the petrol we could have.

We then decided to find a hotel that would change money. After half an hour we found a suitable place and Mel and I went inside. While we were there, ironically a money-changer stopped at our vehicle and asked Mick and Tony if they wanted to exchange any currency.

Constantine is a picturesque town, with a deep gorge running through the centre of it and a suspension bridge linking the two sections. Before leaving the town we decided to cross the bridge to take some photographs. Fortunately we found another filling station and topped up with oil, fuel and water. We purchased enough engine oil for several oil changes as it was so cheap.

We left Constantine by the same route that we had entered by for a short distance and then turned off to the right for the town of Batna. We were now heading south towards the Sahara Desert. Almost as soon as we turned off onto the Batna road we noticed the difference in the surrounding countryside. Gone were the rolling hills and mountain ranges. Now there was bare rock and dry ground, with a marked absence of olive groves or any other trees and no cultivation of crops, just the occasional house with goats or donkeys in the yard, or even a few sheep.

We were soon amongst hills again though, and shortly after passing through Ain-M-Lila, a British built industrial town, we came upon two large salt pans, on either side of the road, one with a splendid reflection of the hills in it. At about 1600 hours we arrived at Batna and took the by-pass around it, heading for the next town of Biskra. We travelled for another hour or so before pulling off the road for the night, rather earlier than usual; but the vehicle was due for an oil change and this seemed the best time to do it. We found a nice soft patch of ground, which is easier on the body when you have to lie on it all night, and also makes it easier to dig a hole to drain the old engine oil into.

Mel, being chief mechanic, proceeded to change the engine oil while the rest of us erected the tents which were up before he had finished. As light was fading we offered to give Mel a hand. Mick poured the new oil into the filler while Mel checked the oil level but to his amazement after 9 pints of oil had been poured in, normally sufficient to fill the sump, the dipstick still showed empty. The next moment we heard hysterical laughter and turned to see Tony rolling helplessly on the ground. He managed to blurt out that Mel had forgotten to replace the sump bung and there were 9 pints of new oil running straight through the engine and into the hole that had been dug in the sand. It was just as well we had purchased plenty of oil back in Constantine.

By the time we had cleaned up, it was dark, there being no twilight in the desert area. On this 3,000 foot plateau that stretches from the north Algerian coast to the start of the Sahara Desert it was decidedly chilly, so we quickly had our evening meal and scurried into the warmth of our tents for an early night. The general pattern of our sleep on this trip, and one which we soon got used to, was in bed as soon as it got dark, and up as soon as it got light — normally around 0430 to 0500 hours. Tony went without supper on this occasion as the main course included biscuits and he had had a nasty experience back in Constantine when found he had been eating a biscuit full of weevils. The memory lingered, so Mick ate his share of biscuits. Weevils are common occurrences in both biscuits and bread in African countries and one just has to get used to it or go hungry.

After one of the coldest night's sleep yet, we were up at 0600 hours to find the temperature already in the upper sixties Fahrenheit, and after a breakfast of 'weevil' biscuits from which Tony excluded himself again, we were soon on our way. After only a short distance, after climbing a small hill, covered in greenery, we came upon a lot of activity around a bridge being built over the main north/south railway line. This bridge will carry the 'col-descarabanes', a stretch of road that will eventually link up with and become part of the Trans-Saharan Highway. A couple of miles further on the narrow tarmac road widens and the green trees and grass give way to a savanna like terrain, with deep craggy rain gullies on both sides of the road running away from the tarmac edges like cracks in a window pane. One of the deeper ruts, parallel with the road, had water in it, which eventually drained into an oasis surrounded by date palms, fresh green grass, and shrubs. There was also a small house with a vegetable garden being tended by a couple of Arabs.

We were now entering the northern limits of the great Sahara Desert, and the people we passed along the roadside were becoming fewer. The fresh green areas were giving way to barren rock and sand, and very soon vegetation would completely disappear, for nothing grows in the sterile Sahara. We wondered what our next night's sleep would be like on the hardening ground and whether we should be able to drive tent pegs into it.

Some 45 miles from our previous resting place we descended from 3,000 feet to 1,000 feet, and suddenly the mountains appeared to close in on the road until we were driving through a small gorge. At the same time the railway which had been running parallel with the road moved right away from us. A short distance further on we reached our first Wadi — a causeway of a sort which often becomes uncrossable when it rains, owing to the road flooding to a depth of up to five feet. It's the ideal place for a car wash as one Arab was demonstrating as we sped past, although here the water depth was only a couple of inches.

We passed through the small industrial town of Fontaine des Gazelles and then through Fermi-Dris-Amor. Alongside the road were signs of the Trans

Saharan Highway, in some places in advanced stages of construction. The terrain was becoming more dry and barren as we negotiated a slight incline that rose between two hills. From the top we looked down on to a long twisting road leading into Biskra just 4½ miles ahead.

It was Friday, the Sabbath in Algeria, and we expected to find everything in Biskra deserted; but much to our surprise there were some shops open so we stocked up with provisions for the long desert stretch ahead. Almost a desert town, Biskra showed signs of rapid expansion with many new buildings being erected, many in the form of housing estates. Having diverged from the main route to enter Biskra, we left the town by the same route to join the road heading for Touggourt.

Biskra to Touggourt

Shortly outside Biskra the railway re-appeared alongside the road. At least this way we knew we could not get lost. There were also signs of greenery again and the mountains opened right up giving us a panoramic view over a large expanse of plain ahead with a dead straight road. Five miles on we passed a very large date plantation with an airstrip alongside after which the greenery gave way once more to hard desert scrubland with only one or two oases in the distance.

The temperature was rising fast and a heat haze had descended, partially obscuring the view. We then came upon a road sign giving the warning 'camels crossing' followed by our first sand dune and then within half a mile, two camels did cross the road. They were heading for a water hole by the roadside, so we stopped, hoping they would pose for the cameras, which they obligingly did.

Now the weather was becoming hotter and hotter, and the nights colder and colder, as we advanced further into the desert, with the mountains gradually disappearing from sight and more and more sand dunes taking their place. The road still remained straight, the sky a clear blue with not a cloud in sight, and the temperature a comfortable 75 degrees F.

The construction work of the Trans Saharan Highway was no longer in evidence as we approached the small town of De-Still with its two track railway siding, and water tower which can be seen from up to 5 miles away. Just beyond De-Still, the road forks, and we took the right hand road sign-posted to El-Meghaier. At the junction electricity pylons join the railway that still runs alongside the road although we saw no sign of a train. There were also one or two flowering shrubs by the side of the road which must have found some moisture in the soil. A little further on the railway crossed the road in front of us, and we had to cross it several times as the track weaved its way back and forth before moving right away again together with the pylons. However, it rejoins the route a few miles further on.

At 1600 hours, with the sun mellowing to the west, almost on the horizon of sand dunes, and shining directly through the offside windows of our vehicle, we passed a sign showing 12 miles to El-Meghaier. The terrain had not changed over the last 50 miles apart from the increasing presence of sand dunes which cover a wider area as the scrub disappears completely.

We passed a large date plantation to our left as we approached El-Meghaier, which is just off the main route, and we diverted into the main town in the hope of finding a filling station. However luck was not with us so we left again, travelling further south along a good tarmac road with sand dunes skirting both sides of the road. It was also noticeable here that the Africa of the Arab was slowly changing to the Africa of the negro. Even though we were still amongst Arabs, their complexion was decidedly darker.

At 1620 hours we passed another road sign giving Touggourt as 55 miles away. Some twenty miles further on we noticed a long line of date plantations and in between them scattered sand dunes and an old desert fort.

We eventually found a filling station at Djamaa and a plentiful water supply so we filled all our petrol and water containers. We did not know when we would next get the opportunity as we were about to enter the desert proper.

As light was fading we decided to call it a day and, just as we pulled off the road, there was our railway track again. We were all up by 0800 the next morning just in time to see our first train go by. Soon we were on the road and after a short while lost the railway track again together with pylons. We came across a couple of sand dunes that had blown across the road during the night, but we were not held up too long as a sand plough was busy clearing a way through.

As we passed two tall radio masts we could see the town of Touggourt in the distance. The railway track joins the road into town and a lot of industrial activity is evident with tons of steel pipes stacked on both sides of the road obviously for a pipeline. As we entered town we passed a group of children playing hopscotch, but once again our main priority was a bank for local currency and, as we would soon be in the desert, some anti-scorpion and snake-bite serum. We had no trouble finding either and were soon fully stocked up. It was while in this town that we were approached by our first fellow traveller, a Swiss, apparently hitchhiking, but we had no room in our vehicle so were unable to help him .

Touggourt to Ouargla

We were soon on our way again to Ouargla 95 miles away. We were now surrounded by sand dunes with the occasional date plantation and also the odd skeleton of a car that had been abandoned some time ago. The sky remained a pastel blue, with not a cloud in sight and the temperature climbed to the eighties fahrenheit. This is a straight road with a good tarmac surface.

At 12.45 the sun shone directly overhead. We thought we were in the middle of nowhere when in the distance appeared a huge oil refinery. Then suddenly we found a 'street trader' by the side of the road, selling the famous 'desert rose', a crystalline/rock substance that forms in all shapes and sizes under the sand; and a little further along we passed some Arabs digging for this same formation. Fifteen minutes later we came to another signpost with Ouargla marked at 50 miles. We stopped here for a while and, on turning over a couple of stones by the side of the road, I found our first scorpion, only a young one but still dangerous and painful should anyone get in the way of its sting. We soon moved on again and further along passed a local inhabitant riding his camel, with a 'spare' in tow.

As we approached Ouargla we passed a military airfield on the left-hand side of the road, with fighter planes at the ready, while on the right were some fairly large sand dunes, ready to be blown into some other position by the desert wind. There was also a large date plantation here and we scrounged a bowl of fresh dates from the plantation workers.

The town of Ouargla is surprisingly large and well equipped, and we had no trouble finding the provisions we needed. There is even a well stocked market, well worth a visit, with picture-postcards on sale at their stationery stalls, and even a stall selling the 'desert rose'. The greatest surprise, however, was when we came across a stall selling fresh 'whippy' ice cream; needless to say we all delved in here. This town is so interesting, and there is so much to see that we stayed several hours longer than we intended and by the time we were ready to move on light was fading so we decided to back track to a large area of sand dunes that we had passed on the way in, and camp there for the night. Maybe in the morning on the way through town again we would find an early morning coffee shop . . . this place had just about everything else.

We soon had the tents up. With the sand dunes and date palms scattered around us, the area made an ideal desert setting, particularly with the sun slowly sinking behind the dunes, seemingly peering at us through the branches of the date palms as it did so, as if to say 'good-night, see you tomorrow'. Something we could bank on now and over the next few weeks.

Soon after we had erected the tents we were surrounded by scores of local children, understandably curious, for it cannot be every day that they are visited by white people camping on the outskirts of their town. We were very cautious as we knew of the light-fingered reputation of the majority of Arab children. They do it for fun but it can cause hardship, especially to people in our position whose items are not replaceable in the desert or, indeed, Africa; so we ensured that someone was watching them all the time. However, it seemed that these had all come from a type of boarding school for, shortly, a couple of grown-ups appeared, respectably dressed. Apparently teachers, they introduced themselves, although we could not understand what they were saying, and then proceeded to make the kids sit at a distance from us on the soft sand in an orderly manner, and observe our activities from there. When darkness fell, they all disappeared as quickly as they had arrived.

The next morning we drove slowly through Ouargla looking for a coffee shop, and very soon found one right on the main route through town so we eagerly stopped there for a while. As we continued our way through the town we noticed that they even have street lighting!

Ouargla to El Golea

Leaving the town behind us, we travelled through an avenue of date palms, then the country opened up again into a wide expanse of desert, with scattered sand dunes and, ahead, a small lake or dam with water in it, and flamingos scavenging round the edges. The road surface was becoming very stony as we passed a small oil well about 8 miles from town.

As we clocked 10 miles out of Ouargla we observed clouds of black smoke in the distance. On both sides of the road small gauge oil pipelines lead away into the distance, presumably to an oil refinery. The road here is still good with a flat tarmac surface as we climbed to 800 ft above sea level. The black smoke was apparently waste oil being burnt at yet another oil refinery that we passed. It rises in a straight column, and then as it reaches a certain height is caught by the breeze and moves off in a horizontal direction for some considerable distance.

Soon we passed a road sign: Ghardaia 140 kilometres (88 miles). This is the next town to head for although our route turns south before reaching it. Sixty-five miles from Ghardaia we passed six Fiat trucks parked, all loaded with large pipes, the first vehicles that day, and just past them a small shack in the middle of nowhere, with a 'Tea' sign outside! However it was shut. Shortly afterwards we were overtaken by the first car we had seen outside a town for a couple of days. The countryside was unchanged, stony and barren, with the odd car tyre or abandoned car body here and there. We passed another desert shack some 35 miles from Ghardaia where the electricity pylons joined the road once more. We were now at 1,000 feet, and more clouds were forming. A couple of shrikes were spotted on the road side and then bedouin tents with their camels wandering close by.

At 11.45 hours we reached the junction: Ghardaia to the right and our turning , El Golea, to the left. From here to El Golea is 155 miles. Right by this junction is a large oil pipe storage yard, and a T.V. booster station. Who would have thought there was a T.V. in the desert?

From here on it is south, south, south all the way, until the desert is crossed. This was what we had been waiting for, one of the highlights of the Trans Africa Safari: the actual crossing of the world's greatest desert, the Sahara. Up to now we had been in semi-desert and savanna, but soon there will be nothing but sand and more sand, mountains, hills and rock intermingled. We will be isolated from civilisation, in a world of our own, where for company we will have only scorpions or the occasional high-flying eagle.

Thirty-five miles south of our junction, I had a surprise for the rest of our group. Every time I have travelled this route I have stopped at this spot. Believe it or not, at this point, Hasai Touiel, where there is nothing but sand for miles, there stands on the left-hand side of the road a brick built café that also offers accommodation for weary travellers! It had changed little since I was last here, and still offered reasonably priced chicken, chips, and salad, with coffee or tea. Meals are served on a table complete with cloth, and can be eaten inside in the shade or outside in the sun. The place is surrounded by trees and at the rear is a swimming pool. Needless to say we stopped here for a meal. We also managed to change some money with a vendor who approached our table and we filled our containers with sparkling clear water.

After lunch we moved on and soon passed the petrol station at Hasse Fahl. We crossed a completely dry wadi and noticed a desert breeze getting up, blowing wisps of sand across our path in an eerie, snake-like way. It is still in the range of the *sirocco* here, a warm wind that blows to the Mediterranean from the Libyan Desert. We pulled off the road mostly to rest the vehicle, and were soon passed by a fleet of seven other overlanders who gave a cheery wave as they sped past. Back on the road we passed through two small plateaux and then had to slow down for a herd of wandering camels. Then we passed three parked Arab driven fuel tankers, with the drivers on the sand on their prayer mats, praying towards Mecca, the setting sun casting their long shadows across the shimmering sand. The T.V. booster masts appeared more frequently now, about 20 miles apart.

At 44 miles from El Golea we passed a lonely yard with a small shack alongside, and two sand ploughs in the yard, so we knew the job of the occupant and reckoned he is kept quite busy at times as we were now experiencing frequent small sand storms.

We pulled off the road for the night to camp at the foot of a small hill covered in weather eroded rock, and had the most difficult time yet in erecting our tents as the ground was rock hard: even using a hammer the tent pegs ended up looking like safety pins. There was a fair old breeze blowing too which made the night cooler. We had covered 250 miles in the day which is good by desert standards. The terrain was still rocky and sandy looking like a lunar landscape, with odd shaped rocks and stones lying about which were probably formed millions of years ago.

After a fairly cold night, the sun was up before us. We had a quick scramble up the hill and a look round — you never know what you may find in areas such as this, where it is quite possible man has never trod before. We found a patch of tiny footprints in a soft area of sand, presumably those of a small bird, and then I found a large area where sometime many years ago a meteorite shower had landed. The meteorites were scattered all over the area, some as big as tennis balls, and it was obvious that they had hit the earth with quite a force as some of them were embedded in other rocks to a depth of a few inches. There were also signs of burning on some of the rocks and some other odd shaped rocks that resembled clusters of rabbit droppings stuck together. They were fairly heavy but not as heavy as some of the meteorite samples we collected as souvenirs.

We got back on the road and soon were only six miles from El Golea. The sky was blue with no clouds, and the terrain was changing slightly to a sandy one again but still with plenty of rock about. We passed another booster mast and small satellite tracking station, then negotiated a sharp bend to the left and found ourselves on the crest of a hill looking down on to El Golea, the largest oasis in the desert. As we drove into the town, the date palms looked strong and healthy. The streets have gutters and kerbs here and there are plenty of houses but no street lighting. We stayed just long enough to restock with provisions and then went on our way again.

El Golea to In Salah

The road is still good flat tarmac as you leave town. We stopped for fuel and water on the way out as the next town is 250 miles away. We travelled out of town through the date palms lining the road and found we were descending into a basin, with a plateau one side and sand dunes the other. We passed a patch of dense scrub that looked like gorse, hiding a water hole, as the road twisted up towards the plateau. Some huge sand dunes and another booster mast could be seen in the distance as we started to ascend the Tademait Plateau which stretches all the way to In Salah 250 miles away. The road here is 1,000 feet above sea level, and rising. It narrows after leaving El Golea, with scarcely room for two vehicles and the surface deteriorates with pot holes in places. However there were signs of road improvements in progress — a bulldozer (goodness knows where he came from) clearing sand off the road. As we clocked 70 miles from El Golea the road surface improved again. The surrounding area is very flat and once again we were in amongst drifting sand. Ahead we saw another TV mast in the distance and, as visibility is so good, we decided to measure the distance to it, which turned out to be 11 miles. It could prove an excellent landmark in a sandstorm. By now clouds partly obscured the sun and we watched the breeze picking up the sand and dancing off with it into the distance, where we could just make out the shape of another oil well.

As the wind strength increased and with it the sand storm, we decided for safety's sake to seek shelter behind a sand dune and let the storm blow over, first of all taking bearings of our position as a severe storm can cover the whole area with sand and even obscure the road. Even as we watched from our sheltered position the wind picked up huge clouds of sand and transported it to some position way off in the distance. After 50 minutes the wind subsided and we were on our way. Although it had not been a bad sand storm, there was nonetheless a thin layer of sand to a depth of about ¼ inch right across the road. The surface of the desert was flat and smooth — so was the road ahead, apart from the odd pothole breaking the surface, and we frequently observed water mirages in the distance both on the road and over the sand.

At 15.15, 90 miles from In Salah, we passed another tracking station to our right, while to the left is another shack-cum-café, but shut. The road here was still straight, but the tarmac surface was fast deteriorating, soon to disappear completely. The breeze continued to blow, sending another cloud of sand across the road in front of us.

At 192 miles from El Golea we slowly started to descend the Tademait Plateau, but not before stopping to admire the majesty of the four flat-topped rocky hills that stood proud out of the sand, across the plain before us. After descending the 1 in 5 gradient from the top of the plateau at 3,000 feet we decided to pitch camp at the base, away from the cold desert wind of the night.

At first light the next morning we were up and ready to strike camp. The temperature at 0730 was 42 degrees Fahrenheit; as we were under the shadow of the plateau, the sun had not yet found us. Stripping the tents was not easy either with the strong wind still blowing, and it took four to each tent, one at each corner, to pack it away. We were back in that lunar landscape with its craters, odd shaped rocks, and plateaus.

Soon we were heading for In Salah, across open plain. Date plantations began to appear again and electricity pylons alongside the road, indications that we were nearing town, and we passed an aerodrome to our left. Then, very suddenly, a sandstorm blew up and we were in the thick of it. Already a sand plough was in action clearing the road so we stopped to let him proceed.

The storm was short-lived and at 0900 hours we entered In Salah, and appeared to be back in civilisation again. The streets have lighting and the houses have TV aerials — even the mud-brick houses. In this town is another tracking station and a military fort, still in use. We located the market place, and much to our surprise found a stall selling hot sugar ring doughnuts which we all tried. The desert is full of surprises! Close by the doughnut stall was an old well with a donkey standing by to haul the bucket. We then proceeded to the only filling station to top up our fuel tanks and water cans, but we had to wait a while as there was quite a queue.

As we left In Salah we realised it was Tuesday and we must try and reach Tamanrasset by Thursday lunchtime as the sabbath starts then and everything closes until Saturday. Tamanrasset is the last town in Algeria; there is not another town for 700 miles so it is essential to top up there with fuel and water for the longest stretch across the Sahara, commonly known as the 'graveyard' stretch.

In Salah to Tamanrasset

As we left the town behind us, and the street lights disappeared, there was a strong desert breeze blowing across the wide tarmac road, this time from the east. Twelve miles out of town we could see nothing around us but sand, and the weather was very hot, in the nineties — and this is winter in the

Sahara. After an hour's driving, ridges and plateaux once again appeared on both sides of the road, which was becoming potholed; this surface can do a lot of damage to a vehicle's suspension and tyres, even a Land Rover, so we had to go carefully.

At Hassi Krening, halfway from In Salah to Arak, we dipped into a large wadi and, emerging from it on the other side, found a slight improvement in the road. A large ridge ran parallel to the road to the left as we made a slight descent to find the terrain opening up into a huge plain again. The height is 1,100 feet above sea level.

About 80 miles out from In Salah we passed a lonely cyclist and our first vehicle of the day, as we headed towards a high mountain ridge. The road weaves and winds its way through the mountains and the surface deteriorates once more. Ahead of us the mountains have a blanket of sand covering them, blown there by the wind, giving some of them the appearance of gigantic dunes.

At 1300 hours it was very, very hot, although the road surface had improved again as a layer of hard sand covered the surface and filled the pot holes. At 122 miles from In Salah the mountain range closed in on the road which was fast giving way to sand so we stopped for a while to engage the wheel hubs to give us four-wheel drive and to check the vehicle over. It was far too hot to work in overalls or any clothing but as we had now become acclimatised to the sun, we had nothing to fear healthwise. Mick and Mel changed the brake shoes while Tony re-arranged the inside of the vehicle and removed much of the desert sand that inevitably finds its way in.

While the others were still busy, I partially climbed one of the sand covered mountains, to take some photographs. From my position halfway up the dune, I could see our group and the vehicle, and nothing else but sand. It was a touching moment even for me who had seen it all before. This was the desert. We were right in the heart of it but who could explain the solitude, the beauty, the wide expanse of sand, mountains, and hills, the clear blue sky. By day or night it is a beautiful place and is best summed up in the words of that famous song from the show *The Desert Song*: Blue Heaven for you and I, Sand, kissing a moonlight sky, A desert breeze whispering a lullaby, and only stars above you . . .

When everything had been checked over and packed away again, we all jumped aboard, only to discover we were bogged down in the soft sand, and even four-wheel drive could not get us out. It was a case of out with the sand ladders and shovels, and dig! Fortunately, it did not take us long to get out of the rut and we were soon back on the road again. We were 145 miles from In Salah.

In this area, we passed through many wadis which, even when dry, can be seen from a long way away by the amount of plant life growing round them. Here there is a slight improvement in the road condition, but the scenery changes slightly. The terrain is once again rocky, and the mountains are crumbling, and surrounded by huge lumps of rock that have rolled down. As we passed over the next rise the whole area was covered with rocks that appeared to have rained from heaven. No matter how many corners you turn, or how many hills you climb, the view over the top, or around the corner is always different. One minute you can see nothing but sand, and the next there is a pure rock landscape.

About 25 miles from Arak we passed the old Tadjemout Fort standing alone by the roadside, and dipped into what must be a huge lake when it rains in this area for there is a large area of green bushes and shrubbery and even small trees. Six miles outside Arak are the beautiful gorges and Arak oasis, and more greenery alongside the road, even small trees again.

As we approached Arak the road suddenly disappeared completely right in front of us, leaving an 8-10 foot drop. It had been washed away by flash floods and torrential tropical downpours that can hit these areas. So we had to backtrack a little and make our way through the sand and rocks until we found the road again — not always as easy as it sounds.

After a small diversion we returned to the road and entered the Arak Gorge, a splendid place, unexpected in the middle of the Sahara desert, with tall sheer cliffs on either side of the road. As you enter the Gorge there is a tin shack on one side of the road labelled 'café', and a few shacks. Running alongside the road is a dried up river bed which had once crossed the road taking that section with it, but this time the wash-away was not too steep and we were able to negotiate the rift. A little further on is the Arak fort, now deserted, and a filling station, the first for 175 miles. Once again the road disappeared, and we had to divert. This is an area of outstanding beauty and never disappoints, but I should not think many people come here for a day's picnic.

As we got farther into the Gorge, the sides opened back and became less steep. At the end of the Gorge the road disappeared once more, this time for a long stretch. There was a marked diversion that took us through broken rock and deep shifting sand and around the back of a mountain. The going became very rough but we had to press on for if we stopped we ran the risk of sinking deeper and deeper into the sand. We could see areas where large trucks had become embedded in the sand. Soon we came to a large sandy area with two routes through it so we selected the marginally better of the two and struggled through the deep sand with all four wheels driving for about 100 yards before coming to a halt in a deep hole with the Land Rover precariously poised at an angle that would take most vehicles over onto their sides. As the vehicle started to topple everyone inside instinctively scrambled over to the driver's side to keep all four wheels on the ground. Carefully, they crawled out of the offside door and I told Mick and Mel to stand on the two steps on the driver's side and lean back as far as they could, clinging to the roof rack. The sand was halfway up the nearside doors, and to get out of this situation we had to drive really slowly and steadily, with Mel and Mick leaning back as far as they could and the offside wheels barely touching the ground. Another mile or so further on we were very pleased to come back on firm ground again after such a scary moment and, deciding we'd had enough for one day, stopped to pitch camp under the shadow of the 4,790 ft tall Mount Tintejert close to our exit from the Arak Gorge.

During the night we heard low growling and scuttling noises outside our tents which kept us awake. When we emerged very carefully next morning, we found that one tent was surrounded by large cat-like foot marks, presumably those of a mountain lion, and the bread that we had thrown away the night before was gone. Also the sardine tins left beside the tent for the night had been licked clean. There were many scorpion tracks around both tents and we felt glad we had not left our tents during the night. There was also evidence of monkeys in the area. Obviously there is plenty of wild life about.

We stripped our tents and packed them away, and so started another day. It had been a chilly night, but the early morning mist disperses quickly and the sun was shining through as we exited from the gorge. The gorge opens out into a plain and then comes the ascent of the Mouydir mountain range.

Well into the desert, and rest time alongside the "road".

By 0930 hours we had climbed to 3,000 feet above sea level and the surrounding area was once again of rock and hills. The edges of the road were sandy, but away from the road are mountains, all different: some conical, some flat-topped, many crumbling and others of a slate-like material. All around is clear evidence of the course the water takes when it rains, with deep gullies down the sides of the hills. All along the roadside here are wrecked vehicle shells, many burnt out.

0945 hours and the temperature had risen to 80 degrees Fahrenheit, the sun blazing down on us from above. The road surface became bad again, broken up in long stretches. Some 40 miles from the gorge the terrain is a flat plain with low mountains to the left covered with a blanket of sand. It looked like a lunar landscape, the holes in the road resembling craters! Eventually the road became so bad that we decided to leave it and drive through the desert on compass. So we took to the sand and roughly followed the direction of other vehicle tracks, making sure not to drive in them. We were still at 3,000 feet and had travelled 80 miles in 3½ hours. We saw a herd of camels in the distance with two white ones amongst them.

As you approach In Ecker Fort, the terrain becomes more stony. This fort is still in use. We stopped at the filling station to top up the fuel tanks and jerry cans and continued on our way. There is a small section of tarred road here, with the sides heavily re-inforced with boulders sealed in heavy wire mesh cages, but in places the road is still washed away and we were forced to drive over the sand again. On the left hand side of the road we passed a fuel dump, which looked like a military installation. The golden sand now looked whiter as it wound its way around the mountains, and we found a small area of scrub following a dried up river bed. At 140 miles from Arak Gorge was another heap of 45 gallon drums and another fuel dump. There was a military base next to this one and a line of electricity pylons fading into the distance. As we passed this base we saw a French Land Rover travelling in the opposite direction and we all exchanged a wave. Five miles up the road is In Amguel, a deserted fort. Close by there are some mud huts and an oasis with a café. The mountains here resemble piles of mud. Just past In Amguel there is a turning to the left signposted to Djanet (625 kilometres, 390 miles) a town in the east Sahara. About 15 miles beyond the Djanet junction is an area with mountains that look more like slag heaps dumped on the sand.

Fifty miles from Tamanrasset there is a fair road again which climbs the rugged Hoggar mountain range. The beauty of this range has to be seen to be believed. The pot holes have been filled in on this stretch of road, not with the usual dirt, but with tarmac. Unfortunately, however, this good road does not last long and soon you are back on sand.

At 1500 hours we passed the small oasis town of Tiet, with its wind powered water pumps, mud and grass huts, and a fort, and shortly after we were back on a road again, with a very good surface, recently laid. Approaching Tamanrasset the plains open out and a little further on is Tamanrasset airport, a civil and military airport combined, close to which is a large army camp. Opposite the airport is a large sandy area so we decided to take advantage of it to camp for the night and enter town first thing in the morning. The driving had been hard and dusty. The air was quite chilly here at 4,800 feet above sea level.

After a cold night we found it still so cold that we dressed in jeans or trousers. At 0800 we were heading for Tamanrasset — named after a beautiful woman — and the geographical centre of the desert. This town is forever expanding, nestled amongst the Hoggar, a rugged mountain range with Assekrem its highest peak at 9,600 feet. High up on Assekrem stands a simple stone building, the hermitage of Father Charles du Foucauld, the French missionary who was murdered by the Touaregs in 1916. This is a site much visited by tourists to the area but a four-wheel drive vehicle is necessary to reach it. In Tamanrasset and the desert surrounding it we met the Touaregs in their famous blue robes, and found it difficult to equate these peace-loving friendly people with their outlaw/robber existence of years gone by.

Entering Tamanrasset, we were surprised at the activity and cleanliness. There were several overlanders about, as this is just about the most interesting town. We stopped for a moment at the monument signifying the geographical centre of the Sahara Desert, before proceeding to a filling station to fill our tanks and jerry cans with fuel. But they had no water.

There is a large market, several good hotels, and streets lined with shops. Along the main street there are kerbs to the roads, street lights, and new buildings being erected everywhere, with a lot of new industry. There is a large post office, even a supermarket, but offering little choice: mainly tinned food, peaches and meat. They do, however, have a large supply of cheese, freshly flown in from Algiers: only two types though, Edam and Cheddar, freshly packed in cellophane, a welcome treat. Another commodity is torches: hundreds of them, and there are long queues of people after them.

We still had to find water so we asked at the police station, where they directed us to the main tourist hotel; but they would only fill one 5 gallon jerry can and then only if we spent the night there. We had to fill 4 x 5 gallon jerry cans, so we had a problem. All we could do was keep asking.

Remember that while in Tamanrasset you must check out with customs and immigration as this is your last town in Algeria. You must have your passports, carnet, and currency declaration stamped for exit and re-convert any currency you have left. At 10.30 we arrived at the frontier police station, and completed the necessary documentation for our departure, but could venture no further without water. We were sent from one petrol station to another without success, and in due course were directed to a well 3 miles out of town. However we could not find it. So back into town and keep asking. Eventually someone we had made friends with earlier in the morning agreed to take us to a well. He told us we would have no chance of getting water from it without him so we took him with us in and out of many small streets and over a lot of waste ground till eventually we came to the well, where we were able to fill all our jerry cans. We took our friend back into town and he directed us to the bakery on the opposite side of the dried-up river bed where we got fresh bread.

Tamanrasset to In Guezzam

Fully equipped, we asked our way out of town, as there are no signposts, and soon we were on the road to In Guezzam, the border town. The road is very good, freshly laid tarmac, and very wide. It is being laid by the army and is a completely new road and part of the Trans Saharan Highway. We passed another tracking station, and then a dried up river bed runs parallel with the road. There are also electricity pylons carrying cables but 13 miles out from Tamanrassset the cables disappear, although the pylons continue! We dipped into a wadi and started the slow descent from 4,500 feet. At 31 miles out from Tamanrasset the road ends, although there are signs of

*Be on your guard in areas of "drifting sands", as what looks like firm sand could be
a depression filled with soft sand and extreme care is necessary to prevent the vehicle
capsizing.*

roadworks and the road continuing much further in the near future.

At 3,250 feet we left the road and took to the river bed. Again all the mountains have a layer of sand on them giving the appearance of sand dunes. Far to our left at 3,000 ft we could still see the road works, with huge baskets or boulders forming the edges, to prevent water erosion. Every couple of miles we passed a road works base loaded with machinery for road building but did not see much work going on, probably because we were now into the Sabbath.

Some 45 miles from Tamanrasset we were still in the dried up river bed but very soon got back on to a tarred section of road again. However it was very badly potholed and corrugated, and it had been a much more comfortable ride in the river bed so back we went. We had seen no traffic since leaving Tamanrasset, and the temperature at 14.30 hours was up to 85 degrees, much warmer than the previous day.

We left the river bed at 64 miles out of Tamanrasset and took to the desert using the compass and following the markers placed 2 kilometres apart. These were sometimes 45 gallon drums, sometimes tall poles stuck in the sand. We passed many more burnt out wrecks of cars, presumably stolen and stripped for parts in the quietness of the desert. Vehicle parts are in great demand here and very expensive. The mountains become scarcer, and there is more open sand at 2,400 feet and 85 miles out of Tamanrasset.

1600 hours. The vast expanse of sand stretched before us epitomising everyone's dream of what the desert looks like: nothing but sand. Occasionally we passed a stony area, with the odd patch of scrub. We moved into softer sand and once more we were following the tracks of other vehicles, when suddenly we came across what looked like pushbike tracks. Pushbike tracks, out here miles from nowhere? The surface became firm again 100 miles south of Tamanrasset, and so smooth that we could hum over the sand comfortably at 60 miles an hour, seeing ahead for a great distance across the barren waste. At 1700 hours there they were again, cycle tracks in the sand, even places where the cyclist had fallen off. The fine pure sand, devoid of stones and rock, had a hard crust but there were soft patches. Dangerous regions for us were where trucks had become stuck and the wheels had dug deeper in the efforts to get out causing quite a hole; holes fill with fresh sand and level off leaving it very soft and dangerous.

The mountains were now few and far between with large flat areas of sand everywhere and a lot of ground vegetation, one type resembling small round pumpkins. We continued to follow the markers, although many of them were lying flat on the ground.

At 124 miles from Tamanrasset there was nothing but smooth hard topped sand, with only the odd soft spot; but we could see far enough ahead to drive round them. It was very comfortable riding at 60 mph over the sand, much more so than on some of the roads! But seeing some of the damage caused by the rain, we were glad it was not the wet season.

Light was fading, and it is foolish to drive in the desert after dark, so we pulled off the route and made camp for the night amongst a patch of 'desert pumpkins', but not before having a game of cricket with some of them.

At 0810 hours next morning still following the tracks, we met our cyclist, a brave Frenchman attempting to cycle across the desert! At least with a cycle he did not have to worry about getting stuck, or running out of petrol. We checked if he was okay; he had plenty of water but was low on food so we let him have some of ours, wished him luck, and continued on our way. At 0830 as we travelled over our sea of sand we could make out trees in the distance. The sun was up and it was warming up nicely. The route markers were now piles of rocks, some painted white, and our height was 2,000 feet.

The sand got softer as we passed through what looked like a graveyard for cars and a bus all burnt out in the sand, then suddenly we were stuck in soft sand, so it was a case of everybody out and push, for we were not in too deep. A few minutes and we were away again. To our left as we moved off were large sand dunes, while to the right were low mountains. Soon we were stuck again, this time in softer sand and much deeper, so we had to use the sand ladders, moving forward about 10 feet at a time, then replacing the ladders in front of the wheels for another 10 feet. It took four or five moves to get back on firm ground and away again. We had some huge sand dunes around us now and even the mountains had sand piled up against them. The road wove in and out and around dunes which the shifting sands had piled in the middle of the track. The surface of the sand was less smooth now and large stones on the surface gave us a very bumpy ride.

1130 hours. We were driving over rock, reducing our speed considerably. Then a sand storm blew up cutting visibility right down. We were now at 1,200 feet and 100 miles from In Guezzam. The temperature outside was over 90° and as we had been doing some hard driving through soft sand, the vehicle was beginning to overheat. We stopped for a while to let it cool down, and also deflate the tyres slightly to give us more flotation and reduce the chances of us sinking into the sand. This works, but the engine has to work even harder and overheats quicker.

At 20 miles from the border the sand had been blown away from the route exposing bare rock. We had to drive over this very slowly and carefully for some miles, with the occasional gust of wind lifting clouds of sand in our path, before finding firm sand again.

In the distance were the trees that signify In Guezzam and the border post. It is a small village with a military post and small military airport. There are several mud huts and an abandoned fort. All of the buildings are probably the homes of the border officials. There is a well and a diesel pump to bring the water up but it is only operated at certain times. There is a filling station, but it seldom has fuel: in fact the driver of a Citroen had been waiting there for fuel for 5 days, so we were glad we had filled to capacity in Tamanrasset and had enough to get to the next main town. There is also one shop here but they have little stock: just sardines, corned beef, condensed milk and soap.

On reporting to the border customs we found them closed from noon to 1600 hours, and as it was only 1330, we parked, had a wash, and sorted out the vehicle. Mel re-inflated the tyres and then we had a look round. At 1500 hours we joined the queue of half a dozen vehicles waiting to cross, hoping the post would open early: it gets dark between 1700 and 1730 and it is forbidden to drive in the desert after dark. We were lucky and we soon had our passports stamped, got through customs and by 1550 were on our way out of Algeria and heading for the Niger border, and Assamaka, the Niger checkpoint 16 miles across the desert.

Niger

Moving away from the border post we passed a lookout tower on a hill to our left. The sand here was very soft so we tried to keep moving, following the markers which were not too clearly defined; but after ten minutes we got stuck, so it was out with the sand ladders and we were away again first time.

Some 10 miles on we came across an army encampment, and a sign with 'Niger Border' on it, but no indication as to which way to go so we had to stop and ask at the camp. On the right track at last we travelled along at 50 mph over flat firm sand, past a herd of camels accompanied by two Arabs. At 1640 we arrived at the Niger border post which is no more than a group of caravans and tents in the desert, miles from anywhere.

There were several other vehicles waiting at the checkpoint — not a good sign — and it made matters worse when we discovered that one group of Swiss travellers had been there a week, and were now out of food and water.

Our turn in the queue soon came, and the officials instructed us to turn *everything* out of the vehicle. They then proceeded to go through it all with a fine tooth comb, including the cases containing our photographic equipment to which they took an instant dislike, particularly the telephoto lenses. Mel and Mick were taken along with all their gear to one of the huts/offices, where the officials went through all the equipment again, and then sent Mel and Mick back without it. They could not speak French, the official language in this country, and a French lady came to their aid, explaining to the officials that they were amateur photographers, and not journalists spying on them as was believed. The officials insisted that Mel and Mick should have photographic visas.

At 1820 hours the border was closed, which meant we were there for the night, along with all the other travellers. We put one of the tents up for the night. There was a brisk breeze blowing which made the tent erection difficult, but we managed eventually. I decided to sleep in the vehicle for security reasons. The wind blew strongly all night but for a change we were warm.

In the morning we had a lay in, as the border did not re-open until 0900 and we did not expect to be allowed to go then in any case. It was Mick's birthday, the first spent away from home, and in the middle of the desert too! The diaries the others were keeping had also been confiscated the night before but returned soon afterwards. However we had to be careful when completing them in case it was interpreted wrongly, so while I kept guard the rest started getting their books up to date, out of sight in the tent. By 0930 the sun was up but there was a severe sand storm blowing, making things very uncomfortable. By 10.30 we were still waiting. These things cannot be rushed so we did nothing else but wait.

Ten minutes later we were approached by one of the policemen who, presumably, had started duty that morning. He looked in the vehicle and counted the seats, then looked at us and figured out we had a couple of spare seats. He then asked me if we had room to take a policeman to Arlit, 132 miles across the sand. Knowing this could be our ticket away from the place, I readily agreed, explaining that our passports were being held together with our photographic equipment. "I will fix that," was the reply, and within a few minutes, we had all our gear back, together with our passports, duly stamped, and our carnet, unstamped as it had to be cleared in Arlit. We waited for the police officer who was to accompany us, and meanwhile his friends began bringing his luggage: drums of oil, sacks of potatoes, gas bottles etc! Spoils of his term of duty presumably, from travellers who did not want to be held up or penalised. As we were very close to our weight limit, we politely refused the gas bottle and some of the oil, explaining our position, keeping our fingers crossed all the time. Fortunately he agreed to leave those items behind. A few minutes later we were ready to move off with our policeman passenger sitting in the back seat next to Mick, his service rifle between his knees.

Assamaka to Arlit

The sand storm was still blowing as we left. We were only too well aware of the dangers involved in driving through a sand storm, but could not lose the opportunity to move away from this particular border post. The sand was soft to start with, and visibility so poor that we were only just able to make out the 45-gallon drum markers. However our travelling companion knew the way well and he corrected us several times as we strayed from the route. The distance between each marker here is about two kilometres. This stretch to Arlit would be our last stretch of the Sahara desert, but I knew only too well that it could be the most treacherous, with large areas of soft sand, sharp rock with thin layers of sand hiding it, and shifting dunes that can enforce long detours. This is a stretch where binoculars are essential.

We had now crossed into the extremely poor, landlocked, semi-desert country of Niger. Soon we would be out of the Africa of the Arab and into black Africa.

By noon we were 24 miles from the border, driving over an area of sand that looked more like a shingle beach with the stones well worn and compressed into the sand. Here we changed direction from north-east to east, heading directly into the sandstorm, but fortunately the markers were now only one kilometre apart. After another mile we changed direction again, this time to head south, and after another two miles we turned south-east.

By 12.30 the storm was clearing a little, with blue sky showing through although the sand was still swirling around us.

We were now passing large sand dunes and the surface was good firm

215

gravel. Some 41 miles from Assamaka we bore south again, and passed an Arab with two children walking through the sand storm. They seemed a long way from home out in the wilderness.

An hour later we lost the markers, but our policeman took over, guiding us over layered rock with a lot of scrub and sand grass amongst it, as we clocked 56 miles from Assamaka. Suddenly the sand storm blew itself out and we could see clearly for miles. Another mile and we were at a 'junction' unsure which route to take, but our policeman knew. However we had not gone far when we were bogged down, so out came the sand ladders, and without too much bother we were free.

After 65 miles the going got tough. The road was up and down like a roller coaster. The high sections were firm, but the storm had filled the dips with soft sand and we had to speed through them to avoid getting stuck, sinking in the sand at times to the depth of our wheels. We cleared the area safely and were soon back on firm shingle again as we passed a pair of ringed plovers foraging in the sand.

At 73 miles from Assamaka we were on good flat smooth desert again, with markers every kilometre. Our height above sea level was still 1,200 feet. Our average speed over the last 90 miles from Assamaka was 25 mph, which was not bad considering what we had been through. There was now the odd tree on our route and we also passed a Touareg with his camel. We had to stop to let the Land Rover cool down and realised we were entering a long belt of small thorn trees — a sign that there must be water around somewhere.

We set off again at 1540, with just 18 miles to go to Arlit. The sand was soft again, and in the distance we could see smoke rising. After 13 miles we passed the source of the smoke, a French-run uranium mine on our right and an airstrip. We also saw our first road signs for some time, followed by a dual carriageway, with dirt surface, presumably constructed for access from the uranium mine to Arlit.

At 1615 we finally arrived in Arlit and our companion guided us to his base, and assisted us in getting our passports cleared for Niger. He then offered his thanks, we all shook hands, and he directed us to a building further up the street where we had to get our carnet stamped.

We were now in a typical African community, with open butchers by the roadside, vendors cooking meat and doughnuts on open fires, buxom topless African women carrying goods on their heads and the baby strapped to their back, and the usual mud huts.

Arlit to Tahoua

At 17.10 we set out for Agadez, 148 miles away, and found we were back on a good tarmac-surfaced road again. We felt pleased as we had successfully achieved one of our main objectives on this trip; the north south crossing of the Sahara Desert. However, after a short distance on good roads, we would be back in the desert again, on a little used and tricky section, as we intended to visit the legendary town of Timbuktoo.

After a wind-less and fairly warm night, we were up at 0700 and after breakfast were on the road for our first complete day's travel in Niger. The countryside was broken savanna 1,800 ft above sea level, with rocky hills on the right. A Thompsons gazelle leapt across the road in front of us, and our road passed through herds of camels, goats, and a few donkeys.

At 53 miles from Arlit we were stopped at a police check point, with permanent barriers right across the road. They checked our passports and we were on our way again. The road remained good, but it passed through rocky terrain with low shrub scattered along the whole area and prolific bird and animal life. We passed a couple of huts made of mud and straw as we dipped into a wadi. The wadis can be seen clearly from some way off on account of the greenery surrounding them, and at that season there were straw huts erected close to the wadi edge in anticipation of the rains.

Some 96 miles from Arlit we passed through areas that looked like agricultural holdings, with fine herds of longhorn steers roaming around. We were now up to 2,000 feet again, and the temperature was 91 degrees.

With an excellent road we soon reached Agadez, an interesting town with its unusual mosque tower and multi-racial inhabitants. This is the main destination of the Touareg caravans, bringing huge slabs of salt, strapped to the sides of their camels, from Bilma, deep in the desert. A much sought after souvenir of this town is the 'Agadez Cross' with a history and tradition stretching back many years. There are one or two good hotels in Agadez and the market is well worth a visit. We tried unsuccessfully to change money here but didn't linger.

As we left the town boundary we were stopped again by a police check who wanted to see the passports and vehicle papers. There are many such checks but with a friendly attitude they should not prove any problem.

The road was still good but the surrounding countryside had changed little over the past 150 miles: still open savanna with shrub and now more larger trees. We were now on the road to Tahoua, at 1,600 feet.

The whole countryside appeared to be in the grip of a severe drought, with everywhere looking very dry, but 50 miles from Agadez we passed a large water hole, with water in it and cattle drinking. The terrain here takes on a different appearance. It is not so flat, and the sand gives way to soil. There is grass on both sides of the road, and large termite hills here and there.

At 1400 hours we approached a casual police check, but the police were sitting under the verandah of their building out of the hot afternoon sun, and waved us on. We were at 2,000 feet and everywhere looked very parched and dry. The roadside is bordered by large trees, but they had few leaves on them. We passed more water holes but they were all dry. Even the cattle were affected by the heat, standing in the road and refusing to move to let us pass. The roads were almost devoid of traffic. We had travelled 160 miles from Agadez and the only vehicles we had encountered were a couple of tourist Land Rovers parked up a few miles back. Out of curiosity, we stopped at a well, surrounded by cattle and found that the depth to the surface of the water was 75 metres. Donkeys worked in relays, hauling the water up.

Around 177 miles from Agadez we passed through the small town of Abalak, with its mud huts, straw 'wigwams', and sun-affected cattle wandering in the road, making sure we detour and drive round them. Just outside this town we passed a pair of beautiful saddle billed storks standing a little way back from the edge of the road.

At 1650 hours having travelled a total of 360 miles over some of the best roads we have been on in Africa we decided it was far enough for the day so pulled off the road for the night. We soon had our tents up and were joined the next minute by one of the locals, armed with an axe over his shoulder and a sword by his side. He appeared to be a deaf mute so we used sign language with him. He had a herd of goats with him, and was obviously the herdsman. We made him welcome at our camp, which seemed strongly advisable as we were probably on his land. He stayed for some while, eating tea with us, and then, as darkness fell, suddenly rose and disappeared into the distance.

We were up at 0700 hours and soon back on our good road. We had not gone far when we passed a couple of fields of maize, and there were also some vegetables growing. Next to the grass huts at the edge of each field were water storage jars, some 10 ft high, and made of clay.

At 38 miles from Tahoua all the plant life looked a lot healthier. There was certainly water here somewhere, for the trees had a greener appearance. We were at 1400 feet, and at 0830 hours the temperature was already 70 degrees. A heat haze restricted visibility but we could see herds of goats just back off the road munching away at some fresh green shoots of grass, and a little further along the road, African women with huge bundles of branches balanced on their heads, presumably heading for their fire.

We were now passing more and more native settlements along the roadside and, in the poorest country in Africa, we were beginning to see how people live. We saw the African women walking round in the most colourful clothing, the men in the field harvesting the maize, thrashing the corn cobs to extract the seed; the women standing next to tall earthenware jars (sometimes the jars are carved from a solid lump of tree trunk) pounding away at corn in the bottom with tall thick poles, grinding it into flour; and the local children, dressed in rags, by the side of the road playing. We passed through a village, and then encountered several wadis and also a few bridges. Each and every bridge or wadi is named and the name is displayed on a plaque a little way along the road as you approach.

We passed through Koloma Baba and then approached Tahoua. At the outskirts of the village are mud huts, so well constructed and baked hard by the sun that they are equal in strength to some brick-built buildings. The local African kids were by the roadside again waving as we passed. We stopped at a police station and asked directions to the bank as we had to change our money to the CFA Franc of Niger.

While Mel and I were in the bank our vehicle was suddenly surrounded by local children, inquisitive to say the least. Mick and Tony were sitting inside the vehicle for safety and soon had dozens of people of all ages around them. It is not often that they find white people driving through their town. Some of the smaller kids were begging, and would have been more than satisfied with a toffee each. Then a couple of girls appeared with trays on their heads loaded with bananas, mangoes and nuts for sale and along came a couple of chaps selling home forged knives and swords. After explaining that they had no money, Tony and Mick lost a lot of the crowd, but a few persisted, eventually giving their wares away, so the two inside the Land Rover ended up with several bananas and nuts. I was inside the bank for well over an hour while the others were enjoying their first taste of a portable African market. As I left the bank, the natives with the knives returned, and I had a look at them. They were very well made but we had such a long way to go yet, and if we were to start carrying knives and things, their possession might be misinterpreted by some border guards.

Driving slowly through the town, we were besieged by children with begging bowls and adults with trays on their heads and an assortment of goodies such as corn on the cob, sugar cane, peanuts, fruit and even cooked meat. We then visited the market to re-stock with provisions, and the scene there was much the same: old women seated on the ground surrounded by piles of oranges, yams, or peanuts; some cooking monkey or goat meat over an open fire, most of them with an adornment of coloured robes, and many with babies strapped to their backs.

After stocking up with provisions, we drove to a small café that we had spotted on the way in for a meal of chicken and rice. Our meal finished, we were besieged by kids outside, so gave them the chicken bones. You would think they had not eaten for months as they bit into the bones like dogs. This was a real eye-opener to starvation and poverty.

Tahoua to Niamey

By 1320 hours we were on our way out of Tahoua and heading for Niamey, the capital of Niger. It is from Tahoua that most overlanders travel south and take the road to Birni Nkonni and straight into Nigeria; but we were travelling west to Timbuktoo on this trip, although we followed the road south for a while. Eleven miles out we were diverted onto a dirt track from the tarmac road as work was in progress building a bridge. The diversion took us round the edge of a maize field and back onto the road. Half an hour later we crossed a newly built bridge, this time with water flowing under it. There were now low hills by the roadside, and plenty of greenery about. We were now at 1100 feet and travelling at 55 mph on a good road.

At 62 miles from Tahoua we passed through the village of Saliva, adorned with the usual mud huts, some square, some rectangular, some circular. Some of them are built on rocks so that they are off the ground, while others have a perimeter wall around them, constructed of mud.

Some 95 miles from Tahoua we passed a large T.V. booster mast; the road veers sharply to the right and westwards to run parallel with the Nigerian border, while a section of road goes straight on to Birni Nkonni and the Niger/Nigeria border control only a few hundred yards away. The heat haze was still with us and the temperature at 1500 hours was 95 degrees. We were seeing more wildlife, with vultures, eagles, rollers and shrikes appearing frequently.

At 1600 hours we passed through another mud hut village: Yaya, with a large water hole and vegetable patches surrounding it. Trees close to the water looked healthy, but those further back appeared parched. Ten miles further we saw a lot of yellow grass growing again. After another four miles we passed through the village of Manseyha and just past this village, we pulled off the road for the night.

Mel had a close shave during the night. He was taken short and made a hasty exit from the tent, torch in hand. While he was standing facing the bushes he felt something run over his foot. Shining the torch on his foot he saw a full grown scorpion scampering away. Mel decided to stay in the tent till daylight in future.

We were up at 0615 the next morning so we could make an early start and, after a quick breakfast, we were on our way. The temperature at this time of morning was 65 degrees. We hadn't gone far when the Land Rover engine started missing, so we stopped and the mechanics had a look at it. Fortunately, it was nothing more serious than a dirty air filter, so after a quick clean we were on our way again.

At 0730 we passed through Kombrey and then Kassari. About 27 miles from our camp site the flat plain became more undulated and there were low plateaux on either side of the road. After 41 miles we passed through Matankari, a fairly large town. The road was still good, enabling us to reach 60 mph. We passed a dead cow by the roadside, disturbing a couple of vultures feeding on its flesh. After 43 miles we came to Badifa, a busy little town, with the women grinding the corn the same way it has been done for centuries. Through this village we saw our first baobab tree. Two miles outside Badifa is another booster mast and close by several round dome-roofed huts on stilts.

Through Bolbol and then, an hour later, Dosso where we were stopped at a checkpoint. They checked our passports and took all our names and passport numbers before we were allowed to proceed. Dosso appeared more modern than some of the towns we had passed through. There were even push bikes in the streets.

After 140 miles we stopped on top of a ridge and looked down onto the next town of Koigorou and the length and breadth of the savanna plain.

We were making very good time on the excellent roads and soon passed a road sign showing Niamey as 30 miles away. High in the sky above us we saw our first swallows, who were in their winter home.

We entered the outskirts of Niamey and, as usual when entering large towns, we were stopped at a road block for passport and car papers check. Niamey sits on the banks of the great River Niger, which has its source in the Loma Mountains on the Sierra Leone/Guinea border, and meanders its way over 2,200 miles through Guinea, Mali, Niger, forms part of the northern border of Benin, and finally enters the sea in Southern Nigeria. This river features prominently in this trip.

Niamey is a busy place, with traffic lights, policemen on point duty, roundabouts, street lights, and kerbs — all uncommon in African towns. Our first objective here was to obtain a photographic visa for our next country, Mali, for I had experienced trouble taking photographs on previous trips. We found our way to the Mali Embassy without too much trouble, but they could not help us and suggested we applied in the first main town in Mali. We then visited the police station for permission to take photographs in Niamey, but the officer we had to see was out till 1700. We tried the banks to change some money but they were all closed until 1600, another 3 hours, and hotels would not help us with money exchange. So in the short time we had been in Niamey we had not done too well. We did, however, find a filling station that had petrol, and filled our main tanks. We then drove to the river bank for a little sightseeing to pass the time until the banks opened. On arrival at the river, we were amazed at the size of it. It must have been 1,000 yards across. We wandered along the bank, watching the locals having a wash, or washing their clothes. We passed quite a few vegetable plots on the river banks, with crops such as lettuce, onions, carrots, cabbages, and leeks flourishing. No shortage of water for the plants here. Further along the bank we came to a small riverside market, selling mainly fish. There was an old horse that seemed to be on its last legs tied to a tree, men, women and children splashing in the water's edge, and wooden canoes carved from a whole tree trunk, some 50 feet long, ferrying passengers across the river.

All African markets have an atmosphere about them, an attraction that appears to draw tourists such as us like a magnet. It is a marvellous experience to walk round these markets, meet people, and talk with them and discover more about their way of life. Nearly all of them want to say "hello", and they all wear an instant smile, despite the poverty in which they are living.

As soon as it was opening time for the banks, we made our way to the nearest branch, and cashed a little money to see us to the border. We then proceeded to the police station. At 1700 precisely the officer arrived, but merely told us we did not require a visa to take photographs in Niamey, so that was that, and we were on our way out of town. We stopped at the "exit" barrier, and handed over our passports for checking. We were then waved through. As time was getting on we only drove a little way out of town before turning off the road and erecting camp for the night.

Niamey to the border

It was a warm night, even sleeping naked on top of our sleeping bags, and when we arose at 0700 the temperature was still 68 degrees. At 0800 it was 78 degrees. We headed north west, towards the Mali border, and another session in the Sahara. The surrounding countryside was very flat, and the road good to Tillabery 75 miles away. We were at 1,000 feet above sea level and occasionally caught a glimpse of the River Niger way over on our left — as it would be for the next 540 miles all the way to Timbuktoo.

We passed through a few small mud hut villages, already in the full swing of their daily routine, herds of goats and cattle roaming everywhere. We overtook an African bus, loaded to capacity, with cattle and goats tied down on the roof rack, which made us wonder just how they got them up there.

At 0930 we drove through Tillabery, a quiet little town with just one or two shops. We stopped at the post office to send mail home, and then continued on our way. As we left we came to the end of the tarmac and were back on a dirt road with a firm surface, fairly well maintained with loose stone coverings in places. However, it was fairly rough. As we travelled along at a steady 30 mph, leaving a huge cloud of dust behind us, we passed a field of sugar cane sprouting from the rich looking soil. We were running close to the river and could see the crops running down to the water's edge, where the natives were poling their canoes against the fast running current.

The river appeared to be in full flood, in stark contrast to some of the areas we had been through. Fifteen miles from town we were on a fairly good road with a loose gravel surface and were able to travel along at 50 mph, but with care for many herds of cattle and goats cross the road to and from the river, tracks that they follow every day, digging deep furrows into the already hard packed ground.

At 11.40 we arrived at the border town of Ayorou, and how different the attitude of the border officials compared with those we had encountered on entering Niger. These were friendly, smiling and courteous. They had a quick look around the vehicle while we bought some freshly cooked goat meat from a local trader, which we shared with the customs officials. After a friendly chat, they opened the barrier and we were on our way after a stop of only fifteen minutes. It was another hour before we arrived at the immigration control, where the attitude of the officials was just as friendly. While they checked our passports, we had a game with the local kids for five minutes and then we were on our way. Goodbye Niger!

Mali

Our first stretch of road in Mali was dirt and heavily corrugated, restricting our speed to around 15 mph. We arrived in Labézanga, Mali's border town at 1340, and while Mel took our passports and car papers into the office, the rest of the group assisted me in topping up our main tank with petrol from the jerry cans. This was a mistake, for the police saw us and, thinking we had some to spare in an area where there is little petrol available, came over and asked us to let them have some. It is very difficult to refuse a person who controls your entry into a country, no matter what he is asking, but we explained as best we could that it was all we had, and luckily for us they did not persist. Then we went to the customs check, where they also wanted to see the car papers, but there were no problems so we were soon on our way again, and were now officially in Mali, another poor country but one of the most interesting in the African Continent. It is an enchanting land, distinguished by its culture, history, scenery and variety of people, bound together by the cool flowing waters of the Niger river.

The port of Mopti, which we did not have an opportunity to visit on this trip, is commonly known as the "Venice of Mali". It is a floating bazaar where native boats from far north and far south meet, inhabited by ornately dressed Fulani girls and Bozo fishermen.

Like Agadez in Niger, this is another melting pot of many different tribes, where traders meet to trade their wares, and where salt slabs are marketed after being brought from the deep Sahara. Farther south from Mopti is Djenne, a historic town dating back to the eighth century, on an island accessible only by boat for three quarters of the year.

Labézanga to Gao

Our road was straight, but very bumpy and corrugated. Most of the wadis are bridged but they are in very poor condition necessitating care. Those wadis that are not bridged are very steep and we had to slow down to walking pace to negotiate them. Forty minutes and fifteen miles later we passed our first

222

mud village. The road was still bad, shaking us all about in the vehicle. Fifteen minutes later we decided we had had enough for one day and pulled off the road. We were all in need of a good wash so we engaged all four wheels of the vehicle and drove in the direction of the River Niger. We could not see it as we left the road but after driving through the undergrowth and shrub for a mile, we arrived at its bank and, after checking the water to ensure it was clean enough, we all stripped off and jumped in. There are so many diseases that can be encountered in African waters that you have to be very careful but, in general, if the water is clear and running, as this was, it should be safe.

After a good soak, we were able to have a look round, and were amazed at the wonderful array of wildlife in the area where we had chosen to camp for the night. We were right on the river bank, but the main flow of water was some way out, the other side of a thick reed bed bordering the river. Out came our binoculars until the loss of daylight defeated us. We noted crested cranes, stone curlews, stone plovers, black hadada, sacred ibis, herons, ducks, geese and many others too numerous to mention. Then, on the other side of a rivulet running into the Niger, about 100 yards from where we were camping, Mick spotted something which gave us all a great deal of excitement — giraffes: about half-a-dozen feeding on the low thorn acacia trees along the water's edge. We all watched these majestic animals until darkness fell when we could hear hippopotamus bellowing from the edge of the reed bed in the river. This was certainly one of nature's wonderlands. Then, as soon as light was gone, we had a chorus of bullfrogs calling from all around us. It was not going to be a peaceful night, but who cared? It was the sort of noise we welcomed and could easily tolerate: the true sound of Africa.

Mel and Mick were up at 0600 the next morning, birdwatching, and the rest of us soon joined them. The birds were still there but the giraffes had gone, and at the water's edge we occasionally saw a frog surfacing for air.

At 0830 we started to move off, sorry to leave this place. We rejoined the road and headed towards Gao. The road was still dirt and very rough, and in the first hour's travel we only covered 18 miles. Then the surrounding countryside took on a gravelly appearance to match the road and the trees and bushes began to look very dry again.

At 1025 we approached the town of Ansongo where we had to stop and clear customs. Mel took in the necessary paperwork and we were soon on our way again. Next was the police check, which we nearly missed as the barrier was open and the place not too clearly marked. There were also many people about, making it more difficult to spot. Having driven past the post, we reversed back and Mel went in with the paperwork, while the rest of us stayed outside telling the border officials what they could not have — they always wanted something from us, normally whatever they could see.

The town of Ansongo is situated right by the river, and we had a splendid view across the water to the reed beds, with the natives in their canoes drifting about cutting the reeds for drying, to be used eventually for roofing their huts.

It was very hot as we left Ansongo. Just outside the town the terrain once again took on a desert appearance with large areas of sand surrounding the bushes and trees. The road was still dirt and very bumpy, although straight, and in places we followed where other vehicles had 'sidetracked' very bad sections by driving into the bush and then back onto the road again when it improved. We kept sinking into soft sandy sections, with the engine sump shield scraping the surface of the sand, but we were fortunate enough not to get stuck. The road was once again running very close to the river and there was a wonderful array of bird life all around us. The temperature at 1100 was 96 degrees and getting hotter all the time although there was a welcome cool breeze. By noon the heat of the day, combined with the hard work of pushing through soft sand, was causing the engine to overheat, so we drove to the top of a small hillock by the side of the road where we could gain the full advantage of the breeze. We manoeuvred the vehicle until the engine faced into the wind and waited, scanning the excellent view of the river through our binoculars. The temperature outside was 108° and we could certainly feel it. Overhead we spotted a couple of rare griffon vultures circling. They obviously knew what the heat does to people!

When the engine temperature was down to below normal, we left our hillock and returned to the road for the final run to Gao. As we approached, we drove through an avenue of palm trees, noticing a small swarm of locusts flying amongst them. We passed the airport and a number of radio masts before being stopped at a customs road block. Mel took the paperwork in and we were soon cleared and instructed to report to police H.Q. in Gao.

As we entered Gao we were back on tarmac road again for a short while, although potholes made it less comfortable than the dirt road. We arrived at the police H.Q. after a long search at 1330 hours, and Mel and I took our passports inside. We wanted photographic visas and hoped to get them here along with the entry pass we needed but the person responsible for signing the passports was away until the next day. We would have to wait. This meant hanging about in Gao, the sort of delay we had been expecting all along but up to now had managed to miss.

We did not want to leave the Land Rover unattended: it is not wise. So we took turns walking round town, visiting the markets, and the riverside. The markets here do not have much in the way of variety: in fact, apart from locally grown peanuts and vegetables, all we could see was tinned pineapple juice and soap. There is, however, a long line of Singer sewing machines manned by the local men and women, busy stitching material of all colours. We then drove to another market by the river which was much the same except that dried fish and meat were on sale — also packets of biscuits, but the price was very high. The children in this town are friendly and not always on the cadge as in most other African towns. In fact they surrounded us and gave us peanuts and sweets and shared their apples and cakes.

With little to do until the next day, and little left to see, we slowly made our way out on the Timbuktoo road to find a camp site for the night. We drove for a couple of miles through the immense palm groves that border the roadside, then left the sand road and headed towards the river, pitching camp right on the edge amongst the palms. There was not the array of bird life of the previous night, but we did have the bull frogs to sing us to sleep.

After a quiet night's sleep in our exotic camp site, we were all up at 0545, had a quick breakfast, took a couple of photographs, and drove back into town to the police H.Q. to collect our passports. However, we soon found out that it was not that easy. Mel went in alone and returned with some forms that had to be completed. We returned the forms and were then told to wait. Apparently the officer who had to sign our passports did not feel like doing it just then, and what could we do about it? Next thing we knew he had gone off for a couple of hours, with our passports still unsigned. Mel spent most of his time walking in and out of the police station, just to let our presence be felt, in the hope that it might prompt them to sign the passports and be rid of us. At noon, it was 107 degrees and scorching hot. At 1300 the officer returned and, after giving him a few minutes to settle down, Mel went in again. He returned almost immediately with our passports duly stamped and signed with both entry pass and photographic visa, but with the discouraging news that we must repeat the process in each main town in Mali, as each town is in a different district and requires a separate pass and photographic visa.

Gao to Timbuktoo

We finally left Gao on the Timbuktoo road, travelling through groves of palm trees. We still had the river in sight and we could make out some large sand dunes on the opposite side. Some 12 miles from Gao we stopped for five giraffes crossing the road and followed them for a while to take some photographs. We were able to get quite close to these majestic looking animals, which were peacefully nibbling at the fresh green leaves of the thorn trees. As we drove on we passed a group of Africans travelling on their donkeys. The terrain was very flat and becoming very dry.

At 36 miles from Gao we had to stop again to let the vehicle cool down. We were on a firm patch of ground but could tell by the parched appearance and cracks that this area is under water when it rains. At 45 miles out of Gao the road becomes very rough, with deep ruts filled with soft sand, and close corrugations, so we took to the dried up lake beds which make for a much more comfortable ride. This section of road is level with or below the level of the surrounding countryside and clearly during the wet season it must be covered with water and impassable.

At 51 miles from Gao the sand dunes began to close in on the road, covering it a foot deep in places and making our progress very difficult. After a couple of miles the sand cleared as we entered the outskirts of Bourem. This is a picturesque village in the middle of an area of sand dunes, a typical desert town, for now we were once again entering the Sahara proper. North of Bourem is pure desert, while to the south is something that most desert towns do not have: a deep, fast flowing river, with all the water imaginable, lush green reed beds stretching out almost to the edge of the current some 150 yards from the river bank. Bourem is quiet, just about on the edge of civilisation, for it is the last 'main' village before Timbuktoo over 200 miles away over the sand. There are no road signs here — in fact the only road is the one we came in on — there are just tracks left by previous vehicles branching out in all directions over the sand dunes. It is easy to see how Timbuktoo entered legend as a place in the middle of nowhere: a town miles from any civilisation or road. We had to find our way to it through 200 miles of wild untamed desert, using only the stars and our compass for navigation. It would be most unwise to follow the tracks of other vehicles: who knows where they lead? There is, however, one big navigational aid: the River Niger. As long as we keep the river to our left, and hopefully in sight, we should not get lost.

It took us three quarters of an hour to find our way out of the village, after going round in circles, driving through people's 'back yards', and at one stage zooming down a track we'd been told went to Timbuktoo only to find the river at the end. Eventually we were away, driving over the sand dunes, and taking compass bearings while on the move for fear of sinking in the sand should we stop. This was going to be the toughest section of the desert encountered on our trip, but we all looked forward to it. Not many people take this route and we could see why.

We took an undulating course over the sand dunes, occasionally dipping into a dried up river or lake bed, which is firmer and kinder on the engine. This is certainly a 4 x 4 route only. After only an hour we had to stop to let the engine cool, and were rather concerned as we seemed to be heading away from the river, but it is impossible to keep the river always in sight because of the thick undergrowth. Riding over the sand is fairly smooth going, but occasionally rock appears on the surface making the going very bumpy. A lot of the time we followed tracks of other vehicles heading in our direction, but they kept splitting up and heading off into the bushes to goodness knows where.

At 15 miles from Bourem we could see the river again over on our left, much to our relief, and made out fishing huts along its edge. The Land Rover was overheating again owing to labouring hard in the soft sand, so we decided to head towards the river for the night. We came to a halt amongst some huts in a fishing village, and were at once surrounded by hordes of friendly African villagers. The village leader came over and introduced himself, and told us in fluent French that we were the first white people he had seen in two years. We once again noticed the wonderful array of bird life here at the river's edge and the village leader, noticing our interest, offered to go out and shoot a duck for our tea. We declined, however, partly because we had no method of cooking it and partly we preferred the duck on the water.

Soon we were in the clear running water for a swim and wash. We were then given a tour of the village. A surprising feature was the vegetable garden, a communal one for the village, containing first class lettuce, onions, and tomato plants.

As darkness drew in the frogs began to sing, and the locals disappeared to their huts. There was a beautiful sunset but there were thousands of mosquitoes about so we soon retired to our tents.

We were up at 0600 the next morning, hoping to get a good start with the Land Rover before the day got too hot. There was a splendid sunrise. By 0630 we were on our way, re-tracing our tracks to the spot where we left the main route, and heading west into the soft sand once more. We were surrounded by trees, shrubs, and sand dunes, and there were car tracks everywhere. The sand was still very soft and we swayed from side to side like a ship in a rough sea as one wheel then another sank into a sand-filled hole. After 20 miles the bushes began to disappear and all we had ahead of us were clumps of grass. After another 10 miles we arrived at a fishing village, losing the route and tyre tracks completely, but after scouting around we found our way again, only to sink straight into a spot of soft sand, much to the amusement of the locals. However, about 25 pairs of hands pushed us and we were on our way again amidst cheers, laughter and waving.

At 0845 we had to stop and sort the back of the vehicle out after 'taking off' on some concealed banks in the sand. It was very tough going and our top speed was 18 mph. Suddenly the tracks split up, one lot to the south and one lot to the north. We assumed that the tracks to the south were going towards a fishing village, so we took those to the north and after a few minutes found a hand-painted road sign nailed to a tree with 'Bamba' on it and pointing back the way we had come. Bamba is the only main fishing village on our route and is right on the river bank.

The sky was clear and the sun blazing down on us. The sand all round us looked smooth and inviting, but there were many dips and holes into which soft sand had blown which we were unaware of until we hit them.

The front wheels took off, throwing us into the air, followed by the back wheels which then threw all our luggage into the air. The sand was so soft that it came up to our hubs, and it was hard going on the vehicle, so we had to stop every 40 minutes or so to let the engine cool. Over the dry lake beds we could put our foot down, but as we came up the other side it was a case of bumpety-bump again, no matter how slowly we travelled. Our average mileage was down to 12 per hour, and we had not seen the river for some time although the tracks and the compass told us we were heading in the right direction. We eventually decided to drive well away from the tracks in the hope that the ride would be smoother for we feared our roof rack was cracking up.

At noon we found our first helpful road sign: 'Timbuktoo 84 miles'. Twenty minutes later we stopped once more to let the engine cool after a long stretch of soft sand. There was a brisk breeze from the north east which speeded up the process.

At 68 miles from Timbuktoo we had the river in sight again as we passed over another dry lake bed with several deep ruts in it, presumably left there by a heavy truck that had travelled this way during the rainy season. No sooner had we cleared the dried up lake bed than we were in soft sand again, and on variable terrain, so had to reduce speed to keep ourselves and the contents of the vehicle in place. When we stopped again to cool off the engine, Mel let the tyres down a little to give us more flotation on the soft sand, and reduce the thrashing the vehicle was getting from the bumpy undersurface. We were now compelled to cool the engine every 10 to 15 miles, so hard was the going. We passed an area where dead trees had been cut down and used to form a stockade surrounding a barren area of land. We could not determine the reason for this and could only guess it was to keep predators away from cattle.

At 1400 we crossed with a vehicle going in the opposite direction, a light truck driven by an African. It was the first we had seen since leaving Gao. At 1530 hours we decided to find a camp site for the night, rather earlier than normal, but after one of the roughest stretches on our journey to date. There was a lot of work to be done to the vehicle, and a lot of sorting out to be done with our luggage, so we turned off the road and headed once more for the river, after first taking a bearing. We had no idea how far away the river was and, after 2 miles, we were on top of a ridge and could see for a mile or so ahead, but no river! So rather than go any farther and get totally lost, we camped there for the night, with only crickets for company.

We were up at 0600 the next morning, and after breakfast were soon on our way again. We had taken a lot of weight off the roof rack the night before and put it inside the car to make the going a little easier. We were not too far from Timbuktoo now, and the road was a little better although there were still some hidden ruts we had to watch out for. There was plenty of grass amongst the trees and a lot of cattle wandering about, as well as camels, while close to the road we saw an eagle perched in a dead tree.

At 0900 we found sand dunes forming and encroaching over the road again, and then ahead we saw the outline of Timbuktoo. We stopped just outside the town to take some photographs, and then travelled the last couple of miles through deep, soft sand into the legendary town. So, after some of the hardest driving we had encountered, we'd finally made it to Timbuktoo, Timbuktu, Tombouctou or Timbuctou! (No matter how it is spelt, it is pronounced the same way.)

Although it is a name that everybody knows, few people realise that it really

The historic Sankora Mosque in Timbuktoo.

exists, and fewer still know exactly where it is. It is a magical name that brings to mind thoughts of a romantic past. It has the Sankora Mosque dating back to the fourteenth century, the houses of past explorers like Laing, Caillé and Barth. But what most strikes visitors to this town is its serenity, tranquillity, and mystique.

The town is expanding all the time but the streets are still of sand, with loose particles blown up against the walls of the houses. Our first priority was to find the police station to obtain permission to take photographs while here. We drove along the main street, passing the Sankora Mosque, and entered the main square where we were surprised to find, of all things, a *supermarket*, a real brick built building! We had a look inside. Although lacking many of the usual supermarket commodities, it was very well stocked with toothpaste, soap, torches, radios, biscuits, crisps, jam, bottled and tinned vegetables, corned beef, and sweets.

We then drove the short distance to the hotel to ask the way to the police station, but not before we had a meal: steak, chips and peas! At the police station I entered with our passports, but it appeared we did not need to register or obtain a visitor's pass, although we decided to do so just to obtain the Timbuktoo stamp in our passports. It took an hour to complete formalities, which included our photographic pass for this area.

Next we looked for a welder to repair our cracked roof rack. Mick is a welder so provided we got the equipment, he could do the job. Outside the police station we started asking for directions, and the very first person we asked took us straight to a welding shop. The equipment, however, looked as if it had come out of the ark, or been in Timbuktoo since its inauguration! The machine had only one setting, there was no proper mask, and the man was electric welding with gas welding goggles. To make things worse, he only had one size welding rod. After one look at the work he was doing, Mick decided to attempt the job himself. At least he could do no worse. Eventually the job was done. It was not perfect but it would have to do until we reached somewhere where we could do the job properly.

Next we found a bakery which was merely a clay oven in the street, and purchased some bread. It tasted sandy, which was not surprising, but apart from that was very nice. We then found the market, but being Sunday there was not much doing there, although we bought some monkey nuts. We then attempted to find a filling station, but soon discovered there wasn't one. However one of the kids we asked knew where we could buy some petrol, so we let him take us. It turned out to be a private house with one single petrol pump outside, the only supply in town, but we could not persuade the owner to open up for us.

Timbuktoo to Niafounké

We decided we had enough petrol to get us to the next town so we began to find our way out and onto the road to Goundam. The first lad we asked offered to accompany us and direct us to the edge of town so we sat him in the centre of the front seat and were on our way. Five minutes later we were on a road; no signposts, so we had to take the lad's word for it, and as it was going in the right direction, we dropped him off and continued on our way.

The road was firm sand and dirt and there were grass and trees spreading out across the plain ahead. This next section of our route would be similar to the last: we would have to find our own way with the use of a compass. The only roads were far to our left and under water, for we were crossing one of the biggest flood basins in Africa, some 300 miles long by 80 miles wide in places, and the Niger was full at this season and spreading over the whole area. However this meant we had only to keep this huge expanse of water to our left and we should not get lost.

The going soon became rough as we wound our way in and out of the bushes and trees, and the sand soon became soft. There were telegraph poles taking a winding course through the bushes, many of which were dead, some burnt down to a pointed stump emerging from the ground. At 1630, 15 miles from Timbuktoo, the route became very busy as we began to pass dozens of donkey caravans, the donkeys loaded down with huge sacks of rice, heading towards Timbuktoo. It seemed we were heading for a heavy rice growing area, the locals taking full advantage of the present ample supply of water. As we passed the last of the donkeys, the tracks we had been following headed into an area of very soft, deep sand, and we had to engage low ratio to crawl through. The vehicle soon started overheating, so we drove off into the bushes and made camp for the night.

The next morning we rose at 0615 hours and were soon back on to the soft sand, which is firmer in the morning before the sun hits it; so it is easier on the vehicle if you can get a good start while it is fairly cool. At 0700 we passed our first donkey caravan of the day, laden with sacks of grain, plodding through the soft sand, staring straight ahead, and oblivious of our presence. We were now driving close to the edge of the Niger flood area, and occasionally crossed dried up areas that indicated the water level was not yet at its highest. From time to time we were only a couple of feet from the water's edge, following tracks of other vehicles only to see them disappear into the water. There were also "puddles" left by the flooding, where the water was not as high as it had been. Luckily the ground around the water's edge was quite firm.

After forty miles we could see our first town, Goundam, in the distance, surrounded by sand dunes, with the approach road very soft. Here we had to get some more money and some petrol. The town was larger than we thought, with some fairly good looking brick-built houses, although the roads are sand. Unfortunately it has no bank and no petrol, so we were in something of a quandary. There is a post office where we mailed some letters home, and asked where petrol might be obtained. Every person we asked had the same answer: "Timbuktoo". Obviously we had made a mistake in not waiting there until the next day and buying petrol before we left. We continued asking, in case someone had a black market supply, but without much luck, so we drove around town a bit asking people with cars, especially those who looked European as they might be more sympathetic to our problem. We eventually found an import/export company who were prepared to let us have a little, but only at £4 per gallon in Mali currency, which we did not have. After two hours we concluded that the cheapest method would be to go back to Timbuktoo, all 53 miles of it, and top up our tanks there, with a lesson well learnt. An alternative was to travel 22 miles off our route to Dire, which we were assured had plenty of petrol (but no bank) then return the 22 miles back to Goundam and continue. At least we knew that Timbuktoo had petrol and a bank.

We were still making up our minds when a Toyota Land Cruiser sped past, driven by a European so we chased after him, waved him down and explained our problem. It turned out that he was an American missionary but, more

230

important, he could help us out with petrol and accept payment in U.S. dollars which we had, so we followed him to his place, a large house right on the edge of the flooded area, and sat talking, drinking Coke, and eating peanuts while one of his servants ran round friends to find who had the cheapest black market petrol. He returned with the news that he could get us 60 litres at 6 dollars for 5 litres, which was a great help, so we gave him our jerry cans to fill as it was not wise to let the "supplier" know that the fuel was for strangers.

While we waited we passed the time by walking around the market along the water's edge, watching the natives poling their canoes in the water. We tried to buy some evaporated milk in the market but we could not find any. When we got back to the house at 1150 the servant had just returned with the fuel. Our new-found friend had had to go out, so we paid the servant in dollars at the agreed rate, and he then guided us onto the right road out of town. The road we were planning to take to Niafounké was flooded so we were directed to a roundabout route via Tonka, crossing a small river before turning south onto a soft sandy road.

We headed off towards the hills in front of us, passing through some dense bush, and then the road became firm soil, but ten miles out from Goundam we were back in soft, but not too deep, sand again. At 1300 we started to climb over a sand dune that stretched right across the road and for 1½ miles to either side of it. There were already tracks leading over it so we felt we should be all right. Once on top we found it was nothing more than a huge sand covered hill, with a splendid view for miles ahead across the plain and the whole flooded area. There was also a wide range of fresh green grass and bushes bordering the route ahead of us.

Now we were on a well worn track, with a light covering of sand over it. On either side of the road were caster oil plants, many in bloom, their scarlet flowers complemented by red tinged leaves. At 10 miles from Tonka the road became very bumpy with a covering of soft sand on the surface, which kept our top speed down to 20 mph. Then, after a couple of miles, we were driving over dry lake beds again until we entered Tonka at 1345.

We passed through the village and just outside there was another large dried up lake to cross, but this one had a gravel causeway. We then passed through a small mud hut village, after which the road became very good and we attained speeds of up to 40 mph on some stretches. On either side of the road were large termite hills, some as high as 5 feet. Suddenly the road veered to the left and we were driving along the water's edge again in deeply rutted tracks for a while, then back on good road again.

We entered Niafounké at 1515, passing between some large sand dunes on the way. By the look of it they had been freshly blown in and some reached to the top of the telegraph poles, leaving just the top of the pole protruding from the centre of the dune. The weather had been a lot cooler lately with the temperature now a comfortable 84 degrees.

Niafounké to Kogoni

From Niafounké the road runs across the flood land to Mopti, and we had planned to take this road. However, with the current level, it was under water and, as there are no vehicular ferries, we were compelled to continue driving around the edge of the floodland.

Just past Niafounké we came to a very rocky area, with a couple of low

Some of the roads in Africa are not even as wide as the vehicle.

rocky hills ahead of us, and a bay running inland for several miles from the flooded area, forcing us to detour right round it, which meant covering about 32 miles to travel two. Our route took us through fields of crops, around the base of the rocky hills, along the water's edge and through very soft sand in which we became stuck a couple of times. It was a slow arduous journey, especially when driving over the rocks, as there is no way round them. We also encountered several gullies up to 2 feet deep, caused by the flood water, and these we had to drive across. However, they were only a foot wide and with the sand ladders we did not have too much trouble, although a couple of times the rest of the group had to get out and give a push.

Fifty-five minutes after starting the detour we reached the top end of the bay where we turned and travelled back in the direction we had come from on the opposite side. These first 16 miles took us nearly an hour but the terrain on this side was much better and, by keeping close to the water's edge where the sand is flat and firm, we were able to travel along at speeds up to 40 mph.

Halfway along we reached a village and the road appeared to end. Once again we had to seek help from the locals, who were only too pleased to point us in the right direction. We were on plain sand with only tracks of other vehicles to guide us. There were plenty of small bushes and grass scattered amongst the sand dunes as we headed directly into the face of the setting sun. At last, we reached the end of our detour, and headed south onto our road once more. We could clearly see the main flood area to our left and decided to drive towards it to camp for the night. In places the undergrowth was so dense that we had to drive straight through it, much of it being young palms. Nearer the water we could hear the beating of drums. As we parked and switched off the Land Rover engine we could hear fainter drum beats coming from across the flooded area several miles away. We then spotted a couple of natives at the water's edge, each with an empty 40 gallon drum. Obviously, they were transferring messages to somebody on the opposite side of the water. For half an hour we watched and listened, until the Africans both disappeared, leaving their 'drums' by the water's edge. As it was now almost dark we hurried to erect our tents for the night.

We were woken at 0600 the next morning by ground squirrels chattering outside our tents and were up soon afterwards, just as the sun began shining through the palm trees. We returned to the road, which was now firm but corrugated and bumpy. After a while the road deteriorated considerably and began breaking up into several routes and weaving in and out of the grass covered dunes. As we travelled along at 1000 feet above sea level with palm trees on one side and the water on the other, we could not help wondering just how many 'tourists' had used this track, which remained firm but very rough, keeping our speed down to an average of 18 miles per hour. Our route took us through several small mud hut villages, with cattle and goat patrolling the perimeter of the flooded area. After thirty miles the road straightened out but became more sandy with some very soft patches here and there, and the occasional bumpy section concealed in sand, throwing us up in the air as we hit it and making quite a mess of our luggage in the back.

We had travelled 60 miles over very rough roads when the town of Léré opened out before us. It is a small town consisting of mainly mud huts and one or two small roadside shops. We stopped at one to restock with provisions before continuing on our way. The road remained rough until about 12 miles from Léré, when the dirt surface improved considerably and we were able to attain speeds of up to 40 mph. After another 28 miles the road became very good with a firm smooth dirt surface, under water at times, and we

233

cruised along at 50 mph. After 6 miles it deteriorated again, with some deep ruts running along it, apparently left by some heavy vehicle when the ground was wet or flooded. We had to slow right down and scraped our sump on the dirt at times. We passed a village consisting of a few straw huts, and observed the local children drawing water at the well. A few miles further on we passed Nampala, shortly after which we found ourselves driving through vast millet plantations.

We soon entered another village, with many of the occupants working the village well, where we stopped for a while. They were using donkeys to lift water buckets and we were amazed at the distance the donkeys walked from the well, and the length of rope used to haul the buckets. Apparently this well was over 100 metres deep, and had no water in it as such but a stream running across the bottom. The only way to raise the water was to station small kids at the bottom with small buckets, filling up the larger buckets as they are lowered. We looked down the well, which was no more than 5 ft in diameter, but could see nothing though we could hear the kids chattering!

The road away from this village weaves its way in and out of trees and bushes and alternates from firm hard dirt to soft sand. 15 miles from our deep well, it led straight into the flooded area and we came to a full stop. We could see no way of driving through as it was too soft and deep, and, as the water ran inland amongst thick bushes and trees, we had no alternative but to back track for half a mile or so and drive round this area through the clearing and to rejoin the track further along.

We now passed through many villages, each small but a hive of activity. The water now seemed more under control, with much irrigation and canals criss-crossing the road. The canals led into paddy fields on both sides of the road where rice was already being harvested. We were surprised to see several push bikes being ridden about as we entered Kogoni and immediately noticed the difference that navigable water brings to an area: the inhabitants are better off and have fuel, food and transport. We stopped at Kogoni market, which had the widest selection of goods we had seen for some time, and were immediately besieged by scores of kids and adults who obviously do not see white people often. We spent quite a while taking photographs, and then proceeded to tour the market. All of the traders were pleased to see us and all wanted to shake hands. The language barrier made no difference as all made themselves clearly understood with sign language. Wares included fresh oranges, tangerines, pineapples and bananas, yams, cassava and onions; also huge sacks of fresh peanuts. The native women are immaculately dressed in brightly coloured robes and before leaving we took a few photographs. It was then time to move on, driving past the plots of fresh, healthy looking vegetables, and the bushy mango trees.

Kogoni to the border

We continued on our way following the route of the canals, occasionally slowing to drive over a hump that is placed close to each lock gate. The road is fairly good with just the occasional deep rut to watch for. We were now heading for Niono.

Beyond all the villages we decided to pitch camp early as we were all in need of a wash, and the clear waters of the canal would give us that opportunity. However, the only clearing we found had been used regularly by cattle plodding to and from the water and subsequently the ground was packed so hard that we were unable to drive one single peg into it. We did have a good wash though, before finding a suitable spot 7 miles on. As soon as the tents were erected we jumped in quick for close to the water there are plenty of mosquitoes about.

By 0700 the next day we had the tents packed away and were back on the road driving through a vast area of paddy fields that stretched for miles ahead. We finally arrived at the end of the canals, and had to start asking directions. The road ahead from here is of fairly firm dirt with small corrugations giving us a speed of around 40 mph. occasionally we passed a small canal or lake, accompanied always by paddy fields or vegetable plots. On our journey to date we could really appreciate the high value of water in these hot regions. A short distance up the road we spotted our first coconut palms all laden with large green coconuts, not quite ripe. Then came a large area of sugar cane and a large processing plant. We stopped for a while to cut some of the juicy cane and trucks of cane passed us, heading for the processing plant, some so laden that they scattered lengths 6-8 feet long all along the road.

We were now approaching Markala, where a dam holds back a large section of the River Niger. As we came to the town, we drove over a large steel bridge wide enough for four lanes of traffic, spanning the width of the Niger. Even at this point, nearly a thousand miles from where we first encountered it, the river is still over 800 yards across, and we stopped to look down and marvelled at the immense amount of water passing beneath the bridge. This bridge doubles as a railway and road bridge, and is also used by pedestrians. We completed the crossing of the bridge, and entered Markala, thus ending our desert travel. From here to the C.A.R. travel on tarmac or dirt roads should be easy going, but we still had to anticipate problems ahead and stay alert at all times.

In Markala we found a filling station, our first — apart from the single pump in Timbuktoo — for 700 miles, and shortly afterwards we were back on a tarmac road. Life goes on much the same here. We stopped to watch a group of about 24 women grinding their grain into flour, and a couple of older women saw us watching and entertained us with a dance before continuing with their labours.

As we passed through Markala and on to the Ségou road, we travelled through an industrial area, with a couple of large textile factories and dozens of push bikes parked outside.

It takes just 25 minutes to reach Ségou, and from first impressions it looks a large town, with all the facilities. We pulled into a filling station to top up with petrol, but they had none. Up the road at another the story was the same. After an hour's search we eventually discovered fuel, but there was a long queue and a large group of Africans around one pump each holding several jerry cans. By joining the queue we did not stand much chance of getting fuel so I sent Mel and Tony, who can exert their size if necessary, with some of our jerry cans, to stand with the group of Africans. It took half an hour but they eventually returned with petrol.

By this time everything was closing for the afternoon siesta which lasts from 1300 to 1600, so we topped up our water bottles and set out on the road to Bla. We passed through Cinzana before crossing a tributary of the River Niger. The road is good and straight with a tarmac surface giving us a speed of up to 50 mph. The next village is Tula, and then we entered Bla. Our plan had been to drive up to San and then on to Mopti, both on the opposite side of the flood area, but as our fuel situation was getting critical we decided to head straight for the border with Burkina Fasso (formerly Upper Volta).

We therefore kept to the Koutiala road and just outside Bla decided to pull off the road for the night, pitching our tents against the background noise of screaming monkeys and whistling crickets. Our journey through the desert to this point had been just over 3,800 miles.

We were woken the next morning by the sound of the local telephone service: African drums. We lay in our tents listening for a while before getting up. The drums continued talking to each other for about an hour. At 0630 we could hear the widow bird faintly echoing its song of woe in the distance. It did not take us long to get back on the road and we were soon passing through the first village. It must have been the main market day for we passed scores of women by the roadside with huge bundles or bowls of grain, or boxes containing some items, all perfectly balanced on their heads.

At 0745 hours we arrived at Koutiala, a fairly busy little place with a large variety of goods. They even have bicycle stalls and a couple of permanently erected shops. In an open clearing of the market was a huge pile of coconuts, with a couple of Africans removing the nut from the husk, and placing each in its own pile, while another African graded them by size. There was also a large selection of fruit, and some lovely looking spring onions, freshly picked. The filling stations had fuel so we topped up the main tanks. As we left town we were up to 1300 feet above sea level, the time was 0900, and the temperature already 88 degrees, the warmest it had been for some days now. We disturbed a kori bustard feeding by the edge of the road, and further along passed a couple of small cotton fields.

There was little traffic on the road to the border, but we passed a couple of cyclists probably travelling from one village to another. At 1010 we reached the Mali border control, where Mel jumped out and took our passports in for stamping. They directed us to customs control. We were finally cleared by 10.30 and on our way to the border with Burkina Fasso at Falamana.

Access to the Koumi village is via a crude log footbridge, not strong enough for vehicles, which has to be negotiated with extreme care.

237

Burkina Fasso
(formerly Upper Volta)

On arrival at the Burkina Fasso police check, Mel did his usual stint with the passports, and we were soon on our way to the customs control which is 25 miles away from the police post. It was 1115 and the outside temperature 98 degrees. The countryside here takes on more of a jungle appearance, with some very tall trees, hanging vines, and thick undergrowth. The roadside villages consist more of straw built huts as opposed to the mud huts we have been used to seeing.

The customs control is in the centre of a small village, and it did not take long to clear us for entry. The officials here were most friendly and helpful. We decided to have lunch here, and walked across the road to a coffee stall, where they accepted Mali money. So we had a 'bowl' of coffee — a dish that must have held a pint filled to the brim for the equivalent of ten pence.

Meanwhile, the vehicle was parked under some huge mango trees on the opposite side of the road, well within our sight and was attracting quite a crowd of inquisitive locals until one of them brushed against it and set off the alarm. Within seconds they were gone, leaving the area deserted.

Bobo-Dioulasso and Koumi

Burkina Fasso is another poor, landlocked country of which the modern capital is Ouagadougou. We were making for the second city of Bobo-Dioulasso. Apart from larger trees the countryside is much the same as Mali although the villages are different. Passing through the village of Bama, we came upon a vast acreage of rice paddies on the outskirts, with several banana trees growing also. We passed Koundougou and arrived in Bobo-Dioulasso at 1400 to find the streets adorned with flags and bunting. It seems that Sunday December 13th marks the anniversary of Independence granted in 1958 and was a public holiday. We hardly hoped to find a bank open but decided to look anyway. We drove around and stopped at the National Bank where they change travellers cheques but were closed until 1530 — an hour and a half wait; so we spent it touring the very large market area directly opposite. This was certainly the largest and best equipped market we had come across. At 1530 we returned to the bank only to be told that they exchanged travellers cheques only in the mornings! Mel span a yarn about our not having any money or petrol, and was taken to the manager, who appeared to take pity and told him to return at 1630, just before they closed, and he would see what he could do. We had no choice as there is no other way to obtain money so passed the time by walking round the market again.

There is evidence that this country is supported by organisations such as Oxfam and African Aid, but items contributed are here in the market, being sold. We noticed that everything is cheap though, with soft drinks such as Coke and Fanta selling for 12 pence, a fifth of what they cost in England.

At 1630 we returned to the bank once more, and by 1700 the manager had changed some travellers cheques for us. We expressed our gratitude and headed for the filling station. There does not appear to be any shortage of fuel here, or vehicles, and the town has more than its fair share of mopeds, the owner of one acting as a guide when we asked the way out of town and the road to Koumi.

Just outside Bobo, as it is known locally, the tarmac road comes to a halt and we were on a dirt road, brick red in colour, as we passed the airport. We decided to stop here for the night as it was getting late.

Next morning we were on the road at 0700, heading for the oldest town in Burkina Fasso and one of the oldest in Africa, dating back several hundred years. Koumi, which takes its name from one of the local rivers, the River Kou, is just 11 miles from Bobo and has no road passing through it. It is situated just off the main Bobo to Orodara red dirt road, and is entered over a couple of crude wooden bridges spanning a couple of deep gullies. We travelled the same red dirt road we had encountered last night. It has a firm surface but is deeply gullied in some places by heavy rain erosion. At 0730 we arrived at Koumi. The bridges are composed of fallen tree trunks, and to cross we had to balance along a single trunk being careful not to slip into the gap between each trunk.

The town looked very ancient and fragile, and we started taking photographs only to discover that photography is forbidden. However we were made welcome wherever we walked, even in some of the huts, and the bakery. We spent most of the morning in Koumi, where the inhabitants live today as they did centuries ago, leaving by the same log bridge.

As it was near lunchtime we decided to return to Bobo, where we found a very clean small roadside café just inside the town. Coffee was the equivalent of 20 pence here but once again was in a large bowl, so we all paid our money and then discovered that the price included a French loaf cut up and spread with margarine. While there we also had a meal of steak and rice. One should be wary of eating meat but the café owner showed us the meat before he cooked it and it did look clean.

The Karfiguela Falls

As we left Bobo once more, we passed the station — a large, very clean complex, with some steam engines and some modern diesel shunters. Apparently the cost of a journey from here to Abidjan on the coast is only

£20. We left Bobo behind at 1300, with a temperature of 107 degrees, and agreed that this is a very interesting town, well worth spending several days in.

The road to Banfora is tarmac with an excellent surface all the way. We were now at 1600 feet above sea level. At 8 miles from Bobo we had to divert for a short stretch as they were constructing a new road bridge. We passed many grass hut settlements amongst the mango and cashew nut trees, and halfway to Banfora ran through the village of Finlaide. Here the railway tracks run parallel with the road, and the scenery takes on a jungle appearance.

At 43 miles from Bobo we found oursleves on the brow of a hill looking down on a sea of green: acres of fields of sugar cane. As we made our descent, we passed the Komoe Rapids/Waterfall. Although almost dry at that moment, it normally cascades from the top of the rocks to our right, passes underneath the road, and continues cascading to our left for about 100 yards. It must be an impressive sight when in flood.

After another 10 miles we entered Banfora and continued straight through and onto the road to Karfiguela, and the Karfiguela Waterfall, the highest falls in Burkina Fasso. It is about ten miles from Banfora to Karfiguela, and we took it steady along the narrow and deeply rutted road that passes through the acres of sugar cane that we had seen from the top of the last hill. Sugar cane requires a lot of water, and this huge area of cane has no shortage. Tall sprinklers constantly spray water over the fields of cane, which towered over our Land Rover to a height of some 10 feet or more. Looking ahead, left, right or behind, we could see nothing but cane. In this south west corner of Burkina Fasso is their largest river, the Black Volta, along with the rivers Kou, Komoe, and Leraba. Farther to the east are the Red Volta and the White Volta. As we travelled along our rough dirt road, we passed a few large marshy areas, and the odd dam, another indication of the plentiful water supply. Then the road forked and as we were not sure which one to take, we waited for someone to pass. Suddenly a young African boy leapt out of the thick hedge with a paw paw held aloft. He set us on the right road and as we started on our way thrust the fruit through the passenger window, dropping it on Mel's lap, and disappeared as quickly as he had emerged from his hedge. At least we had supper!

Another 2 miles and we came to a full stop, a broken decaying bridge blocking our way. Although it would have been feasible for foot passengers to use it, there was no way that a vehicle could cross in its present state and with a drop of 8 to 10 feet into a soft muddy river bed. We left the vehicle and stood looking at it for a while. It seemed we had the choice of leaving the vehicle here and walking to the falls, or returning to Banfora to see if there was another route. Obviously this road was little used, so Mel and I decided to walk along it to see how far the falls were, leaving Mick and Tony with the vehicle. After about three quarters of a mile we came upon the falls. Not a long walk but too far to leave the vehicle unattended on the other side of the bridge.

We returned to the bridge to survey the situation once more. In the river bed were several old rotting palm tree trunks and a few that had been split down the centre. Had these been used on the bridge at some time? If we could lay these trunks across the rail tracks horizontally we might be able to cross. Anyway it was worth a try, but this did not turn out to be as simple as we first thought. Each length weighed several hundredweight and it was just about all that four of us could do even to drag one. We struggled and eventually got three logs on to the top of the bridge and placed them so that they were in line with the wheels, one end of the logs on the shore ends of the bridge and the other end on the centre buttress. Mel then jumped into the driver's seat, taking Tony as passenger for balance (and experience). He kept both eyes on me as I guided him across, indicating whether he should stop completely, or turn the front wheels right or left. Mick stayed behind the vehicle to ensure that the rear wheels exactly followed the front wheels. The bridge was about 30 feet across, and after much shunting backwards and forwards, replacing and repositioning the logs, we eventually reached the other side, much to the relief of all, about 25 minutes later. It was the longest 30 feet we had ever travelled!

Once over the bridge we drove the remainder of the distance to the falls, firstly through a field of tall elephant grass that had encroached on the road, and then through a grove of very large mango trees, finally stopping only a few yards from the falls, and erecting camp for the night.

This done we eagerly stripped off and jumped into the deep pool at the base of the waterfall for a wash and swim. Mel and Tony then did a bit of rock climbing up the waterfall itself. Although not completely dry there was very little water cascading over the falls compared to the torrent that normally races over and Mel and Tony succeeded in climbing to the very top.

This is a very peaceful area. The large rock pool is surrounded by sand thrown up in a bank by the force of the water dropping from the top of the falls some 180 feet up. There are beautiful tropical flowers growing around the edge of the falls, while at the top are a series of cascades, and a large area full of tropical plants and trees that look as if they were once part of someone's garden. Monkeys play in the trees, birds sing all around, and from the top of the falls there is a splendid view of the surrounding countryside for miles around.

As darkness fell, and the birds stopped singing, so the crickets started, and the sound of the cascading water of the falls became clearer, like distant thunder. It was pitch black under our trees, as we lay in our tents, discussing how worthwhile it had all been crossing that obstacle of a bridge. We had bridged a gap and found paradise.

We were woken the next morning by the singing of the birds. I was up at 0600 and went for a walk alone to the top of the falls via a well worn path around the side. It was just beautiful walking along the ridge of rock at the top of the falls. Then I stopped abruptly for there, lying directly in front of me on a rock, was a huge puff adder, soaking up the morning sun. I ran to the edge and called the others but by the time they arrived it had slithered away into the bushes.

We all returned to the vehicle, packed our things away, and were soon on the road to Lobi territory. The Lobi tribe, who are found all along the border between Ivory Coast and Burkina Fasso, are famous for their woven cane and reed baskets, and the older women wear metal discs in their upper and lower lips, although this practice is now discouraged by law.

At 1030 hours with a temperature of 94 degrees, we were on a tarmac road, 15 miles south of Banfora. The new tarmac road runs the whole way to the border, where we arrived at 1130 hours and took our passports into the police post. Five minutes down the road we repeated the procedure at the customs post with no hold up or vehicle checking at either.

Mick, one of our group shows how huge some ant (termite) hills can be. He is 5ft 5in.

Ivory Coast

The Ivory Coast border control appeared to be some distance away — 40 minutes at about 35 miles per hour to the police control, where they merely checked our passports and instructed us to proceed to Ouangolodougou for full passport control.

So at 1300 we were on our way along the dirt road to Ouangolodougou, the first town in Ivory Coast, and after a dusty ten-minute ride we arrived and began looking for the police post, as there are no barriers and no signs indicating police or customs. We eventually found it down a dirt road to the right of the main tarmac road just as you enter town. We took our passports in; police control told us to clear customs at Ferkéssédougou, another 28 miles up the road, and 53 miles in from the border, so off we went. As we drove along the dirt road we passed several women with huge bundles of wood delicately balanced on their heads, and others balancing 5 gallon drums of water. The women certainly work hard on this continent, and they all give a wave to passing tourists.

After 1½ hours we came to Ferkéssédougou, and were waved on by the officers at the police post. A little further along we stopped at the customs control and cleared formalities in a few minutes. We then drove out of town on a good tarmac road looking for a camp site for the night. All of the grassland here had been burnt and there were still signs of burning so we had to take care where we camped. At 1630 the temperature was still 99 degrees as we drove off the road and parked for the night.

Ferkéssédougou to Abidjan

Up at first light the next morning we were soon travelling towards Bouake on a good tarmac road. There was evidence of burning all along the road as everything was very dry, although the trees were getting greener. Humidity increased nearer to the rain forests of the Ivory Coast, and we were not looking forward to experiencing sleepless nights due to the constant perspiration of our bodies in the humid areas.

We reached Tafire, and stopped at a stall for what we tried to make a daily routine: a cup of hot coffee. The stall was attended by a very large African lady, who could speak a little English. There was a small child on the floor, his grubby little hands clawing at her legs, until she pushed him away. He then started crying but after a stern "shut up", he stopped, looked at her, and then started bawling even louder. Mother went to a corner and produced a large stick. His tears dried instantly and there was not a murmur from him all the time we were there. Actions speak louder than words!

By 0930 we were travelling along at 1500 feet, and the trees on either side of the road were becoming very dense, a sure sign that we were approaching the rain forests. At 1000 hours our road became a dual carriageway as we entered the town of Niakaramandougou, where there are street lights, pavements and road traffic signs. We drove straight through this town and were soon back on a single road again, but still with a good tarmac surface.

The next town is Katiola which we entered once more on a dual carriageway. Here we stopped to replenish our fuel supply and food stock. In the large market here there is a good selection of fresh fruit, and we took advantage of this to buy ourselves an assortment of freshly picked bananas, oranges, pineapples and mangos. Just after noon, with the temperature 106 degrees, we headed out of town once more on tarmac but only for a short while, diverting on to dirt as the main road was being widened.

We continued to Bouaké, stopping briefly en route to replenish our fuel supply, arriving about 1330 hours to find a large town with all facilities and a very large market. For the first time on our trip the approach of Christmas was evident, with "Happy Christmas" signs adorning many shop windows, and decorations hanging here and there. We continued on our way, passing a large mosque, and stopping briefly at the largest termite hill we had yet seen — about 12 feet tall.

As we continued on our way, we passed numerous crop fields, mainly maize and tobacco plants, and also many banana and coconut plantations. By 1545 we were in Yamoussoukro, the new capital, 166 miles north of Abidjan. We entered this town on yet another good stretch of dual carriageway, this time recently constructed. The whole town is very modern with many new and large buildings being erected, as befits a new capital. Many of the buildings adopt a space age design, and everything is very clean. We passed a go-cart track, golf course and a large area of land being developed into a parkland with a lake. The tarmac road extends through and beyond Yamoussoukro and into Toumodi.

Ivory Coast is one of the big timber exporting countries of the world, and we were made aware of this by the large number of trucks carrying huge tree trunks trundling along the road. Each one carried only two or three trunks, for they were so huge and heavy. Everything now looked lush and green, and overhead dark clouds began to appear in the sky threatening rain so we began to look for a camp site for the night. Soon we were driving down a dirt track to pitch our tents away from the main road and as we started to erect them a few spots of rain fell. Our first rain since entering the African continent!

The night was very sticky because of increasing humidity and as a result we did not get much sleep and were up before dawn. By the first light we were on our way towards the tarmac main road, halting briefly at a coconut tree we had passed the night before to help ourselves to some fresh coconuts.

As we drove towards Abidjan, we entered the rain forest area. It was still early morning, and the tall green trees were enshrouded in a dense mist.

There was no sun visible but the temperature was very close. Within five miles from our camp site the mist was down to road level and we had to reduce speed considerably and drive with our lights on.

At 40 miles from Toumodi on the Abidjan road we came upon another dual carriageway with an excellent surface. There is a road sign here. "Abidjan 150 kilometres". We were now down to our lowest level since leaving the North African coast: 500 feet above sea level. Some 8 miles further along the dual carriageway we were greatly surprised to find a motorway, and a very good one at that. There are even emergency telephones placed at one kilometre intervals. This new motorway has been cut straight through the jungle, and must have cost a lot of money. There was not much traffic but plenty of pedestrians about, natives carrying baskets on their heads, and a few on pushbikes, all travelling towards us on the same side of the road without much care for their safety. Obviously the new motorway was proving a good way to travel without getting their feet muddy. Nor can snakes hide on the road!

Everything is so different in this country. The scenery is jungle, with high humidity. We passed large numbers of palm trees, mainly the thick stemmed, shortish variety known as the palm oil tree. The oil is extracted from the fruits, which are reddish in colour, the size of dates. This oil is one of the most sought-after commodities in the world, mainly for soaps and cosmetics. A little further along the road we passed through a huge rubber plantation; strapped to each tree, about 3 feet from the ground, is half a coconut shell, open end up, to catch the latex flowing from the angled cuts in the bark.

Eight miles from Abidjan the motorway ends, giving way to a very good dual carriageway. As we entered Abidjan we passed along lines of filling stations with all the major companies represented, and we stopped at one to fill all our tanks as there is a shortage of fuel in our next country, Ghana.

Abidjan is one of the most modern cities in the whole continent — a hive of activity in the centre with ultra modern buildings in the form of offices and hotels, and many gift shops catering for the tourist industry.

Abidjan to Takikroum

As we left Abidjan the storm clouds began forming again, and we had a little rain, this time with thunder, but it did not last long. We were now on our way to the Ghanaian border at Takikroum, passing through dense rain forest and sometimes clumps of bamboo, reaching 20 to 30 feet skyward and meeting across the road. We also passed a couple of coffee plantations, and the aroma from the sweet scented flowers drifted in to the Land Rover.

At one stage we spotted a native in the jungle chopping down a "wild" palm oil palm. We discovered that he was after the sap and stayed for a while to watch him tap it. The sap from this palm when fermented is known as palm wine or, to the locals, "bungi", a very potent local brew. We were still in the jungle area and, apart from the odd vehicle passing by, all we could hear was the screeching of monkeys, the screaming of parrots, and the calls of many birds. We experienced police check points at regular intervals on this stretch of road and soon discovered that they were after truck drivers smuggling goods to the Ghana border. Occasionally we were stopped and our papers checked, but most of the time, when they noticed we were visitors, we were waved on.

Soon we reached the town of Abengourou, the last large town before

In these forests many palm trees grow and this native is preparing to extract sap from a couple of palms, which will be fermented to make ''bungy'' or palm wine.

Ghana, and stopped to stock up with provisions. We had been having trouble with one of our batteries, which did not seem to be holding its charge, so while I bought groceries Mel popped into a garage and borrowed a battery tester. Our suspicions were confirmed. The battery was finished. Although we had a second battery, we needed to replace the broken one soon in case the good one decided to pack up too, for you cannot call out the breakdown truck in the places we were going. Mel enquired about price but at £100 each we decided to try and get a cheaper one in Ghana.

As light was fading we pulled off the road just outside the town to camp. After a hot sticky night we got back on the road again to Ghana at 0730 and, still on tarmac, headed on towards Agnibilekrou where we arrived at 0900. Here the tarmac ends and we were back on dirt roads. There were not many signposts about but a Frenchman came to our assistance and pointed us in the right direction: up the main road a little then fork right onto the Takikroum road, a red dirt road with a few corrugations, but a fairly comfortable drive. A short distance along this road we stopped at a customs post and Mel took our papers in. Clearance did not take long. The police post is another 20 miles along the road and we crossed into Ghana without incident.

In equatorial Africa, once the desert has been cleared, the scenery changes dramatically to one of dense forest with narrow rutted mud roads running through it.

Ghana

At 1030 hours as we drove through the gate into Ghana we could hear Christmas carols being sung. The sound was coming from the local radio station.

The customs and police controls are in the same area here so once we had finished with immigration we were accompanied to our vehicle by the customs officials who gave it a quick check over and then issued us with a clearance form. We were then on our way.

Dormaa Ahenkro to Kumasi

Our first town in Ghana, Dormaa Ahenkro, was only a short distance away, and we reached it after about 10 miles along a good dirt road. Here we were stopped at a check point, but they only took a quick look at our papers and waved us on. In Dormaa Ahenkro we were soon approached by black market dealers wanting to change money, offering up to twenty times the official bank rate. When we tried to buy food we discovered that it was very expensive and the only way to survive seemed to be by dealing on the black market. Things had certainly changed since my last visit. We headed out of town on a dirt road again, and on the outskirts we were stopped at another police check. They had a quick look around the vehicle, and one of the officers decided he wanted a packet of biscuits he could see in the back — but he was out of luck as they were Mel's and he never gives food away! A short distance on we were on tarmac road, very bad with scattered potholes for about 5 miles, then a good surface with granite chips all the way to Berekum.

On the way into Berekum we were stopped briefly at a road check again, and also on the way out. A good tarmac road then continues to Sunyani. On my last visit here a couple of years earlier the buildings were new but already they had become dilapidated. On to Nkwanta and another road block but this time we were waved through. From this point the road deteriorates again, and is badly potholed.

The sun was shining as we headed through Bechem. The tarmac surface between the holes was very good and thick rain forest was still with us on either side of the road. After a couple of miles there were long stretches of road where the tarmac had gone completely. The going was so rough that we decided to call it a day and look for a clearing in the rain forest in which we could camp for the night. We soon found a spot and hurried to erect our tents before we were eaten by the mosquitoes, flies, and other biting insects.

The next morning, after a humid night, we were up at 0600. We emerged from our tents to see a couple of vultures prowling around on the ground outside. As we walked towards them they flew into the trees. There was a heavy mist covering the tops of the trees, hiding them from our view. Not far from the Land Rover, we found a column of army ants on the march: one continuous column, jet black in colour and about an inch wide, composed solidly of ants. Parallel with the column spaced at about 6 inch intervals, were grenadier ants, huge things about an inch long with heads and pinchers the size of the head of a pencil. Their duty was to protect the column and this they did well, making a lunge at us whenever we got too close. Occasionally they were too quick for us: Mel was wearing sandals and one of the grenadiers grabbed his toe causing Mel to let out quite a yell, dropping his camera in the process. There were hundreds of thousands of ants in this column maybe one hundred yards long.

We eventually hit the road again, and it was much better, although the good tarmac surface lasted only 10 miles before we were back amongst the potholes again. We passed a cocoa processing plant, this country being one of the leading growers of cocoa.

We soon arrived in Kumasi, 40 miles from where we camped for the night, and once more were stopped at a road block as we entered. There was little delay, however, and we were soon waved on after showing our papers.

Kumasi to Accra

There are no signs pointing the way to the capital, Accra, so we had to ask around for the right road. As we left Kumasi the road became rough again, very badly potholed, and also very narrow, the edges broken away by heavy trucks and buses. At 30 miles from Kumasi we passed a large palm oil plantation and then another police check but we were waved straight through. We were now regularly passing palm oil plantations, banana plantations, and cocoa farms.

After 60 miles we passed through Nkawkaw and on towards the town of Nsawam. We decided to take this route as the road via Bunsu was impassable in places. As we approached Anguim, we had a range of mountains to our right, and the road was lined with palm oil palms on one side and cocoa trees on the other. We passed straight through this town, and continued on the badly potholed road, weaving in and out of the holes as best we could. Then we fell straight into one and immediately heard the air escaping from one of our rear tyres — our first puncture on the trip to date. We hastily changed wheels and continued on our way.

We soon reached Nsawam and pulled in, hoping to buy some bread. I also had to 'adjust' our roof rack with a hammer as the potholes had caused it to crack up in places. While we were parked up a bus passed us with several small goats standing on the roof rack. Just outside Nsawam the road improved and we had a good surface again all the way to Accra where potholes appeared again.

As we entered Accra we were again stopped at a police check, and then waved through. We arrived in Accra five days before Christmas, and as we planned to spend Christmas with some friends here, we had five days to look around the capital of Ghana, and give the Land Rover a good check over and service in preparation for the next stage of our trip.

It was while in Ghana that we met our first lot of overlanders travelling our route and also planning to spend some time in Ghana. However they were the sort we could do without: the type who know everything there is to be known about travelling; who think that the precautions we take are a waste of time. For instance they had had only the mandatory injections to gain entry into various countries: they had not bothered to have gamma globulin before starting the trip and, when we met them, one member was just recovering from hepatitis!

During our stay we had a good tour of the capital, replaced the faulty battery, shortened and reinforced the roof rack, and gave the vehicle a good service. Then, on December 27th, it was time to move on. We said our goodbyes, and by 1000 hours were away.

We left Accra on a short stretch of motorway, but this soon deteriorated into a potholed road and we had to take it steady again. At Sogakofe we crossed over the Black Volta River, from which point the road improved again and we were back on good flat tarmac with no potholes. At 1415 we reached the Ghana border town of Aflao. Here we completed our exit forms, and Mel took the lot in to be cleared. It took half an hour.

Entry into Togo took a little longer as after about 40 minutes Mel came back to the car with one of the customs officials who wanted to have a look inside. He was very thorough, peering into our camera boxes, first aid box, cases etc., but was soon satisfied and gave us clearance to enter Togo.

The Accra coastline is one of the most interesting parts of the country, with its scores of fishing canoes carved out of whole tree trunks.

Togo and Benin

Togo

As we drove along the excellent Togo roads, we had the sea on one side and the Gulf of Guinea and new modern hotels on the other. We soon decided to pull up somewhere for our first swim in the sea since arriving in Africa. The sea offshore looked calm but there were some very large waves rolling up the sandy beach. We took the Land Rover almost to the water's edge, and after a quick change, all jumped in. There were a lot of African kids already playing at the water's edge and, once they saw us and the plastic football we were carrying, all wanted to join in the fun. They certainly did not lack energy and it wasn't long before they had us all tired out. It was 1700 and would soon be dark so we drove up the road a bit and found a camp site right on the beach.

It was a very humid night, being on the coast, and we were rolling in sweat when we got up at 0700, so we went straight down to the water's edge for a cooling dip in the sea. Then we continued on the road, stopping at a fishing village to watch the natives hauling their huge nets up the golden sandy beach, using a large palm tree as an anchor. A little further on we crossed the White Volta river and shortly afterwards arrived at the Benin border. Togo is a long thin country, which ranges north for 550 miles, yet is only 65 miles wide. Benin has the same dimensions.

At the border we joined the queue to have our passports stamped for exit, which took half an hour. Mel took care of the vehicle's papers, and we were permitted to join the queue for Benin. This was by far the busiest border control we had encountered, and even then we upset the guard controlling the traffic by bypassing the vehicles lined up for clearance. He frantically blew his whistle at us but then gave up when he saw we were tourists.

Benin

Entry into Benin took over an hour but eventually we were through the police and then had to contend with customs control. They wanted to inspect everything, and had all our luggage off the roof rack and opened. Once they realised we were willing to be helpful, the customs officers told us to pack everything away again and be on our way.

As we drove on into Benin, the road was potholed again, and bordered on both sides by groves of coconut palms, with little straw huts on the beach. Some 10 miles into Benin there is a good gravel road and we had a clear blue sky for the first time in ages. The road surface remains good as far as Ganvie, a historical fishing village on stilts in the middle of the River Coulto. Apparently this is a big tourist attraction, but by tribal law photography is forbidden. However, we sneaked a couple.

At 1500 we reached the capital, Cotonou, and stopped to fill up with petrol. It appeared plentiful here so we filled all tanks. We then moved away from the capital to find a camp site for the night, stopping at a huge coconut plantation which we drove through all the way to the beach. The night was the most humid yet and we were glad we had camped on the beach. Although the sea was not really cool it refreshed us and we were soon back on the road and heading for Nigeria.

The road was still very good, but also busy as we drove towards the Nigerian border. Soon we reached Porto Novo, the last main town in Benin. As you leave Porto Novo, the tarmac road becomes gravel on dirt, but still fairly smooth all the way to Igolo, the border town.

We pulled up at the police control while Mel went in with the paperwork, but he was soon back as the officials wanted us all inside filling in forms, so in we went after locking and securing the vehicle. It appeared we had chosen an awkward guard, for he tore up the form Mel had completed, complaining he could not read the writing. For accommodation we always put camping, and he wanted to know what camping is, and where we spent last night. In the end we told him we slept in the car, and he appeared happy with that explanation. Mel then took the vehicle papers to the next counter and they were soon cleared. We then drove the short distance to the Nigerian border control where Mel did the honours once more. This is one border control where we had expected long delays, because of my previous experiences, and straight away Mel had problems. First they would not accept our visa, and then we were told we must wait and see the commissioner, but when he eventually arrived he said everything was all right, much to our relief. In the meantime I had been chatting to the customs officials and making friends with them, exchanging addresses etc. My ruse worked. When our turn came for customs inspection, the official I had been talking to waved us on, saying, as we passed him "Don't forget to write!"

Nigeria

And so we entered Nigeria which has some of the best roads in Africa. It was not long before we were stopped at our first road check. In fact, in the first 20 miles in Nigeria, we encountered five road blocks. We soon reached the town of Otta, where we stopped for some fruit, and then continued to Ifo, a small town and yet another police check. We were waved on and continued towards Abeokuta. At 1600 hours the temperature was still 98 degrees.

Abeokuta to Mokwa

After Abeokuta we began looking for a safe camp site. It was still humid so we didn't expect much sleep. The time is different in Nigeria giving an extra hour's daylight at night and it stays dark an hour later in the morning. Soon the road became quiet with no traffic or people about so we drove off into the bushes, out of sight, and erected tents for our first night in Nigeria, the most densely populated country in the whole African continent. It was a cooler night, but not too comfortable as we were camped on very hard ground.

Back on the road we had not gone 5 miles before we were stopped at a checkpoint, but they merely wished to know where we had come from and where we were going. The road was still good tarmac as we approached Ibadan and another police check on the outskirts. We drove into Ibadan to look for a Land Rover agent, as one of our rear springs was getting weak. On the roads ahead it could go at any time and should really be replaced. We soon found our agent, but unfortunately he did not have the right spring. We would have to try again farther up the road.

We continued through the busy town of Ibadan, one of the main towns of Nigeria, and out on to the road to Oyo. It was a cloudy day with no sign of the sun, but nevertheless warm. The road to Oyo has the odd pothole but was not as bad as some we had been on.

We followed behind two large fuel tankers for a stretch and observed something of the Nigerian way of life. In the space of 20 miles we saw dead dogs in the road, chickens fighting, and overturned artics. Driving through this country is not without risks for Nigerian drivers keep up a hectic pace. Because the roads in Nigeria are good, drivers are apt to put their foot down and hit top speed from one side of the country to the other. Travelling by road, one can expect to see carnage in the form of wrecked trucks, buses, tankers and cars, particularly every time a bend or bridge is approached or where the road narrows; Nigerian drivers do not seem to have mastered the art of slowing down when cornering. Perhaps the high number of wrecked tankers is reason for fuel being in short supply in the northern towns. Another factor contributing to the high accident rate is the amount of alcohol some drivers consume. So be warned: keep a safe distance from other vehicles and drive with care.

At 8 miles from Oyo I pulled up alongside a roadside stall as I had seen some red bananas for sale. These are the sweetest and tastiest of all bananas, and one does not see too many of them about as they are difficult to grow. They are easily identified by their red skin and are almost straight, and a lot thicker than the normal banana. Through Oyo the road was good again, and we passed dozens of stalls selling nothing but tomatoes.

We were now at 1;000 feet. On through Ogbomosho, another busy little town with goats and hens wandering everywhere, and then to Ilorin, stopping at a police check on the way in. In town we discovered a lack of road signs so we had to ask the way: the roads between towns are excellent but in the towns they are very poor.

The scenery was now changing from rain forest to savanna as we drove northwards towards the desert region. At 20 miles out of Ilorin we came to a very dangerous bend with a bridge; the river bed below had more scrap iron than water in it! At 8 miles farther on the road was broken up in places. The temperature at 1430 hrs was 102 degrees with the sun breaking through. At 1520 we passed through Jebba, and, not for the first time on this trip, crossed the River Niger. At 1715 the temperature was still 102 degrees, now with a clear blue sky and bright sunshine, as we drove into Mokwa.

A turning to the left in the centre of Mokwa leads to New Busa and the Kainji Dam, Nigeria's biggest, a distance of 75 miles from Mokwa. West of the Kainja Dam is the Borgu Reserve, home of the Kambriri tribe: the women have heavily scarred bodies and faces, traditionally a sign of beauty, and many of them wear ivory rings protruding from their lower lip. The men of the tribe wear loin cloths, with long swords strapped to their waist. From New Busa, the road swings round to the west of the dam. A ferry for passengers and vehicles crosses the northern reaches where the Niger joins the dam, and then swings back and comes out in Kontagora, where the dirt road rejoins the tarmac.

A visit to a Kambriri village is an experience never to be forgotten. As a whole, Nigeria is a beautiful and interesting country of great contrasts from Lagos in the south — one of Africa's most modern cities — to the northern towns where vultures still scavenge the streets. The Nigerian people are happy yet eccentric, brash yet friendly and there is no better place to meet them than in the lively market places, particularly in Maiduguri. Nigerian markets are difficult to equal anywhere in Africa.

Mokwa to Kano

By 0730 next morning there were already lots of trucks on the road carrying all sorts of commodities from cane to bags of sugar, cattle, and machinery. Entering Kontagora we were stopped at our first roadblock of the day, with little delay. All the filling stations here seemed "dry", but we eventually found the only one in town that had petrol, joined the queue and waited. An hour later we were still in the queue, but Mel and Tony had managed to fill some jerry cans so we made do at that and proceeded on our way.

A couple of miles out of town we found the road blocked by an overturned pantechnicon straddled completely across the road — a typical Nigerian situation, and with several cars already waiting. Fearing a long delay I quickly surveyed the situation, and seeing flattish fields to left and right engaged four wheel drive. Within a couple of minutes we had driven through a field, around the accident, and back on to the road the other side, much to the amazement of all concerned.

At 30 miles from Kontagora the tarmac road became deeply rutted, caused presumably by heavy trucks sinking into the tarmac when it is softened by the hot sun. The rutted section lasts for about 20 miles and then becomes clear for about 5 miles before the ruts appear again. At 75 miles from Kaduna the road becomes very good again, and we were able to cruise along at 50 mph, arriving in Kaduna at 1600. Mick, who had been feeling bad all day, was deteriorating so first priority was to find him a doctor. We pulled into a filling station to refuel and asked the way to the hospital, and whether there was a Land Rover agent (we still needed a spring) and it turned out that the two were within 100 yards of each other. On the way through town we were stopped at a police road check. In towns the police are fairly strict and check documents whilst those on the road outside of towns normally wave you on with a smile. This police officer was rather officious, and had a good look around the vehicle, noticing that our tax disc had expired four months ago. He then wanted to see the carnet, read the date of issue as date of expiry, and started on about that. It took us 10 to 15 valuable minutes to explain things, and eventually he said he would "forgive us" this time, and told us to be on our way. We made a hasty departure. Three miles farther down the road we stopped at the Land Rover agent with about five minutes to spare before they closed. Mel and I rushed inside but they only had the standard spring and we required the heavy duty model. In the meantime Mick, who was waiting outside, was sick again which caused concern to a couple of Nigerians, who came inside to tell me that he was bad. The manager of the Land Rover agent was British, and we obtained from him the address of a nearby doctor — a Nigerian woman doctor, who had done much of her studying in England, at Leeds University. She diagnosed an intestinal infection and prescribed and supplied five different types of tablet, a bottle of intravenous water to drink, and three injections, two of which were intermuscular. Mick's consultation came to N(Naira)62, or £52. By this time it was 1800 and light was fading fast so we drove out of Kaduna to find a camp site for the night, stopping about 12 miles out of town.

The next morning we arose at 0700 after a cool night, probably due to the fact that we were camping on the Kaduna plateau at a height of 2000 feet. It was the first of January. We were into another year.

It was not long before we stopped at our first checkpoint, but the police soon waved us through with a "Happy New Year" greeting. As we drove along on top of the plateau, passing a large forest on our left, we could see little of the surrounding countryside for the Harmattan wind was making everything very hazy. The Harmattan blows clouds of fine dust and sand from the southern region of the Sahara which obscure everything. Visibility was down to less than two miles, as we drove through the savanna scattered with the odd baobab tree.

We entered Kano state and drove through the small town of Kura. The road has a few potholes in it but nothing to worry about. Just outside Kaduna we were stopped at a checkpoint, where they wanted to check our vehicle papers and passports. We then had a friendly chat with the policemen before proceeding on our way. As we entered Kano town we were stopped at yet another checkpoint. Visibility was now under one mile.

Kano is Nigeria's second city and covers a large area, but it is fairly flat with few large buildings. Before driving through we stopped for petrol and were stopped again at a checkpoint on leaving town.

Kano to Maiduguri and the border

We headed out on to the road to Maiduguri. At 25 miles out from Kano we crossed the bridge over the River Hadele at Wudil, stopping for a while to watch the local people below going about their daily chores — the women washing their clothes, the men washing themselves, and the kids playing. The temperature was 98 degrees. We carried on along the now good tarmac road for another 30 miles before pulling off into a small copse to erect camp.

The night was the coldest yet and when we arose at 0700 the temperature was 48 degrees. Mick was still poorly and appeared to be making little improvement despite his medication. So we decided to make straight for Maiduguri, a large town, and seek further medical advice in a hospital there. We were at 1400 feet as we rejoined the road at 0750 hours and made our way towards the first main town of Potiskum, 170 miles away. It was possible to maintain 50 to 60 mph for considerable distances on this good road. Every available piece of land suitable for growing crops is utilised in Nigeria and we passed field upon field of maize, cassava, yams and sugar cane. All plots are small and obviously tended and owned by the family living in grass and mud huts in the corners of the plots. There were also many herds of oxen and goats along the roadside.

At Birnin Kudu we approached our first checkpoint of the day but were waved through. Further along, approaching Kari, the road is slightly potholed but we drove along the hard shoulder that runs along the whole length of the road from Kano to Maiduguri.

The Harmattan was still blowing and the accompanying haze hid the sun but the temperature was nonetheless 90 degrees. In Kari the road terminates in a junction and we turned on to the Potiskum road.

The main road by-passes Potiskum, but on arrival we made our way into town to fill up with fuel, being waved through another police check on the way in. We pulled into a filling station, but they were out of petrol, so we drove along the road a little looking for another one. A little farther was a crossroads with a filling station on each corner, but a queue of cars to our left indicated it was the only one with fuel. Half an hour later, with just one car in front of us there was a power failure. We waited hopefully but after 15 minutes gave up and drove on towards Maiduguri. At 60 miles from Potiskum we entered Damatura, after stopping at the now customary police check, and immediately found a filling station with petrol.

We eventually arrived in Maiduguri at 1500 and immediately set off for the General Hospital in the town centre, and soon had Mick in front of a doctor. After a thorough examination, the diagnosis was enteritis and malaria

— malaria was especially puzzling as we had all been regularly taking prophylactic medicines. The doctor prescribed plenty of fluids and rest, so it looked as if we would be in Maiduguri for a while.

As proper rest cannot be obtained in a tent, we started looking for a hotel and settled for what appeared the most respectable in town: the Lake Chad Hotel. The prices were reasonable too. Three days later Mick was sufficiently recovered to begin travelling again, but during the night Mel became ill so I took both of them to the hospital again, Mick for clearance and Mel for treatment. It turned out that Mel also had a mild dose of malaria, probably picked up at the same time as Mick. The doctor gave Mel two injections and 21 *tablets a day* to take, and prescribed rest. This posed problems as our visas expired the next day so I had to apply for an extension. The cheerful stocky immigration officer could not have been more helpful when we explained our position to him, and asked us to wait while the visa was extended. Meanwhile we got talking to a Roman Catholic priest who was waiting for a transit visa to Tchad and back. The priest and the immigration people knew each other well, and we soon discovered why. In 1945 the priest had left Ireland for Nigeria as a missionary for two years. He is still there.

Six days after our arrival in Maiduguri, everybody was fit enough to travel again. We left town at noon on the road to Bama and the border, first on a dual carriageway for a few miles and then on a bumpy two-lane single carriageway road which was being re-surfaced.

Three quarters of an hour after leaving Maiduguri we reached Bama, crossing over a dry bed, originally the Yetseram running into Lake Chad. Most rivers in this area were dry as this region was experiencing a severe drought. The only filling station in Bama was empty and closed, but a bit further down the road was a large roadside fuel tank with a group of African boys selling fuel from it. We pulled over and filled a few jerry cans. It was a primitive method: one boy operated an ancient hand pump which filled a glass bowl at the top with one gallon; then he released a valve and the petrol flowed down into the tank or jerry can.

Driving through Bama we passed a road gang working on the new road surface and once past them the road became badly broken up with many potholes. At 1400 hours we reached the town of Pulka, where we left the tarmac road and turned left on to a badly corrugated but firm dirt surface heading towards the Cameroon border. We passed several small mud and straw hut villages, and to our right we could see the northernmost extremity of the Mandara mountain range which runs parallel with the border on the Nigerian side. We were driving at a steady 1000 feet above sea level, and at 1430 reached the exit town of Kirawa.

Mel carried the paperwork in for customs clearance, while I took my usual safety precaution of making friends with the customs officer seated outside. This always makes for an easier time in getting through. This particular officer was more interested in our trip than searching the car and when Mel emerged with the papers he waved us on our way without even so much as a glance inside. We then drove a short distance down the road to the police post where they wasted no time in stamping our passports so by 1500 hours we were on our way to the Cameroon border officials.

Cameroon

Once over the border, police check comes first, and after 10 minutes we were officially in Cameroon. The dirt road, corrugated in places, continued and everything around us was parched, even the trees looking half dead in the drought. We passed a couple of harvested cotton fields on the approach to Kourgui, 15 miles from the border, where you have to clear customs. Mel once again took the papers in and before long we continued down the road to Mora. Here we had to ask the way and were directed along the road we were already on and told to turn right where dirt meets tarmac. So we were soon once more on a good surfaced road. The countryside around us was mountainous and rocky. There were a couple of waterholes alongside the road, where a number of storks and hammerkops were paddling, with cattle egrets around the edge. A short distance on and we came across an area of grass that would provide a soft bed for the night so we drove off the road, down a steep bank and parked.

Maroua to Ngaoundéré

At 0800 the next morning we were all up and ready for our first full day in Cameroon. The Harmattan was still blowing and the accompanying haze was hiding the mountains and hills of which we had had a good view the day before. We rejoined the road and began our drive through the savanna, with fields of crops on either side of the road.

Cameroon is a triangular shaped country, the apex in the far north in the centre of Lake Chad. Northern Cameroon is picturesque with the volcanic, rugged Rhumsiki and Kapsiki mountains around Mokolo, adjoining the Mandara range. At the base of these mountains are native settlements, with huts of straw and mud, circular and conical, built by their inhabitants, the Kirdi tribe: a race of people with just about the darkest complexion in Africa, and often seen wandering about with the scantiest of clothing, or more often completely naked.

As we drove south — following the line of crumbling rugged mountains to our right that looked like heaps of boulders dumped there centuries ago — the maize and other crops in the roadside plots looked remarkably green, despite the drought, which had left the river beds and most of the water holes completely dry. As we stopped to watch a native laying the foundations of a new hut, a young lad appeared from the bush beating a home-made drum made out of an empty 5 litre oil can. Our builder drew up plans in the dust to show us how he had to build six huts. One was already finished up to the start of the roof, and he was waiting for the mud to dry as he started on another. All around herds of goats were happily munching away at the remains of harvested crops in the fields.

At 1200 feet we soon found ourselves in the mountains as the road twisted and turned among them. Some were barren, others grass-covered. Then we came to our first police check of the day. This time there was a barrier right across the road, and we stopped against it and waited while Mel took our passports into the 'office'. He soon returned telling us we all had to go in and complete forms, so after locking the vehicle, in we trooped.

The next town is Maroua, and as we proceeded on our way we came to the end of the tarmac road and drove onto a graded dirt road with heaps of rubble piled alongside ready for road improvements. The dirt road took us into Maroua where we had to find a bank to change some of our travellers cheques into local currency. We travelled into town along tree-lined roads and after making some enquiries got to the bank: but we were too late, it was closed. I could see people working inside so made my presence known at the window and was immediately waved around to the rear of the building where an employee greeted me at the door and took me in to the manager. He spoke good English and agreed to change a little money for us, but could not change travellers cheques. Fortunately I still had some French Francs, which he found acceptable — much to our relief as we were getting low in fuel and with, the weekend ahead, would have been unable to buy petrol, food or anything else without local currency. We celebrated our currency exchange with a nice hot cup of coffee, and then made a tour of this very clean and busy town which appeared to be well stocked with all commodities.

It was very hot as we left Maroua and headed back onto the main road. Soon we came upon another police check but all they appeared to want was conversation and we stayed there talking for half an hour during which time one of the two police officers went to a nearby village stall and bought us a Coke each. As we talked to one, the other waved down some of the passing traffic, and we discovered that their main objective was to search for smuggled goods being transported between states. By the time we had finished talking it was time for the two officers to finish for the day and we agreed to transport them to their lodging place a few miles down the road. Some 35 minutes later we reached Figdil, dropped our policemen on the outskirts, and continued on our way. After another half an hour or so we pulled off the road into a secluded spot to camp. For most of the night it was so hot we could not sleep and as we lay there we could hear native drums beating in the distance.

Next morning as we drove along we passed a lot of local women, all with loads on their heads, obviously heading towards a market. African women certainly work hard and it is nothing for them to walk 10 miles to market, sell their wares for a few pence and then walk all the way back again.

Five minutes later we arrived in Pitoa. Here the line of heavily laden African women ended as they filed into the large market place and unloaded their wares. We spent a little while walking around this market, and when we

259

A common sight in Africa is women grinding grain into flour. Women do the hard work while men go hunting.

returned to the Land Rover it was surrounded by young inquisitive kids, hands everywhere, peering through the windows in amazement. It was difficult to get through them to get in so I took a few sweets out of a bag I had bought in the market and threw them on the ground. Immediately the kids dived for them, legs and arms everywhere as they scrambled on the ground for the sweets. We took the opportunity to get into our vehicle and we were away.

We passed a couple of fields of guinea corn as we entered Garoua and a smart looking mosque. We had now descended to 400 feet, our lowest for a long time. There is a very large meat market in Garoua and we had a walk around it, but there were so many flies about that it was difficult to see the meat! After a brief stop we were on our way again. Just outside Garoua we passed over the River Benoué and were surprised to see it flowing and not dry like most other rivers in this area.

The road was still good tarmac, with cotton fields on either side, the pickers hard at work reaping the harvest. We passed through Djola and Tonga, where the road had been re-surfaced recently and even had white lines painted along the centre of it. The next village, Boki, is marked clearly on the map but blink and you will miss it, it is so small. Just outside Boki we passed large areas of land that had been burnt, whether by accident or design we did not know but, considering the drought, it was probably accidental.

Ten minutes later we arrived at a checkpoint and road barrier, but the latter was open and unmanned so we drove straight through. We were now at the edge of the Bénoué National Park, which has an assortment of animals including dik diks, impala, gazelle, ground squirrels, and baboons. We climbed rapidly to a height of 1600 feet and as we reached the top of a ridge had a splendid view of the low plains ahead; but here the tarmac road surface was badly potholed and we had to reduce speed. Although we had passed through several villages there seemed to be an absence of crops in this area, despite the water running under most of the bridges we crossed.

As we travelled further south everything appeared to be greener, and water more abundant. We were now climbing the L'Adamaoua mountain range which rises to over 6000 feet in places. Approaching Karna we were stopped at a police roadblock, but were waved through when they noticed we were tourists. Through Karna and we crossed the River Benoué again. We were now surrounded by mountains, and a few miles farther on the road started climbing into them. We pulled off the road to admire the splendid view of the plains below and let the Land Rover engine cool as the steep climb and the temperature of 96° combined to make it overheat for the first time since the soft sand of the desert. Five miles later we reached the top, at 4000 feet above sea level, and had an incredible view across fields of golden grass, with green trees scattered throughout the plains and into the valleys below. As we began our descent through groves of large mango trees and banana palms, we passed at 3,200 feet a large lake to our right.

Ten miles further on we approached the outskirts of Ngaoundéré, driving into the town along an avenue lined with mature pine trees, passing a busy looking railway yard on the way. We drove straight through town, and out the other side, only stopping at a police check.

Ngaoundéré to the border

Once outside the town we were back on a dirt road but a very wide and

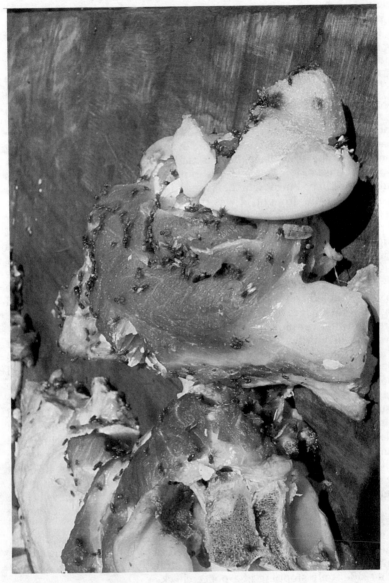

Care should be taken when buying fresh meat in Africa. This is at a butcher's shop in a market place.

smooth one that gave us a fast and comfortable ride. We passed hay drying in the fields and looked down on to the grassy plains from 3800 feet, while along the edge of the road were lines of trees in full bloom. We crossed a fast flowing river, the Vina, and a large cattle complex. The surrounding mountains were now covered with a carpet of fresh green grass, and the scattered villages along the roadside had healthy looking mango trees between the huts. As we approached Dibi the road was corrugated in places, and the trees closed in on us with dense bushland bordering the roadside.

At 44 miles from Ngaoundéré we were up to 4000 feet again, with hot sun shining down on magnificent surrounding countryside. Some 20 miles farther on we reached 4600 feet, and in the distance could see more rugged peaks. The road then descends sharply to 4000 feet and we were engulfed in a sea of green from both sides of the road as we headed south east towards the border with Central African Republic, on a very dusty road. All the villages were surrounded by woven grass fencing, presumably to keep the dust out of the houses. Another 20 miles and we had descended to 3200 feet and passed through a village with plots full of cassava. The road became bumpy with a few dips so we had to proceed with care. At 110 miles from Ngaoundéré the road became badly corrugated and very uncomfortable as we came to a fork in the road and branched left to the next village of Lokoti.

There was so much shrub by the roadside now that it was difficult to find somewhere to pull off for the night then, just before a bridge over the River Lom tributary we spotted a turning to the right which ran down into a grassy area parallel with the river and we decided to see where it went. Keeping the river to our left, we drove about 100 yards to the end, and found a junction and two smaller parts of the tributary joining the main section. At the corner we found just about the most perfect camping spot anyone could hope for: a lush green soft grassy area about 100 feet by 200 feet, surrounded on two sides by bushes and trees while on the other two sides the river, deep, clean and fast running, only about 50 feet wide here, with several large rocks scattered across part of it. German sweet wrappers, French newspapers and empty food tins piled neatly in one corner, partly burned, indicated that we were not the first overlanders to spend the night in this campers' paradise. Indeed, we had not been there many minutes when we saw a large overland truck and a Combi leave the main road and begin to drive down towards us. Then they stopped, reversed out, and continued on their way. Whether they saw us and did not want to intrude, or thought that the truck might not make it along the narrow path, we will never know. It was a pity as we would have liked company: someone to exchange tales with over the camp fire.

The next morning we were up and about at 0630 and it was decidedly chilly at 48°F, and a height of 2800 feet above sea level. We rejoined the dirt road to the C.A.R. border, and 14 miles from camp passed over the main section of the River Lom and the dirt road unexpectedly gave way to tarmac — but only for 7 miles or so. At 29 miles from our camp site we reached Garoua-Bouali, a largish town with three filling stations which all appeared to have fuel, so we filled up at one and continued towards the border control. The police post came first and Mel took the paperwork in for clearing. He soon returned with cards for each of us to complete. The customs control was just across the road so Mel wandered over with our carnet, and soon returned with the papers cleared and we were on our way to the C.A.R. border control 5 miles down the road.

Brightly coloured and clean clothing laid out to dry in the hot sun. Drying normally takes about 5 minutes.

Central African Republic

Five minutes later we left Beloko and the police post, and were shortly away again heading for customs control in the next village; customs clearance took only five minutes.

The Central African Republic survives on its diamond wealth, and is well known for its exotic flowers and beautiful tropical butterflies. It is a country that is memorable to any visitor travelling overland — by the red dirt roads and red soil; by its succulent and wide variety of fruits; and by its native huts, rectangular in shape, contrasting with the circular huts in the other African countries. Bangui, the capital, is like a separate country: before you can enter the capital you have to clear customs and immigration as at any border control. The exact reason for this is not clear but presumably it is because Bangui is a rich modern city compared with the poor under-developed villages in the rest of the country, and some sort of control has to be exerted to prevent all the inhabitants trooping into Bangui to settle.

Our dirt road was good and smooth, enabling us to maintain 40 mph for long distances. As we drove we could see little of the surrounding countryside for we were hemmed in on both sides by dense bush but 27 miles from the border it began to clear and we got our first view of the C.A.R. countryside: a mixture of golds, yellows, and greens.

Baboua to Bossembélé

At Baboua we had to stop at a roadblock, this time not police but customs. We were soon cleared but then had to wait for police check as well. While we sat in the Land Rover, with the outside temperature at 102 degrees, a small whirlwind headed towards us lifting dust, leaves and anything light in its path. Just before it reached our vehicle, it broke up and collapsed. On again, with the road still good but we kept coming across potholed sections which caused us to reduce speed.

At 52 miles from the border we crossed the first of the rickety wooden bridges which are common in this country, then started a long steady descent, affording us a good view of the road ahead of us. We were soon down to 2,000 feet and 76 miles from the border we had to cross another wooden bridge, which did not look at all safe; so we sent Tony ahead to reconnoitre on foot before crossing. Care has to be taken on all of these bridges as they are constructed of timber and some are very old. Safely over we continued on our way, crossing several more bridges before reaching the outskirts of Bouar. Beyond Bouar on the road to Bossembélé we passed a large army camp, where we were stopped to have our papers checked. The road was a little bumpy from here but still with a good firm surface, and we could look out over the rain forest of C.A.R.

At 1500 hours we copped our first kamikaze chicken. Throughout Africa chickens roam freely over the road in every village, presumably not used to too much traffic. When possible we reduced speed until they were clear. But they have a nasty habit when they see you coming of squawking and flapping all over the road, or making a quick dash to the opposite side of the road. Unfortunately, this silly bird caught us unawares.

After Baorc at 154 miles from the border we found road improvements under way with an excellent dirt surface for a while, and at 1700 we reached the town of Yaloké. Half an hour later, when everything appeared quiet and deserted, we pulled off the road to camp for the night. Suddenly, as if from nowhere, we were surrounded by local kids. Goodness knows where they came from, but we could not camp there now and so we moved on. Another 7 miles and we pulled off the road again and waited. Nobody appeared so we took the tents from the roof rack and erected them for the night.

We were up with the sun the next morning and left at 0700. As we passed through the villages we could see the women standing by the log fires outside their huts, with large iron pots suspended over the embers. There were many men, presumably forestry workers, walking along the roadside carrying axes and long knives. We had not gone far before we encountered our first police check of the day. The barrier across the road was locked, and there was no sign of anybody so we had to go and look for them. We managed to find someone who quickly cleared our paperwork and let us pass. At 37 miles from Bossembélé we crossed our first wooden bridge of the day, as usual accompanied by a dip in the road, but the general road surface remained good, slightly corrugated but smooth enough to enable us to drive along comfortably at 50 mph. The sun was just peeping from behind the trees, taking the chill out of the morning air, as we rode the contours of the land. The surrounding rain forest looked green and healthy and stretched out before us for miles with one or two black burnt sections.

At 3 miles from Bossembélé we crossed another wooden bridge, and then entered the town itself, surprisingly on a good tarmac road. Bossembélé is a busy town, and as we drove through, we passed lines of African kids on their way to school, all dressed in identical clothing, most of them with the satchel on their back and the strap around their forehead. On the edge of town we stopped at the police road check for a couple of minutes and then continued out on the good quality tarmac road which we could see stretching ahead of us. It was 0820 hours and the temperature 80 degrees.

Bossembélé to Bangui

Soon we arrived at the small town of Boali. Here we turned left off the tarmac, and drove along a rocky dirt road for a distance of 4 miles, past an African

The spectacular Boali falls in Central African Republic.

school, to the Boali falls, some 300 feet high and one of the greatest spectacles in Central African Republic. It's a sight that should not be missed, particularly when they are in flood. The falls cascade over rocks in a picturesque jungle setting, the river at the base meandering away into the distance. The river is the Mbali, which from here flows into the Oubangi at Bangui, the capital; and the Oubangi in turn runs into the great Congo river.

We returned to the tarmac road and drove on towards Bangui. The sun was partially hidden by a haze now, and as we drove along the trees were getting noticeably larger and denser. The road here is at 1000 feet and passes over the River Mbali, then over the River Mpoko a few miles further on. We were now heading due south and with about ten miles to go to Bangui were stopped at an army/police checkpoint. This time they checked the passports and also did a brief search of the car, delaying us for about 15 minutes before letting us pass. A few minutes later we were on our way to the capital, stopping about 3 miles outside for the customary police and customs control before being allowed in.

Once in town we drove straight down to the edge of the River Oubangi and looked across the wide expanse of fast flowing water at our next country, Zaire. The river must be nearly a mile across at this point, and there was plenty of activity about in the form of canoes traversing the river, and fishermen on the bank hauling their nets.

We decided to spend a couple of days in Bangui, as there is a lot to see and we were not sure from where or when the ferry to Zaire ran. Also we had been unable to obtain visas for Zaire before departure so intended to try and get them at the Embassy in Bangui. First, though, we had to find a hotel for the night.

There are many Europeans in this town, and some directed us to the Independence, near the centre of the town. It is almost next door to a large cake and coffee shop which, we later discovered, is run by a French expatriate. It sells the most beautiful cakes and bread. As we entered the hotel we were besieged by Africans selling boxes of the most exquisite African butterflies, and pictures made from butterfly wings. They also have carved ebony elephants for sale, and we all bought some souvenirs. The hotel itself is clean and reasonably priced.

It did not take us long to find the Zaire Embassy. They issued us with forms to complete and said "Come back tomorrow". It all seemed too easy after the problems we had had in London.

We were all up by 0700 the next morning, heading first for the river to enquire about the ferry. We soon found where it went from but there was no sign of it. Directly opposite the ferry ramp is the French Embassy so we went in there to ask and they referred us to a firm called Socatraf, further along the river bank nearer the town market. Meanwhile we had noticed two very smart looking hotels, the Rock and the Safari, right on the river bank, both closer to the ferry and in an excellent position giving panoramic views over the river and the country of Zaire on the opposite side. It transpired that the Safari was cheaper than the Independence Hotel so we decided to change hotels for the next night. Opposite the hotels was a large area of waste land, an ideal camping spot. In fact there was already a party of Belgian overlanders there with their Dormobile. The waste land is directly below the President's palace, perched on top of 100 foot cliffs, overlooking the river.

Next we went to Socrataf to arrange the ferry. They are in the shipyard on the quay, and I entered the office and paid for our trip across the river. Apparently Socrataf is not the company which owns the ferry, but it owns

A popular craft is carving "dug outs" from whole tree trunks.

tugs that propel it (the ferry engines no longer work). Indeed as we returned to our hotel we saw the ferry crossing the river with a single car on board, propelled by the tug behind.

We had a quick lunch and then set off for the Zaire Embassy. There were our passports, each duly stamped with the Zaire visa we so badly needed in order to continue our journey. The cost was high, but considering the mess we would be in without a visa, we decided it was worth every penny.

Bangui to Loko and back

As we had a couple of days to spare before crossing the river to Zaire we decided to spend the time travelling a little way out of Bangui in search of the pygmies that live about 80 miles south of the C.A.R. capital, in an area bounded by water and little visited.

Heading south on the tarmac road, we were stopped after 6 miles at the customs/police check situated on every road into and out of Bangui. While Mel went to the office with our paperwork, we were approached by a native lad selling freshly baked bread, in the form of turtles and snakes. This unusual bread must have been a new thing in the area for the guards at the police/customs check showed great amusement, particularly at the turtle. Ten minutes later we were on our way again, driving along a good tarmac road in a southerly direction. We crossed a bridge over the wide, fast flowing Mbali river, the same on which the Boali falls are situated. Below the bridge a dredger was at work, lifting loads of gravel and dumping it in canoes tied alongside, which then travel off down the river with their load. A little farther on we entered the rain forest once more, the tall straight trees towering above the road. We passed through several small villages and although the road was still tarmac, it was rather uneven in places, and 27 miles from Bangui the inevitable potholes began appearing, though these lasted only for 5 miles.

At 43 miles from Bangui we arrived at the town of Pissa, passing the bread delivery boy whose cycle was fitted with a 'cage' on the rear carrier, full of french loaves. A police check did not take long and then we proceeded through the centre of town and branched left off the tarmac road onto a dirt road, in very good condition, heading now towards the town of Bouchia. Half an hour later we stopped for lunch by a stream, where several naked girls were splashing about in clear water. We watched them for a while, also hordes of exotically coloured butterflies — perhaps twenty different varieties — landing at the water's edge for a drink.

Now the road became corrugated. We were entering the equatorial region of C.A.R. with the jungle now becoming very dense on both sides of our road. Trees in the native settlements included banana, palm oil, and even bread fruit, coconut and paw paw; and we also passed through several coffee plantations. At 66 miles from Bangui we stopped at a road junction, turning right onto the road to Mbaiki for a very short distance before turning left in Bouchia. Now our road was just a dirt track, heading south towards Loko and the ferry to take us across the River Lobaye and into pygmy territory. This road goes through some enormous coffee plantations and a few palm oil plantations, remnants of colonial days, but now rather run down and dilapidated. The large houses, or mansions attached to the plantations are also dilapidated, but feature some splendid architecture. The track we followed weaves its way through the coffee bushes and palm trees for about 15 miles from Bouchia, and takes you back into another world, when the area was a thriving industry making millionaires of the Europeans who owned the plantations.

This track, which is of single car width, is badly rutted, mainly by the torrential rainfalls common in this country, which turn it into a river bed, and our speed was reduced to about 10 miles per hour. Occasionally the surface improved enabling us to travel a little faster, but we did not dare to go too fast in case we missed a turning; you are constantly turning left, right, and left again, and always asking directions to Loko in the absence of signposts. We found a banana palm growing by the road side, and cut ourselves a bunch of bananas, being very careful to avoid the juice that seeps from the stem, for it leaves indelible black marks on everything it touches. Even the 'stainless' steel knife we used was left with a black stain on the blade. At 6 miles along this road and 72 miles from Bangui, we passed a very good football pitch, surrounded by palm oil trees. The pitch had fresh green grass on it, and was on the edge of one of the few villages in this area, probably one that sprang up from a worker's encampment back in the plantation days. Opposite this football pitch is a large rubber plantation, now derelict, the trees too old for production and the plantation overgrown with weeds and small shrubs that have sprung up by themselves. A reminder of days gone by was the heavy scarring on the lower trunks of the trees in the form of diagonal lines where the bark was once cut to extract the latex. The odd tree still had the catching cup secured to it, now full of dust, leaves, and other debris.

Three miles down the road we came to a crossroads with signposts pointing to every location except Loko! We had to ask directions again, and were soon back en route driving along a flat dusty road for a couple of miles before hitting the rutted sections again. The aroma of coffee bushes in flower came drifting in through the open windows of the Land Rover, but then we were once again driving through thick jungle. We came to a crude log bridge, looking very unstable, and crossed with extreme caution. One mile up the road we crossed another, and then another, and then we passed a group of natives no more than four feet tall: we had found the first of the pygmies. They were heading towards Loko, their village.

It is only in the C.A.R. and Zaire that it is possible to find pygmy locations, and even then one must travel deep into the jungle to encounter these small people who are very shy, and suspicious of the white man. The pygmies live on the wild fruits and vegetables of the jungle, and any wild animal that comes within the range of their bow and arrow. Many have now become assimilated into Bantu villages and locations scattered throughout Central Africa, but others still live with their own tribes and by travelling deep into the jungle one can have the experience of meeting them in their original environment.

As we reached the Lobaye river the ferry was beached on the opposite side, some 150 yards across, so we hailed the captain and, after a session of frantic waving and gesticulating, we heard the engine start and it made its way over to us. The pygmies we had passed back along the road were now waiting with us and allowed us to take some photographs, appearing quite unperturbed as we clicked away with our cameras. Once across we arranged to be taken back in about 5 hours' time, and set off for the village of Loko. There was no road and we had to make our own way across the scrubland that separated us from Loko.

On arrival in the village we were soon stopped by the Mayor, who introduced himself to each of us in turn. Surprisingly he was Bantu, not

The word "modesty" has different connotations in Africa, and these girls in Central African Republic were only too pleased to be photographed after we discovered them splashing about in a stream.

pygmy. It seemed there were quite a few Bantu living here. Some of the shy pymies soon emerged, and we strolled casually through Loko learning about their way of life. It is only a small village and we soon came to the end. A new road is being cut through the jungle linking Loko with the only other village in this area, Bongoumba, about 12 miles away so we decided to drive there along the river bank. We found the village to be little more than a couple of mud huts so we drove down to a couple of canoes in the river, where once another ferry ran across, and had a dip in the cool inviting water. The locals soon came running down to warn us that the River Lobaye is crocodile infested so we were soon out again! We made our way back to the ferry along the freshly cut dirt road, hordes of beautifully coloured butterflies drifting across our windscreen as we drove along.

We arrived back at the ferry at 1630 hours after an enjoyable day in pygmy territory to find the skipper waiting for us. Mel, Mick and Tony wanted to cross the river in a dug-out canoe, paddled by one of the pygmies, so I offered to take the Land Rover across alone. However when they all got in, they found the water was just about lapping over the edges and, as the river was full of crocodiles, Tony opted out and came over with me. On the way back I learnt that we were the first vehicle to cross on the ferry for several weeks. There is no charge on this or any other ferry in C.A.R. or Zaire, as they are classed as 'roads' and accordingly are free; but it is common amongst tourists to tip the skipper and crew.

After we had left the ferry to the waves and cheers of the crew and the many villagers who had crossed to bid us farewell, the ferry promptly returned to the centre of the river and put on a show for us, zig-zagging back and forth, and then turning circles in the centre of the river before bidding us farewell and sailing once more to the opposite bank. We then took off down the road to look for a camp site for the night.

Up at first light the next morning we were serenaded by toucans and hornbills as we packed the tents away. We set off back to Bangui, travelling along the bumpy rutted dirt track, and then taking a different route back via M'Baiki and the tarmac road. Approaching Pissa we were waved straight through the check point and soon after crossed the River Mbali once more, with the dredger still at work loading gravel into the canoes.

The Bangui ferry

We arrived back in Bangui at 0930 and went to the market for provisions, coming away with a parking ticket as well for parking in a prohibited area right outside the market. We booked in at the Safari Hotel for the night and got cleaned up for our journey next day through Zaire. We also took the opportunity to re-arrange the goods packed in the Land Rover to avoid any damage as there were some very rough roads ahead. The rest of the afternoon we spent lazing on the sandy river bank outside the Rock Hotel.

The next day we were up bright and early checking everything over in preparation for our crossing into Zaire. First of all we had to enter the docks via the main gate opposite the market, and clear passport control. We all had to complete an immigration card before our passports were stamped. The next stage was to drive to the ferry departure point and clear customs. Mel took the carnet into the building while I enquired about the tug as there was no sign of it. It seemed it was on its way from another job and as Mel came out with the carnet we could see it in the distance coming up river towards us. However, instead of pulling in by the ferry, it stopped short and went into the docks. We waited. It was an hour later when tug and ferry eventually arrived and drove the ramp up the slope. The skipper then beckoned us on and we slowly negotiated the steep slope down to the ferry. Ours was the only vehicle on this crossing, and soon the ferry pulled away, slowly edging its way up river against the strong current: it had been an enjoyable stay in the Central African Republic. The ferry sailed past the Rock Hotel, and then through the narrow gap in the river opposite the Safari Hotel.

Zaire

The ferry crossing the Oubangi takes 15 minutes so we were soon in Zaire, formerly the Belgian Congo — the 'darkest Africa' of Stanley's explorations. This was to be one of the toughest sections of our trip with roads practically non-existent; we would have to travel 1,800 miles along what are little more than dirt tracks, very badly rutted, which flood completely when it rains. We would have to cross many rotten wooden bridges, some of which would require re-building or repairing before they could be used. Around us would be lush emerald green jungle with trees that can tower to a height of 200 feet or so, covered with creepers and other vegetation, surrounded by a lower tree layer and shrubs and tall bamboo. There would be many ferry crossings over the deep, fast-flowing Zaire river or one of its numerous tributaries, and diversions if we discovered that a certain ferry had stopped operation — quite a common occurrence. If it rained we might be driving through water as high as the bonnet of the vehicle, bridging gaps in the track where the torrential rains had washed large sections away; and negotiating fallen trees, and flattened bamboo which block tracks after every rainstorm. Other problems would be acute shortage of fuel and the difficulty of finding a camp site in thick jungle where clearings become overgrown in just a few days. We had filled all available fuel containers and tanks before leaving C.A.R., as the only station which might have fuel is in Kisangani, and even then the chance is remote. There is little road transport in Zaire, particularly in the north, the main means of transportation being by air or river.

Apart from all this, Zaire is still one of the most interesting and exciting countries to visit in the whole of Africa. Much of the country is still unexplored, therefore presenting a challenge to any overlander. We would delight in the thick green jungle vegetation, encroaching on us so quickly in places that it would cut out the light completely. We would marvel at the beautiful flora to be found along the roadside, and the exquisite array of butterflies: perhaps we would even be lucky enough to see Papillon, the world's largest butterfly with a wing span of up to 10 inches, dark red with black markings. Very high humidity might prevent us getting much sleep at night but we would be able to lie awake and listen to the constant calling

275

River ferries in Zaire are crude but effective, often consisting of a wooden platform on oil drums propelled by rope from the opposite bank. This one took us to the land of the pygmies.

of the crickets, monkeys, or various birds. Our journey through this country would be unforgettable, all the more so because of the hospitality and extreme friendliness of the Zairean people.

Zongo to Bogilima

Zongo is the border town in Zaire where you have to clear customs and immigration after the river crossing. Customs and immigration were mere formalities: they did not check the vehicle but the immigration officers left their office to wish us 'Bon Voyage'!

In the first hour we managed to travel only 10 miles on the bumpy one-car track. Our top speed was only 12 mph and we were down to walking pace at times. In fact, one could travel faster on foot on some of these roads. We hoped nothing large would need to pass us for it would be an extremely tight squeeze. All round was dense jungle, and tropical butterflies drifted across the windscreen. After the first 12 miles the road improved slightly enabling us to reach 20 mph at times. At 22 miles from Zongo we crossed our first wooden bridge and came to a junction where we had to ask the locals for directions to Boyabo. They soon put us on the right road.

We were at 1500 feet and the road was very rocky. The jungle had opened out slightly giving us a good view of the lush green countryside, with acres of elephant grass in front of us and rolling hills in the distance. In the second hour we managed 15 miles and the road then improved, enabling us to reach 25 mph at times. We passed through an avenue of palm oil trees, crossing another wooden bridge, and noticed the appearance of bamboo along the roadside. We met a column of army ants, the second we had seen, and passed through many small villages in clearings in the jungle, all with chickens and goats running free, and banana palms and bread fruit trees growing around the huts.

The road continued to improve and in the third hour we managed to travel 16 miles. At a fairly large village we overtook a cyclist with two goats strapped to his pannier rack, both alive and looking very uncomfortable. Then we passed our first motorised transport in Zaire, a motor bike, and noticed puddles in the road as if it had rained recently. In each village we had passed women had rushed to the edge of the road, with a large pineapple or perhaps a hand of bananas held aloft that they wish to sell, and it became evident that this is their sole income. The jungle began to engulf the road again as we crossed two wooden bridges in quick succession and began to look for somewhere to camp. Not far up the road we were lucky enough to come across a large clearing in the jungle where trees had recently been cut for their timber, so we drove in and pitched camp for the night.

We were up the next morning to the screeching of monkeys and hornbills, with the sun shining down on the clearing. As soon as we drove out onto the road, though, we lost the sun owing to the tall vegetation overhanging the road. The road was still bumpy and rutted, and after 8 miles we came across an unsignposted junction and had to ask directions. Past a group of disused plantation homes and 3 miles on we came upon another junction, asking directions once more. The road widened and had a gravel surface with rain gullies in amongst the corrugations, keeping down the distance travelled in the first hour to 16 miles. We passed another column of army ants on the march, and a couple of old plantations with very old coffee bushes still growing, then drove through a village where each hut had a grass mat outside with a layer of coffee beans drying in the sun.

At 90 miles from Zongo we crossed our first steel bridge followed by another wooden one and then came to another unmarked junction. The road was now hard packed clay with deep ruts in places and our speed dropped to 8 to 10 miles per hour.

The villages consist of two lines of huts with the road running down the middle, and every village we passed through looked immaculately clean. Often we saw the woman of the hut out with her broom sweeping away dead leaves and other debris. The village children seemed to know we were coming for they lined the roadside waving and shouting with an accent combining African and French: "Hello Toureest". Sound in the jungle carries a long way so they probably heard our Land Rover coming long before we reached them. Once we stopped to watch an elderly man weaving a basket out of split bamboo, and before long we were surrounded by children and adults welcoming us.

At 110 miles from Zongo the road became very badly rutted for long sections, with very deep ruts in places caused by heavy vehicles sinking in the soft mud during the rainy season. Our speed now was between 2/3 mph and 12 mph varying with the road conditions. We were also now encountering quite a few log bridges.

At 10.35, 135 miles from Zongo and just over halfway between Libenge and Kungu, we came to our first river crossing, only to discover after driving down the ramp to wait for the ferry, that it "went up river", as the natives said, and no longer operated on this section. This sort of occurrence in Zaire is not unusual, but it creates a great deal of inconvenience, for we now had to backtrack for nearly one hundred miles

There was an old steel floating pontoon in the river, and we wondered if there was any way we could utilise it to get us across, but without any power to propel it the situation seemed hopeless. The river is deep, fast flowing, and nearly 200 yards wide and we did not have enough rope to pull us across. So there was nothing for it but to turn round and head back towards Libenge. Alas on turning we became embedded in the soft sandy mud; but the locals soon rallied round and dug us out and we were on our way.

At 1500 hours, 4½ hours later, we passed last night's camp site, and in twenty minutes were at the road junction for Bogilima and Gemena. According to the locals, the ferry was running at Bogilima although there was no crossing marked on the map. We would have to wait and see!

The Bogilima road had a fair red dirt surface, corrugated in places, and we reached speeds of up to 30 mph along it although we were down to 10 mph at times. At 13 miles we came to a road junction: left fork for Bosobolo, right fork for Bogilima — a road still rutted, with tall elephant grass on either side. At 17.15 we reached Bogilima, driving straight through to the river where, much to our relief, we found the ferry to be operational! We were 47 miles from last night's camp site, but had travelled 187 miles in the day: 140 miles wasted. The ferry dropped its ramp and we drove on, the only vehicle for this crossing.

Bogilima to Gemena

At the other side we immediately began looking for a camp site as it was now 1800 hours. The jungle was dense, making it impossible to find anywhere to pitch our tents. We passed a village with a crude football pitch, but it was

278

In Zaire, the only way across rivers is by ferry, when they are running — and that is only when more than one vehicle wishes to cross. On this one we waited for three hours before departure. These ferries should not be approached direct, but rather at an angle as the ramps are very steep and you are liable to become stuck on a direct approach.

being used so we carried on. Then we came across a sort of layby, right on the roadside, with huge piles of gravel in it — obviously road repair material. We drove in and managed to find a clear spot just large enough to erect two tents. Just before dawn, we discoverd that this gravel store had not been a good choice for we were woken at 0530 by the heavy sound of machinery and peered out to find a bulldozer-type vehicle coming to remove some of the gravel. We hastily got out and demolished the tents in record time before the JCB did. At 0600 hours we were on the road to Gemena.

Mick was taken ill during the night and still did not feel too good so we took it steady for a while. The trees and road were shrouded in mist, and we were unable to travel at more than 10 mph owing to the badly corrugated road surface. We came up behind a lorry that had stopped on the road with a puncture, and just managed to squeeze past. We managed to travel only 15 miles in the first hour, the mist slowly lifting to give us a clearer view ahead. In every village we passed through there were hordes of locals, particularly children, waving and shouting at us as we drove by, with their usual "Hallo Toureest". If by chance they were a little way back from the road and we did not see them, they would shout frantically until they attracted our attention and we waved to them.

At 44 miles from the ferry crossing at Bogilima the road improved greatly and we were able to drive along at up to 40 mph, passing through several small villages almost hidden by the dense jungle. Another 10 miles on we reached the outskirts of Gemena. The General Hospital is situated on the main road, on the left hand side, and I took Mick in for a check as his condition had deteriorated. The doctor gave him a thorough examination and diagnosed malaria again. Mick was given an injection of quinine and a box full of tablets and told to rest. There was no room in the hospital so we asked the doctor to recommend a clean hotel. He guided us to the Hotel Bonne Auberge run by a Flemish colonial, which turned out to be the only hotel in the town; it appeared to be a well-maintained two-storey building but when we looked at the rooms they were filthy: beds with dirty mattress and no sheets or blankets, and no running water, hot or cold. Also the place was rat infested. However, there was nowhere else to go, and Mick had to have rest, so we had no choice. A room cost £7 a night excluding meals. We took our own blankets and sleeping bags up to the room, and then left Mick in bed while we tried to find a bank.

The bank was just a few yards along the road from the hospital, but when we tried to change travellers cheques, we were informed that they only exchanged cash. This transaction was going smoothly until I produced the customs currency declaration. Suddenly the bank decided that it could not change cash either, refusing to give a reason. Fortunately, an expatriate living in Gemena then approached me and offered to change cash and travellers cheques at the normal bank rate; I willingly agreed as it was the only way to get any money to pay for our accommodation, food and petrol.

The next problem developed when we tried to buy petrol. There was none in town at any of the filling stations, and would be none in the forseeable future. We decided to seek out our friendly expatriate who, we learned, ran a large pharmacy in the centre of town, to ask where we could get petrol, and he directed us to friends of his who run a large cotton/coffee growing concern. Apparently they had their own supply of petrol delivered direct to the company for the many vehicles they use in their business. They were willing to sell but quoted a price 3 times the normal. In fact we had enough petrol to get us a good way across Zaire, but decided to fill our main tanks even at this inflated price. It is always best to fill up whenever possible as you never know when and where petrol or diesel will be available. Expatriates are usually able to help out though, and there are groups of them in most Zaire towns.

Back at the hotel, we found Mick asleep, but had to take Mel to the hospital to see the doctor as he was now feeling sick. His was also malaria again but very mild so he was just given some tablets to take. We explained to the doctor that there was not a drop of water in the hotel room so he lent us a 10 gallon plastic drum and directed us to a pump. He also gave us a gallon of drinking water.

At 1830 that evening the doctor arrived to re-vaccinate Mick and check on his condition; for the whole time Mick was bad, the doctor called morning and evening. At the worst stage, Mick seemed almost at death's door, being badly dehydrated, and not eating anything. Then, a couple of hours before the doctor was due to put him on a drip feed, he started drinking coffee, and this heralded his recovery. For all his trouble the doctor made no charge. In fact all we had to pay for was the hotel and medicines from the pharmacy.

During our stay in Gemena which lasted a week, nothing much else happened. I was becoming concerned that our stay in Gemena was also prolonging our stay in Zaire, and bringing us closer to the approaching rains, which can play havoc with the roads. Although we had no rain we had seen lightning in the distance and heard the occasional roll of thunder. However, we had to wait until everyone was fit.

Seven days, 14 injections, and umpteen dozen tablets later, Mick was fit enough to travel again after his second bout of malaria in a month. His last evening in Gemena, he was able to have a good meal in the hotel restaurant in preparation for travelling again the next day. We were up at 0600, and on the road at 0700, with the sun just rising. Gemena was a poor though attractive town, but we were all pleased to get away from the dirty, rat- and cockroach-infested hotel, and back on the road again.

Gemena to Binga

It was a sandy road leading from Gemena, but the surface was good and we were able to reach 25 mph. We passed miles of coffee plantations on the road to Akula and our next ferry crossing. Friends we met in Gemena had advised us to take this road instead of travelling via Businga, despite it being marked on the map as a poor road, and so far so good.

An hour and ten miles from Gemena there were some long hard clay sections of road with occasional sandy patches. Once more we heard the familiar "Hello Toureest" as we waved our way through many villages, and it became obvious that this is the most popular route for overlanders.

After 40 miles the road became firm but corrugated, with not much sand. The dense green jungle gradually gave way to rubber tree plantations. At 70 miles from Gemena we slowed down to 10 mph on a very badly rutted section of road and maintained this speed for the remaining four miles to Akula and our ferry over the River Mongala.

Entering Akula, there was evidence of recent heavy rain, with the dirt road more of a mud pit and deep holes in it filled with muddy slime. We reached the river where the ferry was still running, so joined the queue and waited for our turn to embark. Meanwhile, the road workers we had met in Gemena met up with us again, and told us that a 150-yard section of the road on the other side of the river had been completely washed away by heavy rain, and there was no way to pass until the hole was filled. Already trucks loaded with soil were on their way across, so we thought we would take a chance. The ferry docked, running its ramp up the river bank, and just as we drove on we saw our first Papillon butterfly, swooping low over our heads before flitting off across the river, its flight so easy and graceful.

On the opposite bank, the ferry was unable to get really close, leaving us a drive of about 35 feet through water a foot deep. In addition the ramp had an angle of more than 45 degrees making disembarkation difficult, so Mel and Tony found some planks for me to drive down. Unfortunately the ferry driver suddenly decided that he could wait no longer and with our vehicle only halfway down the ramp he moved off. Our spare wheel mounted on the rear door caught the ramp as the vehicle slid, and partially ripped our rear door off. We spent the next hour trying to fix it and did not make too bad a job of it, though later when we had the proper tools we would have to do it again.

Soon we reached the spot where the rain had washed the road away. There was another Land Rover in front of us with two girls and two boys in it, and we pulled up behind them to wait. Our fellow travellers had everything including the kitchen sink in their vehicle. In fact they had so much stuff inside that two of them had to travel on the roof rack! We were delayed for four hours by this hole on the road and eventually continued on our way at 1500 hours.

Back in Gemena we had been told by the cotton growers that there was fuel available from the growers' association in the little town of Binga, so we decided to try and make it there for the night. The first four miles were very bad with deep ruts, and holes, and our maximum speed was 5 mph. At 6 miles from the Mongala river ferry the road improved enough to enable us to travel at 30 mph for some distance but at 22 miles it became badly rutted again all the way into Diobo. Here we turned left onto the road to Binga, passing through acres of rubble and palm oil plantations, the majority belonging to Lever Brothers or Dunlop. We also passed some coffee plantations along the excellent dirt road towards Binga.

Some 39 miles from the ferry we arrived in Binga and stopped outside a large building where there were a lot of white people to enquire about petrol. Apparently we were too late: it was 1800 hours, and they were all going home, but one of them told us to return the following day when they would let us have some fuel. He then invited us to his house for a drink and we gladly accepted. Chatting in his house, we learned more about the way of life out in this desolate area. He then led us along the dark dusty roads to a friend who runs the Catholic mission, where we could camp for the night. We soon erected our tents, and the French missionary let us use his kitchen to make ourselves coffee before going to bed.

By 0540 the next morning, we were preparing for an early start, and by 0640 had found our way to the petrol office. The procedure is to pay at the offices of the planters, and then take a voucher to their private petrol supply. They asked how much our tank held, how far we had to go, and how many miles to the gallon, in order to decide on a quota, for the supply is not plentiful. We got 15 gallons for which we were very grateful.

Binga to Aketi

As we drove along the smooth dust roads, through the acres of palm and rubber trees, we passed groups of children on their way to school, and several forest workers armed with their machettes or pangas. At 0700 the temperature was 78 degrees. We arrived in Mbokutu and turned left on to the main road to Lisala some 85 miles away, where we would see the great River Zaire for the first time. This road was fairly good, although rutted in places, and we travelled at 25 mph for most of the time, although 25 miles from Binga the road became more uneven, reducing our speed somewhat. We were still travelling through plantations, but passing few villages now, some of which appeared deserted. There were now some holes in the road filled with water from the recent rains, which we tried to avoid, not knowing how deep they were or what lay beneath the muddy water.

At 69 miles from Binga the badly rutted road descends a steep hill, then climbs again through an area of very soft sand. At the top of the sandy section is a lot of hard rock embedded in the road, to be negotiated with care. We then observed a rare sight in this country, a road sign! Lisala 23 kilometres (14 miles).

Some 82 miles from Binga the road stretched out ahead of us, still bordered by the unchanging jungle, save for the odd clearing for native settlements and their crop fields. At 5 miles farther on we crossed a large, old wooden bridge, and entered Lisala, turning right off our road towards the river. At last we had come to the notorious Congo, now the River Zaire; all we could see was water and, on the opposite side, jungle. For those seeking a primitive but enjoyable river trip, vehicles and passengers can be shipped from Lisala up river to Kisangani, a journey which is quite an experience in itself.

We immediately began asking around for petrol, hoping to fill our tanks again, but had no luck at all in this town. We could not even find drinking water. So we headed back on to the road that leads to the next town of Bumba. At 10 miles out of Lisala we climbed a hill and from the top looked down upon the huge River Zaire meandering its way through the dense jungle. Eight miles on we crossed a wooden bridge over a fast flowing deep river, whose water looked surprisingly clean. Our road was smooth but dusty with the occasional sandy section. The jungle began to engulf the road, huge bamboos arching over it, their fronds leaning against the trunks and branches of trees on the opposite side. At 37 miles from Lisala we passed through a very pretty village surrounded by tall palm oil trees. As we drove through, the goats ran to one side, but the chickens scampered all over the place attempting suicide beneath our wheels. This time we managed to miss them all.

At 1345 we were in Modjamboli, 56 miles from Lisala, where a road sign showed Bumba 41 miles. The road was still surprisingly good and the going smooth. At 1500 we crossed a rickety wooden bridge and entered the town of Ebonda, passing an old disused steam engine by the side of the road. There was a road sign: Bumba 7 miles. Soon afterwards we entered Bumba and started looking for cars driven by white people, a potential source of supply for petrol. We soon found one driving a Land Cruiser, and he directed us to his company, Scibe Zaire, which was down on the river bank. It seemed to be quite a big company in this part of Zaire. We soon found it and Mel went to enquire about petrol. Next thing we knew he was opening the large double gates and beckoning us in. It was our lucky day. We were allowed 140 litres — more than enough to fill all our tanks and jerry cans. The price

It is not unusual in equatorial Africa to find a huge tree blocking your path, particularly after a rain storm. This one took half an hour to cut and roll away.

was high, 5 times normal, but this is not important when petrol is as scarce as it is here.

Topped up with fuel and water, we headed out of the town of Bumba at 1700 hours planning to find a camp site. The skies were black, and 20 minutes later the heavens opened and a deluge of water engulfed us. The rain had arrived, my worst fear. Driving slowly along the slippery road, aquaplaning in all directions, it soon became apparent that we would be lucky to find a dry camp site tonight; the choice was to keep driving, or wait for the rain to stop — which seemed unwise as roads tend to get washed away. Already rain was finding its way into the vehicle and I was driving with my accelerator foot full of water.

It was now nearly dark and we were driving through a sea of bamboo, blocking the road in front of us, forced down by the weight of water. The rain restricted visibility considerably as we pushed our way through the bamboo branches, which sprang back behind us. They beat against the windscreen, threatening to break it, and played havoc with our paintwork. Then only five miles farther on came what I had dreaded: a huge hardwood tree across the road, completely blocking it. Four other vehicles were stopped and fortunately a group of locals was already hacking into the tree. It does not take them long to clear a tree with their axes, hard as the wood is, for they work as a team and have plenty of experience. Incidentally, while waiting for the road to be re-opened, it's wiser not to park under or near a standing tree, lest that too comes crashing down as the gushing water washes the soil from its roots. An average jungle hardwood weighs in the region of 50 tons and would do more than scratch the paintwork!

After half an hour the locals managed to chop through the tree. From saplings by the roadside they cut lengths of wood about 8 feet long and four inches in diameter so that everyone could heave together and lever the huge section of trunk blocking the road to one side.

We set off again. The rain had formed a 'river' on one side of the road, a gulley filled with muddy rushing water. As this road, like most in Zaire, was wide enough for only one vehicle, we drove very slowly for some way at an angle of 45 degrees with the water over the tyres on one side of the vehicle. A mile farther on we came upon another tree across the road but it was cleared just as we got there. We had been travelling in the rain for two hours but had covered only 13 miles! More bamboo, and then more, then a whole curtain of bamboo across the road almost blocking it; although we were following large trucks which had helped flatten the bamboo, it was still very thick and even with our headlights full on we could not see through it. The trucks ahead of us must have been used to these conditions for they were travelling much faster than we were, and their tracks in the mud were washed out. Judging by the road, and the leaves, branches, and bamboo littering it, we were now in the area where the storm had hit hardest.

We were now well away from any habitation and well out on the road to Aketi. Suddenly, we saw the feared red tail lights ahead and pulled up behind a line of trucks and other vehicles. It had stopped raining so Mel and I took a walk towards the front of the queue, feeling our way in the dark through drooping branches, soaked with rain. After passing four trucks we stopped: in front of us was the expatriate in the Land Cruiser whom we had met in Bumba. He had left Bumba 1½ hours before us on a non-stop trip to Aketi, over the roads he knew like the back of his hand, but this was as far as he had got. A few yards farther we found the reason. A massive tree had blocked the road — a dead tree so the wood was not easy to cut through. Already some of the drivers had tried and blunted their axes, with no way of sharpening them. We could only wait for someone to come along with a sharp axe. So we prepared to sleep in the vehicle as some of the other drivers were already doing. As we sat in our seats, slowly dozing off, we watched an incredible display of lightning, lasting some 20 minutes, rivalling the best firework display.

We awoke the next morning at 0530 to the sound of metal on wood. Already the locals were chopping away at the tree trunk and were halfway through. Reinforcements must have arrived during the night. We now had quite a line of local vehicles behind us as well as in front.

At 0800 hours the trunk eventually crashed to the road and, although we were a hundred yards back in our vehicle, we felt the vibrations as the wood hit the ground with a tremendous crash. We all jumped out to help lever the trunk to the side of the road, and shortly afterwards were moving again, through the puddles and rain gullies 2-3 feet deep. We still had to contend with drooping bamboo. It took us 1½ hours to cover 13 miles from the fallen tree. At one point we came to a bridge with many of the timbers missing, and had to reconnoitre on foot and then "re-build" it before we could cross. The condition of the roads was indescribable. They had to be seen to be believed.

At 32 miles from Bumba, the bamboo still arched across the road but there were signs of improvement. The ruts were now few and far between, and the surface was undulating. We crossed another bridge and eventually arrived in Aketi as the sun came through.

Aketi to Kisangani

Once through Aketi the road became very soft and we could manage only 10 miles per hour through our bamboo jungle. We reached a railway bridge doubling as a road bridge, and eased our way across it. There was a small village on the other side, and then a crude log bridge, after which the road improved considerably and we drove along at 30 mph. We passed a road sign: Buta 74 kilometres (46 miles). Another 10 miles and the road became potholed, reducing our speed again to 15/20 mph. We crossed another bridge before entering the outskirts of Buta at 1520 hours.

After Buta we were on the road to Banalia and another ferry crossing. This section of road was in good condition and we were able to maintain speeds of 40 mph for long distances, travelling through a bamboo archway for a couple of miles at the start. Alas, we rammed two chickens in the space of 5 minutes, unable to do much to avoid them at 40 mph, and leaving a cloud of feathers in the road behind us. We were now 36 miles from Buta and we had been travelling an hour. Dusk was falling, so we began looking for a camp site.

At 1740 hours we crossed the River Tele. The road is bounded by dense jungle which made it difficult to find a suitable place to camp so we kept on driving. As darkness fell, I switched on the headlights and spotlights only to find the spotlights very dim; so we pulled up to investigate and discovered they were full of water, probably as a result of driving through deep water filled ruts.

At 1945 we reached the River Aruwimi to find the ferry waiting to load for the five minute crossing to Banalia, so we drove straight on. Once on the other side we drove straight through Banalia, still looking vainly for

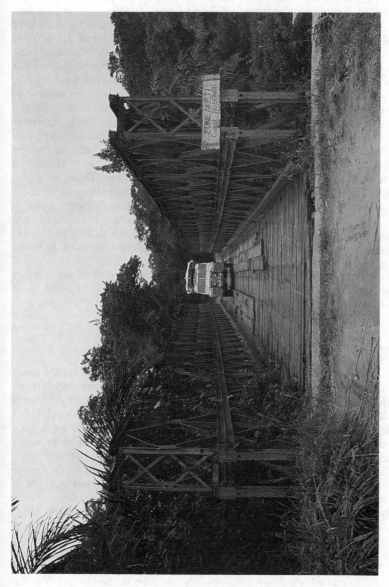

Many jungle bridges are very rickety and have to be patched up before crossing with care.

somewhere to camp, so ended up pulling in to the side of the road and spending the night in the vehicle.

The next morning we were all up at 0530, and by 0630 were on our way to Kisangani. The road is good, firm packed clay with a layer of gravel over it. We crossed a long steel and timber bridge over the River Lindi and a few miles farther on crossed our last river before Kisangani, entering this large town at 0730. As usual, we headed straight for the centre in search of a bank, and soon found one just opening, so we exchanged some travellers cheques for local currency, the Zaire. Our next job was to get some petrol, if possible, but all the filling stations we had passed had been closed. We eventually found one station open and joined the queue, hoping that the supply would not run out before we got to the pumps. While in the queue we got talking to some locals and learnt that our watches must go forward an hour.

We reached the fuel pumps and managed to fill both main tanks, but the attendants would not fill our jerry cans so we drove round the block, siphoned the fuel out of the tanks into the jerry cans, and then returned to fill the tanks again. It meant rejoining the queue, but it did not take too long and was worth it to fill all our containers and tanks at the normal price.

Kisangani is worth a stay for a couple of days, if not more. There are some good and fairly cheap hotels, serving good meals at reasonable prices. Topping the list is the fish straight from the River Zaire and very fresh — especially the kapitan fish commonly known as the Nile perch. Fish are frequently caught weighing 100 lb or more, and a kapitan steak is delicious. There is also an excellent market and no shortage of provisions of all sorts. It is a good place to stock up.

While in Kisangani a visit to the Wagenia fishermen, perched on poles in mid-river, to observe their unique method of catching fish, is a must. And the celebrated Stanley Falls should not be missed.

Kisangani to Beni via Mt Hoyo

We left Kisangani on the road to Wanie-Rukula. This is tarmac for 14 miles to Madula where we turned off towards Bafwasende, for we wanted to drive through the Ituri forest and glimpse the rare okapi, a creature half zebra and half antelope, that was only discovered in recent years. (This is also the best route for Mount Hoyo, another interesting spot to visit.) So we were back on a red dirt road in good condition with just one or two potholes to avoid and passing through some coffee plantations at 1200 feet above sea level. The villages appeared very quiet as we hummed along at 50 mph. Jungle edged the road on both sides, and bamboo archways appeared in front of us every so often. We passed a couple of natives selling dead monkeys, recently shot and ready for skinning and the pot. We crossed over another wooden bridge 38 miles from Kisangani, and the road remained good although we had to watch for the odd pot hole.

At 75 miles from Kisangani we crossed a fast flowing river, and stopped to watch some natives on the river bank below, hard at work digging out tree trunks to make their dugout canoes. The bamboo drapes itself along the water's edge on both sides of this river, tops arching into the water.

Some 20 minutes later, at 1500 feet, we heard a hissing coming from the rear of the vehicle and found our fire extinguisher had set itself off with the vibration. Nothing too serious, though, and we soon corrected matters.

The jungle was thicker than ever, and it was looking as if we would have to sleep in the vehicle again, when we came to a disused quarry, surrounded by towering trees. As we erected the tents we could hear the screaming of monkeys, and looked up to see them swinging amongst the tree tops.

We were up at 0600, to a cloudy sky although there had been no rain. The road remained good as we started on our way with only occasional potholes. As we approached Bafwabalinga, however, the road deteriorated and we were running over corrugations with potholes every few yards, but beyond Bafwabalinga the road improved again as we climbed a hill amongst towering bamboo.

The sun was still hidden in the clouds as we passed a road sign showing Nia Nia 78 kilometres (49 miles) near a couple of closed down filling stations. In places we were passing over broken up tarmac on the road — so there had at some time been tarmac sections. We then climbed a long hill where the road was very bumpy with rocks scattered across the surface, passing a palm oil plantation, and shortly afterwards the road became similar to the old cobblestone roads, shaking the vehicle about as we rumbled along for 2 miles. At the end of the stones we were faced with some deep ruts.

We came to the River Ituri, a continuation of the River Aruwimi, and had to wait at the bridge while repair men re-laid the wooden planks on the steel girders. This made a change for we normally did it ourselves!

We arrived in Nia Nia and pulled up outside a small café hoping to buy a Coke, but ended up having a meal of rice, potato, and monkey meat. Very nice it was too. Then back onto the bumpy road with another cobbled section. We passed through a village with several coffee bushes in full bloom, and the beautiful scent drifted in through our open windows. There was less bamboo now, but more banana palms. We still had the towering trees of the jungle though, and halfway between Nia Nia and Mambasa we passed through villages where there were a number of pygmies walking about. We attempted to photograph them but they wouldn't have it and ran to hide in the trees.

A few miles up the road we stopped to admire the scenery and water fall at the Station de capture d'Epulu, where the okapi is frequently seen. This spot is a reserve and has a well-maintained camp site with a full time warden. There is also a small shop. We passed the bridge over the river, pausing to photograph and admire the falls, and then entered another area of bamboo. The road was fairly good and we managed speeds up to 30 mph. We spotted several baboons in the road, but they ran and hid in the bush as we approached. As we reached 2200 feet above sea level and began to descend a rutted hill, the rain started.

It was really teeming down as we entered Mambasa. We wanted to take a a jungle road from there to Beni, but on asking the locals we learned that recent heavy rains had washed a lot of the road away. In any case the ferry halfway along the road was no longer running, so we headed out on the road towards Komanda with the rain still falling. At 1930 the rain eased off just as we came to a clearing in the jungle so we pulled in and quickly erected the tents for the night.

The rain stayed away for the rest of the night, and we arose at 0600 the next morning. The air was moist, the mist hanging from the trees like lace curtains. The roads were still wet and muddy, very rutted and soft, and soon after leaving our camp site we passed a lorry stuck in the mud at the side of the road, but there was little we could do to help. Rocks exposed by the rain and deep gullies had to be negotiated very carefully. We crossed the River Ituri again, over a bridge with a plaque affixed to one of the girders

After a central African rainstorm, the ruts and dips in the road fill with water, sometimes to a depth of 2 or 3 feet, causing quite a hazard. On occasions like this it is best to send a travelling companion ahead to determine the depth before driving through.

showing the date it was built: 1948! This was the third time we had crossed the Ituri, and each time there had been plenty of deep fast flowing water. We were now passing some healthy looking herds of cattle roaming the road, and chewing at the elephant grass along the side.

As we entered Komanda the sun broke through for the first time in two days. Ahead of us we could see the start of the famous Ruwenzori mountain range, the legendary "Mountains of the Moon": a natural wonderland of alpine flowers, masses of thick mosses and lichens forming a carpet for as far as one can see, with bamboo, ferns, and giant lobelias.

In Komanda we turned right on to the Beni road, and nine miles along this dirt road took a narrow dirt road to the right that leads to Mount Hoyo. The road starts off well but then becomes very rough, passing over a couple of crude wooden bridges on its climb to the hostel at just over 3000 feet, which is as far as vehicles may go. The hostel is like paradise in a wilderness. It is very clean and well maintained, with an excellent restaurant, and kept smart and tidy. One may sleep in the main building, or in one of the bungalows, and the view out over the jungles of Zaire is breathtaking. There are always pygmies wandering about here, taking advantage of the tourist, and selling trophies such as bows and arrows, tortoise shells, animal skins, and musical instruments. They are only too pleased to be photographed, but it is advisable to negotiate the fee in advance to save any embarrassment. We stopped here for a while and had a delicious omelette. Looking through the visitors book, we noted an entry by an overland party that read: "Just reached here after 8 weeks crossing Zaire during the rains, four times our planned travelling time. Never again in the rainy season!" This speaks for itself.

Mount Hoyo, with its snow-capped peaks, is one of the most beautiful areas of the whole continent and has an irresistible magnetic force. It teems with wildlife. Amongst its intriguing damp, dark caves and crystal clear waterfalls, are the Venus Falls, a short distance above the hostel, within easy walking distance through the damp undergrowth and not to be missed. Up here, far away from the humid atmosphere of the jungle below, the caves can be decidedly cold. In fact, one of the caves close to the hostel is used as a cold store!

After an enjoyable visit to Mount Hoyo, we descended the dirt track again and re-joined the main road to Beni. Two miles along the Beni road we crossed a bridge over the River Loya. There was a lovely blue sky above us, with one or two white fluffy clouds, as we passed a line of palm oil trees, all full of weaver bird nests. At 30 miles from Komanda, on an improved section of the road, we were up to 3000 feet again, and travelling at 30 mph along a smooth surface. This lasted for 22 miles, then we were once again driving over a bone-shaking cobbled road, reducing our speed to 10 mph. After 8 miles it gave way to a normal dirt road with corrugations for 3 miles before giving way once more to 3 miles of cobble.

We approached Oysha and the road improved to smooth hard dirt. Oysha appeared to be a small town, but from the time we passed its first buildings to the time we left the last of the buildings behind our speedometer clocked 10 miles — and we drove straight through with no detours. It is a large coffee centre; spread along the main street are lines of scales for weighing sacks of coffee berries. Sacks were being delivered for weighing, some individually on someone's back, others by the cart load. It is not surprising that coffee flourishes here since coffee bushes like altitude; only a few miles away is Uganda, once one of Africa's greatest coffee growing countries.

Between Oysha and Beni the road can be described as fair and dusty, becoming tarmac as it enters Beni, a colourful town at the foot of the Virunga mountain range. From here we would head east to the border with Uganda. But first we had to obtain more petrol, as the fuel situation in Uganda at present is pretty hopeless. If possible we wanted to buy enough to get us across Uganda and into Kenya where there is no shortage.

We drove 3 miles through Beni looking for fuel but without success. Most people we asked advised us to try Butembo, and although this was off of our route, we decided to try it as it is only 25 miles down the road. So we headed out of Beni.

Beni to Butembo and back

The dirt road took us through a countryside of lush green grass, acres of it, intermingled with mao and mango trees. At 5 miles from Beni we climbed to 3800 feet, driving along laid stone roads again for a couple of miles. Ten miles from Beni we reached 4000 feet, and enjoyed a splendid view of the jungle on one side of the road, and the Virunga range of mountains on the other. The fresh green colour of all the vegetation testifies to the frequent heavy rainfall here.

As we approached Butembo, on a dusty dirt road with several rocks breaking the surface, we drove into a severe rain storm. It really poured down and sent all of the Africans scurrying for shelter but it stopped just as we drove into Butembo. It was 1700 hours and would soon be getting dark so we immediately began looking for petrol but all the filling stations we tried were empty. There had to be a fuel supply here somewhere because of the amount of vehicles about. Butembo is a big town, with a wide main road and we travelled the whole length on foot asking for petrol. Eventually someone agreed to let us have a little from his own supply but wanted payment in Zaires, which proved difficult as we were about to cross into Uganda and had run our Zaires right out. Nor were there any banks open at that time of day. Our friend then suggested we change money in the Hotel Kiryo on the edge of town, which in any case was only a short distance from where he lived. Although the price he wanted was very high, the highest yet, we had to have fuel.

The hotel gave us the impression that we were somewhere in Europe. It is a very clean, tidy place and, apart from the staff, is full of white people. As it was now getting dark we decided to book in for the night, and made our reservation. We then enquired about changing money, but learned we would have to arrange this with the manager who would not be back until morning. However, a woman overheard our conversation, and kindly offered to introduce us to a friend of hers who would shortly be arriving — the manager of the local Commercial Bank! When he arrived we explained our position, but he could not help us until morning when the banks were open, and then could exchange only cash and not travellers cheques. He advised us not to change our money at the bank anyway for we would only get the normal rate. He offered to introduce us to a friend, in fact a Roman Catholic missionary from France, who would change our money on the black market and give us double the bank rate. "He will also change travellers cheques if they are in dollars," said the Bank Manager. We could hardly believe our ears: the Bank Manager telling us not to change money at the bank, and then sending us to a Roman Catholic Father who changes on the black market!

We were given directions, and it did not take us long to find the mission

Here Mick poses with a pygmy family on Mount Hoyo. Mick is 5ft 5in.

and our money-changer. It was dark when we arrived and we found him in his office — counting money! He was a white Frenchman who spoke little English, but we managed to get by with our limited French and exchanged all of the money we needed, getting a little more for the cash than we did for the travellers cheques. The Father also gave us an address of a company that would supply us with petrol at a cheaper rate than we had already been offered and he gave us a letter of introduction.

We had no idea why the priest should dabble in the black market, but we noticed that the mission was a large place, and appeared to have a hospital attached to it, so our guess was that he needed international currency to purchase drugs for the hospital. We did not bother to ask questions. We returned to the hotel for the night, with lightning flashing all around us, but as yet no rain.

At 0800 the next morning we were on our way to fill up with petrol. The black market rate we received for our money made the petrol price appear reasonable. Changing travellers cheques in Zaire is a rare experience, so our luck must have been really in. We drove into town, turning left off the main road, into the yard of our petrol supplier, and within 20 minutes had both tanks and all of our jerry cans filled.

At 0845 we were on our way out of Butembo heading back towards Beni, over the stony mountain with the cobbled road, and once again past the breathtaking scenery. We passed some roadside market stalls and stopped to purchase some of the fresh fruit on sale: tomatoes, oranges, passion fruit and bananas, before continuing on our way. Beyond a grove of palm oil trees we entered Beni once more on the short section of tarmac road, reaching the roundabout in the centre of town. Here we turned onto a very bad rutted dirt road heading towards the Uganda border.

To the border via Virunga National Park

Five miles along this road, slowly descending, we arrived at a barrier. It was the entrance to the Virunga National Park that we had to drive through. We signed the entrance book, and then continued along the slightly improved dirt road, with tall elephant grass on either side. We were now down to 2,800 feet. Six miles into the park we crossed a fast flowing river, the Semliki, and the dense bush bordering the road opened out to give us a splendid view across the parkland of grass covered hills and, in the background, the Ruwenzori mountains, their tops hidden in the clouds.

We passed the occasional native village, surrounded by plots of bananas, cassavas, yams, maize and the like. A little further on we made a diversion left to Mutwanga, situated at 3000 feet. This village, the main base for mountaineers and climbers of the Mountains of the Moon, is set picturesquely right at the base of the mountains. A wide variety of plants and other vegetation rambles over huge rocks that hundreds, even thousands, of years ago were part of the mountain peaks. Crystal clear and icy cold streams trickle through the terrain, seeking the easiest route. Mutwanga is 8 miles off the main road, which we rejoined after a brief visit and continued towards Uganda.

The road was now becoming very uneven and we had to negotiate the humps and bumps very slowly at speeds ranging from 5 to 15 mph. At 55 miles into the Virunga park we stopped on the crest of a hill and looked out over the fields. Down below us lay the Semliki river and we could make out the heads of hippopotami bobbing about on the surface. Everything looked so fresh and green. Up to now the dense elephant grass and bushes bordering the road had prevented us from enjoying such a splendid view.

We had only travelled 12 miles in the last hour owing to the poor road condition, but it was now showing signs of improvement. At 63 miles into the park we made another diversion, heading right to Ishango on the shores of Lake George, in an unspoilt and rarely visited beauty spot. It offers a captivating landscape looking out over the surrounding countryside and across the vast lake. As we drove towards Ishango, the bushes and elephant grass thinned out considerably and we were able to see for miles across the wide open plains. We passed herds of impala with their young, and numerous warthogs with their piglets following close behind in single column formation. Out across the fields to our right we had our finest view yet of the Ruwenzori, the white fluffy clouds swirling around their peaks. We passed water buck, francolin, and more impala, with a single buck chaperoning his herd of 30 to 40 does. There were some huge euphorbia cacti and then a few buildings came into sight, marking Ishango and the end of the road — a total of 16 miles from the main road through some interesting and breathtaking scenery. Perched on the chimneys were marabou storks. We paid our fee for the park, and then walked to the edge of the cliff and looked down onto the lake, a couple of hundred feet below. All along the water's edge were thousands of water birds: ibis, storks, herons. The water was alive with hundreds of hippos, and on a sand bank a little further along the bank we could make out crocodiles, basking in the sun.

The border is only 3 miles from where we re-joined the main road, and within a few minutes we were there, all of us reluctant to leave one of the most interesting and exhilarating countries yet. We arrived at the Zaire border control at 1710 hours and they had just closed, but, with the usual smile and extended hand that we had received throughout the whole of Zaire, they opened up and within a couple of minutes we were cleared and on our way to the Uganda control 3 miles down the road.

Some bridges double as road and rail bridges.

Uganda

Although the Uganda immigration were prepared to open up to clear us, the customs had gone home so we had to wait for morning. The officials offered to let us camp amongst their huts, an offer we readily accepted for it was a long time since we had camped on soft grass. A couple of them gave us a hand and were quite amused for it appeared they had not seen quite such small tents before. They insisted on trying them out for size as soon as they were erected. Just as I had prepared the tea, one of the officials brought over 6 fresh eggs that his wife had just hard boiled for us, a very welcome gift. The Ugandans are just as friendly as the Zaireans. It was not long before we were all in bed anticipating a night's sleep that not many people experience for although this border post is situated at 3000 feet it is slap bang on the equator and we were splitting the northern and southern hemispheres!

During the night the heavens opened and it teamed down with rain, but we managed to stay dry in our tents. Thunder and lightning accompanied the rain, lighting up the whole area. At 0700 the rain eased off, and the birds began singing to herald the rising sun now showing itself through breaks in the clouds. The border opens at 0800, so after we had packed the tents away we walked around to see how wet the road was. It was a dirt road currently being re-scraped and although the surface was in excellent condition, the layer of dust left behind by the scrapers had turned to mud, and local workers' cars were sliding all over the place. This section of road will eventually link up to become part of the Trans African Highway.

We prepared to leave our camp site amongst the huts that are home for the customs and immigration officals. The huts are the usual circular shape with a conical roof, but constructed of steel and aluminium, and are supplied by the government for the border officials. However, we learnt that the border officials prefer the customary mud built homes. It seems that these steel huts are very cold at night, too hot during the day, and very noisy when it rains. The officials applied to the government to have mud huts built but were refused, so they all got together and put straw roofs on the steel huts to make them more homely. They also wanted to plaster the sides with mud but this was not allowed.

The border to Mbarara

At 0800 the border opened and Mel soon cleared the paper work, and we set off to join the main road into Uganda. However, as our front wheels touched the main road the back wheels sank into the mud at the edge and we were stuck. Even in four-wheel drive we got nowhere. Water running along the gutters made it impossible to dig mud out from the rear wheels to insert our sand ladders. No sooner did we dig out a shovelful of mud than the water rushed another lot back into the hole. To make matters worse it started pouring with rain again.

Tractors and bulldozers were parked at the edge of the road but the roadwork crew had not turned up for work and the vehicles were locked, so there was no way we could use them. About 20 local people helped push but it made no difference. After two hours of pushing, digging, and heaving, we suddenly thought of trying the sand ladders under the front wheels and, believe it or not, within a couple of minutes we were out, and slip-sliding our way along the muddy road on a very erratic course even using four-wheel drive. We were all smothered in mud as was most of our gear, so we stopped a couple of miles along the road to have a wash in a stream.

The road we were on would make an excellent motorway with the addition of tarmac, for it was wide enough for at least four lanes of traffic and had an excellent surface. Six miles from the border we could see Lake Edward in the distance and, to the left and right grass covered mountains and rolling plains. Ten miles from the border we were stopped at an army road check. They were looking for smugglers and wished to inspect the vehicle and our papers. They did a thorough job but were quite friendly and helpful when they realised we were tourists. While talking to them we discovered we should put our watches forward an hour.

We were now well into Uganda and, for the first time since leaving England, were driving on the left hand side of the road. 14 miles from the border we were on a good tarmac road again, a real luxury. However, it only lasted for a short distance, and we were soon back on a parallel dirt road as road improvements were being carried out. Two miles farther on tarmac resumed with a heavily chipped surface. Ahead of us we could see Lake George, and a little more rain fell as we entered the Ruwenzori National Park, formerly the Queen Elizabeth National Park and one of the best national parks in East Africa.

At 25 miles from the border we crossed the equator line and stopped to take some photographs of the sign. From the roadside we looked out across the waters of Lake George and could see hippopotami on the water's edge. We were now driving across a flat plain at 2500 feet, with herds of impala on both sides of the road. We drove 17 miles across these National Park plains, then the road bends to the left as it approaches Bushenyi, and begins to climb, giving a breathtaking view over the land we had just crossed. The road climbs for 16 miles to 4500 feet. The rain had now stopped and the sun broke through the clouds for the first time that day, as we looked down over the jungle below, surrounded by mountains, with green fields scattered here and there.

We were passing many banana plantations, and the occasional tea plantation. The road here was not so good: still tarmac but breaking up in places leaving some deep potholes. At 1430 we reached Mbarara. There was still much evidence in this town of the fighting that occurred when Idi Amin was ousted, for this was one of the first towns that the Tanzanian invasion forces had entered and it was clear that they had met resistance in this garrison

There is no mistaking the spot where you cross the equator in Uganda.

town. Life was back to normal but the damage remained. We changed some money in a bank and then continued on our way towards Kampala, the capital.

Mbarara to Kampala and to Kenya

All along the road there was evidence of unrest and fighting, with damaged buildings and frequent road checks. There was not much traffic on the roads apart from buses, and the countryside was very green and hilly. Potholes were now more frequent as we approached Masaka, passing a pineapple plantation and more tea plantations. Again there were many damaged buildings, particularly hotels, and another police check. We were experiencing these every few miles and although brief, and normally friendly, it was an inconvenience as we had to wait our turn behind other vehicles. Then we came upon a policeman who wanted to go to Kampala, and he mentioned that with him on board we would be able to drive straight through most of the checks; so we agreed to take him along. His company proved invaluable as we were waved through one police check after another, only rarely having to stop for any length of time. At Nabusanke we crossed the equator again and were back in the northern hemisphere.

The roads throughout were generally good with just the occasional patch of potholes, but as we approached the capital, Kampala, we had to reduce speed considerably as the roads were very badly potholed. We arrived in Kampala at 1905. We had intended to remain on the outskirts and camp but had promised to get our policeman in to Kampala, so had to modify our plan. It was already dark and after dropping him off we began looking for a hotel, but it did not prove as easy as we had expected. Everyone was helpful but the first five hotels we tried were full of refugees, and others were damaged as a result of the fighting and closed. Eventually we were offered a single room in the Fairways Hotel. It also was full but the proprietor did not like the idea of us wandering the streets late at night and so managed to squeeze us all in.

We arose at 0700 the next day and were soon on the road and heading towards the Kenya border. At 13 miles from Kampala we approached our first police check of the day, but were waved straight through. A few yards farther up the road we passed a group of smartly dressed school children walking to school. Our road was lined with banana palms and we passed by a couple of tea plantations and several coffee plantations. Still ahead of us were the rolling hills.

At 0830 we arrived in Jinja where the Victoria Nile culminates in the Owen Falls Dam before entering Lake Victoria. This is a dramatic sight. Here is a large hydro electric station that supplies Uganda, and much of Kenya, with electricity.

We were still travelling at 3000 feet and the tarmac road remained good. There were pine forests on the approach to Iganga where we stopped for a while to have a look around the busy market. On the way out of Iganga we were stopped once more at a police check. We then had a steady run on a good, quiet road to the Uganda/Kenya border, 147 miles from Kampala, arriving at 1145. Mel as usual dealt with the paper work, and we were soon cleared by the Ugandan side and on our way in to Kenya.

300

Kenya

Entering Kenya you have to produce all your money and travellers cheques so that the officials can make a note for currency control. After this formality we were then cleared and passed through immigration and into Kenya.

Our arrival in Kenya did not signify the end of our trip but did herald the end of the hard travelling for we were now in one of the more developed countries of Africa, where the majority of roads are tarmac. The capital, Nairobi, is clean and modern, and everything is available with very few shortages. Kenya is one of the biggest tourist attractions on the African continent; it has first class game parks, white sandy beaches bordering on the warm waters of the Indian Ocean, deserts, snow-capped mountains, lakes, extensive shopping facilities and good transport. All of the hotels are first class, no matter where they are situated. No matter what your choice of pastime, you will find something to amuse you in this country.

Kenya straddles the equator, and right on this line is the constantly snow-capped Mount Kenya, with its twin peaks and huge glaciers. Featured on the Kenya/Tanzanian border is Africa's highest mountain, the legendary Kilimanjaro. Lakes Naivasha, Baringo, and Nakuru are world-famous for their birdlife, especially flamingoes, and these are only three of the bird sanctuaries. Just south of Lake Baringo is Lake Bagoria with its gushing hot water springs. Mombasa is an island on the coast and the main coastal resort, but there are others such as Malindi and Kilifi. Between Mombasa and Nairobi, a distance of 300 miles, is the Tsavo National Park, one of the world's largest, with up to 20,000 elephants roaming in vast herds. The centre of activity, though, is Nairobi where the best hotels are. Nairobi is situated at 5,500 feet above sea level and accordingly has a pleasant climate. A lot of overlanders make this their destination. Petrol and spares are plentiful, the roads are good and not too busy, and around the capital are a couple of good camp sites, particularly in the City Park.

Anybody wishing to travel further than Kenya must spend two or three weeks in the country for you need special permission to cross the border with Tanzania and this takes 2 or 3 weeks to obtain. Why is this? In the late seventies a dispute arose between Kenya and Tanzania regarding tourism.

Apparently tourists were flying into Nairobi, using all Kenya's facilities, and then travelling to Ngorongoro and other Tanzanian game reserves with Kenyan operators just for the day. This was depriving Tanzania of much sought after foreign currency. So Tanzania closed all borders with Kenya. Now any tourist wishing to cross from Kenya into Tanzania or vice versa must have written permission from both the Tanzanian Police Commissioner and the Kenyan Police Commissioner. The Kenyan Police will not issue a permit until they see the Tanzanian permit. (Note: Since the author undertook this trip the border has been re-opened but travellers would be wise to check on the current situation when making plans.)

We had decided to stay a month in Kenya before going on our way and we took the opportunity to give the vehicle a good overhaul in preparation for the last stage of our trip. When our time came to leave Kenya it was with regret after a very enjoyable and eventful stay.

We were on the road at 0645 in the morning heading towards Namanga, the border town about 103 miles south of Nairobi. We took the Mombasa road for a few miles and then turned right at the Namanga junction.

On we drove watching the gazelle, zebra and impala feeding and roaming the plains. At Kajiado the scenery changed, the plains giving way to shrub covered hilly land. In the distance were mountains and, way across in the clouds, we could just make out the unmistakable shape of Mount Kilimanjaro with its snow-covered slopes. At 4800 feet we drove through the Masai township of Bissel, surrounded by foothills, and passed several Masai tribesmen, in their ochre stained robes, carrying long spears, tending their cattle. Down to 3900 feet we approached the border as the sun broke through for the first time that day. To our left we could still see Kilimanjaro, an awe-inspiring sight indeed. We arrived at Namanga and filled up with fuel at one of the many filling stations, for fuel is not plentiful in Tanzania, and then proceeded towards the border post. Here we had to report to immigration, customs, and then police control, which took around 30 minutes. We were then cleared and on our way into Tanzania.

Nairobi, Kenya, is one of Africa's most modern cities.

Tanzania

Over the border in Tanzania the countryside looks much as it does in Kenya: hilly, with low bush and the occasional yellow thorn acacia tree and baobab. The road was tarmac and very good as we headed towards Arusha. By the roadside sheep and cattle grazed.

Arusha to Babati

At 68 miles from the border post we reached Arusha after passing coffee plantations and banana palms on the approach and, judging by the puddles and areas of mud it looked as though they had had heavy rain here recently. Our first stop was the bank where we had to obtain some Tanzanian currency and, this being a large town, we hoped to top our tanks right up with petrol. However, the first three stations we visited had no petrol; but then we found a Total station with a supply, although there was a long queue. We joined the queue, sitting in our vehicle and watching some fighting which had broken out on the other side of the petrol station as hundreds of Tanzanians struggled to get a gallon of paraffin, which was also in short supply. After a while the police arrived with their dogs to restore order.

We managed to top up the main tank, which gave us sufficient fuel for a few hundred miles, so we left Arusha heading east towards Lake Manyara. The road on this route is mainly dirt and murram, but we decided to take it as the one through Dar Es Salaam, although tarmac, is badly broken up with many potholes; it is alway better to travel on even or corrugated dirt than risk the vehicle on potholes that sometimes cannot be seen until you drive into them.

We were crossing open plains again with rolling hills here and there. The road was very bad: tarmac, broken up along the edges, leaving only a section in the centre wide enough for one vehicle and even that badly potholed.

At 2000 feet we passed the beautiful Lake Manyara. It is well worth diverting here for a visit to the Ngorongoro Crater, one of the largest complete walled volcanic craters in the world with a diameter of over 10 miles. The crater has long been extinct and is now filled with wildlife in abundance.

Just past Makuyuni, at a spot about 50 miles from Arusha, the tarmac ended completely and we were on a gravel road, fairly well maintained but very heavily corrugated, with the corrugations very close together. Over on our right was the wall of the great Rift Valley which we would continue to travel along for some considerable time.

Occasionally we passed a large baobab tree (*Adansonia Digitata*) or sausage tree (*Kigelia Pinnata*), and the beautiful jacaranda (*Jacaranda Acutifolia*) which is evident in game parks both here and in Kenya. These three and the fever tree (*Acacia Zanthophloea*) are the commonest trees in Africa and easily identifiable by the amateur. The baobab, nicknamed the upside-down tree by David Livingstone, is identified by its shape, which does indeed resemble a tree planted upside down with its roots sticking up in the air. It is seldom seen in leaf. It is one of the most extraordinary trees in the world, and one with the largest circumference. It is also one of the longest living trees with specimens reaching 2000 years old. The sausage tree is identified by its odd looking, huge sausage-shaped fruits weighing around 6 to 7 pounds each. It is the wood of this tree that is used to make the 'pounders' that one regularly sees African women using to pound their grain, while the trunk is used for dug-out canoes. The jacaranda could rank as the most beautiful tree in Africa, with a profusion of violet blue flowers covering it in a mass of colour before the leaves appear. The yellow fever, or yellow thorn acacia, is identified by its yellow bark and huge spreading shape, reaching a height of 50 feet. It is often found close to water, but one particular specimen grows in the centre of Nairobi. If when you are in Kenya, you are invited for a coffee at the thorn tree, it means a restaurant by this name in the centre of which is a large Acacia Xanthophloea, planted some time ago, and its trunk is the traditional spot for leaving messages for friends.

We arrived in Babati, a fair sized town surrounded by mountains, and immediately began our search for petrol. We spent two hours, enquiring at every likely and many unlikely sources but without success. At that point, a young lad came up to us with a gallon can full of petrol and offered it to us for the high price of £3.50. Although it was expensive we accepted as it was the only fuel we were likely to get in this town. When we asked him where he'd got it and whether there was more he refused to say — so perhaps he'd pinched it from his father's car! There are two filling stations in this town, and the Esso station owner said he was expecting fuel in two days' time, but someone else told us he had been saying that for the past three months.

Babati to Dodoma

We left town two hours after arrival, passing their reservoir on the way out. The road surface was much better now, the corrugations gone, and we just had the odd pothole to contend with. Large trees lined the roadside as we drove through a small valley with the hills towering above us.

At 12 miles out of Babati we began an ascent up a mountain range, with mud huts at the roadside as opposed to the brick buildings in Babati. Banana palms were growing around the huts. On top of the mountains the trees were very dense, their dark green leaves contrasting against the bright blue sky. The road surface became murram but five miles later at 5000 feet the surface was corrugated for a couple of miles, ending at a point where the road had recently been graded and scraped leaving an excellent smooth surface of dirt. Once we reached the end of the scraped section, ten miles on, we were stopped at a check point but were soon waved on.

Some 50 miles from Babati we began a long twisting descent at the bottom of which a flatter section of terrain stretched out before us, with a vast area of maize and little brick-built homes dotted everywhere. We also crossed a dry river bed. Seven miles farther on the trees gave way to grassy pastures and crops as we began another ascent. There must have been rains recently as everything looked very green. The road surface remained good but stony in places where rain had washed the surface dirt away.

We entered Kondoa Irangi, a modern looking town, and once more began asking for petrol. No luck at all here so we continued on our way. There are lots of baobab trees in this area, particularly around the outskirts of Kondoa Irangi. The road was corrugated again making for an uncomfortable ride. We cleared the town boundary and began looking for a camp site. We were very low on petrol so it was essential to find somewhere the next day that had a supply.

We spent the night 21 miles from Dodoma, the new capital of Tanzania, and were up at 0730 the next day and soon out on the road. At 15 miles from the town this road develops a sandy surface for a while, and passes an area of young grape vines. At 7 miles from town it becomes tarmac and we switched off the engine and coasted down the hill in an effort to save fuel. On the approach to Dodoma we passed more grape vines. We stopped at the first filling station but they had no fuel. We had to find fuel somehow so we flagged down a passing Range Rover with a white driver, and he sent us to the local council offices, known as D.D.D. where fuel rationing is controlled and permits issued. Here we found that fuel could only be purchased on Mondays, Wednesdays, and Fridays, if they had it; as it was Friday with no fuel anywhere it looked as if we would have to wait until Monday to go farther. Nevertheless there had to be fuel somewhere so we toured the town in the hope of finding a private supply, and happened to pass a British company based in Dodoma: George Wimpey. We pulled up and entered the offices where Mel and I explained our position to the person in charge. He was sympathetic to our cause, and offered to take Mel back to the council offices, where he knew the person in charge of fuel distribution and might be able to get us some where we had failed. Half an hour later they returned with the news that one of the filling stations would have a supply of fuel arriving very shortly — surprise news even to Wimpey — so we followed two of the Wimpey company cars to the filling station where the fuel was due to arrive. News spread fast and there were already about 20 cars queueing. The tanker, when it arrived, was only a small one and from our position in the queue it did not look hopeful, but the Wimpey boss took Mel over to the garage owner and explained we were tourists and friends of his, and instantly we were beckoned to the head of the queue with an attendant ready at the pump. We could hardly believe our luck. We were limited to 70 litres, but that was enough to get us to the main Dar-es-Salaam/Zambia highway where there is plenty of fuel. In less than no time we were on our way again, after expressing sincere thanks to "Mr Wimpey".

Dodoma to Mbeya and the border

The road out of town is dirt with occasional rocks protruding through the surface making the going rather bumpy. It is also corrugated in places although the width is enough for three lanes of vehicles. At 32 miles from Dodoma we still had the tree covered mountains with us, and many crops were being cultivated along the roadside. Some 47 miles out the road narrows to a single lane with thick bush either side, and the surface is of sand.

At 86 miles from Dodoma, much to our surprise, we came to a section of tarmac road, two lanes wide, and we passed a large lake between a dip in the mountains. We rounded a bend to find a recently built dam in our path, the Matela Dam, and also a new power station. This explained the tarmac road. We were stopped at the approach to the dam by police who asked us to sign a book before crossing. We also had to sign out on the other side.

Our laterite surface lasted for 17 miles, then we rejoined the dirt road for two miles, after which it was laterite with corrugations again for 5 miles. Then we were back to the rough dirt road. Everything along the roadside was now looking very dry, and we crossed several dried up river beds.

We were now 120 miles from Dodoma and approaching the Kipengere mountain range as we began a steep ascent up a rough, twisting, pebble covered road, bordered by thick trees and bushes. Climbing from 2400 feet to 3400 feet we looked back on a beautiful sight of thick forest-covered hills with valleys in between stretching as far as the eye could see.

Our rough, rock strewn road levelled out at 3900 feet and the surface took on a sandy texture, with flowering cactus plants at the roadside. We now had a long range of tree-covered mountains ahead of us — an impressive sight. The hard road surface was almost like stone but fairly smooth as we began to climb again. At 161 miles from Dodoma we rejoined the tarmac on the approach to Iringa at 4700 feet, and passed an airfield to our left. The road continued to weave its way through the mountains to Iringa, where we immediately began looking for fuel, for light was fading. The first filling station was closed, and the second about to close, but they allowed us in and we filled all of our tanks and jerry cans to capacity. What a change after the difficulties we had been having! We recalled that on the way into Iringa we had passed a nice looking restaurant on the right called Ya Kapti, so we returned there for a meal.

We then left town, finding an excellent tarmac highway at the bottom of the escarpment. After a few miles we pulled off at the edge of a maize field for the night, erecting our tents to a chorus of crickets singing under the half moon at 5000 feet above sea level.

The next morning we had a faulty ignition switch which delayed our departure. We feared the whole unit might have burnt out but on dismantling it found that a wire terminal had worked loose at the back. It took only a few seconds to replace it and soon we had the switch re-assembled, and were on our way again towards the Zambian border. We continued to climb to 5900 feet and had a splendid view of the tree-covered mountain range, with fields of golden sunflowers between.

At 40 miles beyond Iringa we passed through acres of pine forests first on one side of the road, and then the other, which went on for ten miles. Then as we topped the next hill, we had a splendid view of what lay ahead: flat, green countryside, with swamps and shallow lakes in the dips between the fields.

We arrived in Makumbako, still running with the mountains, now approaching the highest point of the Kipengere. At Igawa we began to veer away from the main range of mountains and descended a steep course to 4000 feet. The road was still in excellent condition, tarmac and wide enough for three lanes of traffic. At 166 miles from Iringa we passed the highest point of the Kipengere Mountains to our left, an impressive sight with two high waterfalls enhancing the beauty.

Another 35 miles and we entered Mbeya, hoping to top our fuel tanks up. However it was Saturday and, although the stations had fuel, they were not allowed to sell it at the weekend. We did not propose to wait until Monday, as fortunately we were not desperately short of petrol so we took a trip to the Mbeya market which I remembered from previous visits as large and comprehensively stocked. As we left Mbeya we passed the smart new railway station under the shadow of the grass covered southern end of the Kipengere range. Farther along the road there was a giant new textile mill under construction with what looked like a new mining complex alongside. The surface of the road was not so good and had some potholes in places.

At 58 miles from Mbeya we arrived at Tunduma and the border with Zambia. Here we all had to go into the office to complete the immigration forms. As it was Saturday, and most places close in Tanzania on a Saturday, we were asked for 25/- each "overtime money", but we explained the situation away saying we had no Tanzanian shillings left and we were "let off". Good-humoured ignorance is always the best policy in such situations. Our passports and carnet stamped, we entered Zambia to repeat the procedure.

Zambia

Immigration at Nakonde was no trouble, but when it came to customs clearance the fun started. We had to complete several forms, and then produce every penny we had with us for the customs officers to count and enter on forms. They then decided that they had given us the wrong forms and we had to start all over again. When it came to the carnet, although it was valid for Zambia, the words '''valid in Zambia'' were not actually stamped on it (not that they should have been) so they would not accept it. They told us that we would have to lodge a deposit before entry, which I agreed to do, as it was only a few pounds and we had no alternative. We were then told that we would need insurance for our vehicle and all of the contents. We all nodded in unison. After all the palaver, they finally said we could go, but they forgot to take the money for the carnet deposit and the insurance on the vehicle and I "forgot" to remind them, so we did not do too badly particularly as these had been issued! All in all it took us two hours to clear Zambian customs but we soon gained one back as Zambian time is one hour behind Tanzanian time.

Nakonde to Lusaka

Just as we moved away from the border it hurtled down with rain from storm clouds that had developed while we were inside the customs building. A short distance from the border was a filling station on our left so we pulled in to get some petrol. The African woman running the place told us she did not have any and when we asked how far it was to the next filling station, all we could get from her was "too far", so we left it at that and continued on our way. The rain really teemed down, thunder and lightning with it, and we drove 28 miles before we cleared it. We then pulled off the road for the night on to a dry patch of ground.

We were all up at 0600 the next morning as I wanted to seal the windscreen before we went anywhere. The vibration on the dirt roads must have worked the glass loose and it had leaked badly. I pumped some Sealastic around the edges as a temporary measure while the others dismantled the tents.

The road was tarmac and very good as we got under way with a blanket of cloud above us. We hummed along quite comfortably at 50 mph. We could not see much of the countryside as the road was bordered by forest or tall grass which obscured our view completely. The road was very quiet and almost devoid of traffic. We had a few spots of rain but it did not come to anything.

At 240 miles from the border we came to our first town with petrol; Mpika. Here we topped up our fuel supply and for the first time could see beyond the road as the trees cleared giving us a view across the fields to the hills bordering the Luangwa Valley.

Some 85 miles from Mpika we passed a turning on our right that leads to the Livingstone Memorial, and to Lake Bangweulu, the largest lake inside Zambia. We also passed a small lake where a couple of African kids at the roadside were selling fish. About 24 miles farther on we came to a large power station under construction, beyond which, no matter which way we looked, the countryside was a mass of trees.

At 4800 feet we entered the village of Serenje, which also has a filling station, and a few miles outside town we drove into an old quarry for the night. The sun was still shining and we had some drying out to do after yesterday's rains. The ground was a bit hard but after scraping some of the larger stones away we found a sandy base on which to erect our tents.

I was awake at 0515 the next morning and soon had the others up. There was no sun shining when we hit the road and the sky had a light covering of cloud. There were still masses of trees bordering our route. Sixty miles from our camp site we came along to a large junction with tall street lights. To the right is the main road to Ndola and the main cluster of Zambian copper mines, whereas we turned left and headed towards Lusaka, the capital.

A short way from the junction we passed Kapiri M'Poshi, a busy little town with shops and a filling station along the main road, and scores of people on their way to work, presumably in the mines. As we left this town the trees were sparser enabling us to see farther across the countryside. At 42 miles along the road we entered Kabwe at 3800 feet, a large town with all facilities — banks, restaurants etc. — and seemingly a large white community. I changed some money at the bank, and then we proceeded to top up the fuel tanks.

We then carried on towards Lusaka, passing a large lead and a zinc mine on the outskirts of Kabwe. Once again trees lined the roadside although they were less dense and soon gave way to open fields with acres of sunflowers, and some dairy farms with healthy looking cattle roaming around.

We entered Lusaka on a dual carriageway, with street lights and traffic lights, something we had not seen much of lately. There were multi-storey buildings, and everything you expect to find in a capital. It reminded us of Nairobi, being just as modern and clean and maybe busier. The shops, however, are not quite so well equipped, and luxury items, such as films and other photographic articles, seemed expensive. We found a supermarket and stocked up with provisions but the range of food they had was not all that good; we could not find any tinned milk, something that we relied on a lot.

Lusaka to Livingstone and the Victoria Falls

Leaving Lusaka, we drove on and through Kafue, a small mining town. We passed copper and iron mines, then crossed over the river Kafue. We were now down to 1500 feet, the lowest we had been for a long time, as we headed towards the great Kariba Dam. We drove on through the low rugged mountains until we saw Lake Kariba to our right. A couple of miles from the dam we pulled in at a customs/police check. As we did not intend to enter Zimbabwe at this point, but merely visit the dam, we left our passports, to be collected on our return, and the officials let us through.

Gazing out at the dam wall we were amazed at one of the world's greatest engineering feats. The Kariba Dam, completed in 1960, took the Italians seven years to build. Thirty Italians lost their lives in the construction of this dam and a chapel in their remembrance is erected on the Zimbabwean side. The dam is a great source of power for both Zambia and Zimbabwe. We stood on the road across the top of the dam and looked down on to the river Zambezi 460 feet below, meandering its way through a solid rock valley.

Our visit over, we made our way back towards the customs post to collect our passports, and then to a bar at Siavonga for a cool refreshing drink. While in the bar I spotted what looked like a giant plastic orange on the counter, only it was not plastic, it was real and larger than a football. I learnt that it was grown just up the road by a priest who apparently had larger ones still on his tree. Apparently, its enormous size was mainly pith and the actual fruit was no larger than a normal large orange. We then made our way to the lake side and erected our tents for the night, amongst hungry mosquitoes.

We were all up the next morning in time to watch some of the fishing boats return to shore with their catch of a small whitebait-type fish for the Zambian market. We then set off, heading back towards Lusaka before branching to the left on to the road to Mazabuka and Livingstone.

As we reached Mazabuka the countryside became remarkably flatter. The mountains had gone, as had the trees bordering the roadside, and in their place were planted fields of sunflowers, maize, and grass. Our tarmac road was good. We drove through Monze, passing huge maize silos and orange plantations on the way into town and then, a few miles further on, Pemba. In Choma we stopped at a smart café for lunch and found it clean and efficiently run. Choma is a small, tidy agricultural town.

At Kalomo we stopped for petrol, passing a tobacco farm on the way into town. The sun was still shining through the clouds, and the road still excellent tarmac. It is surprising that there is not more traffic on the Zambian roads for they are certainly in tip-top condition.

We finally arrived in Livingstone, another clean, tidy town catering mainly for the tourist for this is the main Zambian town for visitors to the Victoria Falls. We stopped to ask a policeman directions to the falls and he offered to accompany us and show us the way. The falls form the border between Zambia and Zimbabwe, and we were intending to cross the Victoria Falls bridge over the Zambezi to reach our next country. As we approached the bridge we could see the massive wall of spray thrown up by the cascading water from a couple of miles away, and as we reached the bridge it was as if drizzle had started to fall, with the spray drifting across our path and soaking everything in its wake.

We soon reached the Zambian border control and Mel took in the paperwork. Within a couple of minutes we were all cleared for departure and were on our way to the Zimbabwean control.

Zimbabwe, Botswana, South Africa

Our entry into Zimbabwe was quickly accomplished. Zimbabwe is an invalid country on the carnet so we had to make a deposit before being allowed entry, but it only came to a couple of pounds.

First priority was a visit to the majestic splendour of the Victoria Falls — a must for any tourist to this part of Africa, whether an overlander or not. To miss it would be unforgivable and something you would always regret. It is unbelievable that one of the world's most feared and powerful elements could appear so beautiful. A short distance from the Falls is one of the world's largest baobab trees, the circumference so large that three double decker buses could easily wrap themselves around the trunk, which has a girth of over 60 feet at ground level. Another worthwhile place to visit is the crocodile farm on the shores of the Zambezi.

Victoria Falls to Plumtree and the border

We then drove the short distance into the town of Victoria Falls in time to cash some money at the bank. We exchanged our money in a couple of minutes which must be a record for this trip as the whole procedure normally takes hours. The roads in Zimbabwe are of excellent quality, tarmac throughout, and little used by other traffic. The sun was out as we headed south towards Bulawayo at a comfortable 50 mph.

Some 65 miles from Victoria Falls we crossed the dried up river bed of what was once the Delta River on the approach to Wankie, Zimbabwe's coal mining town. The countryside so far had been hilly, but as we approached Wankie the hills thinned out and we were soon in almost flat countryside. Wankie, although a colliery town, is very clean and colourful. The poinciana or flame tree (*Delonix Regia*), whose strikingly beautiful flowers turn the whole tree into a scarlet umbrella as they burst into bloom, lined the roads, enhancing the beauty of the area.

After Wankie we began travelling through dense bush countryside, crossing the now dry Luksoi River 100 miles from Victoria Falls. The bush and trees along the roadside were now looking very dry.

At Gwaai River the clouds formed and within a few minutes we got a few spots of rain but hardly enough to wet the road as we were stopped at a police check on the outskirts. However we were waved on when they saw we were tourists.

We stopped at Lupani for fuel, but the filling station was empty. We continued on our way, now looking for a camp site for the night. The roads are bordered by grass verges about 30 feet wide on each side, and beyond the verges is the dense bush with a barbed wire fence separating the two, obviously to keep animals off the road, but making it difficult to find somewhere to camp.

Eventually we found a break in the fencing and drove into the bush where a clearing suited our purpose admirably. We had a fairly warm night snug in our sleeping bags, and were up again at 0700 the next morning with the wind blowing. We were soon on the road heading for Bulawayo where we arrived 30 minutes later and took a tour of town and then a walk around the shops. It is another very clean and tidy town with a very large white contingent, most of the shops being run by white people, and everything, particularly food, inexpensive. We found a filling station and attempted to fill our tanks but were limited to 30 litres so we took that, travelling to the next filling station for another 30 litres.

We were now heading for the Botswana border, 70 miles away. We crossed the Khari river which was completely dry. The surrounding bush also looked as if it could do with some water. The road remained good tarmac and there was a railway running alongside as we headed towards Plumtree and the border.

Botswana control to Gaberone

It took us only 1¼ hours to reach Plumtree, situated at 4000 feet, and a few minutes later we were at the Zimbabwe/Botswana border. Mel took the paperwork in while the rest of us waited outside and within a very short while we were on our way out of Zimbabwe and heading towards Botswana. Halfway between the two border controls the tarmac road ended and we were back on dirt roads again. Everything still looked dry, the only green being roadside cactus plants, and even they looked pretty sorrowful. The River Shashi forms the border and that too was dried up.

At the Botswana control things did not go quite so easily. First, we all had to enter the building and complete the forms; then they would not accept our insurance saying we had to buy theirs. We had a bit of fun with them as I produced a $100 travellers cheque to pay for the insurance which totalled about $2, but they could not change it. It was worth a try and might have saved us looking for a bank. In the end I gave the officers a $20 travellers cheque. We were then cleared for entry and also had made some useful change for purchasing food or petrol, for we were not likely to have an opportunity to change any more money until we reached Francistown 60 miles away.

Although we started off on a dirt road, it was very good, having recently been scraped, and there were no bushes or trees at the roadside to block our view across the semi-desert bordering the road. In places there were lots of bare rocks protruding through the road surface making the going a little bumpy, but nothing too serious, It looked as if this road would soon be tarmac for there were lots of vehicles parked up belonging to Marples Ridgeway, the British roadbuilders, together with piles of gravel, steel reinforcement mesh, and scrapers.

In fact when we had travelled 52 miles from the border we found ourselves on newly laid tarmac, an excellent two carriageway road, running for the remaining 5 miles into Francistown. There, we topped up our fuel tanks, exchanged some more money at the bank, and then continued on our way, still on a good, new tarmac road, with the edge of the Kalahari Desert on our right. We crossed three more dried up rivers, indicating that this country was in the grips of a severe drought, for these three — the Rivers Shashi, Thilede, and Thlotstane — are normally fast flowing sources of water.

Some 60 miles from Francistown, with the sun sinking fast, we pulled off the road to camp for the night in the bush.

We were all up at 0600 the next morning on what could be a sad day for us all, for it was to be the last day's travelling on this trip before we reached South Africa at the end of our journey. It was a cold night with the temperature down to 50° Fahrenheit indicating that we were in a desert region again.

We rejoined the main road and had not gone far when we were stopped at a cattle disease control post, but they merely took a note of our registration number and let us continue on our way. The road remained good tarmac as we hummed along at 50 mph at 2800 feet. There was a low mountain range to our left, and the sky was one grey blanket of cloud. The land to the sides of the road was now taking on more of a desert appearance. We crossed several dried up river beds, and were occasionally stopped at disease control points before entering Mahalapye. Here we purchased some provisions and immediately we noticed the strong South African influence in this country, as all of the food and drink appeared to be imported from South Africa.

We travelled out of town on a tarmac road, now with a clear blue sky above us and the sun beaming down. The road surface was in such excellent condition that in less than no time we were approaching the capital of Botswana, Gaberone. The capital gives the impression of being a small place, but is very modern, particularly in the centre, and actually is fast-growing, as is the whole of the country with the recent discovery of extensive diamond mines from which stem most of its wealth. However the commodity more valuable than diamonds, water, is in very short supply.

Gaberone into South Africa and the final leg

We did not stay long in Gaberone and were soon on our way out of town, passing the new hotels being erected, as we headed for the border with South Africa. Red rock mountains to our right were covered in a healthy looking green with one or two maize fields at the roadside. We drove through Lobatse, still on a tarmac surface, and still crossing dry rivers, and then passed through Pitsani with its four giant maize silos alongside the railway line. The countryside is very flat here, and very open, with just one or two bushes breaking up the fields of yellow grass.

Some 82 miles from Gaberone we arrived at the Botswana border control and Mel, for the last time, took in our paperwork. We all had to complete an exit form, and within a few minutes were on our way out of Botswana. At the South African control the procedure was repeated, but here we all had to report to the office and complete two rather lengthy forms. We were at the border control for 30 minutes and then, without any search of the vehicle, left the border town of Ramatlabama, and drove through the independent state of Bophuthatswana and into South Africa at the end of a long overland journey.

Our journey to Johannesburg, the end of our trip, took just 4 hours. Ironically, just 20 miles from our destination we were stopped by South African Police for exceeding the speed limit!

Thus our journey came to an end, after 172 days driving across the African continent through 20 African states, and covering 17,717 miles. This had been my fourth trip but each one is different and all the time there is something to be learnt. There will be others.

Appendix A
Diplomatic missions

The nationalities listed in these pages are the most widespread amongst overlanders. If your nationality is not listed, any of the other nationalities' representatives will assist you in finding your representative.

Embassies, High Commissions and Consulates in African Countries

	ALGERIA	BENIN	BOTSWANA	BURKINA FASSO
BRITISH	Residence Cassiopée Batiment "B", 7, Chemin des Glycines, Algiers. Tel: 605601	None. Apply British High Commission, Lagos, Nigeria.	High Commission, Private Bag 23, Gaberone. Tel: 2483-5.	None. Consul & Ambassador reside in Abidjan. See Ivory Coast.
IRISH	None	None	None	None
FRENCH	6, Rue Larbi Alik, Algiers. Tel: 604381	B.P. 966, Cotonou. Tel: 300824	None	French Embassy, P.O. Box 504, Ouagadougou.
WEST GERMAN	165, Chemin Sfindja, B.P. 664, Algiers. Tel: 63.48.27	7, Route Inter-Etats, B.P. 504, Cotonou. Tel: 31.29.67.	I.G.I. House, The Mall, Gaberone, P.O. Box 315. Tel: 5.31.43.	German Embassy, P.O. Box 600, Ouagadougou.

	ALGERIA	BENIN	BOTSWANA	BURKINA FASSO
AMERICAN	4, Chemin Cheikh, Bachir, Brahimi, Algiers. Tel: 60.14.25/9	Rue Caporal, Anani Bernard, Cotonou. Tel: 31.26.92/3	P.O. Box 90, Gaberone. Tel:53982.	American Embassy, P.O. Box 35, Ouagadougou.
CANADIAN	27, Bis rue d'Anjou, Hydra, Algiers. Tel: 606190.	None. Apply Ghana.	None. Apply Zimbabwe	Canadian Embassy, P.O. Box 548, Ouagadougou. Tel: 32093
AUSTRALIAN	None	None	None. Apply Pretoria, South Africa.	None
NEW ZEALAND	. . . . . . Apply	to	British	Embassy . . . . . .

Embassies, High Commissions and Consulates in African Countries

	CAMEROON	C.A.R.	EGYPT	ETHIOPIA
BRITISH	Embassy, Winston Churchill Avenue, B.P. 547, Yaoundé. Tel: 22.05.45 & 22.07.96.	Hon. Consulate, (Mr. Copperman), Diamond Distributors Inc., B.P. 469, Bangui. Tel: 610513 & 613911. Home No: 610529.	Ahmed Raghab Street, Garden City, Cairo. Tel: 20850-9. Also at 3, Sharia Al Mina, Roushdy, Alexandria (T.47166)	Fikre Mariam, Abatechan Street, P.O. Box 858, Addis Ababa. Tel: 113055.
IRISH	None	None	2, Sharia Maarouf, Cairo. Tel. 55069.	None
FRENCH	Avenue Ahmadoo-Ahidjo, P.O. Box 1631, Yaoundé. Tel: 220901.	Boulevard de Gaulle, P.O. Box 784, Bangui. Tel: 613000.	5, Rue el Fadl, Box 1777, Cairo. Tel: 813 657.	Quartier Kabaia, B.P. 1464, Addis Ababa. Tel: 110066 & 110373.
WEST GERMAN	B.P. 1160, Yaoundé. Tel: 230056	B.P. 901, Bangui. Tel: 614765 & 610746.	5, Rue Mirah, Alexandria. Tel: 845475.	None

320

	CAMEROON	C.A.R.	EGYPT	ETHIOPIA
AMERICAN	B.P. 817 Rue Nachtigal, Yaoundé. Tel: 221633	Avenue President Dacko, Bangui. Tel: 7050/1.	5, Sharia Latin America, Cairo. Tel: 28211/9	Entoto Street, Addis Ababa. Tel: 110666.
CANADIAN	1st floor, Stamatiades Bldg. Ave. de l'Independance, Yaoundé. P.O. Box 572. Tel: 22.02.03.	None. Apply Cameroon.	6, Sharia Mohamed Fahmi el Sayed, Garden City, Cairo. Tel: 23110 & 23119.	African Solidarity Insurance Building, Unity Square, Addis Ababa. P.O. Box 1130. Tel: 448335/6.
AUSTRALIAN	None	None	1097, Corniche el Nil, Garden City, Cairo. Tel: 28190 & 22862.	P.O. Box 137, Addis Ababa. Tel: 44 44 88 & 45 65 36
NEW ZEALAND	. . . . . . Apply	to	British	Embassy . . . . . .

Embassies, High Commissions and Consulates in African Countries

	GABON	GHANA	GUINEA	IVORY COAST
BRITISH	Batiment Sogame, Boulevard de l'Independance, BP 476, Libreville. Tel: 72.29.85.	High Commission, Barclays Bank Building, High Street, Box 296, Accra. Tel: 64651.	(Hon. Consul) Magus Ltd., BP 158, Conakry, Guinea. Tel: 43705-8.	3rd Floor, Immeuble "Les Harmonies", Angle Boulevard, Caroe et Ave. Drive, Jamot Plateau, Abidjan. Tel: 22.68.50.
IRISH	None	None	None	None
FRENCH	Rue de la Marie, B.P. 2161. Tel: 722477.	12th Road, off Liberation Ave., P.O. Box 187, Accra. Tel: 28571.	B.P. 373 & 570, Conakry. Tel: 41655.	Rue Lecoeur, Quartier du Plateau, Abidjan. B.P. 1385. Tel: 32249.
WEST GERMAN	Ave. Alfred Marche, P.O. Box 299, Libreville. Tel: 722790.	Vallderosa Lodge, No.4, off 7th Ave. Extension, Northbridge, P.O. Box 1757, Accra. Tel: 21311.	B.P. 540, Conakry. Tel: 441506.	11, Ave, Joseph Aroma, Abidjan. Tel: 324747.

	GABON	GHANA	GUINEA	IVORY COAST
AMERICAN	Boulevard de la Mer, Libreville. Tel: 72.20.03/4	Liberia/Kinbu Roads, Accra. Tel:66811.	2nd Boulevard and 9th Avenue, Conakry. Tel:415.20/4.	5, Rue Jesse Owens Avenue, Abidjan. Tel: 32.46.30.
CANADIAN	3rd Floor, SCI Du Stade, Blvd Pasteur, Libreville. Tel: 724154 & 724169.	115, Independence Avenue, P.O. Box 1639, Accra. Tel: 28555 & 28502	Grand Hotel de l'Independance, P.O. Box 99, Conakry. Tel: 445019.	Trade Centre Bldg., 23, Noguès Avenue, Abidjan. Tel: 322009.
AUSTRALIAN	None	Milne Close, Off Dr Amilcar Cabral Road, Airport Residential Area, P.O. Box 2445, Accra. Tel: 77972.	None	None.
NEW ZEALAND	. . . . . Apply	to	British	Consul . . . . . .

Embassies, High Commissions and Consulates in African Countries

	KENYA	LIBERIA	LIBYA	MALAWI
BRITISH	Bruce House, Standard Street, Nairobi. P.O. Box 30465. Tel: 335944.	Embassy, Mamba Point, PO Box 120, Monrovia. Tel: 221055 & 221107.	None. Apply Tunisia or Egypt.	Lingadazi House, PO Box 30042, Lilongwe. Tel: 731544; also Victoria Avenue, PO Box 479, Blantyre. Tel: 633022.
IRISH	Norfolk Hotel, P.O. Box 40064, Nairobi.	None	None	P.O. Box 462, Downs House, Victoria Avenue, Blantyre. Tel: 34851
FRENCH	French Embassy, P.O. Box 41784, Nairobi.	94, United Nations Drive, Monla Pairl, P.O. Box 279, Monrovia. Tel: 221122.	Rue Ahmed Lafli Soad, P.O. Box 312, Tripoli. Tel: 72380.	P.O. Box 30054, Lilongwe. Tel: 730377.
WEST GERMAN	Embassy of Federal Republic Germany, P.O. Box 30180, Nairobi.	P.O. Box 34, Monrovia, Tel: 261460	Sharia Mon, Hassan El Mashai, P.O. Box 302, Tripoli. Tel: 33827.	Convention Drive, Capital City, Lilongwe. P.O. Box 30046. Tel: 731266.

	KENYA	LIBERIA	LIBYA	MALAWI
AMERICAN	American Embassy, P.O. Box 30137, Nairobi.	United Nations Drive, Monrovia.	Shari Mohammad Thalirt, Tripoli. Tel: 34021/6.	P.O. Box 30016, Lilongwe. Tel: 30396 & 30166.
CANADIAN	Canadian High Commission, P.O. Box 30481, Nairobi. Tel: 334033/6.	None. Apply Ghana.	None. Apply Tunisia.	None. Apply Zambia.
AUSTRALIAN	Australian High Commission, P.O. Box 30360, Nairobi.	None	None	None
NEW ZEALAND	Apply British High Commission	. . . . . Apply	to British	Consul . . . . .

Embassies, High Commissions and Consulates in African Countries

	MALI	MAURITANIA	MOROCCO	NIGER
BRITISH	Hon. Consul, P.O. Box 1708, Bamako, Tel: 22.46.46.	BP 214, Nouakchott. Tel: 528.28.	17, Boulevard de la Tour Hassan, BP 45, Rabat. Tel: 20905/6; also 60, Boulevard d'Anfa, BP 762, Casablanca. Tel: 261440/1.	Vice Consulate, PO Box 942, Niamey.
IRISH	None	None	None	None
FRENCH	Square Patrice Lumumba P.O. Box 17, Bamako. Tel: 222951.	Boulevard Maritime, P.O. Box 15, Nouakchott. Tel: 2248.	49, Allah Ben Abdullah, P.O. Box 139, Rabat. Tel: 63824.	French Embassy, Niamey. Tel: 72.24.31.
WEST GERMAN	B.P. 100, Bamako, Tel:223299.	P.O. Box 372, Nouakchott. Tel: 51032 and 51722.	P.O. Box 235, Rabat. Tel: 35232.	German Embassy, Avenue General de Gaulle, Niamey. Tel: 72.25.34.

	MALI	MAURITANIA	MOROCCO	NIGER
AMERICAN	Rue Testard/Rue Mohamed, Bamako. Tel: 246.63/4.	P.O. Box 222, Nouakchott. Tel: 52660 & 52663.	7, Ave de Marrakech, Rabat. Tel: 30361/2	American Embassy, Niamey. Tel: 72.26.61/2/3.
CANADIAN	Office of Canadian Embassy, Koulikouro Road, P.O. Box 198, Bamako. Tel: 222-36.	None. Apply Senegal.	13, bis, Rue Jaafar As Sadik, B.P. 709, Rabat-Agdal. Tel: 71375/77.	Canadian Embassy, Niamey. Tel: 72.36.86.
AUSTRALIAN	None	None	None	None
NEW ZEALAND	Apply to British Consul	. . . . Apply	to British	Embassy . . . . . .

Embassies, High Commissions and Consulates in African Countries

	NIGERIA	RWANDA	SENEGAL	SIERRA LEONE
BRITISH	11, Eleke Crescent, Victoria Island, Private bag 12136, Lagos. Tel: 611654 & 611934	Avenue Paul VI, BP 356, Kigali. Tel: 5905 & 5219.	20, Rue du Docteur Guillet, BP 6025, Dakar. Tel: 217392, 215208 & 210971	Standard Bank Building, Lightfoot Boston St., Freetown. Tel: 23961-5
IRISH	New Africa House, 4th Floor, 31, Marina, Lagos. Tel: 25769.	None	None	None
FRENCH	1, Queens Drive, Ikoyi, P.O. Box 567, Lagos. Tel: 603300.	40, Ave. du Deprite-Kanuzani, P.O. Box 53, Kigali. Tel: 5225.	1, Rue El Hadj Amadou Assane Ndoye, Dakar. Tel:21.01.81	13, Lamina Sankah St., P.O. Box 570, Freetown. Tel: 22477
WEST GERMAN	15, Eleke Crescent, Victoria Island, P.O. Box 728, Lagos. Tel: 611011.	8, Rue de Bugarama, P.O. Box 355, Kigali. Tel: 5222 & 5141	43, Ave. A Sarraut, Dakar. Tel: 22.48.84	Santanno House, 10, Hows Street, P.O. Box 728, Freetown. Tel: 22511/2

	NIGERIA	RWANDA	SENEGAL	SIERRA LEONE
AMERICAN	7, Eleke Crescent, Victoria Island, Lagos. Tel: 57320	Blvd de la Revolution, Kigali. Tel: 5601	BIAO Building, Place de l'Independance, BP 49, Dakar. Tel: 26344/5 and 22143	Cnr Walpole and Siaka Stevens Street, Freetown.
CANADIAN	Niger House, Tinubu Street, P.O. Box 851, Lagos. Tel: 72.36.86/7	Office of Canadian Embassy, Akagera Street, P.O. Box 1177, Kigali. Tel: 3210 & 3278.	45, Boulevard de la République, Dakar. Tel: 21.02.90.	None. Apply Nigeria.
AUSTRALIAN	P.O. Box 2427, Lagos. Tel: 25981/2	None	None	None
NEW ZEALAND	Apply to British Embassy	. . . . Apply	to British	Consulate . . . . . .

Embassies, High Commissions and Consulates in African Countries

	SOUTH AFRICA	SUDAN	SWAZILAND	TANZANIA
BRITISH	5th Floor Nedbank Mall, 145/147 Commissioner St., P.O. Box 10101, Johannesburg. Tel: 331-8161.	New Aboulela Building, Barlaman Avenue, P.O. Box 801, Khartoum. Tel: 70760-6 & 80191	Allister Miller Street, Mbabane. Tel: 42581-6.	Permanent House, Independence Avenue, P.O. Box 9200, Dar-es-Salaam. Tel: 29601 (10 lines)
IRISH	9/10 London House, 21, Loveday Street, Johannesburg. Tel: 836-5869	None	None	P.O. Box 655, Dar-es-Salaam. Tel: 20301.
FRENCH	Kine Centre, 111, Commissioner Street, Johannesburg. Tel: 21-3468	P.O. Box 377, Khartoum. Tel: 77619	None	Baga Mayo Road, B.P. 2349, Dar-es-Salaam. Tel: 68601.
WEST GERMAN	Consulate General, 16, Kapteijn Street, Johannesburg. Tel: 725-1519.	53, Sharia El Baladia, Block No. 8 D.E., Plot 2, P.O. Box 970, Khartoum. Tel: 77995 & 77990.	None	Investment House, 10th floor, Somara Ave., P.O. Box 9541, Dar-es-Salaam. Tel: 23286 & 26417.

	SOUTH AFRICA	SUDAN	SWAZILAND	TANZANIA
AMERICAN	Consulate General, Kine Centre, 111, Commissioner St., Johannesburg. Tel:21-1681.	Gamhouria Avenue, Khartoum. Tel: 74611 & 74700.	P.O. Box 199, Mbabane. Tel: 2272/4	National Bank of Commerce Building, Dar-es-Salaam. Tel: 22775.
CANADIAN	P.O. Box 26006, Arcadia, Pretoria, Tel: 487062	None. Apply Egypt.	None. Apply South Africa.	Pan Africa Insurance Bld., Independence Avenue, P.O. Box 1022, Dar-es-Salaam. Tel: 20651
AUSTRALIAN	Standard Bank Chambers, Church Street, Pretoria. Tel: 37051	None. Apply Egypt.	None.	Bank House, 4th floor, Independence Avenue, P.O. Box 2996, Dar-es-Salaam. Tel: 20244
NEW ZEALAND	Apply British Consulate General.	. . . . . . Apply	to British	Embassy . . . . . .

Embassies, High Commissions and Consulates in African Countries

	TCHAD	TOGO	TUNISIA	UGANDA
BRITISH	Avenue de Brazza Socopao du Tchad, BP 751, N'Djamena. Tel: 2932	Hon. Correspondent, Mr P. Morgan, Société F.M. Barshall, B.P. 2290, Lome. Tel: 21.34.26.	5, Place de la Victoria, Tunis. Tel: 245.100 & 245.324	10/12 Parliament Avenue, P.O. Box 7070, Kampala. Tel: 57301/4 & 57054/9
IRISH	None	None	None	None
FRENCH	Rue du Lieutenant Franjais, B.P. 913, N'Djamena. Tel: 2576.	Rue Bissagne, B.P. 337, Lome. Tel: 2576/7	1, Rue de Hollande, Tunis. Tel: 245700.	None
WEST GERMAN	B.P. 983, N'Djamena. Tel: 3090 & 3137	B.P. 1175, Lome. Tel: 212370	18, Rue Félicier Challaye, P.O. Box 35, Tunis. Tel: 281246 & 281255	P.O. Box 7016, Kampala. Tel: 56767/8

	TCHAD	TOGO	TUNISIA	UGANDA
AMERICAN	Rue du Lt. Col. Colonna D'Oranan, N'Djamena. Tel: 3091/4	Rue Pelletier Caventou, Lome. Tel: 2991.	144, Ave de la Liberté, Tunis. Tel: 282566.	None
CANADIAN	None. Apply Cameroon.	None. Apply Ghana	3, Sénégal Street, Palestine Place, P.O. Box 31, Tunis. Tel: 286-577	None. Apply Kenya.
AUSTRALIAN	None.	None.	None.	None. Apply High Commission, Nairobi, Kenya.
NEW ZEALAND	. . . . . Apply	to	British	Embassy . . . . . .

Embassies, High Commissions and Consulates in African Countries

	ZAIRE	ZAMBIA	ZIMBABWE
BRITISH	9, Avenue de l'Equateur, 5th floor, Kinshasa. P.O. Box 8049. Tel: 23483-6 & 23280	Independence Ave., P.O. Box 50050, Lusaka. Tel: 215315.	High Commission, Stanley House, Stanley Avenue, P.O. Box 4490, Harare. Tel: 793781.
IRISH	None	P.O. Box 338, Lusaka. Tel: 72532 & 73171.	None.
FRENCH	Av. Rép. du Tchad, Kinshasa. P.O. Box 3093 & 7385. Tel: 22669 & 25566	Unity House, Cnr Kalunjila/Freedom Way, P.O. Box 30062, Lusaka. Tel: 212917	Immeuble Pal House, 67, Jameson Avenue, P.O. Box 1378, Harare. Tel: 792707.
WEST GERMAN	201, Av. Lumpungu, Kinshasa. P.O. Box 8400. Tel: 26933 & 26934.	P.O. Box 50120, Lusaka. Tel: 217449 & 217667.	None.

	ZAIRE	ZAMBIA	ZIMBABWE
AMERICAN	310, Av. Aviateurs, Kinshasa, P.O. Box 697. Tel: 25881-4.	P.O. Box 1617, Lusaka. Tel: 50222	172, Rhodes Avenue, P.O. Box 3340, Harare. Tel: 794521
CANADIAN	Edifice Shell, Corner Bld. du 30 Juin & Avenue Wangatta, Kinshasa. P.O. Box 8341. Tel: 22706 & 24346	1st Floor, Barclays Bank North End Branch, Cairo Road, P.O. Box 31313, Lusaka. Tel: 75187/8	45, Baines Avenue, P.O. Box 1430, Harare. Tel: 793801.
AUSTRALIAN	None. Refer British Embassy.	None. Apply Dar-es-Salaam, Tanzania.	None
NEW ZEALAND	None. Refer British Embassy.	None. Refer British Embassy or Consul	None. Refer British Embassy or Consul.

Consuls/Embassies of African countries based in London

Algeria 54 Holland Park, W11 3RS. Tel: 01-221 7800/4

Angola None. Apply Portuguese Consulate, 62 Brompton Road (3rd floor), SW3 1BJ. Tel: 01-235 6216.

Benin 125-129 High Street, Edgware, Middlesex. Tel: 01-951 1234

Botswana 162 Buckingham Palace Road, SW1W 9TJ. Tel: 01-730 5216.

Burkina Fasso 150 Buckingham Palace Road, SW1W 9TR. Tel: 01-730 8141.

Burundi None. Nearest: Square Marie Louise 46, Brussels 1040. Tel: 230-45-35 & 48.

Cameroon 84 Holland Park, W11 3SB. Tel: 01-727 0771/2/3.

C.A.R. None. Apply French Consulate General, 24 Rutland Gate, SW7 1BE. Tel: 01-581 5292.

Congo (Brazzaville) None. Nearest: 37 bis, Rue Paul Valéry, 75016 Paris. Tel: 500-60-57.

Djibouti None. Nearest: 70, Boulevard Pereire, 75017 Paris. Tel: 622-04-49 & 58.

Egypt 19 Kensington Palace Gardens, W8 4QL. Tel.01-229 8810/8/9.

Ethiopia 17 Prince's Gate, SW7 1PZ. Tel: 01-589 7212.

Gabon 48 Kensington Court, W8 5DB. Tel: 01-937 5285/9.

Gambia 60 Ennismore Gardens, SW7 1NH. Tel: 01-584 1242/3.

Ghana 38 Queen's Gate, SW7 5HT. Tel: 01-584 6311.

Guinea None. Nearest: 24 Rue Emile Menier, 75016 Paris. Tel: 553-72-25 & 28.

Guinea Bissau (Port Guinea) None. Nearest: Avenida Praia de Victoria, 41-2° Lisbon. Tel: 53-34-55.

Ivory Coast 2 Upper Belgrave Street, SW1X 8BJ. Tel: 01-235 6991.

Kenya 45 Portland Place, W1N 4AS. Tel: 01-636 2371.

Lesotho 16a St. James's Street (1st floor), SW1A 1EU. Tel: 01-839 1154.

Liberia 21 Prince's Gate, SW7 1QB. Tel: 01-589 9405.

Libya Embassy currently closed.

Malawi 33 Grosvenor Street, W1X ODE. Tel: 01-491 4172.

Mali None. Nearest: 89 Rue du Cherche-Midi, 75006 Paris. Tel: 548-58-43.

Mauritania None. Nearest: 5 Rue de Montevideo, 75016 Paris. Tel: 504-88-54.

Morocco (including Tangier) 49 Queen's Gate Gardens, SW7 5NE. Tel: 01-584 8827.

Mozambique None. Apply Portuguese Consulate, 62 Brompton Road (3rd floor), SW3 1BJ. Tel: 01-235 6216.

Niger None. Nearest: 154 Rue de Longchamps, 75116 Paris. Tel: 504-80-60.

Nigeria 56/57 Fleet Street, EC4Y 1JU. Tel: 01-839 1244.

Rwanda None. Nearest: 101 Boulevard St Michel, 1040 Brussels. Tel: 734-17-63 & 735-31-18.

Senegal 11 Phillimore Gardens, W8 7QG. Tel: 01-937 0925/6

Sierra Leone 33 Portland Place, W1N 3AG. Tel: 01-636 6483.

Somalia 60 Portland Place, W1N 3DG. Tel: 01-580 7148/9.

South Africa 16 Charles II Street, SW1Y 4QU. Tel: 01-839 2313. Also Trafalgar Square, WC2N 5DP.

Sudan 3 Cleveland Row, St James's, SW1A 1DD. Tel: 01-839 8080.

Swaziland 58 Pont Street, SW1X OAE. Tel: 01-589 5447/8.

Tanzania 43 Hertford Street, W1Y 8DD. Tel: 01-499 8951.

Tchad None. Apply French Consulate General, 24 Rutland Gate, SW7 1BE. Tel: 01-581 5292

Togo 20 Wellington Court, 116 Knightsbridge, SW1X 7PL. Tel: 01-584 1948.

Tunisia 29 Prince's Gate, SW7 1QG. Tel: 01-584 8117.
Uganda Uganda House, 58-59 Trafalgar Square, WC2N 5DX. Tel: 01-839 5783.
Zaire 26 Chesham Place, SW1X 8HH. Tel: 01-235 6137.
Zambia 7-11 Cavendish Place, W1N 0HB. Tel: 01-580 0691.
Zimbabwe Zimbabwe House, 429 The Strand, WC2 0SA. Tel: 01-836 7755.

Appendix B
Government representatives & African motoring organisations

Government representatives

Egypt
— Minister of Tourism, 110, Rue Kasr el Aini, Cairo.

Ivory Coast
— Minister of Tourism, Immeuble Alpha 2000, (P.O. Box 184), Abidjan.

Kenya
— Principal Immigration Officer, P.O. Box 30191, Nairobi.
— Chief Tourist Officer, Ministry of Tourism, P.O. Box 5466, Nairobi.
— Licensing Officer, Registrar of Motor Vehicles, P.O. Box 30440, Nairobi.

Morocco
— Office National Marocain du Tourisme, 22, Avenue d'Alger, P.O. Box 19, Rabat.

Mozambique
— Minister of Foreign Affairs, Avenue Antonia Enes No.4, Maputo.
— Department of Immigration, P.O. Box 614, Maputo.

Senegal
— Secretariat d'Etat au Tourisme, 3e étage, Ave. Jean-Jaurès X Peytavin, Immeuble KEBE extension, Dakar.

Tanzania
— Principal Immigration Officer, P.O. Box 512, Dar-es-Salaam.
— Licensing Officer, P.O. Box 332, Moshi.
— Licensing Officer, P.O. Box 222, Arusha.
— Licensing Officer, P.O. Box 4000, Tanga.

Uganda
— Principal Immigration Officer, P.O. Box 7165, Kampala.
— Licensing Officer, P.O. Box 7031, Kampala.

Zaire
— Office National du Tourisme, Coin Boulevard du 30 Juin et Avenue de Kitona, Kinshasa.

Zambia
— Chief Immigration Officer, P.O. Box RW 300, Lusaka.

Zimbabwe
— Chief Immigration Officer, Private Bag 7717, Causeway, Harare.

African motoring organisations (affiliated to AIT and/or FIA)

Algeria
— Touring Club d'Algerie, 1 Rue Al-Idrissi, Alger.
— Fédération Algerienne du Sport, d'Automobile et du Karting, 99 Boulevard Bouakouir, Alger.

Egypt
— Automobile et Touring Club d'Egypt, 10 Rue Kasr al Nil, Cairo.
— Automobile et Touring Club d'Egypt, 15 Rue Salah Salem, Alexandria.

Ethiopia
— Automobile Club Eritreo, Via Guistino de Jacobis No. 4-6-8, P.O. Box 1187, Asmara.

Ghana
— Automobile Association of Ghana, Fanum House, 1 Valley View, Labadi Road, P.O. Box 01046, Christiansborg, Accra.

Ivory Coast
— Fédération Ivoirienne du Sport, Automobile et Engins Assimilés (F.I.S.A.), 01 B.P. 3883, Abidjan.

Kenya
— Automobile Association of Kenya, Nyaku House, Hurlingham, P.O. Box 40087, Nairobi.

Libya
— Automobile and Touring Club of Libya, Maidan Al-Ghazala, P.O. Box 3566, Tripoli.

Malawi
— Automobile Association of Zimbabwe Agent, Blantyre Insurance & General Agencies, Livingstone Avenue, P.O. Box 333, Blantyre.

Morocco
— Touring Club de Maroc, 3 Avenue de l'Armée-Royale, Casablanca.
— Royal Automobile Club Marocain, Ain Diab, Corner Avenue de la Côte-d'Emeraude & Rue Mimizan, Casablanca.

Nigeria
— Automobile Club of Nigeria, 24 Mercy Eneli Surulere, Lagos.

Senegal
— Automobile Club du Sénégal, Immeuble Chambre de Commerce, Place de l'Independance, Dakar.

South Africa
— Automobile Association of South Africa. AA House, 66 De Korte Street, Braamfontein, P.O. Box 596, Johannesburg.

Tanzania
— Automobile Association of Tanzania, Cargen House, Maktaba Street, P.O. Box 3004, Dar-es-Salaam.

Tunisia
— Touring Club de Tunisie, 15 Rue d'Allemagne, Tunis.
— National Automobile Club de Tunisie, 29 Avenue Habib-Bourguiba, Tunis.

Zaire
— Fédération Automobile du Zaire, Hotel Okapi, B.P. 28, Kinshasa 1.

Zimbabwe
— Automobile Association of Zimbabwe, 57 Samora Machel Avenue, P.O. Box 585, Harare.

Appendix C
Conversion tables

Length

1 inch = 25.4 millimetres (mm)   1 millimetre = 0.039 inches (in)
1 foot = 0.305 metre (m)   1 metre = 3.281 feet (ft)
1 mile = 1.609 kilometres (km)   1 kilometre = 0.621 miles (ml)

Kilometres to miles

Kms	Mls	Kms	Mls	Kms	Mls
1	0.62	11	6.83	30	18.64
2	1.24	12	7.45	40	24.85
3	1.86	13	8.07	50	31.07
4	2.48	14	8.69	60	37.28
5	3.10	15	9.32	80	49.71
6	3.72	16	9.94	100	62.14
7	4.34	17	10.56	200	124.28
8	4.97	18	11.18	500	310.70
9	5.59	19	11.80	1000	621.40
10	6.21	20	12.42	2000	1242.80

Miles to kilometres

Mls	Kms	Mls	Kms	Mls	Kms
1	1.60	11	17.70	30	48.27
2	3.21	12	19.31	40	64.37
3	4.82	13	20.92	50	80.46
4	6.43	14	22.53	75	120.69
5	8.04	15	24.13	100	160.93
6	9.65	16	25.74	200	321.86
7	11.26	17	27.35	250	402.30
8	12.87	18	28.96	500	804.65
9	14.48	19	30.57	750	1206.90
10	16.09	20	32.18	1000	1609.30

Metres to feet

M	Ft	M	Ft	M	Ft
1	3.28	6	19.68	20	65.60
2	6.56	7	22.96	50	164.00
3	9.84	8	26.24	100	328.10
4	13.12	9	29.52	250	820.25
5	16.40	10	32.80	500	1640.50

Feet to metres

Ft	M	Ft	M	Ft	M
1	0.30	6	1.83	20	6.08
2	0.60	7	2.13	50	15.20
3	0.90	8	2.43	100	30.50
4	1.22	9	2.74	250	76.25
5	1.52	10	3.04	500	152.50

Millimetres to inches and inches to millimetres

mm	in	mm	in	in	mm	in	mm
5	0.19	100	3.90	1	25.4	6	152.4
10	0.39	200	7.80	2	50.8	7	177.8
20	0.78	250	9.70	3	76.2	8	203.2
25	0.97	500	19.50	4	101.6	9	228.6
50	1.95	1000	39.00	5	127.0	10	254.0

Weight

16 ounces	= 1 pound (lb)	1000 grams	= 1 kilogram (kg)
1 ounce	= 28.35 grams (g)	1 gram	= 0.035 ounces (oz)
1 pound	= 0.454 kilograms (kg)	1 kilogram	= 2.205 pounds (lb)

Ounces to grams and grams to ounces

g	oz	g	oz	oz	g	oz	g
25	0.87	200	7.00	½	14.17	8	226.80
50	1.75	250	8.75	2	56.70	10	283.50
75	2.62	500	17.50	3	85.05	12	340.20
100	3.50	750	26.25	4	113.40	14	396.90
150	5.25	1000	35.00	5	141.75	16	453.60

Pounds to kilograms and kilograms to pounds

lb	kg	lb	kg	kg	lb	kg	lb
½	0.227	10	4.54	1	2.20	10	22.05
2	0.908	20	9.08	2	4.41	20	44.10
3	1.362	25	11.35	3	6.61	25	55.12
4	1.816	50	22.70	4	8.82	50	110.25
5	2.27	100	45.40	5	11.02	100	220.50

Volume (capacity)

1 gallon = 4.546 litres (l)
1 pint = 0.568 litre (l)
16 pints = 1 gallon (gal)

1 litre = 0.22 gallon (gal)
1 litre = 1.76 pints (pt)
1 litre = 1000 millilitres (ml)

Litres to gallons

L	Gal	L	Gal	L	Gal
1	0.22	11	2.42	25	5.50
2	0.44	12	2.64	30	6.60
3	0.66	13	2.86	40	8.80
4	0.88	14	3.08	50	11.00
5	1.10	15	3.30	60	13.20
6	1.32	16	3.52	75	16.50
7	1.54	17	3.74	100	22.00
8	1.76	18	3.96	200	44.00
9	1.98	19	4.18	500	110.00
10	2.20	20	4.40	1000	220.00

Gallons to litres

Gal	L	Gal	L	Gal	L
1	4.54	11	49.94	25	113.50
2	9.08	12	54.48	30	136.20
3	13.62	13	59.02	40	181.60
4	18.16	14	63.56	50	227.00
5	22.70	15	68.10	60	272.40
6	27.24	16	72.64	75	340.50
7	31.78	17	77.18	100	454.00
8	36.32	18	81.72	200	908.00
9	40.86	19	86.26	400	1,816.00
10	45.40	20	90.08	500	2,270.00

Millilitres to pints and pints to millilitres

Ml	Pt	Ml	Pt	Pt	Ml	Pt	Ml
25	0.044	250	0.44	½	0.284	6	3.40
50	0.088	500	0.88	2	1.13	8	4.54
75	0.132	600	1.05	3	1.70	10	5.68
100	0.176	750	1.32	4	2.27	12	6.81
200	0.352	1000	1.76	5	2.84	14	7.95

Fuel consumption

1 mile per gallon   =   0.354 kilometres per litre (km/l)
1 kilometre per litre   =   2.825 miles per gallon (mpg)

Miles per gallon to kilometres per litre

Mpg	Km/l	Mpg	Km/l	Mpg	Km/l
6	2.12	16	5.66	30	10.62
8	2.83	18	6.37	35	12.39
10	3.54	20	7.08	40	14.16
12	4.24	22	7.78	45	15.93
14	4.95	25	8.85	50	17.70

Kilometres per litre to miles per gallon

Km/l	Mpg	Km/l	Mpg	Km/l	Mpg
3	8.47	8	22.60	13	36.72
4	11.30	9	25.42	14	39.55
5	14.12	10	28.25	15	42.37
6	16.95	11	31.07	16	45.20
7	19.77	12	33.90	17	48.02

Power

1 horsepower (hp)   =   745.7 watts (W)
1 watt (W)   =   0.0013 horsepower (hp)

Altitude (effect on horsepower)
Engine performance will be reduced, in some cases drastically, the higher the altitude that you drive at. To counteract this you fit different jets to the carburettor of your vehicle. Most vehicle manufacturers are able to supply an assortment of jets for different altitudes. Without the correct jet for the altitude you can expect to lose approximately 3% of your engine power per 1,000 feet altitude. (See table)

Altitude	% of normal horsepower at sea level	Altitude	% of normal horsepower at sea level
Sea level	100	5,000 feet	83
1,000 feet	96.25	6,000 feet	80
2,000 feet	93	7,000 feet	77.5
3,000 feet	89.5	8,000 feet	75
4,000 feet	86	9,000 feet	72

Thus it is advisable to carry a selection of jets with you. Without them you will find that whereas you would normally cruise along at 60 mph at sea level, this will be reduced to 40-45 mph at 7,000 to 8,000 feet.

Country capitals and altitudes

Algeria — Algiers, sea level
Benin — Cotonou, sea level
Botswana — Gaberone, 4,208 feet
Burkina Fasso — Ouagadougou, 1,010 feet
Cameroun — Yaoundé, 897 feet
C.A.R. — Bangui, 1,410 feet
Congo — Brazzaville, 1,002 feet
Egypt — Cairo, 65 feet
Gabon — Libreville, sea level
Ghana — Accra, sea level
Ivory Coast — Yamoussoukro, sea level
Kenya — Nairobi, 5,448 feet
Liberia — Monrovia, sea level
Libya — Tripoli, sea level
Malawi — Lilongwe, 3,499 feet
Mali — Bamako, 1,574 feet
Mauritania — Nouakchott, sea level
Morocco — Rabat, sea level

Mozambique — Maputo, sea level
Niger — Niamey, 639 feet
Nigeria — Lagos, sea level
Rwanda — Kigali, 2,591 feet
Senegal — Dakar, sea level
Sierra Leone — Freetown, sea level
South Africa — Pretoria, 4,592 feet
Sudan — Khartoum, 1,239 feet
Swaziland — Mbabane, 3,749 feet
Tanzania — Dar Es Salaam, sea level (Dodoma, new administrative capital)
Tchad — Ndjamena, 967 feet
Togo — Lomé, sea level
Tunisia — Tunis, sea level
Uganda — Kampala, 3,719 feet
Zaire — Kinshasa, 1,006 feet
Zambia — Lusaka, 4,250 fet
Zimbabwe — Harare, 4,824 feet

Velocity (speed)

| 1 mile per hour (mph) | = | 1.609 kilometres per hour (kph) |
| 1 kilometre per hour | = | 0.621 miles per hour. |

Miles per hour to kilometres per hour

Mph	Kph	Mph	Kph	Mph	Kph
5	8.04	15	24.13	35	56.31
7	11.26	17	27.35	40	64.36
9	14.48	20	32.18	50	80.45
11	17.69	25	40.22	60	96.54
13	20.91	30	48.27	70	112.63

Kilometres per hour to miles per hour

Kph	Mph	Kph	Mph	Kph	Mph
7	4.34	20	12.42	50	31.05
10	6.21	25	15.52	60	37.26
12	7.45	30	18.63	80	49.68
15	9.31	35	21.73	100	62.10
18	11.17	40	24.84	120	74.52

Gradients

On most modern maps, gradients are shown as a percentage. This chart gives you the modern percentage method against the older "one in" feet method.

Gradient in feet	%	Gradient in feet	%
1 in 5	20	1 in 15	6.6
1 in 6	16.6	1 in 16	6.2
1 in 7	14.3	1 in 17	5.9
1 in 8	12.5	1 in 18	5.5
1 in 9	11.1	1 in 19	5.3
1 in 10	10	1 in 20	5
1 in 11	9.1	1 in 25	4
1 in 12	8.3	1 in 30	3.3
1 in 13	7.7	1 in 35	2.9
1 in 14	7.1	1 in 40	2.5

Temperature

- To find degrees Fahrenheit from degrees Celsius (Centigrade):

$$(°C \times 9 \div 5) + 32$$

- To find degrees Celsius (Centigrade) from degrees Fahrenheit:

$$(°F - 32) \times 5 \div 9$$

Celsius/Fahrenheit chart

°C	°F	°C	°F	°C	°F	°C	°F
-10	14	1	33.8	12	53.6	23	73.4
-9	15.8	2	35.6	13	55.4	24	75.2
-8	17.6	3	37.4	14	57.2	25	77
-7	19.4	4	39.2	15	59	26	78.8
-6	21.2	5	41	16	60.8	27	80.6
-5	23	6	42.8	17	62.6	28	82.4
-4	24.8	7	44.6	18	64.4	29	84.2
-3	26.6	8	46.4	19	66.2	30	86
-2	28.4	9	48.2	20	68	31	87.8
-1	30.2	10	50	21	69.8	32	89.6
0	32	11	51.8	22	71.6	33	91.4

Tyre pressure

Many countries now use the metric form of measuring tyre pressures, ie. kilograms/sq. cm. A few use atmospheres. This table will assist you in selecting the correct pressure for your tyres.

lb per sq. in.	Kg per sq. cm.	Atm.	lb per sq. in.	Kg per sq. cm.	Atm.
10	0.70	0.68	32	2.24	2.18
12	0.84	0.82	34	2.38	2.31
14	0.98	0.95	36	2.52	2.45
16	1.12	1.09	38	2.66	2.58
18	1.26	1.22	40	2.80	2.72
20	1.40	1.36	45	3.15	3.06
22	1.54	1.50	50	3.50	3.40
24	1.68	1.63	55	3.85	3.74
26	1.83	1.77	60	4.20	4.08
28	1.96	1.90	65	4.55	4.42
30	2.10	2.04	70	4.90	4.76

1 pound/sq. in.   = 0.070 kilograms/sq. cm.
1 pound/sq. in.   = 0.068 atmospheres (atm.)
1 kilogram/sq. in. = 14.223 pounds/sq. in.
1 atmosphere   = 14.696 pounds/sq. in.

I am Man

When game is short
the tiger leaves for better hunting grounds.
When air grows chilled
the winged fly to warmer air.
And if the grass won't grow
or burns or withers in the drought,
all the herbivorous migrate.
I am Man . . . . . I too will go.

No one has ever told me why.
No answer ever satisfied this crazy,
bursting, lusting thing that forces me
to go away from home.
But I am eager to learn and I must go.

I must go so I can learn.

And I will travel round the world.
And I will soak myself with other people's strangeness.
And if I gag on their strange foods
or turn my nose from their strange smells
I will learn their foods can be my foods,
their smells my smells.
For I am learning about Mankind.

And if I look in awe upon their sights
and fill with wonder at their histories
I will learn their sights were also made for me,
their histories are my histories.
For I am learning about Mankind.

And if I hurt their pride with clumsiness
or break their hearts with thoughtlessness
I will heal them with respect
and mend them with my understanding.
For I have learned to love Mankind.

For I have learned
that all the world's peoples are my peoples.
And all the world is One.

Author untraceable.